Accession no.
36213023

Contempora

WITHDRAWN

WITHDRAWN

WITHDRAWN

D1615537

Edinburgh Textbooks on the English Language – Advanced

General Editor
Heinz Giegerich, Professor of English Linguistics, University of Edinburgh

Editorial Board
Laurie Bauer (University of Wellington)
Olga Fischer (University of Amsterdam)
Willem Hollmann (Lancaster University)
Rochelle Lieber (University of New Hampshire)
Bettelou Los (University of Edinburgh)
Robert McColl Millar (University of Aberdeen)
Donka Minkova (UCLA)
Edgar Schneider (University of Regensburg)

TITLES IN THE SERIES INCLUDE:

A Critical Account of English Syntax: Grammar, Meaning, Text
Keith Brown and Jim Miller

English Historical Semantics
Christian Kay and Kathryn Allan

A Historical Syntax of English
Bettelou Los

Morphological Theory and the Morphology of English
Jan Don

Construction Grammar and its Application to English
Martin Hilpert

A Historical Phonology of English
Donka Minkova

English Historical Pragmatics
Andreas Jucker and Irma Taavitsainen

English Historical Sociolinguistics
Robert McColl Millar

Corpus Linguistics and the Description of English
Hans Lindquist

Contemporary Stylistics: Language, Cognition, Interpretation
Alison Gibbons and Sara Whiteley

Visit the Edinburgh Textbooks in the English Language website at
www.edinburghuniversitypress.com/series/etoteladvanced

Contemporary Stylistics

Language, Cognition, Interpretation

Alison Gibbons and Sara Whiteley

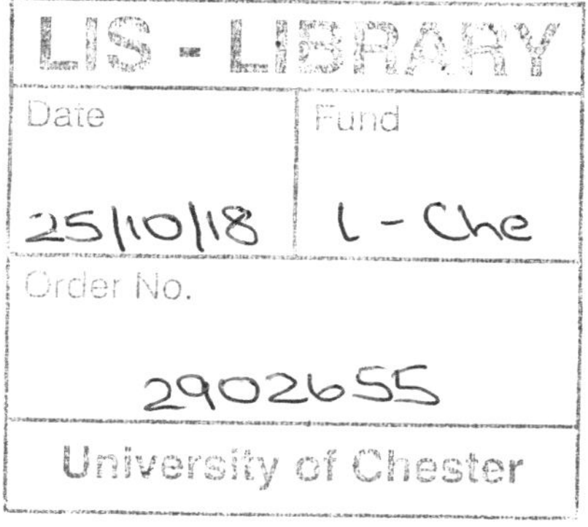
LIS - LIBRARY
Date 25/10/18
Fund l - Che
Order No. 2902655
University of Chester

EDINBURGH
University Press

Edinburgh University Press is one of the leading university presses in the UK. We publish academic books and journals in our selected subject areas across the humanities and social sciences, combining cutting-edge scholarship with high editorial and production values to produce academic works of lasting importance. For more information visit our website: edinburghuniversitypress.com

© Alison Gibbons and Sara Whiteley, 2018

Edinburgh University Press Ltd
The Tun – Holyrood Road,
12(2f) Jackson's Entry,
Edinburgh EH8 8PJ

Typeset in Janson MT by
Servis Filmsetting Ltd, Stockport, Cheshire,
and printed and bound in Great Britain

A CIP record for this book is available from the British Library

ISBN 978 0 7486 8276 8 (hardback)
ISBN 978 0 7486 8277 5 (paperback)
ISBN 978 0 7486 8278 2 (webready PDF)
ISBN 978 0 7486 8280 5 (epub)

The right of Alison Gibbons and Sara Whiteley to be identified as the authors of this work has been asserted in accordance with the Copyright, Designs and Patents Act 1988, and the Copyright and Related Rights Regulations 2003 (SI No. 2498).

Contents

Figures

Tables

Permission acknowledgements

Grateful acknowledgement is made to the following sources for permission to reproduce material previously published elsewhere. Every effort has been made to trace the copyright holders, but if any have been inadvertently overlooked, the publisher will be pleased to make the necessary arrangements at the first opportunity. All literary works and extracts are included in this book either in accordance with fair use or through grant of permission, as detailed below.

Chapter 2: Foregrounding

Jeffrey McDaniel's poem 'don't touch it!' was reproduced from his (2008) collection *Endarkenment*, University of Pittsburgh Press, p. 34. Permission granted by author.

Permission for e. e. cummings' poetry was granted: 'The Mind's('. Copyright 1938, © 1966, 1991 by the Trustees for the E. E. Cummings Trust, from COMPLETE POEMS: 1904–1962 by E. E. Cummings, edited by George J. Firmage. Used by permission of Liveright Publishing Corporation.

Chapter 3: Phonemes to sound patterning

Permission to print – McCaffery, S. (2000) 'Sixteen' [originally published in *Intimate Distortions* (1979)], *Seven Pages Missing: Volume One: Selected Texts 1969–1999*, Coach House Books, p. 138 – granted by Steve McCaffery.

The extract from Filippo Tommaso Marinetti's 'Zong Toomb Toomb' translated by Elizabeth R. Napier and Barbara R. Studholme comes from *Marinetti: Selected Poems and Related Prose*, Yale University Press, and is reprinted with permission from Yale Representation Ltd.

Louis MacNeice's poem 'River in Spate' from MacNeice's *Collected Poems*, published by Faber & Faber has been published with permission from literary, film, and TV agents David Higham Associates.

Chapter 4: Morphemes to words

'Space Sonnet & Polyfilla' by Edwin Morgan from his *Collected Poems* (1990 [1977]: 341) is reprinted with permission from Carcanet Press.

Chapter 5: Phrase to sentence

Matthea Harvey gave permission for the reprinting of her poem 'In Defense of Our Overgrown Garden', originally published in her (2000) collection *Pity the Bathtub Its Forced Embrace of the Human Form*, published by Alice James Books.

Chapter 11: Varieties and invented languages

Permission to reproduce 'Received Pronunciation' was granted by the author Sally Goldsmith. The poem appears in: A. Lehoczky, A. Piette, A. Sansom and P. Sansom (eds) (2012) *The Sheffield Anthology: Poems from the City Imagined*, Sheffield: Smith/Doorstop, pp. 93–4.

Permission to reproduce quotations from Dialectable greetings cards was granted by Julia Harrison of Dialectable Ltd.

Chapter 12: Figure and ground

Permission to reproduce 'The House Is Not the Same since You Left' was granted by the author Henry Normal. The poem appears in: Normal, H. (1993) *Nude Modelling for the Afterlife*, Newcastle upon Tyne: Bloodaxe Books, p. 21.

Chapter 15: Cognitive grammar and construal

Charles Causley's 'I Am The Song' is reproduced with permission of the author and publisher. The poem is from *Collected Poems 1951–2000*, published by Picador (2000).

Chapter 17: Text-worlds

Permission to reproduce 'Hypothetical' was granted by the author Maria Taylor. The poem appears in S. Hannah (ed.) (2014) *The Poetry of Sex*, London: Viking, pp. 45–6.

Chapter 18: Negation and lacuna

Faber & Faber granted permission for the reprint of Julia Copus' poem 'This Is the Poem in which I Have Not Left You', originally published in Copus' (2012) collection *The World's Two Smallest Humans.*

Chapter 19: Analysing the multimodal text

Permission to use extracted words from *13, rue Thérèse* (2011) as well as reproduce the image of page 5 in Figure 19.1 was granted by Hill Nadell Agency and the author Elena Shapiro: Copyright 2011, Elena Mauli Shapiro. Used by permission of the author.

Ilona Chavasse, Rights Director of Oneworld Publications, granted permission to reproduce pages 1 and 25 from *Illuminae: The Illuminae Files_01*, on behalf of the authors Amie Kaufman and Jay Kristoff, Copyright 2015; Published by Rock the Boat, an imprint of Oneworld Publications.

Blast Theory granted permission for the use of the three screenshots from *Karen*, shown in Figures 19.4 and 19.5.

Acknowledgements

It has taken us quite a long time to write this book; too long, because so many things have happened along the way – new houses, new jobs . . . basically, life happened! And because the book has taken so long, we have accrued many debts.

First and foremost, the team at Edinburgh University Press have been supportive and patient throughout. Thank you to our original commissioning editor, Gillian Leslie, and the editorial team – Jenny Peebles, Richard Strachan – and to Laura Williamson for her ongoing commitment and enthusiasm for the book as we prepared to submit it.

In writing this book, we were committed to analysing (and therefore sharing with our readers) poems and fiction that we enjoy. Since many of these works are contemporary, we have on several occasions had to obtain permissions. Thanks to the English Research Committee at De Montfort University and to the Humanities Research Centre at Sheffield Hallam University for helping to cover some of the permissions costs; thanks also to the authors who gave permission freely and whose work has inspired our analyses.

Thanks to students who read draft chapters and gave us their feedback on the book as learners; in particular thanks to Lauren Anstey, Chelsea Humphries, Ashleigh McCann, Liam Moffat, and Louella Murfin. Thanks also to the students on the 'EGH317 Investigating Real Readers' module at the University of Sheffield for helping to test out and reflect upon the reader response methods covered in Chapter 22 and allowing us to use some of their think-aloud responses in this book.

Our thinking and writing has benefited from our connections with the Poetics And Linguistics Association (PALA) and the International Association of Literary Semantics (IALS). We also feel privileged to be part of the Cognitive Poetics Research Group (CPRG) based in Sheffield. We are particularly indebted to friends and colleagues who suggested literary texts, or read, reviewed, and gave advice about chapters in this book: Alice Bell, Kathy Bell, Joe Bray, Sam Browse,

Will Buckingham, Joanna Gavins, Chloe Harrison, Jane Hodson, Chris Hopkins, Anu Koskela, Jessica Mason, Louise Nuttall, Simon Perril, Joe Phelan, Stephen Pihlaja, Keith Scott, and Peter Stockwell. Thanks also to all those who have politely inquired about the book's progress and offered encouragement and support along the way.

Part I

Introducing contemporary stylistics

1 Contemporary stylistics

1.1 What is stylistics?

Stylistics is the integrated study of language and literature. Often, these areas of study are treated like separate concerns. For example, in further education ('A' Levels) and onwards, it is currently possible to study English literature or English language without the other; that is, as though they are unrelated. Nevertheless, literature is made, fundamentally, of language. Contemporary stylistics studies literature by drawing on theories and ideas from the study of language, and provides insights into the structures and functions of language in use. Sometimes stylistics is called **literary linguistics**, but in this book we use the term 'stylistics' to refer to this integrated approach. As we discuss below, stylistics has a long history and has been developed through the combined influence of a number of different sub-fields in linguistics and literary criticism. Our subtitle – *Language, Cognition, Interpretation* – was chosen because this book is designed to provide you with the toolkit to analyse language, connect your linguistic analysis to literary interpretation, and, in turn, relate both language and interpretation to the cognitive processes involved in reading. We call this contemporary stylistics, but such a name raises the questions: *What is stylistics?* and *What makes it so contemporary?* This section seeks to answer the former question with a brief history of stylistics as an academic field of study.

In contemporary stylistics, **style** is fundamentally concerned with the relationship between linguistic form and literary meaning and interpretation. Verdonk explains that 'style' derives from the Latin word ***stilus***, originally meaning an ancient writing instrument made of metal, wood, or bone (2006: 196). The etymological origin of 'style' as a writing instrument provides insight into why readers and critics often speak of 'a writer's style'. Indeed, the term 'stylistics' originates from the discipline's very early interest in discussing the 'style' of different authors. Verdonk argues that it is likely that the evolution of the meaning of the word 'style' was extended from 'an instrument for writing' to 'a manner of writing', first in the literal sense of 'a writer's characteristic way of shaping letters', and next in the figurative and deeper sense of 'a writer's characteristic mode of expression in terms of effectiveness, clarity, beauty and the like' (2006: 196). This latter meaning of 'style' is at the heart of classical Latin **rhetoric** (1200 BCE to sixth century CE) in which the words *elocution* and *stilus* were used interchangeably. Classical rhetoric is one of the earliest precursors of stylistics as a discipline. Rhetoric focuses on the ways in which language can be used to impress and to persuade. Contemporary stylistics takes from rhetoric its interest in form, emphasis on context, and consideration of the social and emotional effects of language.

Although rhetoric was most concerned with the composition of speech, stylistics has privileged writing. This is the result of another of its central influences, **European Structuralism**, particularly **Russian Formalism**, a school of literary criticism that developed in Russia around 1915 and was later based at **the Prague School** in the 1930s. The approach was considered formalist because it focused on the devices of language (the form) in literature. Central figures included Roman Jakobson, Jan Mukařovsky, and Victor Shklovsky. A major contribution to stylistics from Russian Formalism is the concept of defamiliarisation, which forms the basis of the stylistic framework of foregrounding, introduced in Chapter 2.

As Carter and Stockwell (2008: 292–5; following Fowler 1981) outline, from the 1920s onwards, in the United States, **structural linguistics** – developed by Leonard Bloomfield – paved the way for analysing the metrical patterns in poetry, whilst in the late 1950s Noam Chomsky's **generative grammar** (also know as **phrase structure** and **transformational grammar**) facilitated systematic, descriptive analysis of phrases, clauses, and other syntactic structures. Because early stylistics developed in the 1960s and 70s from interdisciplinary contact between linguistic and literary criticism, this fusion of influences resulted in an approach to text analysis that continued to possess the precision of descriptive linguistic methods whilst gaining insight into the ways in which formal structures of language can create literary effects and interpretations. This descriptive approach to language can be felt in the frameworks discussed in Chapters 3–5. Roger Fowler's career demonstrates the interdisciplinary transition in the sense that his work moved from the analysis of language using transformational grammar to exploring the linguistic analysis of literary works. Around the same time, M. A. K. Halliday developed his own social semiotic approach, called **Systemic Functional Linguistics**. This was founded on the notion that language is a situational system of choices, and these choices have socio-cultural and ideological functions. Halliday's notions of register and transitivity are discussed in Chapters 6 and 10 respectively.

Developments in linguistics in the 1970s and 80s, exemplified by Halliday's work, championed the study of language *in use* in everyday interactions, rather than solely as an abstract structural system. Meanwhile, within literary criticism, **reader response theory** argued that literary meaning is generated through the interaction between texts and readers, rather than being inherent within a text. Combined, these literary and linguistic influences had a profound effect upon stylistics, which, since the 1970s has been concerned with the study of texts in context, viewing readers as active constructors of textual meaning.

As a discipline, stylistics thrived in the late twentieth century: in 1981, Geoffrey Leech and Mick Short published *Style in Fiction*, a seminal work on the principles and methods of stylistics; in the 1990s, a series of edited collections, with the subtitle *From Text to Context*, showcased stylistic analyses of poetry (Verdonk 1993), fiction (Verdonk and Weber 1995), and drama (Culpeper et al. 1998). The key stylistics journals appeared throughout this period too: the first issue of the *Journal of Literary Semantics* appeared in 1972, whilst *Language and Literature* was established in 1992.

Stylistics has never been a discipline to stand still. It is a progressive discipline, meaning that it continually seeks to refine and update its principles in line with new knowledge in relevant fields. When, at the end of the twentieth century, the cognitive revolution brought into focus the psychological dimension of language, stylistics reinvented itself as **cognitive stylistics** (Semino and Culpeper 2002) or **cognitive poetics** (Stockwell 2002a) (the terms are interchangeable). In doing so, the discipline integrated the insights of the cognitive sciences into an understanding of how we read the linguistic structures that form literary texts. The cognitive development of stylistics is the focus of Parts IV and V of this book.

We have thus far introduced the discipline of **stylistics**, which has arisen from a melting pot of influences: rhetoric, Russian Formalism, structural linguistics, Systemic Functional Linguistics, and the cognitive sciences. In the next section, we explain how stylistics has continued to evolve since the early twenty-first century into what we call contemporary stylistics.

1.2 How is it contemporary?

The title of this book carries the premodifier 'contemporary' to describe stylistics for a number of reasons. Firstly, our use of 'contemporary' designates the scope of this book. As noted above, stylistics is formed from a variety of influences, but the most recent and significant shift in the discipline came as a result of the aforementioned 'cognitive turn' in the 1980s–90s. For years, this cognitive linguistic strand of stylistics has been considered a sub-discipline of stylistics – a supplement or development of the more well-established analytical approaches. This view of stylistics, divided into a mainstream and a cognitive approach, is no longer tenable. Cognitive frameworks have an undeniable explanatory power and offer new perspectives on the questions that have always interested stylisticians.

In many universities, traditional and cognitive branches of stylistics are taught separately (that is how we both learnt them) using separate textbooks. Indeed, it is possible (though becoming less likely) for stylisticians to be well versed in either one or the other, rather than both. We believe that, in the future, all stylisticians need to be versed in the full range of approaches. This book brings together both traditional, well-established ideas in stylistics and relatively newer, cognitively informed ideas. Additionally, this book introduces other recent advances in stylistics such as corpus analysis and reader response methods. In doing so, this book supplies you with a more complete picture of the state of *contemporary* stylistics, a discipline that draws on a range of linguistic theories in order to achieve multi-faceted analytical possibilities. This book therefore delivers a state-of-the-art picture of what stylistics looks like in the early twenty-first century. For us, contemporary stylistics involves choices between linguistic and cognitive linguistic frameworks, and this book gives you the information you need to begin orienting yourself in this new terrain. Those of you who are unfamiliar with the history of the discipline need know only that we aim to provide you with a complete, up-to-date picture of what stylistics is in the twenty-first century so far.

Our second motivation for the use of the premodifier 'contemporary' in our title is the fact that we have chosen to focus predominantly on literary texts written in the modern and contemporary period – from the twentieth century to the present day. It is important to note that a stylistic approach can be used to investigate literature from *any* historical period – and indeed, occasionally we do discuss older works such as Samuel Richardson's (1740) *Pamela, or Virtue Rewarded*, Jane Austen's (1813) *Pride and Prejudice*, 'The City in the Sea' by Edgar Allan Poe (1831), and Emily Brontë's *Wuthering Heights* (1847). Historical works have received extensive attention in stylistics, and there is even a sub-discipline called 'historical stylistics' (for instance, see Adamson 1999; Auer et al. 2016; Bray 2014a; Busse 2014). We believe that you should use stylistics to examine your literary passions, and the contemporary focus of this book reflects our interests as contemporary literary scholars. We have also tried, in choosing which literary works to analyse, to include a range of texts. Stylistics is interested in language and literature in the widest sense: including canonical and non-canonical texts, those regarded as highbrow or lowbrow, popular or experimental.

Finally, our book is about stylistics as a diverse and current approach, so our use of the word 'contemporary' is also designed to emphasise that stylistics is a discipline of the now and of the future. Stylistics offers a unique, interdisciplinary approach to the combined study of language and literature, and it is for this reason that it is becoming increasingly more central to all levels of English education. Contemporary stylistics has a long history and one of the things that makes it such a fascinating, vibrant approach is that it is always evolving: frameworks are constantly tested and updated, new ideas from linguistics and related disciplines are incorporated and applied. It will be up to you, the next generation of stylisticians, to steer its future development. In this sense, stylistics will always be – and always was – contemporary.

1.3 The structure of this book

This book is organised to reflect key dimensions of the integrated study of language and literature. Part I (this chapter) introduces stylistics and offers a brief overview of the discipline. Part II familiarises you with the study of literature *as* language. It begins, in Chapter 2 on 'Foregrounding' by introducing Russian Formalist ideas about linguistic patterns in literary uses of language. As the chapter shows, foregrounding forms the bedrock of a stylistic approach (and foregrounding is returned to in cognitive terms in Chapter 12 on 'Figure and ground').

Language is a complex phenomenon, formed from multiple, interconnected levels. It is made up of spoken sounds (phonemes) which form meaningful units (morphemes) that can be combined to make words (lexemes) and which are then built up into sentences (syntax); sentences, in turn, form utterances (spoken turns) or texts that perform functions in human interaction (discourse). The major **levels of language** are set out in Table 1.1. Chapters 3–6 address these levels starting with the micro and working upwards to a more macro perspective: considering sounds in Chapter 3, words and their constituent parts in Chapter 4, and sentences in Chapter 5. As the final chapter in Part II, Chapter 6 shifts scale to consider linguistic meaning (semantics) and discourse. In doing so, Chapter 6 shows how linguistic choices can make a text coherent, create meaningful connections across a text, and orientate a text in terms of genre or topic.

Table 1.1 Language analysis and branches of linguistics

Levels of language	Branch of Linguistics
The sounds and pronunciation of spoken language	Phonetics and Phonology (study of phonemes)
The patterns and shapes of written language on the page	Graphology (study of graphemes)
The construction of words from smaller units	Morphology (study of morphemes)
The words that are used; the vocabulary of a language	Lexical analysis, Lexicology (study of lexemes)
The combination of words to form phrases and sentences	Grammar and Syntax (study of phrases, clauses, and sentences)
The meanings of words and sentences	Semantics (study of meaning and meaning-relations)
The way words and sentences are used in everyday situations	Pragmatics, Discourse Analysis (study of meaning in context)

Part III 'Literature as discourse' covers stylistic frameworks developed from the linguistic sub-disciplines of pragmatics and discourse analysis that revolutionised linguistics in the 1970s. Chapter 7 applies conversation analysis and politeness theory in the analysis of fictional dialogue and the social relations and power dynamics between characters. Although literary dialogue is invented or scripted, readers' understanding of everyday communication guides the inferences they make about characters' communicative interactions. Thus, a stylistic analysis of fictional conversation can be revealing.

Following this, Chapters 8 and 9 continue to explore characters' thoughts and feelings. Chapter 8 considers voice and narration in prose and poetry, outlining the different textual strategies that can be used to present speech, thought, and writing. Chapter 9 then explores the way that attitude is represented through the use of modality and through the depiction of characters' points of view. Chapters 10 and 11 both explicitly connect linguistic analysis with social and/or ideological meaning: whilst Chapter 10 draws on Halliday's Systemic Functional Linguistics to examine the linguistic representation of actions and events, Chapter 11 draws on the study of accent and dialect in sociolinguistics in order to examine the way that non-standard varieties of language can be portrayed in literary texts. Overall, the chapters in Part III demonstrate the way linguistic features influence readers' impressions and reactions to characters and social categories.

In Part IV 'Text as cognition', we shift focus to stylistic frameworks that have developed out of the 'cognitive revolution' that began in the 1980s–90s. The first chapter of Part IV can be seen to revisit foregrounding (first discussed in Chapter 2). However, the newer framework of 'Figure and ground', which is the subject of Chapter 12, augments foregrounding with the insights of cognition, visual perception, and studies in attention. A major belief in the cognitive sciences is that our perceptions and our minds are inextricably linked to our bodies. The way we think is motivated by our concrete, embodied existence in the world. This is the principle of **embodiment**. In this view, our minds are embodied systems. The embodied and experiential dimension of language processing is essential to Chapter 13's discussion of cognitive deixis, in which language is seen to encode our position in the world and thus linguistic structures can stimulate readers to imagine narrative worlds from within a particular viewpoint.

For cognitive stylisticians, the insights of cognitive science lend stylistics a more empirical and erudite understanding of how readers experience texts. Indeed, Carter and Stockwell argue that the 'literary "work" only exists in the mind of a reader; this fact should be at the forefront of stylistic practice' (2008: 300). For instance, Chapter 14 draws on Artificial Intelligence research, specifically theories of the way in which language involves and stimulates our existing knowledge structures, such as our knowledge of the steps involved in eating at a restaurant, or our ability to differentiate between, say, an onion and an apple. Not only do we draw on these knowledge structures in order to go about our daily lives, a reader's background knowledge is also key in the reading process. Chapter 15 on cognitive grammar continues to focus on readers' experiential processing of language, exploring how grammatical structures encode psychological construal.

The psychological dimension of language is explored further in Part V 'Reading as mental spaces'. In Chapter 16, we consider the metaphorical dimension of language and cognition, whilst Chapter 17 explores the ways in which readers imagine characters and worlds based on the linguistic cues of a text. Chapter 18 hones in on a specific linguistic and conceptual structure – negation – and investigates its effect on readers' imaginative interpretations.

The two chapters in Part VI 'Reading as experience' consider the experiential dimension of reading. In Chapter 19, the focus is on texts that feature other modes. Stylistic analysis therefore also accounts for the graphological style or layout of text or the inclusion of images (photographs, drawings, etc.) in order to understand how these different modes impact on the reading experience and the ways in which readers derive interpretations. Chapter 20 'Understanding emotions' suggests that linguistic structures – like focalisation – enable readers to model the minds of characters and resultantly experience emotional connections with those characters (or indeed to resist them).

In the penultimate part of this book – Part VII 'Reading as data' – we introduce some empirical approaches to the analysis of literary texts and literary experience. Empirical approaches are those that involve collecting data about texts or reading experiences and using this data to direct or support a stylistic analysis. Accordingly, Chapter 21 offers an introductory step-by-step guide to the analysis of literary texts using computer tools. Subsequently in Chapter 22, we introduce some methods that can be used to investigate other readers' responses to literary texts.

Each chapter provides a list of keywords and phrases, highlighting the important terms and concepts covered. These are complemented by a summary of the chapter, and a list of activities you can undertake in order to develop your knowledge and put what you have read into practice. Each chapter also details further reading and references for the ideas that are introduced, so that you can continue to explore stylistics through independent research.

Finally, Part VIII concludes the book. Chapter 23 'Future stylistics' reflects upon the stylistic toolkit now available to you as a result of reading this book and working through the activities. Beyond this, we highlight the current trends in present-day stylistics research and point to areas for future development.

1.4 The principles of stylistic analysis

Stylistics involves the application of linguistic theories and frameworks in the analysis of literature. Depending on the interests of the analyst and the aims of the research project, a stylistic analysis seeks either to say something interesting about literature using theories and frameworks from language, or say something interesting about language using evidence and examples from literature. Often, both sides of this exchange are possible.

The best way to gain an understanding of what a stylistic analysis should look and feel like is to read widely in stylistics and to have a go at it yourself! Each chapter in this book contains several examples of stylistic analysis and these can act as a guide for you. The further references point you towards more examples whilst the activities will encourage you to test your own analytical skills and reflect upon your findings.

Stylistic analysis proceeds according to certain conventions, which Simpson (2014 [2004]: 3–4) summarises as 'the three R's': rigour, retrievability, and replicability. These are indeed the bedrock of any good stylistic analysis. Stylistic analyses are rigorous because, rather than being formed from a collection of ad hoc impressions and disorganised ideas, they proceed according to 'an explicit framework for analysis' (Simpson 2014 [2004]: 3). A framework is a systematic collection of terms and ideas that assist you in noticing and commenting upon the language of a text. The rigour of a stylistic analysis comes also from the close, systematic consideration of each part of a chosen text in turn.

Stylistic analyses are retrievable because they make use of sets of terms and criteria that are recognisable to and agreed upon by the wider community of stylisticians. Because there is consensus about the meanings of terms, it is possible for others to, as Simpson (2014 [2004]: 3) puts it, follow the 'pathway' of your analysis and see your workings. Although stylistics involves a lot of specialist terminology, stylisticians do not employ these terms in order to baffle or impress with complex rhetoric; rather, stylisticians aim to be clear and transparent in their discussion of the language of literature. As such, stylistic analyses also seek to be replicable – in the sense that they seek to show you how conclusions have been reached so that you could test them out yourself if you so wished.

One of the common misconceptions which we often encounter in those new to stylistics is the idea that it is all about labelling parts of texts using the metalanguage provided by a particular framework. Whilst labelling and categorising aspects of a text's language is a part of the process of a rigorous stylistic analysis, it is most definitely not the end point. Stylistics is a form of literary criticism: that is, it is interested in wider issues of meaning, interpretation, culture, and society. Stylistic analyses also involve tapping into your own reactions to texts, your own intuitions about their effects and meanings, and your own observations about their role in our wider culture. Integrating your subjective interpretations with attention to a text's language, and making connections between form and effect, is where the art of stylistics lies.

Further reading and references

Good overviews of the development of stylistics and cognitive poetics are: Bradford (1997), Burke (2014b), Busse and McIntyre (2010), Carter (1982), Gavins and Steen (2003), Stockwell (2002a: ch. 1), Toolan (2014), Wales (2006, 2014). Other good introductions to the tools and practices of stylistic analysis include: Blake (1990), Burke (2014a),

Carter (2010), Chapman (1973), Clark (1996), Gregoriou (2009), Jeffries and McIntyre (2010), Leech and Short (2007 [1981]), Simpson (1997, 2014 [2004]), Stockwell and Whiteley (2014), Toolan (1990, 1992a, 1998), Verdonk (2002), Wales (2006). Wales' (2011 [1990]) *A Dictionary of Stylistics* is an excellent glossary of key terms; see also Nørgaard et al.'s (2010) *Key Terms in Stylistics*. For more advanced reading in debates about the principles and practice of stylistics, see: Lecercle (1993) and Wales (1993); the Fowler–Bateson debate, reprinted in Fowler (1971) and Simpson (2014 [2004]: 149–57); Mackay (1996) and Short et al. (1998); Fish (1980 [1973]) and Toolan (1996 [1990]).

Useful edited collections on Russian Formalism and the Prague School are: Erlich (1965), Garvin (1964), Lemon and Reis (1965), and Matejka and Pomorska (1971). Bloomsfield's influential book *Language* (1984 [1933]) is a good place to start if you wish to learn more about structural linguistics. Similarly, Chomsky sets out his theory of transformational grammar originally in *Syntactic Structures* (2002 [1957]).

A good introduction to Reader Response Criticism is Tompkins' (1980) edited collection *Reader-Response Criticism: From Formalism to Post-Structuralism*. For works by the major reader response critics and reception theorists, see: Culler (1975), Fetterley (1977), Fish (1980 [1973]), Freund (1987), Holland (1975), Holub (1984), Iser (1974, 1978), and Jauss (1982).

Part II

Literature as language

2 Foregrounding

2.1 The development and devices of foregrounding

In everyday conversation when we speak of 'foregrounding' something, we generally mean to highlight it, to draw attention to it. This is not dissimilar to how foregrounding is used in stylistics. Foregrounding refers to the ways in which certain aspects of a text can be made to stand out or appear prominent through forms of textual patterning. As such, foregrounding is the psychological effect of certain textual devices. In this way, foregrounding works to control readers' attention and is important in the generation of literary interpretations.

Foregrounding derives from the work of the Russian Formalists, in particular from the work of three key figures: Viktor Šhklovsky (1917), Bohuslav Hávranek (1932), and Jan Mukařovsky (1932). In 'Art as Technique', Šhklovsky argued that while the everyday processes of perception and cognition are 'habitual' and therefore become 'automatic', the function of art – including poetry and prose – is to force a re-perception in the reader, that is for the reader to see the familiar in a new light. He claims, 'The technique of art is to make objects "unfamiliar", to make forms difficult, to increase the difficulty and length of perception because the process of perception is an aesthetic end in itself and must be prolonged' (1965 [1917]: 12). In this way, Šhklovsky proposed the concept of **defamiliarisation** (translation by Lemon and Reis in 1965 from the original Russian 'ostraneniye' – to estrange, to make strange), the essence of which is that art and literary language should not only draw attention to their own artfulness and constructedness, but also attract and hold that attention in the creation of literary meaning for the reader.

Hávranek and Mukařovsky of the Prague School built on the concept of defamiliarisation in the 1930s, and it is from their work that the term 'foregrounding' stems (translated by Garvin in 1964 from the original Czech 'aktualisace' – actualisation). Hávranek, for instance, defines foregrounding as 'the use of devices of the language in such a way that this use itself attracts attention and is perceived as uncommon, as deprived of automatization, as deautomized' (1964 [1932]: 10) while Mukařovsky similarly asserts: 'Foregrounding is the opposite of automatization' (1964 [1932]: 19). All three critics – Šhklovsky, Hávranek, and Mukařovsky – were interested in the formal devices of language that could be used to defamiliarise and to foreground stylistic structures and literary meanings.

As a stylistic technique, foregrounding works across the linguistic levels introduced in Chapter 1 (phonological, morphological, lexico-grammatical, semantic, and graphological). Thus, it is an essential concept in stylistics and, while it is introduced in this chapter, it will resurface throughout the book. As a form of textual patterning, foregrounding occurs through either similarity and correspondence, that is through **parallelism** and the **repetition** of a pattern, or through a rupture or break in a pattern, known as **deviation**. Jeffries and McIntyre (2010: 31–2) describe parallelism as 'unexpected regularity' and deviation as 'unexpected irregularity'.

2.2 Parallelism and repetition

Parallelism and repetition are means of *creating* textual patterns, and may occur on micro or macro scales. A repeated pattern could be as small as the repetition of a single word. For example, Sheila Heti's (2013) short story 'The Cherry Tree' begins:

> That winter, all the plums froze. All the peaches froze and all the cherries froze, and everything froze so there were no fruits in the spring.

The repetition of the verb 'froze' four times in these two opening lines emphasises the severity of the frost. Moreover, this emphasis is enhanced by the iteration of the phrase 'all the [fruits] froze'. By using a different fruit in each instance alongside the repetition of 'all', the frost is shown to have been widespread. Additionally, Heti fashions her opening paragraph with a neat symmetry. The noun 'everything' continues to build a picture of the frost's expansiveness, but is then juxtaposed with the consequence of the frost: the freeze on 'everything' and 'all fruits' in 'winter' led to 'no fruits' in 'spring'.

As we have started to see then, repetition can go beyond the recurrence of a single word by taking the form of a repeated structure. Steve Martin's novel *The Pleasure of My Company* tells the story of a man in his thirties named Daniel whose life, and desire to find love, is severely complicated by the fact that he suffers from obsessive compulsive disorder. Clarissa, a student psychologist, has become one of several women who find themselves the source of Daniel's affections. On one of Clarissa's twice-weekly visits to Daniel's house, the following episode occurs (2003: 31–2):

> Then something exciting happened. Her cell phone rang. It was exciting because what crossed her face ranged wildly on the map of human emotion. And oh, did I divide that moment up into millionths:
>
> The phone rang.
>
> She decided to ignore it.
>
> She decided to answer it.
>
> She decided to ignore it.
>
> She decided to check caller-id.
>
> She looked at the phone display.
>
> She turned off the phone and continued speaking.
>
> But the moment before turning off the phone broke down into further submoments:
>
> She worried that it might be a specific person.
>
> She saw that it was.
>
> She turned off the phone with an angry snap.
>
> But this submoment broke down into even more sub-submoments:
>
> She grieved.
>
> Pain shot through her face like a lightning strike.
>
> So, Clarissa had an ex she was still connected to. I said, "Clarissa, you're a desirable girl; just sit quietly and you will resurrect." But wait, I didn't say it. I only thought it.

In this scene, Martin uses repetition to generate a sense of both characters' thought processes. The initial repetition of 'She decided to . . .', for instance, serves (ironically) to highlight Clarissa's indecision as to how to deal with the phone call. Her mental struggle is made particularly evident in the alternating verbs which contradict each other ('answer' vs. 'ignore') as well the repetition of 'ignore' to show that Clarissa mentally revisits this idea.

The various structural repetitions employed by Martin, on the other hand, work to offer insight into Daniel's mind. The repeated placement of 'She' in grammatical subject position and at the start of so many sentences shows the focus of Daniel's attention on Clarissa and foregrounds her reactions. Moreover, each reaction is foregrounded graphologically as a self-contained textual fragment in the form of single-sentence paragraphs, thus giving a sense of the way in which Daniel's obsessive compulsive mind dissects the details of human interactions. Such attention to detail is further accentuated in Daniel's description of his perception of the event into 'millionths', 'moments', 'submoments', and 'sub-sub-moments', the latter three expressions being particularly remarkable for the way in which, through the course of the episode, 'moments' is prefixed by 'sub-'. This example shows how foregrounding might be used by writers to portray a character's **mind style**. Fowler (1977: 103) defines mind style as 'any distinctive linguistic presentation of an individual mental self'. Mind style is not always a result of foregrounding, but in this example the textual patterns communicate a sense of the minutiae of Daniel's cognitions.

Syntactic parallelism is a significant form of structural repetition in which a syntactic structure is repeated or placed in parallel. In Lynne Tillman's short story 'Living with Contradictions', she writes in one sentence 'He didn't want to fight in any war and she didn't want to have a child' (2002: 81). Here, Tillman uses syntactic parallelism (in this case 'He didn't want to [X]' with 'she didn't want to [Y]') to generate a contrast between the priorities of two characters in a relationship, though what is also interesting about this example is that the things that both characters do not want make them anti-conformist to gender expectations. In this way, Tillman uses syntactic parallelism to create both structural contrast and internal incongruity in a way that enacts the contradictions of her story's title.

At its most extended, foregrounding in the form of syntactic parallelism can be used as a structural device in itself. Jeffrey McDaniel's (2008) poem 'don't touch it!' provides a case in point:

don't touch it!

if you touch it, it will melt
if it melts, it will leave a stain
if it leaves a stain, you will always remember it
if you always remember it, it will block the road
if it blocks the road, you will have to climb over it
if you have to climb over it, you will become superstitious
if you become superstitious, you will cover the mirror
if you cover the mirror, you will forget to get dressed
if you forget to get dressed, you will walk around naked in public
if you walk around naked in public, you will get aroused
if you get aroused, you will touch it

Evidently, McDaniel arranges 'don't touch it!' using a repeated syntactic formula: If [X], [Y] will . . . / If [Y], [Z] will . . . /, and so on. In doing so, McDaniel not only endows the poem with rhythm and momentum as it is read but also uses the conditional conjunction 'if' to create a cause-and-effect relationship between the two clauses in each line. The game or conceit of the poem is, of course, that in the course of its eleven lines it moves full circle returning the reader to the 'touch' that is forbidden in the title and first line. While the suggestion to 'touch it' (or not) at the start of the poem is semantically ambiguous though, by the time the final line arrives it has taken on crude connotations, through association with being 'naked' and then 'aroused'.

Syntactic parallelisms tend to suggest to readers that there is a relationship between the two parallel structures. In this way, readers are coerced into seeking interpretive associations between elements. Such semantic connections may be relationships of contrast as in the line from Tillman's 'Living with Contradictions' or they may be relationships of correspondence as we have seen in McDaniel's poem. Either way, syntactic parallelisms invite readers to consider the meaningful rapport between elements and use such meaning as they construct their textual interpretations.

2.3 Deviation

In contrast to repetition and parallelism, deviation draws attention through its difference. On deviation, Mukařovsky speaks of it as 'the intentional violation of the norm' (1964 [1932]: 18). Deviation works by disrupting or departing either from readers' expectations or from a pattern established by the text. This is essentially a division between **external deviation** and **internal deviation**.

External deviation is a violation of the norm in terms of the everyday rules of language. Such deviation would therefore be unusual in any text. A good example of external deviation can be seen in the poetry of e. e. cummings, and indeed even his published name is deviant in its refusal to use the standard capitalisation employed in the writing of names. Let's turn to a poem by e. e. cummings from his 1938 volume *Collected Poems* for evidence of external deviation (line numbers are our additions for analysis):

The Mind's(

i never you never
he she or it

never we you and they never
saw so
much heard so much smelled so much

tasted
plus touched quite so And

How much nonexistence
eye sed bea
yew tea mis
eyesucks unyewkuntel fingelstein idstings
yewrety oride lesgo eckshun
kemeruh daretoi
nig
)Ah,Soul

As in the presentation of his name, cummings' poem is externally deviant in its almost total use of lower case and lack of punctuation. In contrast, when capitals are used they are foregrounded since they stand out against the background norm of the text. In other words, while lack of punctuation is an external deviation from normal language use, the capitals are internally deviant since they diverge from the rules established within the text itself. In cummings' poem, the capitals occur in six words at three key locations: 'The Mind's' in line (L) 1, 'And / How' at the exact half-way point in the poem crossing L8–9, and in 'Ah,Soul' in the final sixteenth line. Foregrounded through capitalisation, these points provide significant frames for understanding this particular poem.

In the first section, upon entering the parenthesis (L2–8), cummings introduces a plethora of subjectivities through pronoun referents ('he she or it') followed by descriptions of exhaustive sensory accounts: 'never / saw so / much heard so much smelled so much / tasted / plus touched quite so'. The repetition of 'so much', composed of intensifier and an adverb with a semantic underpinning of 'more', suggests that the senses are overwhelmed as does the internally deviant appearance of 'plus', which further emphasises the concept of 'more'. The midpoint of the poem in 'And / How much nonexistence' signals a transition. While 'And / How much' appears to continue the concept of 'more', the reference to 'nonexistence' emphasises the intangibility of these sensory experiences. If we relate this sensory overload back to the foregrounded word in the opening line, 'Mind's', this first section might be interpreted as the human mind's (hence the many pronouns – this is a human experience) inability to totally comprehend, cognise, and absorb ethereal sensations.

The second section of the poem (L9–15) then descends into 'nonexistence' with nonsense words. These are both externally deviant since they are not standard spellings of words and internally deviant since they are a new feature in relation to the preceding text. While some of these are incomprehensible, others suggest potential meanings as readers attempt to make sense of them. Reading aloud for instance, some 'words' or 'phrases' appear to be open to homophonic interpretation: 'eye sed bea' might through sound be a rendering of 'I said be'; 'unyewkuntel' may be 'and you can tell'; 'lesgo' for 'let's go', 'eckshun' for 'action' and 'kemeruh' for 'camera'. You could try to decode this whole section in this way, but it seems more important that the poem shifts in its second half from something clear and easily processed by the mind towards something less certain and more experiential – here, experienced sonically. As such, this latter half might be interpreted as relating to the 'Ah,Soul' which follows the closing parenthesis. Taken as a whole then, cummings uses both external and internal deviation in order to foreground significant meanings. While internal deviation enables cummings to provide interpretive frames for readers, cummings employs deviation at an orthographical level to develop the extended meaning of his poem, which charts a journey from a cognising mind to an experiencing soul.

cummings' poem begins to show how internal deviation relies on the established rules, norms, and patterns of a text in order to be deviant and therefore to be effective in foregrounding. Take, as another example, the beginning of Deb Olin Unferth's self-titled short story 'Deb Olin Unferth' (2007: 21):

> No one in Wyoming thinks that Deb Olin Unferth is a fuckup.
>
> No one in Alaska, Nebraska, Texas, or Kentucky thinks that Deb Olin Unferth is a fuckup. Nobody in Morocco, Hungary, or anywhere in the Sahara thinks that Deb Olin Unferth is a fuckup. Nobody in Mexico.
>
> There may be someone in Alabama who does. There may be someone in New Hampshire. Maine. Members of her family may (Phoenix, Chicago).

The shock of the first line, with its expletive, initially appears deviant and foregrounded. However, the text quickly establishes a repeated pattern with the recurrent constructions that follow in the second paragraph ('No one in [X] thinks Deb Olin Unferth is a fuckup'). While the subject shifts from 'No one' to 'Nobody', this change is not too notable and therefore does not evoke strong foregrounding. Similarly, there is slight deviation in the shorter final sentence of the last paragraph, 'Nobody in Mexico', but since the rest of the sentence is omitted (e.g. 'Nobody in Mexico [thinks that Deb Olin Unferth is a fuckup]'), this too is not strongly foregrounded. In this second paragraph, Unferth also uses phonological repetition with the rhyming in the second line of 'Alaska' and 'Nebraska'. There is also the lexical repetition of Unferth's full name which, in its three-part form, is lengthy. Used in the title too, 'Deb

Olin Unferth' is clearly foregrounded as the topic of this short story as is the question, implicitly raised by the negation, of whether she is or is not 'a fuckup'. It is in the third paragraph, then, that the strongest internal deviation occurs: 'There may be someone in Alabama who does.' This sentence introduces 'someone' in contrast to the earlier 'No one' and 'Nobody', and is structurally deviant because of the use of 'may'. The final sentence given in the extract above displays the most internal deviance since it provides a more definite source for the opinion than previously, and moves the place references into parenthesis: 'Members of her family may (Phoenix, Chicago).' The effect of this is to create the suggestion that the preoccupation as to whether 'Deborah Olin Unferth is a fuckup' or not stems from the fact that some members of her family may hold this opinion.

Internal deviation is reliant on the features of the surrounding text and often works in conjunction with repetition and parallelism. Whether external or internal, deviation ultimately works to break the expectations of readers and draw attention to itself as a point of significance.

2.4 Foregrounding and character experience

As you might expect from its title, much of the action in Lee Rourke's (2010) debut novel *The Canal* takes place along the towpath of a canal, a graffiti-strewn and polluted stretch between Hackney and Islington in East London. The narrator, suffering from or perhaps embracing boredom, claims a bench and settles in (2010: 5–6):

> It was good sitting there, watching the world go by – saying nothing, doing nothing, thinking nothing. It was really good. I noticed that one office worker in particular, dressed in a light blue shirt and pink tie – both obviously expensive – kept getting up from his desk and walking over to another desk about ten to twelve times per hour. He looked stressed. He would stand at the other desk – a woman was sitting at it – for about three minutes, looking at her flat screen monitor, and then he would traipse back to his own desk. I had been watching the two Canada geese that had been floating back and forth, constantly giving me the eye – like they were expecting me to feed them. Back and forth. Back and forth. Back and forth. The office worker in the blue shirt and pink tie would shoot off one way and the two Canada geese would paddle by in the opposite direction. Back and forth. Back and forth. Back and forth. Maybe ten or twelve times per hour. Maybe more. I think I stayed on the bench watching the two Canada geese, the man in the blue shirt and pink tie and his fellow office

> workers for three or four hours or so, I'm not sure. Just counting them, watching their repetitive movements. I probably would have stayed there all day if it wasn't for the old lady who had suddenly joined me. She had no teeth, only a black hole for a mouth. She kept asking me over and over and over again in a slurred northeast London brogue.
>
> "Do you like the canal, then? Do you like the canal, then? Do you like the canal, then? Do you like the canal, then? Do you like the canal, then? Do you like the canal, then? Do you like the canal, then? Do you like the canal, then? Do you like the canal, then? Do you like the canal, then? Do you like the canal, then? Do you like the canal, then? Do you like the canal, then?"

The narrator's inactivity is underscored at the start of the extract with the repetition of a parallel structure, a continuous verb followed by the abstract noun 'nothing': He is 'saying nothing, doing nothing, thinking nothing'. This, however, is clearly pleasing to the narrator, since he says 'It was good' and then 'It was really good', a repetition with added intensifier for evaluative emphasis. His attention is occupied by two concurrent figures: 'the two Canada geese' and the male office worker with the 'blue shirt and pink tie'. The repetition of these two noun phrases (see Chapter 4), three times each, makes the images of them vivid for readers (an idea which will be explored further in Chapter 12 on 'Figure and ground'). Moreover, the movement of both the geese and the office worker is particularly foregrounded through the repetition of the adverb phrase 'back and forth'.

The repetition of the adverb phrase 'back and forth' is significant in that it suggests that office work is composed of monotonous routines. The mundane tedium of such white-collar work is also emphasised by the repetitions of 'desk', as the office worker moves between his own desk and the desk of his female colleague. Throughout the extract, there are also numerous references to time ('about ten to twelve times per hour', 'about three minutes', 'Maybe ten or twelve times per hour', 'three or four hours or so'). While there are repeated words, such as 'about' and 'per hour', within these phrases, they are not exact repetitions. Nevertheless, as repeated references to time they create semantic repetition and work to offer a frequent reminder of time passing, though the narrator's sense of time is evidently hazy and inexact. The foregrounding of 'back and forth' along with these fuzzy temporal markers provide weight to the narrator's later claim that he is uncertain of how long he sat on the bench watching the geese and office workers, but he did so, 'Just counting them, watching their *repetitive movements*' (our emphasis).

The action is then interrupted as the narrator is joined by an 'old lady'. The old lady is foregrounded by Rourke's use of metaphor, describing her as having 'only a black hole for a mouth'. Deplorable in its depiction, the 'black hole' is thus somewhat deviant on a semantic level. The repetition of 'over and over and over again' further foregrounds the old lady. When her speech is represented at the end of the extract, it is an unmistakeably deviant repetition of the question: 'Do you like the canal, then?' thirteen consecutive times. Though it looks deviant at first glance, however, the extremity and duration of the repetition means that it quickly loses readers' attention. Most readers are unlikely to read each iteration of 'Do you like the canal, then?' with equal concentration, and are thus more likely to begin to scan this passage. This is because the concept of newness is important in foregrounding and capturing attention. This pattern therefore quickly becomes part of the background of this section of text.

Ultimately, a foregrounding analysis of this passage of Lee Rourke's *The Canal* shows up the ways in which the author uses repetition to depict the living boredom of the narrator and the tedium and feeling of futility that white-collar office work may provoke.

Keywords and summary

Defamiliarisation, deviation (internal, external), parallelism, repetition, syntactic parallelism.

Foregrounding is the psychological effect produced by instances of repetition, parallelism, or deviation. Repetition, parallelism, and deviation can occur across linguistic levels of a text, and we have given some examples of such patterns in the analyses above. To summarise the devices of foregrounding, below is a short indicative list of some of the ways in which repetitions, parallelisms, and deviations may occur.

Phonological: Repetitions of particular sounds such as sibilants, liquids, plosives, or fricatives; devices of sound patterning such as alliteration, consonance, and assonance; deviations in sound choices; using rhyme and meter for emphasis (see Chapter 3).

Graphological: Using typographical devices such as a change in type face/font; the presence of italics, capitalisation, bold, or spacing for emphasis; the presence of unconventional punctuation or the lack of punctuation; the use of colour.

Morphological: Unusual forms of derivation or of breaking words up into distinct morphemes (see Chapter 4).

Orthographical: Deliberate misspellings of words for morphological and/or semantic effects.
Lexico-grammatical: Repetitions of words or phrases, syntactic parallelisms, deviant syntactic structures (see Chapters 4 and 5).
Semantic: Cohesive lexical choices, unusual naming, innovative descriptions and novel metaphors, neologisms (see Chapter 6).

Many of these forms of foregrounding will be revisited in subsequent chapters. As such, your understanding of foregrounding will be extended throughout this book.

Activities

1. Find a poem that uses repetitions and syntactic parallelisms. Identify the linguistic structure of the various patterns. What is the function of these within the poem? Are there any deviations, and if so are they used at important moments? How do the various repetitions, parallelisms, and deviations work together to help you form an overall interpretation of the poem?
2. Find a children's book or think back to your favourite childhood text. Such texts – take Dr. Seuss books, for instance – often employ lots of foregrounding. Look at how the text works. Why do you think this is the case?
3. Techniques of foregrounding are often thought to be employed more intensely in poetic texts, though as we have seen in this chapter fictional prose also makes significant use of foregrounding devices. Find a text from another genre – newspaper report, magazine article, political speech, etc. – and consider how it uses repetition, parallelism, and deviation. Does it? and to what end?

Further reading and references

The concepts of defamiliarisation and foregrounding which form the foundations of the contemporary stylistic understanding of this framework stem from Russian Formalism and were put forward in three central essays: Šhklovsky (1965 [1917]), Hávranek (1964 [1932]), and Mukařovsky (1964 [1932]). Another significant Russian Formalist whose ideas have strongly influenced stylistics, including the theory of foregrounding, is Roman Jakobson: see his collected works (1987). For useful edited collections on Russian Formalism and the Prague School, which include the essays above, see: Erlich (1965), Garvin (1964), Lemon and Reis (1965), and Matejka and Pomorska (1971).

Important work and good overviews of foregrounding can be found in: Douthwaite (2000), Leech (1969, 2008), Leech and Short (2007 [1981]), Levin (1962), Short (1996), and van Peer (2007). Stockwell (2000b) provides a discussion of syntactic parallelism in surrealist poetry. Discussion of foregrounding at the level of graphology can be found in: Short (2000) and van Peer (1996). In 2007, the journal *Language and Literature* produced a special issue on foregrounding: *Language and Literature* 16(2). Gregoriou (2007, 2011) has written on deviance in crime fiction and the contemporary novel. Anyone specifically interested in style in cummings poetry is advised to read: Cureton (1979, 1981, 1986), Simpson (1997: 25–56; 2014 [2004]: 52–5), Terblanche (2010), van Peer (1987), and Webster (1999).

Empirical studies and discussions of foregrounding are: Emmott et al. (2013), Miall and Kuiken (1994), Sanford and Emmott (2012), van Peer (1986), and van Peer et al. (2012 [2007]).

The concept of mind style, also mentioned in this chapter, comes from Fowler (1977, 1996 [1986]) and has since been explored in stylistics by Leech and Short (2007 [1981]), Black (1993), Bockting (1994), Semino and Swindlehurst (1996), Hoover (1999), Semino (2002a), Boase-Beier (2003), Gregoriou (2003), Hoover (2004), Leech (2007), Semino (2007), and Gregoriou (2014). Computational and corpus studies of mind style have been conducted by McIntyre and Archer (2010). McIntyre (2005) has also considered how mind style works in drama while Montoro (2010a, 2010b) has considered filmic representations.

3 Phonemes to sound patterning

3.1 Phonology and stylistics

In linguistics, **phonetics** is the study of speech sounds. For instance, both the words 'cat' and 'phone' consists of three sounds (notice that sounds do not have a one-to-one correspondence with orthographic letters). Each individual unit of sound is known as a **phoneme**. The International Phonetic Alphabet (IPA) is used to describe sounds, with each character representing a different phoneme (for example, the IPA characters for the sounds in 'phone' when pronounced with a British RP accent are [f] [əʊ] and [n]: /fəʊn/). Phonemes are grouped into consonant and vowel sounds and described in terms of how they are physically produced. Consonants are classified based on their *manner* and *place of articulation*; that is, the way in which the airflow moves up from the lungs through the vocal chords to the mouth and/or nose as well as its constriction by the shaping of the tongue and lips. Vowel sounds, on the other hand, are categorised by the tongue's relative height (high/closed, low/open) and positioning in the mouth (front, middle, back) along with whether the speaker's lips are rounded or spread.

Phonology is the study of patterns of speech sounds. Stylisticians are interested in how writers might deliberately manipulate speech sounds for aesthetic effects. When identifying sounds, it is always a good idea to consult the IPA chart (easily available online). However, some phonetic groupings often discussed in stylistic analysis are listed in Table 3.1.

Phonological analysis in stylistics means investigating the ways in which the sonic properties of a text contribute to the literary experience. The auditory quality of language is precisely the point of some poems. Sound poetry, for instance, is a genre defined by the fact that it privileges sound over all other elements, including semantics and syntax. A poet who is often seen as part of this tradition is Steve McCaffery. Born in Sheffield (UK), McCaffery later moved to Canada where he became a central figure in the avant-garde poetry scene. In his

Table 3.1 Phonetic groupings often used in stylistic analysis (based on phonetic descriptions in Fromkin et al. 2014: 189–223)

Name of sound pattern	IPA characters	Linguistic description
Fricatives Fricatives are created through the obstruction of airflow in such a way as to cause friction.	Labiodental fricatives [f] : as *f* in *feel* [v] : as *v* in *veal*	For labiodental fricatives, the friction occurs at the lips and teeth, leaving only a narrow opening from which air escapes.
	Interdental fricatives [θ] : as *th* in *thin* [ð] : as *th* in *then*	Interdental fricatives are created through friction between the tongue and the front teeth.
Sibilants Sibilants are characterised by similar acoustic, rather than articulatory, properties and include some fricatives and affricates. In all cases though, sibilants involve a friction that produces a hissing sound.	Alveolar fricatives [s] : as *s* in *seal* [z] : as *z* in *zeal*	Alveolar fricatives are formed through friction of air between the tongue and the alveolar ridge at the top of the mouth behind the teeth.
	Palatal fricatives [ʃ] : as *sh* in *mission* [ʒ] : as *jh* in *measure*	Friction between the tongue and palate at the top of the mouth behind the alveolar ridge creates palatal fricatives.
	Palatal affricates [tʃ] : as *ch* in *chin* [dʒ] : as *j* in *gin*	Palatal affricates require the raising of the front of the tongue to the palate. While they evoke a similar effect to fricatives, affricates involve an initial stop closure of air followed by its gradual release.
Glottals Glottals are produced primarily using the glottis, the opening between the vocal chords in the larynx (at the base of the back).	Glottal fricative [h] : as *h* in *hen*	For this glottal fricative, air flows through the opening between the vocal chords (known as the glottis) and pharynx and past the tongue and lips as they prepare to sound a vowel (which always follows [h]).

Liquids Liquids are an acoustic category that involves raising the tongue to the alveolar ridge and a small degree of obstruction to the airflow in the mouth.	Alveolar lateral approximant [l] : as *l* in *leaf* Alveolar central approximant [r] [IPA ɹ] : as *r* in *reef*	No actual friction occurs with approximants, but the tongue is raised to the alveolar ridge in a manner that approximates fricational closeness. For [l] the tip of the tongue is raised while for [r] the tip of the tongue is curled back.
Plosives (Stops) Also a form of stop, plosives involve the complete oral obstruction of the airflow for a short period before its release.	Bilabial plosives [p] : as *p* in *pill* [b] : as *b* in *bill*	Bilabial plosives involve stopping the airflow in the mouth through closing the lips.
	Alveolar plosives [t] : as *t* in *till* [d] : as *d* in *dill*	Alveolar plosives stop the airflow with the tongue at the alveolar ridge.
	Velar plosives [k] : as *c* in *cap* [g] : as *g* in *gap*	Velar plosives are produced by raising the back of the tongue to the velum (the soft palate at the top-back of the mouth) and completely obstructing the airflow.

1979 collection *Intimate Distortions*, McCaffery performs acts of phonetic translation – what he calls 'allusive referential' – in which he rewrites a source text through 'an associative-semantic method', choosing words for his revised poem through forms of linguistic relation and connotation. In the case of poem 'Sixteen' (2000: 138), such a method results in a new text that foregrounds the sounds of language:

Sixteen

the scene seen.
heards   men of the night
almost wherever you collect
the sounds.
i heard sheep you herd sheep.
i see scenes you see seas.
you wave a hand i hand
a wave to you.
your sea seen
i see seas
icy   seas

In 'Sixteen', McCaffery plays with three homophonic pairings – **homophones** being words which sound the same: 'scene'/'seen', 'heard'/'herd', and 'see'/'sea'. One of the words within the pairs is consistently a perception word (auditory perception in 'heard', and visual perception in 'seen' and 'see'). Such a choice is interesting since, given that sound poems are designed to be read aloud, the homophones work to generate misperceptions for listeners. This is particularly evident in McCaffery's use of 'heards' in L2: it is most likely to be initially understood as 'herds' because 'heards' is not a grammatically standard form. Moreover, by using homophones, McCaffery not only creates a degree of confusion for readers/listeners, he also creates the impression of semantic similarities between words that sound the same, as is the case in the opening line 'the scene seen': a 'scene' is a visage that is looked at, in other words it is a panorama that is 'seen'. In L5–8 McCaffery uses three syntactic parallelisms, with the final parallelism 'you wave a hand i hand / a wave to you' playing with grammar and word class with both 'hand' and 'wave' acting as noun and verb in the parallel structures (lexico-grammatical analysis is the topic of Chapters 4 and 5). The final three lines of the poem feature a tongue-twisting cluster of sibilants [s] and close with two homophonic phrases: 'i see seas / icy   seas'. While being composed of different words, these two phrases toy with **word boundary misperception**. The auditory difficulty of isolating the boundaries between these words mean that 'i see seas' and 'icy seas' sound like identical phrases. The sonic repetition of the two phrases caused by word boundary misperception thus makes it difficult to discern the syntactic roles and structural relationships of words in such instances.

McCaffery's poem uses sound effects to enact a game of sound and sense. This poem is less about generating a specific overall meaning, and more about the play of sound itself. Even so, this brief stylistic analysis of 'Sixteen' begins to show the way in which sound can be an important feature of style.

3.2 Onomatopoeia, consonance, and assonance

There are a number of ways in which a poet or writer can use the sonic properties of language to enhance a text. Below is an extract from the Italian Futurist Filippo Tommaso Marinetti's sound poem 'Zang Tumb Tumb', originally written between 1912 and 1913, and published in full in 1914 (2010 [1914]: 69; this version, 'Zong Toomb Toomb', is a translation from the original Italian). The poem is an account of Marinetti's own experiences as a reporter of the fighting between the Turks and Ottomans in the Battle of Adrianople in the first Balkan War. This particular extract is part of a sequence called 'Bridge'. The use of bold font is the author's original emphasis:

> you three level your
> machine guns that's it sit get your heads
> down behind your 3 death cameras do
> you understand racket squawking I know
> Turkish do you hear them shouting a saw
> a saw straw burn burn heavy cable
> crunch creak **crrr** the saw **tatatatatatatata**
> aim well **splash** turk 80 kg. into the wa-
> ter **splash** another one 120 kg.
> at least **tatatatatata** very good 2 3 5 turks
> 600 kg. **splash** **splash**
> cluster of turks **kerspslash-splash** to sat-
> isfy you dear Maritsa dazzle **zong-toomb-**
> **toomb** the machine-gun's-had-it 2 more
> keep it up keep it up **tatatatatata** water-
> ing cans of bullets machines to stitch up
> the atmosphere ripped by the axes **zah-**

> **zoo-zah-zoo-zoo** the bridge **cruuuunnch** creak-
> ing of its ribs very long long
> **thrrrrrobbing** of the cable Maritsa 120,000
> cu.m. pressure against the bridge to split
> it **zah-zoo-zah-zoo** **tatatatatata** **kring-**
> **striadiiiiii-ooooz** turks rage fury sobs

In the extract, Marinetti uses the sounds of language in order to evoke the sound and experience of this moment of war. Most immediately obvious as you begin reading is the lack of punctuation, which Marinetti uses to give a sense of the scene as a barrage of noise and a tumult of co-occurring experiences. A key feature of this extract, and of 'Zang Tumb Tumb' generally, is its use of **onomatopoeia**, a lexical item which portrays a correspondence between speech sounds and sounds in the world. Most of these are marked out graphologically in bold font. The first onomatopoeia in the extract, though, 'squawking' is not emboldened. It is used as a derogatory description of the voices of the Turks as they hurriedly plan to destroy the bridge, 'shouting a saw a saw straw burn burn'. Attridge (1988: 127–57) makes a distinction between **lexical** and **non-lexical** varieties of onomatopoeia. '[S]quawking' is a lexical onomatopoeia since it takes the form of a recognised word or verbal structure. In contrast, non-lexical onomatopoeia are made-up words (neologisms).

The next onomatopoeic description features both varieties: 'heavy cable crunch creak **crrr**'. Whilst 'crunch' and 'creak' are lexical onomatopoeia, 'crrr' is non-lexical. This also features **alliteration**, where co-occurring words begin with the same letter and/or sound. Here, it is achieved through **consonance** – an adjacency of consonant sounds – in the repetition of the velar plosive [k] which in the latter three iterations is paired with the alveolar central approximant [ɹ]: 'cable crunch creak crr'. This example demonstrates the way in which onomatopoeia works to imitate sounds through language. In this instance, Marinetti employs both repeated onomatopoeia and consonance to mimic the sound of a bridge cable as it struggles under the weight of the soldiers. Similar to consonance, another form of sound effect achieved through repetition is **assonance**, though now it is a repeated vowel sound. An example of this was seen earlier in 'a saw a saw straw', which repeats the [ʊə] vowel sound.

The next onomatopoeic moment is '**tatatatatatatata** aim well **splash** turk 80 kg. into the water'. It features the non-lexical onomatopoeia 'tatatatatatatata' which imitates the sound of machine gun fire through the repetition of two short sounds: alveolar plosive [t] coupled with the short open vowel [a]. It also uses the lexical and sibilant onomatopoeia 'splash' as a Turk, having been shot, falls from the bridge to hit the water.

Moreover, to demonstrate the sound of a number of Turkish soldiers hitting the water, Marinetti uses non-lexical and lexical onomatopoeia together in '**kerspslash-splash**'. The distinction between lexical and non-lexical forms is not wholly absolute, as we can see in words such as '**cruuuunnch**' and '**thrrrrrobbing**', where additional letters have simply been inserted to emphasise certain existing phonic qualities.

Onomatopoeia is a form of **iconicity**, that is a seemingly natural resemblance between the linguistic form of a communicative sign and its meaningful content. Iconicity is a perceived impression of relation between form and meaning and can occur across linguistic levels. Other auditory forms of iconicity, occurring through sound clusters and meter, will be discussed in sections 3.3 and 3.4.

3.3 Phonaesthesia and the phonaesthetic fallacy

Phonaesthesia is the study of sound symbolism, that is the way in which the sounds of words may be linked to their meanings. The term '**phonaestheme**' was coined by Firth (1930) to describe the way in which particular sounds or sound clusters appear to be linked with certain meanings. To exemplify this, Firth (1930: 185) cites English words beginning with *sl-* (the alveolar fricative [s] paired with alveolar lateral approximant [l]) such as 'slack', 'sloppy', 'slither', and 'slay', to name a few. For Firth, the *sl-* words he mentions all carry negative connotations, thus the consistency of related meaning allows the inference that the *sl-* sound has an inherently pejorative meaning. Similarly, Allan (1986) discusses the consistency of *fl-* to signify sudden movement (as in 'flail' and 'flap') and of *-ash* to suggest violent impact (as in 'crash' and 'smash').

All of these examples are monosyllabic, as are the majority of so-called phonaesthemes in English, and show that the phonaesthemic element can occur at different points in the syllable. A **syllable** is a phonological unit that is comprised of one or more phonemes. Structurally, it can be divided into three parts: **onset (O)**, **nucleus (N)**, and **coda (C)**. Syllables do not necessary contain all parts (ONC) but they must have a nucleus, which is typically a vowel. Thus, the indefinite article 'a' is an example of a minimal syllable since it only contains a nucleus. The nucleus is the central sound of a syllable and can be preceded by an onset and/or succeeded by a coda. The onset is the starting sounds of a syllable and is usually a consonant sound. *Sl-* and *fl-* (discussed above) are therefore onset phonaesthemes, whereas the *-ash* sound is an NC phonaestheme.

While phonaesthesia is a valid area of linguistic study, the evidence for phonaesthemes is not definitive. Studies into the possible reality of phonaesthemes (cf. Bergen 2004; Myers-Schulz et al. 2013) remain inconclusive and therefore unreliable as a form of linguistic data while discussions of, and any evidence for, the relationship between acoustic properties and emotional judgements is extremely vague in terms of semantic meaning.

It is therefore accepted in stylistic analysis that there is no direct or exact connection between the sounds of a word and its meaning. This is known as the **phonaesthetic fallacy**: the relationship between lexical sounds and meaning is arbitrary. As an example, look at the following sentences:

(a) *She whispered sweet caresses.*
(b) *The wasps swarmed crazily.*

Both sentences, which describe different narrative events, use similar sound patterning. Both are dominated by sibilance but also include the voiced labial-velar approximant [w] and velar plosive [k]. Nevertheless, despite the likeness of sounds, the meaning of the sound patterning differs for each sentence. In (a), sibilance is used for iconic effect, to give the text the acoustic sound of the whispering that is being described; in (b), iconicity is still at work but this time it imitates the sound of the swarming wasps. We might also note that while (a) has positive connotations, the iconic representation of wasps in (b) is likely to be interpreted with negative connotations. Thus, the idea of sounds having inherent emotional value is problematised by our example. This comparison makes clear that when considering the phonaesthetic quality of a literary text, stylisticians must always rely on narrative context in order to link linguistic form to literary meanings and interpretations.

3.4 Rhyme and meter

Born in Belfast in 1907, Irish poet Louis MacNeice was educated in England where he read and was influenced by the Modernist poets whose work he criticised for being obscure and difficult. Rather, he believed, poetry should reflect the life of the poet and the world around him. To achieve this, in his poetry MacNeice often demonstrates an acute awareness of sound patterns, using the sensory qualities of language and particularly its sonic properties to bring the places he describes to life in the imagination of the reader. Consider MacNeice's poem 'River in Spate' (1966 [1925–9]: 5–6):

River in Spate

The river falls and over the walls the coffins of cold funerals
Slide deep and sleep there in the close tomb of the pool,
And yellow waters lave the grave and pebbles pave its mortuary

And the river horses vault and plunge with their assault and battery,
And helter-skelter the coffins come and the drums beat and the waters flow,
And the panther horses lift their hooves and paw and shift and draw the bier,
The corpses blink in the rush of the river, and out of the water their chins they tip
And quaff the gush and lip the draught and crook their heads and crow,
Drowned and drunk with the cataract that carries them and buries them
And silts them over and covers them and lilts and chuckles over their bones;
The organ-tones that the winds raise will never pierce the water ways,
So all they will hear is the fall of hooves and the distant shake of harness,
And the beat of the bells on the horses' heads and the undertaker's laughter,
And the murmur that will lose its strength and blur at length to quietness,
And afterwards the minute heard descending, never ending heard,
And then the minute after and the minute after the minute after.

'River in Spate' depicts coffins being carried along by a river. Reading the poem, you should have immediately noticed that the phonological dimension of language is used to create iconicity. In this analysis, we'll consider how MacNeice organises sound patterning, rhyme, and meter to create the sounds of the river he describes.

From the opening line, the sounds of the river are brought to the reader's attention through rhyme. In L1, rhymes occur between the words 'falls', 'walls', and 'funerals'. '[F]alls' and 'walls' are forms of conventional or **end rhyme**, differing only in their onset sounds. This is why when describing syllable structure (remember ONC from section 3.3) nucleus and coda together form a subsyllable unit that is called **rime** (note, the different spelling). The end rhyme is used here as **internal rhyme** since it occurs within a single line of the poem. '[F]unerals' compounds the internal rhyme, finishing the line with the NC/rime in its final syllable '-rals'. Also featuring an alliteration in the form of consonance with the repetition of velar plosive [k] in 'coffins of cold', L1's sonic composition (in particular its internal rhyme) gives 'River in Spate' an immediately rhythmical feel.

L2, 'Slide deep and sleep there in the close tomb of the pool', features internal rhyme too with 'deep' and 'sleep'. In addition, there is **reverse rhyme** in '<u>Sl</u>ide' and '<u>sl</u>eep' which involves a match between at least the initial consonant cluster or onset (O) but can also involve the nucleus (ON). L2 slows the rhythm previously established in L1 though, through long stressed vowels: [i:] in 'sleep' and 'deep', [əʊ] in 'close', and [u:] 'tomb' and 'pool'. L3, 'And yellow waters lave the grave and pebbles pave its mortuary', continues the use of long vowels with the assonance of [eɪ] in 'lave', 'pave', and 'grave'. Given the content of the line, describing the river as the grave for the coffins, the slowing rhythmical effect these long vowels create might be linked to the theme of death. We can also start to notice a pattern with MacNeice mixing softer sounds such as sibilants and liquids ([r], [s], [l]) with harsher plosives ([k], [t], [p]) in all three lines.

The combination of soft and harsh sounds is a continuous feature of the poem. In L4, 'And the river horses vault and plunge with their assault and battery', the plosives work to quicken the rhythm. This is particularly evident in the parallel structures 'vault and plunge' and 'assault and battery', which represent the force of the river through the plosive stops [t], [p], and [b] and the internal rhyme of 'vault' and 'assault'. Sound patterning is once again iconic and, paired with the metaphor of 'horses', shows the river gathering force as it speeds up. The retroflex plosive stop [t] works similarly for rhythmical effect in 'helter-skelter' in L5, aided by the glottal [h] which seems to launch this rhythm. MacNeice's iconic rendering of the river makes it appear to become more ferocious with the consonant velar plosive [k] in 'coffins come' and the plosives [d] and [b] in onset positions in 'drums beat'.

L6 and 7 draw heavily on internal rhyme and assonance. In L6 MacNeice uses two internal rhymes, 'lift' and 'shift' and 'paw' and draw', but fluctuates between the longer back vowel [ʊə] of the latter two lexemes and the short closed vowel [ɪ] in the former pairing. [ɪ] is then subject to assonantal repetition in 'blink', 'chins', and 'tip' in L7 which also features the iconic phrase 'rush of the river' that uses liquid [r] with sibilant [ʃ] to perform the action it narrates. A similarly soft sound pattern is seen in 'quaff the gush and lip' in L8 which again uses sibilant and liquid phonemes as well as quelling the harsh plosive [k] through an onset pairing with approximant [w] (note also, the NC rhyming of 'gush' with L7's 'rush', and 'lip' with L7's 'tip'). The latter half of L8 is dominated by harsh plosives ([d], [k]), a predominant sound patterning that continues into L9 with lots of reverse rhyme and consonance across the two lines. L10, however, softens again with sibilants and liquids.

In L11, sibilant [s] and the approximant [w] are used for iconic effect: 'The organ-tones that the winds raise will never pierce the water ways'. In L12–13 MacNeice speaks of 'the fall of hooves', 'the distant shake of harness', 'the beat of bells on the horses' head', and 'the undertaker's laughter'. The noise of these noun phrases, particularly the onomatopoeia 'beat', is at odds with MacNeice's lament that this is 'all they [the corpses] will hear'. Incidentally, 'all they will hear' contains **half rhyme**, where the final consonant cluster (the coda) matches, with the repetition of the lateral approximant [l]. Given that 'River in Spate' was written between 1925 and 1929, this contradiction and the content of the noun phrases morbidly suggests that MacNeice's 'corpses' may be victims of World War I. The final three lines (L14–16) seem to phonologically soften with the repetition of the nasal [m], liquid [l], and sibilant [s] and [ð] as the corpses come to a final resting point in the river.

The final aspect of this sound patterning analysis is **meter**. When stylisticians speak of metrical patterning they are referring to the way in which poetic lines are organised into weak or unstressed (-) and strong or stressed (/) syllables. When a pattern is repeated across a line, it therefore creates poetic **rhythm**. There are five types of meter, as shown in Table 3.2.

The basic unit of rhythm is known as a **foot**. The number of times the foot is repeated gives the meter its name. Thus, iambic pentameter (which you're probably most familiar with since Shakespeare tended to use it in verse) is five repetitions of a weak strong two syllable foot. A line with only one foot is called monometer; two feet is dimeter; three is trimeter; four is tetrameter; five is pentameter; six is hexameter; seven is heptameter; eight is octameter; and so on.

Table 3.2 Types of poetic meter

No. of syllables per feet	Meter	Description	Depiction
Two-syllable feet	Iambic	A weak syllable followed by a strong syllable	- /
	Trochaic	A strong syllable followed by a weak syllable	/ -
	Spondaic	Two strong syllables	/ /
Three-syllable feet	Anapestic	Two weak syllables followed by a strong syllable	- - /
	Dactylic	One strong syllable followed by two weak syllables	/ - -

In 'River in Spate', MacNeice does not maintain metrical patterning with any real consistency. In L1–2, for instance, no regular pattern can be observed. In L3–4, however, we can detect iambic octameter:

```
3  And yel | low wa | ters lave | the grave | and peb |
     -  /     -  /      -  /       -  /       -  /
   bles pave | its mor | tuary
     -  /       -  /     - /
4 And | the ri | ver hor | ses vault | and plunge | with their |
   -     -  /     -  /      -  /        -  /          -  /
  assault | and bat | tery,
     -     /  - /    - /
```

You may, however, have noted the additional weak syllable at the start of L4. Typically placed at the beginning of a poetic line (or indeed, verse), this is known as an **offbeat**, which Simpson claims 'can act like a little phonetic springboard that helps us launch into the metrical scheme proper' (2014 [2004]: 17).

L5 returns to inconsistent meter. Indeed, exactly half of the poetic lines in 'River in Spate' are not metrically regular (L1, 2, 5, 9, 10, 11, 12, 14). Others appear to have some degree of regularity, as is the case with L7 (which features two iambic feet, five anapestic feet, and an ending iamb) and L13 (which opens with three anapestic feet but then slips into inconsistency):

```
7  The corp | ses blink | in the rush | of the riv | er, and out |
     -  /      -  /       - -  /        - -  /       - -  /
   of the wat | er their chins | they tip
     - -  /      - -  /          -  /
13 And the beat | of the bells | on the hor | ses' heads |
     - -  /        - -  /        - -  /       -  /
   and the und | ertaker's laughter,
     - -  /       - / -  / -
```

Overall, however, 'River in Spate' has a degree of consistency. The lines always contain either seven or eight stressed syllables, and the remaining lines are all iambic – in hexameter in L8, octameter in L3 and L15, and octameter but with an initial offbeat in L4 and L6. L16 is also in iambic octameter with two offbeats, though neither offbeat appears at the line beginning as we might expect. Look at the closing two lines:

```
15 And af | terwards | the min | ute heard | descen |
     - /     -  /      -  /      -  /       - /
   ding, nev | er end | ing heard,
     -  /      - /      -  /
```

16 And then | the min | ute af | ter and | the min | ute af |
 - / - / - / - / - / - /
ter | the min | ute af | **ter**.
 - - / - / -

At the end of 'River in Spate' as the sound patterning discussed earlier appears to soften and fade, MacNeice sets up iambic octameter only to disrupt its rhythm at the very end (emboldened).

Thinking of 'River in Spate' as a whole then, this sound patterning analysis demonstrates that MacNeice uses the phonological level of language to iconically create the tumultuous motion, the stops and starts, of the river itself. 'Spate' means both a sudden flood within a river as well as the quick succession of lots of things coming together. The sonic properties of MacNeice's poem illustrate this, with changing meter and internal rhymes creating fluctuating rhythm, while the sound clusters move swiftly between harsh plosives and softer sibilants and liquids. Moreover, the poem contains numerous references to sound itself, from the beating drums in L5 to the crowing corpses in L8, the chuckling cataract in L10 to the organ-tones of the wind in L11. These sounds, and all the others in the poem, are discordant and clashing. They depict the river as an unpredictable and formidable force and make the reader's experience of both the poem and the river a kind of 'assault and battery' on the ears.

Keywords and summary

Alliteration, assonance, consonance, homophones, iconicity, meter (foot, iambic, trocaic, spondaic, anapaestic, dactylic), offbeat, onomatopoeia (lexical, non-lexical), phonaestheme, phonaethesia, phonaesthetic fallacy, phoneme, phonetics, phonology, rhyme (end, internal, reverse, half), rhythm, syllable (onset, nucleus, coda, rime), word boundary misperception.

Throughout this chapter, we've explored the ways in which writers can manipulate the phonological properties of language for literary effects. From using onomatopoeia, alliteration and assonance, and dominant sound clusters, to rhymes and metrical patterning, writers can enrich the stories they tell by using techniques of sound patterning to create iconicity. The key thing for any stylistician is not to interpret such sounds or devices as indicative of any one thing. The literary interpretations you draw from sound patterning must be attentive to narrative context.

Activities

1. Choose a poem, and perform a homophonic translation. So, try to substitute each word in the original text with a homophone or at least a similar sounding word. How does this make you think of the relationship between words differently?
2. Look at either (a) two literary examples in which the same or similar sound clusters are being used (e.g. sibilance) or (b) two texts that focus on the same subject. For the latter, for example, you could compare Matthew Arnold's poem 'Dover Beach' with Sylvia Plath's poem 'Berck-Plage', both of which describe the sea. Perform a phonological stylistic analysis of your two poems and compare them. How does your comparative analysis show up the validity of the phonaesthetic fallacy? For (a) how are the same sounds used in the creation of different meanings?; for (b) how are different sounds used to evoke similar meanings or iconic representations?
3. Choose a poem on which to perform your own sound patterning analysis. For instance, you could look at another poem by Louis MacNeice such as 'Snow' to see how he uses sounds in a new context. Is there phonological iconicity in the poem you chose? Alternatively, you could choose a poem with a more regular meter and identify what it is.

Further reading and references

For a full discussion of onomatopoeia, see: Attridge (1988). Attridge's work is also excerpted in Simpson (2014 [2004]: 183–90). For those interested in theories of phonaesthemes, see: Allan (1986), Bergen (2004), Firth (1930, 1957), and Anderson (1998) who discusses phonaesthemes as forms of iconicity. Myers-Schulz et al. (2013) also provide an interesting discussion of the possibility of inherent emotion qualities to speech sounds. Stylistic consideration of rhyme, meter, and sound patterning can be found in Attridge (1982), Barney (2010), Fabb (1997, 2002), Jeffries and McInytre (2010), Leech (1969), MacMahon (2007), Simpson (2014 [2004]), and Thornborrow and Wareing (1998). For formalist work on phonology, see: Jakobson (1987) and Jakobson and Waugh (1979)

A good introduction to iconicity is Fischer and Nänny's essay (1999b) while edited volumes published by the *Iconicity Research Project* offer a good sense of the variation of work on iconicity: see Fischer and Nänny (1999a), Maeder et al. (2005), Müller and Fischer (2003), and Nänny and Fischer (2001). For analysis of iconicity in poetry and literary prose, see: Cureton (1981), Halter (1999), Ljungberg (2001), Richter (1985), and Webster (1999). Central work in stylistics and linguistics on iconicity has been undertaken by Leech and Short (2007 [1981]: 233–43), and Ungerer and Schmidt (1996: 250–5). Burke (2001) has considered the effect of iconicity on literary emotion.

4 Morphemes to words

4.1 Words

In the previous chapter, our stylistic analyses concentrated on the linguistic units of sound called phonemes. Phonemes come together to form more meaningful units – morphemes (which we'll begin to discuss in section 4.2) and words. Words have different grammatical functions depending on their lexical category or **word class**.

There are two types of word class: major and minor word classes. Major word classes are often also called lexical words or content words and may already be familiar to you: nouns, often characterised as 'naming words', primarily designate people or things (e.g. *boy*, *cat*, *table*); lexical verbs, considered as 'doing words', tend to express actions, processes, and events (e.g. *walked*, *write*, *thinking*); adjectives, as 'describing words', impart attributes or traits (e.g. *beautiful*, *red*, *bright*) and can be made comparative (*brighter*, *stronger*) or superlative (*strongest*, *worst*); adverbs, as optional parts of speech that modify or 'add to the verb', typically provide further information about manner, place, or time (how, where, when) (e.g. *slowly*, *somewhere*, *today*). In contrast, minor word classes are sometimes called grammatical words or function words. Many of these resurface in analyses throughout the book, but some categories of minor word class include:

- articles/determiners (e.g. definite: *the*; indefinite: *a*, *an*)
- conjunctions (e.g. coordinating: *and*, *but*, *so*; subordinating: *because*, *although*)
- modifiers and intensifiers (e.g. *rarely*, *very*, *extremely*)
- prepositions (e.g. *for*, *in*, *off*, *on*, *out*, *to*)
- personal pronouns (e.g. personal: *I*, *you*, *he*/*she*; impersonal: *it*, *one*)
- possessive pronouns (e.g. *my*, *our*, *your*, *his*/*her*)
- relative pronouns (e.g. *who*)
- demonstrative pronouns/demonstratives (e.g. *this*, *that*)

- auxiliary verbs/auxiliaries (e.g. *be, do, have*)
- modal auxiliary verbs/modals (e.g. *will, could, might, must*)

In stylistics, the analysis of minor grammatical word classes is just as important as that of major word classes. Indeed, the way that grammatical words combine with lexical words is often of great interest to stylisticians. This is partly because words exist in structural relationships. A noun such as 'book' could be used within a larger noun phrase such as 'the useful stylistics book'. In this case, the noun 'book' has been introduced by the definite article 'the' and **pre-modified** by two adjectives 'useful' and 'stylistics'. It could also be post-modified, for instance, as 'the useful stylistics book with the cool cover' where a prepositional phrase has been appended after the noun. Despite the presence of other word classes, 'the useful stylistics book' is a noun phrase because in the context of a sentence it would occupy the grammatical slot reserved for nouns and because 'book' is the **head** or most important word. Phrases can take various grammatical forms: as well as noun phrases, for example, there are also verb phrases. A verb such as 'read' could be part of a verb phrase such as 'has read'.

A familiarity with lexical word class allows you to be systematic in understanding how words function in their literary context. The beginning of Grace Nichols' (1984: 31) poem 'Shopping', for instance, features a list:

> I'm guilty of buying too little food
>
> 1 carton milk
> 1 carton juice
> 1 half chicken
> a little veg and fruit

Although the opening line of 'Shopping' provides context with which to interpret the four following lines as a shopping list, such an interpretation is strengthened by acknowledging that the list effect is also the result of stylistic composition. It reads like an itemised list because of its graphological layout and because each of the four lines is composed as a noun phrase. Moreover, the **ellipsis** (deletion) of the preposition 'of' in 'carton [of] milk' and 'carton [of] juice' as well as the missing determiner in 'half [a] chicken' enhance the sense of the list as notation. In this way, paying attention to word classes contributes to the rigour and replicability of stylistic analysis; it is rigorous because it involves paying close attention to the composition of the text's language, and replicable because stylistic analysis is transparent, allowing others to see how you have reached the conclusion that the text can be interpreted as a shopping list.

Looking at another example, the opening to Elizabeth Hickey's (2005) novel *The Painted Kiss*, further demonstrates the value of lexical analysis. *The Painted Kiss* is an art-historiographical fiction, a subgenre that takes the act of painting or the lives of painters and paintings as the central theme. Despite their fictionality, art-historiographical fictions are nevertheless grounded in history. *The Painted Kiss* imagines the romance between Viennese painter Gustav Klimt and the fashion designer Emilie Flöge. The story is written from Flöge's first-person perspective and, although it features flashbacks of her younger self in the late nineteenth century with Klimt, the present story now takes place in late World War II with Flöge as an older woman who has left war-torn Vienna for the relative safety of the countryside. The first chapter is headed with the location 'Kammer am Attersee' and dated 'October 21, 1944'. It begins (Hickey 2005: 1):

> When I left Vienna, I took one thing: a thick leather portfolio with a silver buckle. I departed quickly and had to leave many things behind. A rosewood cabinet Koloman Moser made for me. Twelve place settings of Wiener Werkstätte silver, designed by Hoffman. My costume collection. One of Fortuny's famous Delphos gowns. A pale yellow bias-cut satin gown by Madame Vionnet. Paul Poiret's sapphire blue harem pants and jewelled slippers. And the paintings. The most precious of all, they were too large and unwieldy to be taken on the train.

Whilst clause types will be discussed in the next chapter, it is useful here to note that the first sentence opens with a subordinate clause ('When I left Vienna'). The main clause, which imparts the most important information, is 'I took one thing'. The vagueness of the noun 'thing' and the singularity of the numerical adjective 'one' – in combination with the clause structure which delays the information – results in the foregrounding of this mysterious 'one thing'. The colon then functions to introduce a list, though the list is itself composed of only one item: 'a thick leather portfolio with a silver buckle'. The importance of this portfolio is further emphasised not only by its status as the sacred 'one thing' that Flöge has taken with her from Vienna, but also by the detail with which it is described. The noun 'portfolio' is pre-modified by two adjectives 'thick leather' as well as post-modified by the prepositional phrase 'with a silver buckle'.

In contrast to the 'one thing' Flöge saved, the second sentence explains that there were 'many things' that she did not take. Despite the lack of the colon punctuation mark, what follows is a list of these abandoned objects. Each item is presented as a noun phrase, with numeration and pre- and post-modification continuing to imply the importance of each object. Proper nouns also appear in many of the lists – names such as 'Koloman Moser', 'Wiener Werkstätte', 'Hoffman', 'Fortuny', 'Madame Vionnet', and 'Paul Poiret'. These proper nouns represent the names of famous artists and designers in Vienna in the period, but even without this knowledge readers are able to deduce that these are brands of a sort and thus the use of proper nouns suggest the considerable monetary value of the objects. An exception to this comes in the form of the noun phrase 'my costume collection'. Flöge was herself a designer. Thus, the possessive pronoun 'my' suggests not only her personal ownership of the collection but, in this context, it also indicates to the reader that she is herself an important name amongst the contemporaries already mentioned. The final item in the list of objects left behind is foregrounded through deviation: 'And the paintings' is the only noun phrase to be preceded by a conjunction ('And'). Graphological deviation is also involved through the separation of this noun phrase into a new sentence fragment. Consequently, the graphological separation and the conjunction 'And' suggest to readers that these paintings are in fact of much greater significance to Flöge than the valuable antiques listed. Moreover, conspicuous in its comparative lack of detail, the use of the definite article in 'the paintings' suggests that Flöge is remembering specific paintings and that they need no introduction. Indeed, the final sentence of the extract clarifies this by referring to the paintings as 'the most precious of all'.

The openings to both Grace Nichols' poem 'Shopping' and Elizabeth Hickey's novel *The Painted Kiss* use noun phrases in order to communicate important meaning. In 'Shopping', the noun phrases are used to represent a shopping list stylistically, whilst the way in which Hickey structures the noun phrases in the opening to *The Painted Kiss* imparts important information to readers about the narrator's emotional attachments to the objects. Paying attention to word classes within stylistic analysis is therefore important since it shows how writers can use lexical structures to express literary meanings. The grammatical analysis of phrases and sentences will be the subject of Chapter 5. In the next section of this chapter, we will consider the internal structure of words.

4.2 Morphemes

Words are composed of morphemes. A **morpheme** is a minimal unit of meaning. Some words are composed of only one morpheme, like 'pen', 'read', and 'homage'. These are 'monomorphemic' or **simplex words**. The word 'when' is also a simplex word since it cannot be

LIBRARY, UNIVERSITY OF CHESTER

broken down into smaller meaningful units: 'wh', 'whe', and 'en' are not meaningful constituents and even though 'hen' is a real word, it does not appear within 'when' in a meaningful way. Words are built up from morphemes. When words contain more than one morpheme, we call them polymorphemic or **complex words**. Putting the two morphemes 'read' and '-ing' together, makes 'reading', a word composed of two morphemes; 'un-', 'present', and '-able' can be combined to make a three morpheme word 'unpresentable'; and so on.

A single morpheme that can stand alone as a word is known as a **free morpheme**: 'pen', 'read', and 'homage' are all examples. In contrast, **bound morphemes** cannot occur on their own, and make meaning by attaching to other morphemes: 'un-', '-ing', and '-able' in our examples above are all bound. These particular morphemes are all **affixes** because they affix to other morphemes. Affixes that precede other morphemes such as 'un-' are **prefixes** while those that succeed other morphemes are **suffixes** like '-ing' and '-able'. Although they don't really occur in English, we can also speak of **infixes** inserted within another morpheme and **circumfixes** that affix around other morphemes. The process of word creation is known as **productivity**. Thus, when speakers use morphological rules to build words, for instance through affixation, this is productive.

The poet e. e. cummings, whom we encountered in Chapter 2, is well known for his techniques of morphological deviation. For instance, look at these opening lines from another of his poems, 'unlove's the heavenless hell and homeless home' (1994 [1958]: 765):

> unlove's the heavenless hell and homeless home
>
> of knowledgeable shadows(quick to seize
> each nothing which all soulless wraiths proclaim
> substance;all heartless spectres,happiness)
>
> lovers alone wear sunlight.

In the first line, we can see two cases of morphological deviation: 'unlove' and 'heavenless'. In the former, cummings adds the prefix 'un-' while in the latter cummings adjoins the suffix '-less'. In essence, cummings is practising **derivational** morphology, creating new words out of existing words (notice that 'unlove' remains a noun whereas '-less' changes the word class of 'heaven' from noun to adjective in 'heavenless'). However, although the morphological rule is sound ('un-' and '-less' do serve the derivational function of creating new words), 'unlove' and 'heavenless' are less recognisable as words (they are more externally deviant) than other similar constructions in the poem, such as 'homeless', 'soulless', and 'heartless'. While in linguistic terms, 'unlove' and 'heavenless' are less productive, readers can still interpret meaning in this poem. In the poem's opening, cummings refutes love through the negative prefix 'un-'. By describing it tautologically as a 'heavenless hell' and a 'homeless home', cummings implies that unloving is an uncomfortable and lonely experience. Love, in contrast, is cast as a precious state in cummings' metaphor, 'lovers alone wear sunlight'.

The lexico-grammatical analyses offered thus far in this chapter – of Grace Nichols' 'Shopping', Elizabeth Hickey's *The Painted Kiss*, and e. e. cummings' 'unlove's the heavenless hell and homeless home' – begin to demonstrate the ways in which an understanding of word class and morphology can support stylistic analysis. These brief analyses reveal how writers use the linguistic composition and function of words for meaningful and often playful purposes.

4.3 Morphological deviations

Following Plett (2010), we can distinguish four main strategies of morphological deviation: addition, subtraction, permutation, and substitution. These processes are used to make words which are externally deviant, therefore unusual and foregrounded. These processes are detailed in Table 4.1. Thus far in this chapter, we have only seen one form of morphological deviation: addition through affixation. Although in this section we will look at another literary example, we will not discuss every form of morphological deviation. Table 4.1 therefore provides illustrative examples from literature of the various morphological processes (many of the examples are taken from Plett 2010).

Dylan Thomas' (1954) radio play *Under Milk Wood: A Play for Voices* is considered one of the Anglo-Welsh poet's greatest works. He worked on it intermittently over a ten-year period and completed the first draft shortly before his death in New York in 1953. The play is often heralded as one of the best examples of Thomas' unique and innovative literary style, showcasing his love of words and sound. The opening to *Under Milk Wood* is, according to the directions, delivered '(*very softly*)' (1954: 1) by the first voice whose words set the scene in Thomas' fictional Welsh village, Llareggub (1954: 1–2):

> To begin at the beginning:
>
> It is spring, moonless night in the small town, starless and bible-black, the cobblestreets silent and the hunched, courters'-and-rabbits' wood limping invisible down to the sloeblack, slow, black, crowblack, fishing-boat-bobbing sea. The houses are blind as moles (though moles see fine to-night in the snouting, velvet dingles) or blind as Captain Cat there in

Table 4.1 Forms of morphological deviation (developed from Plett 2010: 147–82)

Strategy		Linguistic technique	Examples
Addition	Affixation	Prefix (initial)	*fore-* ('*foresuffer*': T. S. Eliot) *un-* ('*unlove*': e. e. cummings)
		Infix (medial)	*-ar-* ('*cursorary*': William Shakespeare)
		Suffix (final)	*-someness* ('*bearsomeness*': James Joyce) *-less* ('*heavenless*': e. e. cummings)
	Compounding	Noun + Verb	'warp-drive'
		Adjective + Verb	'*Newspeak*': George Orwell
		Verb + Adjective	'*spindizzy*'
Subtraction	Clipping	Fore-clipping	'*brella*' (for 'umbrella': James Joyce)
		Back-clipping	'*ad*' (for 'advertisement')
	Lexical blending		'*smog*' ('smoke' + 'fog') '*brunch*' ('breakfast' + 'lunch')
Permutation	Inversion: inverting the grammatical order		'*upbrought*' (for 'brought up': Edmund Spenser) '*upjump*' (for 'jump up': James Joyce)
	Tmesis: interpolating an element		'*how dearly ever parted*' (where 'however' has 'dearly' inserted: William Shakespeare)
	Chiastic reordering across two words		'*Gentes and Laitymen*' (instead of 'Ladies and gentlemen': James Joyce)
Substitution			'*almonthst*' ('almost'/'month') '*prapsposterous*' ('perhaps'/'preposterous): both James Joyce

> the muffled middle by the pump and the town clock, the shops in mourning, the Welfare Hall in widow's weeds. And all the people of the lulled and downfound town are sleeping now.
>
> Hish, the babies are sleeping, the farmers, the fishers, the tradesmen and pensioners, cobbler, schoolteacher, postman and publican, the undertaker and the fancy woman, drunkard, dressmaker, preacher, policeman, the webfoot cocklewomen and the tidy wives. Young girls lie bedded soft or glide in their dreams, with rings and trousseaux, bridesmaided by glowworms down the aisle of the organplaying wood. The boys are dreaming wicked or of the bucking ranches of the night and the jollyrogered sea. And the anthracite statuses of the horses sleep in the fields, and the cows in the byres, and the dogs in the wetnosed yards; and the cats nap in the slant corners or lope sly, streaking and needling on the one cloud of the roofs.
>
> You can hear the dew falling, and the hushed town breathing. Only *your* eyes are unclosed to see the black and folded town fast, and slow, asleep.

Under Milk Wood begins with a grammatical fragment, 'To begin at the beginning'. Whilst there is no deviation here, the repetition of 'begin' shows the process of morphological derivation. 'Begin' is used first in the infinitival verb phrase 'To begin' before appearing in nominalised form in the noun 'beginning'. More interestingly in terms of morphology, in *Under Milk Wood* Thomas makes extensive use of **compounding**, a process of word creation produced by combining two (or more) words or free morphemes. The first compound in *Under Milk Wood* is 'bible-black', created by compounding two nouns, or noun ('bible') with adjective ('black') depending on the contextual construal of 'black'. Whilst 'bible-black' functions as an adjective, it is less clear what its referent is. That is, because Thomas uses commas to make the coordinated adjective phrase ', starless and bible-black,' parenthetical, the adjective phrase could be read as either post-modifying the noun phrase 'small town' or as pre-modifying 'the cobblestreets'. Thus, 'starless and bible-black' appears to serve a double function, potentially describing both the town and its streets.

Thomas continues to use the adjective 'black' in two more compounds, 'sloeblack' and 'crowblack', which further describe the night's darkness. In the noun phrase 'the sloeblack, slow, black, crowblack, fishingboat-bobbing sea', Thomas repeats the adjective 'black' once individually and twice as the head of the two compounds. He also incorporates homophonic play (making 'sloeblack, slow, black' sound like repetition) and assonance (of the [əʊ] vowel which continues in 'crow') to give this description a rhythmical delivery that is iconic of the movement of the sea itself. '[F]ishingboat-bobbing' is an even more complex compound. The compound noun 'fishingboat' is composed of a present participle adjective ('fishing') and noun ('boat'). It is hyphenated with 'bobbing' to form a present participle adjective which pre-modifies 'sea' and uses the image of moving fishing boats to further suggest the sea's up and down motion. As the first voice continues, another morphological deviation arises in the adjective 'snouting', which acts as a pre-modifier in the noun phrase 'the snouting velvet dingles'. '[S]nouting' is created through affixation with the *-ing* suffix added to the noun 'snout'. Another deviant compound at the end of this second paragraph is 'downfound' which is particularly powerful because it has to be said with careful emphases due to the thrice-repeated diphthong [aʊ] in 'downfound town'.

The third paragraph starts with the orthographically deviant imperative 'Hish'. Many of the sleeping inhabitants of the town are cited using compound nouns: 'schoolteacher', 'postman', 'undertaker', 'dressmaker', and 'policeman'. These have become commonplace in English and are not deviant as we no longer interpret them to be creative neologisms (new words). 'The webfoot cocklewomen', however, is more unusual and therefore does attract attention. In the second sentence of the third paragraph, 'Young girls lie bedded soft or glide in their dreams, with rings and trousseaux, bridesmaided by glow-worms down the aisle of the organplaying wood', the compound noun 'bridesmaid' undergoes affixation with the addition of the *-ed* suffix in order to form a past-tense verb which is used in a passive construction: 'bridesmaided by glow-worms'. Additionally, 'glow-worms' is a compound noun while 'organplaying' is a compound adjective made from combining a noun and continuous verb. In contrast to the 'soft' dreams of the girls, the boys 'are dreaming wicked', an expression featuring subtraction with the omission of the adverbial suffix *-ly* (The boys are dreaming wicked*[ly]*). They dream of the 'jollyrogered sea' in which Thomas takes the proper noun 'Jolly Roger' which refers to the infamous skull-and-crossbones pirate flag (though Thomas uses it without capitalisation), adding the suffix *-ed* to form a new past-participle adjective. The last compound in the extract is 'wetnosed', formed from the adjective 'wet' and 'nosed' (the latter derived from adding the *-ed* suffix to the noun 'nose').

The final paragraph of the extract features less deviation (1954: 2; original emphasis):

> You can hear the dew falling, and the hushed town breathing. Only *your* eyes are unclosed to see the black and folded town fast, and slow, asleep.

This features direct address to the reader, which is emphasised through the italicisation of the possessive pronoun in 'Only *your* eyes are unclosed'. Thomas' use of 'unclosed' is interesting: *unclosed* means open, but its atypical use of the negative prefix *un-* makes harder work for the reader.

The opening to *Under Milk Wood* is rich in morphological deviation particularly compounding and affixation. Such intensity of deviation and by extension foregrounding means that *Under Milk Wood* cannot be read or listened to (remember it was written as a radio play) in an automatised way. It slows down your reading and the unusual language makes it feel highly poetic. It also works to make the town that Thomas describes seem unusual. Llareggub is a strange seaside town, an eccentric dwelling place only '*your* eyes are unclosed to'.

4.4 Morphological play in concrete poetry

Edwin Morgan was a Scottish poet, born in Glasgow in 1920. He received a number of awards and honours for his poetry: in 1999, he became Glasgow's first Poet Laureate, a position he held until 2005; in 2000, he received the Queen's Gold Medal for Poetry; and he was the National Poet for Scotland from 2004 until his death in 2010. His work is highly eclectic in style, but from the 1960s onwards Morgan often produced concrete poetry. 'Space Sonnet & Polyfilla' (1990 [1977]: 341) is one such example. The poem appears as two pieces – one entitled 'Space Sonnet', the other 'Polyfilla' – which despite their separation are indivisible:

Space Sonnet & Polyfilla

SPACE SONNET

A1 It's t   delirium's avai   le
A2 on tap when   r the light level   ks
A3 below w   reas   finds accep
A4 The whole   ht appa   us gives the shrinks
A5 excuses to   date stra   jacket form,
A6 and   n deep   Mars they're hard at work.
A7 We only ca   e from t   solar storm,
A8 and   w we're half   to the frenzied jerk
A9 of w   they c   their penal ther
A10 I d   't re   what it was I was
A11 n   r to forget. Guard! it's st   too bright!
A12 I   t to ride the swa   g canopy
A13 with mile-   gh eleph   , I want wet gauze
A14 to roll in, and l   ls of vul   ite!

POLYFILLA

B1   rue   lab
B2   eve   sin
B3   hat   on   table

B4 tig rat
B5 up it
B6 eve in
B7 me her he
B8 no way
B9 hat all apy
B10 on member
B11 eve ill
B12 wan yin
B13 hi ants
B14 ape can

As the title suggests, 'Space Sonnet' is a fourteen-line sonnet. The title is also a play on words, with 'Space' indicating both the poem's setting on Mars as well as the fact that Morgan has extracted parts of words and left graphological spaces in their place. These extractions are then presented in the second sonnet 'Polyfilla', where they sit in the same graphological location as they would in the poetic line from which they have been extricated. Consequently, in order to read the full text of 'Space Sonnet & Polyfilla', readers have to add the particles of 'Polyfilla' into the lines of 'Space Sonnet'.

Taken together, the two pieces communicate a rather surreal narrative. Combining both pieces, the poem reads:

C1 It's true delirium's available
C2 on tap whenever the light level sinks
C3 below what reason finds acceptable
C4 The whole tight apparatus gives the shrinks
C5 excuses to update strait jacket form,
C6 and even deep in Mars they're hard at work.
C7 We only came here from the solar storm,
C8 and now we're halfway to the frenzied jerk
C9 of what they call their penal therapy
C10 I don't remember what it was I was
C11 never to forget. Guard! it's still too bright!
C12 I want to ride the swaying canopy
C13 with mile-high elephants, I want wet gauze
C14 to roll in, and lapels of vulcanite!

In this version, the particles from 'Polyfilla' have been underlined. The truth of the poem's strange and fantastical setting on Mars is hard to ascertain, since the poetic voice's mention of 'penal therapy' and emphatic call to a 'Guard!' raises questions about the speaker's sanity; such uncertainty is perhaps enhanced by the poem's form with the spaces in 'Space Sonnet' and the textual fragments in 'Polyfilla' suggesting a disordered mind.

Morgan's choices of what to extract as textual fragments in 'Polyfilla' experiment with morphological structure. Simpson, in his discussion of the intersection between graphology and morphology in e. e. cummings' poetry, argues that graphological features such as line breaks and white space 'intersect subtly with patterns at the level of morphology' (1997: 47). In e. e. cummings' work this is the result of dividing words into two parts across line breaks, while in Morgan's poem it results from extraction. Building on Simpson's analysis of cummings, we can consider four different effects of Morgan's textual extractions. The first is morphologically unproductive in that a word is split with neither the remaining letters in 'Space Sonnet' nor the extracted fragment in 'Polyfilla' resembling free morphemes. This is the case in L4 and L9 where the words 'tight' and 'therapy' have 'tig' and 'apy' extracted into 'Polyfilla' leaving 'ht' and' ther' in 'Space Sonnet'. In contrast, a second effect is that both the extraction and remaining letters are free morphemes existent in the original word. This is true of 'update' in L5 which becomes 'up' in 'Polyfilla' and 'date' in 'Space Sonnet'.

Both the third and fourth effects rely upon illusion. In the third, a word is divided so that both parts *resemble* morphemes. We can see this in the division of 'remember' in L10 into 're' and 'member'. Whilst *re-* is a commonplace prefix in English and *member* is a word, these are not constituent morphemes of *remember*, which is in fact a simplex word. The fourth effect creates the illusion that the fragment in 'Polyfilla' is a free morpheme, leaving incoherent letters in 'Space Sonnet', such as the extraction of 'rat' from 'apparatus' (L4). Moreover, although the fragment in 'Polyfilla' reads like a recognisable morpheme or word (e.g. 'rat'), the complex does not actually exist within the context of the original word. This is the most common of Morgan's techniques and as a result, we can even start to see themes emerging. For instance, in addition to 'rat' (from 'appa<u>rat</u>us') in L4, 'ants' (from 'elephants') in L13 and 'ape' (from 'lapels') in L14 all masquerade as free morphemes from the semantic field of animals; in L7, a cluster of pronouns seems to arise ('me', 'her', 'he'). Across lines, we also find fragments that we'd expect to co-occur: 'eve' and 'sin' in L2 evoke the biblical myth whilst 'no' and 'way' in L8 collocate as an emphatic interjection.

Ultimately, the fragments in 'Polyfilla' and the meanings they suggest to readers add another layer to the poem. In doing so, they boost the effect of the poem as the direct voice of a troubled mind, struggling to make meaning either in a disturbed state and/or under the interplanetary pressures of excess light on Mars.

Keywords and summary

Addition, affixation (prefix, suffix, infix, circumfix), complex words, compounding, derivation, ellipsis, head, morphemes (bound, free), morphology, noun phrase, permutation, simplex words, subtraction (blending, clipping), word classes.

This chapter has considered the ways writers can exploit the morphological structure of words in literary contexts. In the poems of e. e. cummings and Edwin Morgan explored in this chapter, morphological fractures were used playfully to create new meanings whilst Dylan Thomas used affixation and compounding to enrich the linguistic texture of *Under Milk Wood.* Such deviations emphasise the value of analysing morphemes and words in stylistic analysis but even without such deviations, and as the brief discussion of Grace Nichols' poem 'Shopping' and Elizabeth Hickey's novel *The Painted Kiss* demonstrates, recognising word classes and morphological structures contributes to the rigour and replicability of stylistic analysis.

Activities

1. Find a poem that features several noun phrases such as Edwin Morgan's 'Off Course' (analysed by Carter 2014 [1989]) or write a list of at least ten film and/or book titles that are composed of noun phrases (e.g. *The Italian Job*). Rewrite the noun phrases so that all of the articles are indefinite (e.g. 'a' rather than definite 'the'). In what ways does a small alteration like this change the meanings? Are there some noun phrases that need the definite article?
2. Find an e. e. cummings poem and look at how he has dissected words within your chosen poem. As you do so, try to categorise the way in which words have been divided into morphemes following the system used by Simpson (1997) and in section 4.4 of this chapter. How does cummings' dissection of words into productive or unproductive morphemes affect how you read the poem?
3. Think of a feeling, sensation, thing, person, group, or event which does not have a single word to describe it. Have a go at inventing a word for it using the strategies in Table 4.1, for example:

   'Students who work part-time and study full-time'
   'That feeling on a winter's day when you're glad the sun is out but it is also shining annoyingly into your eyes'
   'The muck you have on your shoes after going to a nightclub'
   'That feeling when you've dropped something really small and you are struggling to pick it back up again'

'Flicking ahead to the end of a novel to find out what happens before you've finished it'

What kind of strategies work best? Why?

Further reading and references

Good linguistic introductions to morphology and word class can be found in Eppler and Ozón (2013: 17–80) and Fromkin et al. (2014: 33–75).

The discussion of morphological deviation in this chapter is founded on Plett's discussion of morphological figures in *Literary Rhetoric* (2010: 147–82) and further influenced by Leech (1969) and Stockwell (2000a). For work on cummings' style including morphological deviation, see: Cureton (1979, 1981, 1986), Simpson (1997: 25–56; 2014 [2004]: 54), van Peer (1987), and Webster (1999). Additional stylistic accounts of morphological composition and word classes in literary contexts can be found in: Carter (1993, 2014 [1989]), Dummet (1993), Freeman (1995), Leech and Short (2007 [1981]), Simpson (2014 [2004]: 116–20) Traugott and Pratt (1980), and Wright and Hope (1996).

5 Phrase to sentence

5.1 Phrases, clauses, and sentences

In section 4.1 of the last chapter, we learnt that words exist in structural relationships. That is, words are built into phrases. You were given examples of noun phrases (NP) and verb phrases (VP): both 'Sara' and 'the enthusiastic lecturer' are noun phrases; 'read' and 'has read' are both verb phrases. The most important word determining a phrase's grammatical character is called the **head** whilst the other elements are **dependents**. In these noun phrases, 'Sara' is the head with no dependents while 'lecturer' is also the head but this time it has dependents in terms of a determiner 'the' and a pre-modifying adjective 'enthusiastic'. 'Read' is the head of both verb phrases but the auxiliary verb 'has' is a dependent.

Phrases are built into clauses and clauses into sentences. The chapter introduces you to types of clause and sentence structure, following Eppler and Ozón (2013: 147–89), and shows you how to use this knowledge in stylistic analysis. The basic clause in English is made from a noun phrase followed by a verb phrase. We can talk about the different elements of a clause (such as noun and verb phrases) in terms of their functions. Usually, the first noun phrase in a clause functions as the grammatical **subject** (S). Everything else is considered to be the **predicate**, which must contain a verb phrase at least. Thus, the simplest form is a sentence such as 'Sara read' where the proper noun 'Sara' is the subject and the verb 'read' is the predicate. To this we could also add information about what Sara was reading: 'Sara read the book'. The predicate is now 'read the book' and is composed of a verb phrase as well as a direct object represented by the noun phrase 'the book'.

The verb phrase is the most important element in clause structure because it dictates what other clausal elements or **complements** are required. It also therefore dictates the structure of a clause. There are several basic composition structures for clauses and these are known as **complementation patterns**.

Table 5.1 Standard complementation patterns in English (based on Eppler and Ozón 2013: 149)

Complementation pattern	Verb type	Examples
S + V	Intransitive	Sara concentrated.
S + V + DO	Transitive	Sara enjoyed the book.
S + V + IO + DO	Ditransitive	Sara gave Alison the book.
S + V + DO + OC	Complex-transitive	Alison thought the book boring.
S + V + SC	Copulative	Alison is bored.

In 'Sara concentrated', the past-tense verb 'concentrated' is **intransitive**. This means that it does not require any other clausal elements to be grammatically complete. This is also true of other intransitive constructions such as 'The wind blew' or 'The door opened'. **Transitive** constructions, on the other hand, do require a complement in the form of a **direct object** (DO). Direct objects usually take the form of noun phrases, as is the case in our example 'Sara enjoyed the book': 'the book' is the DO.

While complementation patterns account for obligatory complements, there can also be additional elements within a clause that are not required. These are called **adjuncts** and they are optional elements. They provide more information but can be added or removed without affecting the grammaticality of a clause. For instance, to the intransitive clause 'The wind blew', we could add the prepositional phrase (PP) 'from the East': 'The wind blew from the East'. To our transitive statement, we could insert an adverb: 'Sara enjoyed the book greatly'.

As the prefix suggests, **ditransitive** constructions require two objects, which we differentiate by referring to one as the direct object and the other as **indirect object** (IO). In our example 'Sara gave Alison the book', the book is the DO and 'Alison' is a typical IO as a recipient of the action represented by the verb. Both DO and IO are expressed as noun phrases, but sometimes indirect objects are embedded within prepositional phrases, altering the ordering of clausal elements. In this case, we could rewrite the clause above as 'Sara gave the book to Alison'.

A complex-transitive verb also requires two elements: a direct object and what is known as an **object complement** (OC). The role of an object complement is to express more information about the DO. Thus, in our example the OC 'boring' describes Alison's feeling about the DO 'the book'. The final verb type creates a **copulative** construction. Typically, this complementation pattern is reliant upon the copula 'to be' and its related forms such as 'is' and 'was' (when used as main verbs rather than auxiliaries). However, it is also the result of lexical copulative verbs such as 'become', 'seem', and 'appear'. Copulative constructions offer more information about grammatical subjects and therefore the clause element that they insist upon is a **subject complement** (it complements the subject, so to speak). In our example 'Alison is bored', 'bored' attributes a property to the subject 'Alison'.

The complementation patterns discussed in this section have been illustrated with examples, all of which are **simple sentences**. Simple sentences are composed of only one clause. In the next section on coordination and subordination, we'll discuss how sentences can be composed of more than one clause.

5.2 Coordination

The five simple sentences from Table 5.1 all contain only one clause and a basic S+V(+) complementation pattern. However, sentences and the information they express can be constructed in more complicated ways than an SVO structure. For instance, sentences can (and often do) consist of more than one clause. A useful method for deciding how many clauses there are in a sentence is to count the number of lexical verbs. If there is one lexical verb, then there is usually only one clause; if there are two lexical verbs, then there must be two clauses; and so on.

Clauses can be linked through two processes: coordination and/or subordination. **Coordination** involves joining two or more independent clauses or phrases. For example, sentences (a) and (b) below are both simple sentences consisting of one clause. In sentence (c), however, they are coordinated using the conjunction 'but'.

(a) Sara enjoyed the book.
(b) Alison was bored.
(c) Sara enjoyed the book <u>but</u> Alison was bored.

Conjunctions are typical markers of coordination. In (c) 'but' joins the transitive clause 'Sara enjoyed the book' with the copulative clause 'Alison was bored'. Because the clauses are coordinated, neither depends upon the other and therefore they have equal importance.

When coordination occurs through the use of overt lexical markers such as conjunctions, it is called **syndetic** coordination (for instance, 'and', 'for', 'or', 'so', 'yet'). On the other hand, **asyndetic** coordination occurs without lexical markers but through other means such as punctuation. We can see examples of both forms in the opening to E. Lockhart's young adult fiction *We Were Liars* (2014):

> Welcome to the beautiful Sinclair family.
>
> No one is a criminal.

> No one is an addict.
> No one is a failure.
> The Sinclairs are athletic, tall, and handsome. We are old-money Democrats. Our smiles are wide, our chins square, and our tennis serves aggressive.

We Were Liars starts with a greeting, which is then followed by a series of copulative constructions. The first three are simple sentences and all cast 'No one' as the subject in order to negate the subject complements which are undesirable attributes. Thus, members of the Sinclair family are model citizens and successful individuals. In 'The Sinclairs are athletic, tall, and handsome', both asyndetic and syndetic coordination is used. Note, though, that this is still a simple sentence since there is only one lexical verb, the present-tense plural form of the copula, 'are'. The conjunction 'and' and use of commas coordinates subject complements in the form of adjectives ('athletic', 'tall', 'handsome'). What about the final sentence? It also uses a combination of asyndetic and syndetic strategies but does it coordinate phrases or clauses?

> *Our smiles are wide, our chins square, and our tennis serves aggressive.*

The answer is that it coordinates three clauses. However, because the lexical verb 'are' is elided in the second and third clauses, it may have been a little harder to spot.

A third form of coordination is **polysyndetic** coordination, which involves the significant repetition of a conjunction (usually 'and') to coordinate elements. Polysyndetic coordination is often a feature of author Cormac McCarthy's style. The following sentence is from his post-apocalyptic novel *The Road* (2006: 3). As you read it, count the lexical verbs and decide how many clauses there are:

> He pulled the blue plastic tarp off of him and folded it and carried it out to the grocery cart and packed it and came back with their plates and some cornmeal cakes in a plastic bag and a plastic bottle of syrup.

As you can see, McCarthy repeats the coordinating conjunction 'and' six times. On the first four occasions this works to coordinate clauses. Unusually, the subject is missing in all but the first clause. However, this is because the subject is identical to the first ('he') and is therefore deleted through the process of ellipsis to avoided repetition. There are therefore five clauses as shown below, with the lexical verbs underlined (how did you get on?):

1. He <u>pulled</u> the blue plastic tarp off of him
2. [he] <u>folded</u> it

3. [he] carried it out to the grocery cart
4. [he] packed it
5. [he] came back with their plates and some cornmeal cakes in a plastic bag and a plastic bottle of syrup.

There are also two instances of 'and' in the final clause. These coordinate noun phrases ('their plates', 'some cornmeal cakes in a plastic bag', 'a plastic bottle of syrup'). The noun phrases themselves are embedded in the adjunct prepositional phrase that begins 'with their plates and . . .'.

In this extract, polysyndetic coordination is not necessary but a stylistic choice McCarthy has made. The effect in this instance is to emphasise the mundane life the characters lead in this post-apocalyptic world. Try rewriting McCarthy's sentence, removing as many 'ands' as possible. This form of textual intervention will help you to consider the different stylistic effects between polysyndetic and asyndetic coordination.

In this section, we've looked at coordination, which can occur at both the level of the phrase and at the level of the clause. When coordination works to coordinate independent clauses, sentences can no longer be said to be simple in syntactic terms. Rather, they are **compound sentences**.

5.3 Subordination

Whilst coordination serves to join independent clauses, **subordination** involves the combination of an independent clause with one or more dependent clauses. These are called **complex sentences**. Here are two examples:

(d) Although Sara enjoyed the book, Alison was bored.
(e) The students like big words, because big things are cool.

Like compound sentences, these complex sentences still contain two clauses. In these examples, both clauses also have their own subject and verb elements. So what makes them complex? Well, the first clue is that they both contain subordinating conjunctions: 'although' and 'because'. Other subordinating conjunctions include 'after', 'as', 'before', 'if', 'since', 'until', 'when', 'whether', 'while'. These mark the clause they introduce as dependent or subordinate. Thus, in (d) 'Although Sara enjoyed the book' is the subordinate clause because it cannot stand alone, whereas 'Alison was bored' is the main clause. Now look at (e) and decide which is the main and which is the subordinate clause.

As well as counting the number of lexical verbs, another method for identifying complex sentences is by looking at the verb form.

Subordinate clauses often contain non-finite verbs (e.g. not marked for tense). Eppler and Ozón (2013: 178–9) ientify three varieties:

1. Base or infinitival form – with (full) or without (bare) *to*:
   - *I asked him to leave.*
   - *I made him leave.*
2. -ed participle form:
   - *Intimidated by Pauline, he left.*
3. -ing form (*gerund*):
   - *Leaving the party made him sad.*

However, subordinate clauses can omit the verb such as in the sentence 'Pauline left after Jack'. Ellipsis takes place in the second instance, but as a subordinating conjunction 'after' brings the clause to our attention ('after Jack [left]'). Another example of a verbless subordinate clause is 'Only a child, eight-year-old Einstein was very clever.' Here, the subordinate clause is 'Only a child'. As an attribute of Einstein, it acts like a subject complement and thus we can think of it as missing a copulative verb (e.g. 'although he was only a child').

Subordinate clauses often typically act as a constituent element of the main clause. Thus, they can act as sentence elements (subjects, objects, subject complements, and adjuncts), as in the example 'Leaving the party made him sad' where the subordinate clause 'Leaving the party' occupies the subject position in the main clause, 'made' is the verb element, 'him' is the object', and 'sad' is an object complement because it gives us more information about 'him'. Subordinate clauses can also act as phrasal elements (post-modifiers of noun and adjective phrases or complements of prepositional phrases). The latter is the case for **relative clauses**, which function to post-modify a noun. Relative clauses are usually introduced by relative pronouns (hence the name!) such as 'that', 'who', 'which', 'whose'.

(f) Alison was bored by the book [that] Sara read.
(g) The man who mugged Joan was dangerous.

The relative pronoun can also sometimes be omitted. This is the case with (f) above, but not with (g).

We have covered a lot of information about sentences in this chapter. Some key things to remember are: practise identifying lexical verbs as this will help you to identify clauses; look out for coordinating and subordinating conjunctions in sentences; be aware that some parts of sentences may be elided; and appreciate the intricate structures-within-structures that form sentences! You can always refer back to the explanations above to help you in your own sentence analyses. Finally, as well as identifying the structure of sentences, as stylisticians we must also consider their literary effects.

To conclude this section then, let's return to Cormac McCarthy's *The Road* (2006: 3). In doing so, we can develop the analysis we started at the end of section 5.2. Sentences have been numbered for ease of analysis:

> (1) When he got back the boy was still asleep. (2) He pulled the blue plastic tarp off of him and folded it and carried it out to the grocery cart and packed it and came back with their plates and some cornmeal cakes in a plastic bag and a plastic bottle of syrup. (3) He spread the small tarp they used for a table on the ground and laid everything out and he took the pistol from his belt and laid it on the cloth and then he just sat watching the boy sleep. (4) He'd pulled away his mask in the night and it was buried somewhere in the blankets. (5) He watched the boy and he looked out through the tree toward the road. (6) This was not a safe place.

The extract begins with a complex sentence. The subordinate conjunction 'when' introduces the subordinate clause before the main copulative clause 'the boy was still asleep'. By using this structure, McCarthy makes 'the boy' the most important subject of the sentence and, in doing so, shows readers how important the boy is to the third-person character 'he'. As discussed previously, sentence (S) 2 is a compound sentence composed of five clauses that use polysyndetic coordination to suggest continuous action performed by the character and the relative monotony of his daily routine.

S3 is another complex sentence. The main clause is transitive: 'He spread the small tarp'. However, the DO is a noun phrase that has been post-modified by a relative clause with 'that' omitted: 'they used for a table on the ground'. This relative clause offers further description of the tarp and suggests not only the function of the tarp but also its regularity of use. S3 is then extended with three coordinated clauses ('and laid everything out and he took the pistol from his belt and laid it on the cloth') before concluding with a complex structure 'and then he just sat watching the boy sleep'. The subordinate structure here occurs with the use of the present participle form of the verb 'watching', and again emphasises the main character's focus upon the boy. S4 and S5 are both compound sentences composed of two clauses each. Whilst S4 describes the boy's sleeping state, S5 demonstrates the main character's split attention on both the boy and the road.

The final sentence (S6) 'This was not a safe place' is a copulative construction.

This extract from *The Road* is relatively short; it consists of only six sentences. Nevertheless, there are two important outcomes to an analysis of its sentence structures. Firstly, it shows how syntactic constructions can create particular stylistic effects: in this context, the use of compound and complex sentences contributes to the representation of the main character's life as a bleak but perpetual series of small actions. The simple sentence (S6) is foregrounded by its brevity: it is a dramatic and brief moment of pause for the main character and highlights to readers the danger of the characters' situation. Secondly, the analysis of sentence structure shows how McCarthy highlights particular aspects of the fictional world and thus prompts certain literary interpretations. For instance, the boy is clearly important to the main character. This is immediately signalled by the fact that 'the boy' is the subject of the main clause in S1 as well as in the first independent clause of compound S4. Moreover, when 'the boy' is not the subject of a main clause, McCarthy ensures that he remains an important focus as the direct object of the main character's watchful eye. In this way, McCarthy uses style and sentence structure to create meaning, narrative tension, and readerly intrigue.

5.4 Poetic syntax

In this section, we'll consider how sentence structure interacts with poetic form, specifically the way in which sentences and phrases are completed (or not) within the boundary of a poetic line. When a sentence or phrase is completed at the end of a poetic line or when a poetic line ends at a grammatical boundary (often indicated by punctuation), the line is said to be **end-stopped**. In contrast, **run-on lines** continue the syntactic structure from one line onto the next, a feature known as **enjambment**.

In some instances, enjambment can create syntactic ambiguity: when sentences are enjambed, readers may find it difficult to construe the syntactic use of a word at the line-ending. This is known as **double syntax**, where a line-ending or line-starting word initially seems to function in one syntactic role as it is read, but its succeeding content suggests that it is being used in an alternate syntactic role. In Furniss and Bath's (2007 [1996]: 81) words, 'syntax becomes "double" when the word or phrase at the line ending can be taken as belonging grammatically either with what comes before or with what comes after'. Consequently, both understandings of the double syntax exist in readers' minds. Matthea

Harvey's (2000: 29) poem 'In Defense of Our Overgrown Garden' contains six instances of double syntax. See if you can spot them as you read the poem:

IN DEFENSE OF OUR OVERGROWN GARDEN

Last night the apple trees shook and gave each lettuce a heart
Six hard red apples broke through the greenhouse glass and
Landed in the middle of those ever-so slightly green leaves
That seem no mix of seeds and soil but of pastels and light and
Chalk x's mark our oaks that are supposed to be cut down
I've seen the neighbors frown when they look over the fence
And see our espalier pear trees bowing out of shape I did like that
They looked like candelabras against the wall but what's the sense
In swooning over pruning I said as much to Mrs. Jones and I swear
She threw her cane at me and walked off down the street without
It has puzzled me that people coo over bonsai trees when
You can squint your eyes and shrink anything without much of
A struggle ensued with some starlings and the strawberry nets
So after untangling the two I took the nets off and watched birds
With red beaks fly by all morning at the window and reread your letter
About how castles you flew over made crenellated shadows on
The water in the rainbarrel has overflowed and made a small swamp
I think the potatoes might turn out slightly damp don't worry
If there is no fog on the day you come home I will build a bonfire
So the smoke will make the cedars look the way you like them
To close I'm sorry there won't be any salad and I love you

None of the lines end with punctuation, so the completeness of each line is dependent on readers' interpretations of syntactic units. L1 appears to be end-stopped. L2 offers explanation to the previous metaphor – that red apples fell from the tree and thus looked like 'hearts' when they landed amongst the lettuces – and is enjambed with the conjunction 'and' coordinating verb phrases across lines. Whilst L3 initially appears to be end-stopped, the next line continues the sentence with post-modification to the noun with a relative clause: 'leaves / That seem . . .'. The first instance of double syntax doesn't appear until the transition from L4–5:

> That seem no mix of seeds and soil but of pastels and light and
> Chalk x's mark our oaks that are supposed to be cut down

The polysyndetic use of 'and' at the end of L4 serves to coordinate nouns, thus 'Chalk' at the start of L5 initially appears to function as the final noun in this list. However, as the line continues it becomes apparent that 'Chalk' is performing a double syntactic role. It is also being used by Harvey as pre-modifying adjective in the subject of a new sentence 'Chalk x's mark our oaks . . .'.

The second instance of double syntax occurs across L7–8 where the poetic voice states 'I did like that'. In this clause, 'I' is the subject and 'did like' is the predicate. 'Like' is a transitive verb that requires an object so it initially seems as though 'that' is the direct object of the verb, referring anaphorically back to the 'espalier pear trees'. The continuation of syntax in L8, though, suggests that 'that' also signals the start of what is known as a ***that*-clause**, a subordinate clause that fills a nominal position (of subject or object):

I	like	that / they looked like candelabras . . .
Subject	Verb	Object

That-clauses differ from relative clauses (which were introduced in section 5.3): *that*-clauses take the role of a compulsory element in the sentence as subject or object. Returning to Harvey's poem, we can see that whilst 'that' initially appears to perform the syntactic role of anaphoric DO, upon further reading it seems that it also performs another syntactic role as the start of a *that*-clause. It is therefore an instance of double syntax.

The pronoun 'it' at the start of L11 is the third case of double syntax, functioning both as anaphoric reference to Mrs. Jones' cane and as subject in the sentence 'It has puzzled me'. 'A struggle' in L13 is a noun phrase, which likewise ends its preceding sentence and acts as opening subject to the next. A similar effect takes place in the fifth instance of double syntax: 'The water' at the start of L17 is a noun phrase embedded in the prepositional phrase 'of / the water' (L16–17) as well as the head noun of the larger noun phrase 'The water in the rainbarrel' which is the subject of the predicate 'has overflowed'. The imperative 'don't worry' at the end of L18 is the final occurrence of double syntax, originally seeming to refer anaphorically to 'the potatoes' before the conditional conjunction 'if' launches a subordinate clause at the start of L19 for which 'don't worry' would act as the main clause.

We have focused here on grammatical analysis, but it is always important to link linguistic features to their overarching literary significance. The six cases of double syntax in 'In Defense of Our Overgrown Garden' are playful and complex but they work not only to double syntactic functions and meanings. They can also be read as a form of iconicity in the poem. Like the overgrown garden, the poem itself appears overgrown, with the boundaries between poetic lines and sentences

Table 5.2 Sentence types and clause combination

No. of lexical verbs	No. of clauses	Combined through . . .	Sentence type
1	1		Simple
2 or more	2 or more	Coordination	Compound
2 or more	2 or more	Subordination	Complex

growing into each other, so to speak.

Keywords and summary

Clauses, complement, complementation patterns, coordination (syndetic, asyndetic, polysyndetic), double syntax, enjambment, iconic syntax, object (direct, indirect), object complement, phrases (head, dependents), predicate, relative clauses, sentences (complex, compound, simple), subject, subject complement, subordination, that-clauses, verb types (complex-transitive, copulative, ditransitive, intransitive, transitive).

This chapter has offered an introduction to some key aspects of syntactic analysis. Section 5.1 described clause elements (such as subject, verb, and object) and explained that different verb types create different complementation patterns. Moving from simple sentences to the subject of coordination and subordination, it was shown that the number of lexical verbs determines the number of clauses. The number of clauses, the type of clause, and how those clauses are joined together determines the type of sentence. This is summarised in Table 5.2.

The analyses in this chapter, particularly of Cormac McCarthy's *The Road* and Matthea Harvey's 'In Defense of Our Overgrown Garden', demonstrate the value of syntactic analysis for stylistics. Syntactic structures can create meaning, emphasis, and stylistic texture.

Activities

1. Look at the following ten sentences, all of which are book titles. Through the process of counting the lexical verbs, how many clauses is each sentence composed of?

   Never let me go. (Kazuo Ishiguro)
   Elizabeth is missing. (Emma Healey)
   All I really need to know I learned in Kindergarten. (Robert Fulghum)
   I was told there'd be cake. (Sloane Crosley)
   This isn't the sort of thing that happens to someone like you. (Jon McGregor)

I still miss my man but my aim is getting better. (Sarah Shankman)
Do androids dream of electric sheep? (Philip K. Dick)
I have no mouth and I must scream. (Harlan Ellison)
You shall know our velocity. (Dave Eggers)
When you look like your passport photo, it's time to go home. (Erma Bombeck)

2. Below is the opening to the novel *A Modern Family* by Socrates Adams (2013). The passage consists of two sentences:

   > A television presenter drives around a town in England. He stops at red lights, beeps at inconsiderate drivers, correctly applies his brakes, accelerates efficiently, observes the highway code, considers suicide, steers, checks all three mirrors, starts, stops, moves.

   How many clauses are in each sentence and therefore what type of sentences are they (simple, compound, complex)? If there is coordination or subordination present, does it happen at phrase or clause level?

3. Think about the following sentence from Brian Castro's (2009 [2003]: 62) novel *Shanghai Dancing*, which describes a hedonist dance:

   > The foxtrotting crowd spilled out of the small church at midnight laughing and singing and whirling and jiving.

   How is the sentence composed in syntactic terms? Thinking of the concept of iconicity that we discussed in Chapter 3, in what sense could you describe this as iconic?

Further reading and references

A good guide to phrase structures and syntactic analysis is Eppler and Ozón (2013), on which this chapter's account of clauses is based. For stylistic analyses that focus on lexis and grammar, see: Carter (1993), Kennedy (1982), Simpson (2014 [2004]), and Wright and Hope (1996: 1–161). Further reading on iconicity was suggested in section 3.7, though it is worth highlighting that iconic syntax is the focus of Cureton (1981) and Richter (1985). The term 'double syntax' stems from Ricks (1963) and is further described by Furniss and Bath (2007 [1996]).

6 Register, lexical semantics, and cohesion

6.1 Register

Chapters 2–5 have introduced ways of applying descriptive linguistic analysis in the study of literary language. The final chapter of this Part of the book considers ideas from the study of linguistic meaning. Linguistic meaning and style are highly dependent on social context. As such, we begin this chapter by exploring **register**, a term suggesting that different styles of language are used in different contexts. Register refers 'to a variety of language defined according to the situation' (Wales 2011 [1990]: 361). Halliday (1978) suggested that register comprises three situational features: mode/medium, tenor/tone, and semantic field:

Mode/Medium: The form of communication, primarily distinguishing between the modes or channels of speech and writing, though we can also recognise the medium (e.g. face-to-face, print, digital).

Tenor/Tone: The social relationship between participants, particularly the roles of addresser and addressee (e.g. orator/audience; writer/reader; narrator/narratee), which can be observed in the tone's relative formality or informality.

Semantic Field: The meaning relations and subject matter (sometimes called the domain), which can be identified in the language of the text. Text-type (e.g. speech, novel, poem, magazine, email, tweet) is evidently a factor here, as is genre. In the recipe genre, for instance, we'd expect there to be field-specific vocabulary (lexis from a particular semantic field, e.g. cookery), such as the names of herbs and spices and directive verbs such as 'whisk', 'bake'.

Epistolary novels (written as a series of documents, most often letters) are a very clear example of how register works in a literary context. Look, for instance, at the start of the first letter in Samuel Richardson's eighteenth-century epistolary novel *Pamela, or Virtue Rewarded* (2009–13 [1740]):

> Dear Father and Mother,
> I have great trouble, and some comfort, to acquaint you with.

Richardson emulates the medium of the written letter within the novel. Furthermore, as a result of the letter format, the historical grandeur of the language, and Pamela's daughterly devotion and respect for her parents, the writing is rather formal in tone. There is also what might be called a 'high' culture register here: 'to acquaint you with' is a rather elaborate phrase in contrast to a more modern equivalent such as 'to tell you about'. In part, this is the result of the Latinate etymology of 'acquaint' ('trouble' and 'comfort' both have Latinate roots too); in contrast, the words in the suggested modern equivalent are Germanic in origin (looking up words in an etymological dictionary or the *Oxford English Dictionary* (OED) will give you this information). In their discussion of register and vocabulary, Wright and Hope make this very point (1996: 208):

> Because of the historical associations of Old French with the court and the law, and of French and Latin with learning, words derived from these sources tend to have a higher, that is more formal, register than Old English or Old Norse ones.

Additionally, the archaic syntax of Pamela's statement, 'I have great trouble, and some comfort, to acquaint you with', and the high, formal register add to the historical flavour of the piece as experienced by twenty-first-century readers.

Now, let's compare *Pamela* with another epistolary novel: the start of *The Perks of Being a Wallflower* by Stephen Chbosky (1999: 3). *The Perks of Being a Wallflower* is not only a more contemporary piece of literature but as a young adult fiction, it has a different target readership:

> Dear friend,
> I am writing to you because she said you listen and understand and didn't try to sleep with that person at that party even though you could have.

Whilst the medium is the same as in *Pamela*, the tone clearly differs. It is much less formal. Such colloquial register is the effect, in this case, of two factors. Firstly, the vocabulary is restricted to common words; and secondly, the sentence is syntactically extended with two instances of the coordinating conjunction 'and', two subordinating conjunctions ('because', 'even though'), and a nominal *that*-clause in 'she said you listen' (with 'that' omitted). (In fact, if you want to test how well you got on with syntactic analysis in the last chapter, identify the number of clauses in this sentence!) The register in just this brief opening to *The Perks of Being a Wallflower* consequently offers useful information to readers. The tenor of the discourse characterises the narrating 'I', a character called Charlie, as a non-adult character due to his unsophisticated use of language. Additionally, the euphemism 'sleep with' to reference sex and the mention of the 'party' might fit with readers' expectations for coming-of-age fictions (implying that Charlie isn't a child, but a teenager).

The way that vocabulary such as 'sleep with' and 'party' creates certain impressions has to do with our knowledge of the context in which these sorts of expressions are typically used: the lexical sets used in texts can evoke particular semantic fields. If you were reading a text that began with the adjunct 'Once upon a time', for instance, what type of text would you expect it to be? Using the three variables of register, take a moment to write down some ideas about 'Once upon a time'. Think particularly about its semantic field: what genre of text is it? What are the main characters like?

Most likely, your comments relate to the genre of fairy tales: you may have written that you'd expect the mode to be that of a written text (though the phrase is also suggestive of oral storytelling), its tenor would be relatively formal due to the genre often having a moral dimension but with language designed for children to understand ... And what about the semantic field? Are you expecting old-fashioned language? Princes and princesses? A world set in a far-off land? This exercise works because 'Once upon a time' is such a well-known **collocation**, that is a sequence of words that often co-occur and in this case in the same context – the opening to a fairy tale. The collocation therefore has strong semantic associations.

'Once upon a time' is also the opening to Roxane Gay's novel *An Untamed State* (2014: 3):

> Once upon a time, in a far-off land, I was kidnapped by a gang of fearless yet terrified young men with so much impossible hope beating inside their bodies it burned their very skin and strengthened their will right through their bones.
>
> They held me captive for thirteen days.
>
> They wanted to break me.
>
> It was not personal.
>
> I was not broken.
>
> This is what I tell myself.

The novel opens with an adjunct element containing two prepositional phrases, both of which evoke the semantic field of fairy tales. Such narrative expectations, though, are quickly disrupted when the main clause states 'I was kidnapped by a gang ...'. Both the verb 'kidnapped' and the noun 'gang' belong to a very different lexical set; there are associations of violence in these words, not happily-ever-after.

Literary works can therefore shift registers to create particular effects. **Re-registration** is one such technique, whereby supposed documents such as newspaper articles or letters are reproduced within literary contexts. Epistolary novels are therefore examples of re-registration. In his discussion of register shifts, Leech (1969: 49–51) also discusses **register-mixing**: when a range of different registers and varieties are used within a single text. The beginning of *An Untamed State* is an example of register-mixing, mixing what we might call a fairy-tale register with a register more readily associated with crime. Looking at the extract, note which words you think belong to each lexical set.

In *An Untamed State*, there is a clear motivation for Gay's use of register mixing. The register shift in the main clause 'I was kidnapped . . .' creates semantic deviation and is consequently more shocking to readers. Moreover, having clearly endured a harrowing experience, the narrator appears to be trying to find a way to understand what has happened to her and to maintain her own sense of self-worth. The negated copulative constructions 'It was not personal. / I was not broken' thus portray the narrator's refusal to be weakened by the event. The final sentence: 'This is what I tell myself' is therefore a poignant admission. It suggests not only that the fact of being 'not broken' is a lie, but that the very use of the fairy-tale register is a means for the narrator to mask her pain and to reason that this experience has happened for some sort of higher purpose.

6.2 Lexical semantics: Synonyms and antonyms

Another aspect of linguistic meaning that is useful in stylistic analysis is lexical semantics. Semantics is the study of meaning; thus it follows that lexical semantics is concerned with the meaning of words and the sense relations between them. As a result of its evolution, the English language is particularly rich from the point of view of lexical semantics. Originally a West Germanic language, English came into contact with Latinate languages through the influx of French words after the Norman Conquest in 1066 and later as a result of the deliberate learned use of romance vocabulary (Latin, Greek, and French, as well as Italian and Spanish) during the cultural renaissance of the early modern period. It is for this reason that considering the etymology of words can inform our knowledge of the tenor of discourse (as we briefly demonstrated above in section 6.1).

The diverse history of English also explains why there are numerous **synonyms**, that is words with similar meanings. If we consult *Roget's Thesaurus*, 'acquaint' and 'tell' are listed as synonyms, alongside other verbs such as 'inform', 'impart', 'apprise', 'advise', 'enlighten'. Synonyms, though, do not have identical meanings. Think, for instance, about 'tell' and 'advise': what is the difference between *telling* and *advising*? And what about context? Consider the following uses:

(a) Sara told Alison that she'd done the washing-up.
(b) Sara advised Alison that she'd done the washing-up.

Which verb, *told* or *advised*, sounds more natural? Why would you choose to use one over the other? Evidently, register and lexical semantics are interrelated.

In literature, synonyms can be used to avoid monotonous repetition of a lexeme. See if you can spot the synonyms in the following lines of 'The City in the Sea' by American Romantic poet Edgar Allan Poe (1992 [1831]: 964). The poem imagines a dreadful sunken city at the bottom of the ocean:

> For no ripples curl, alas!
> Along the wilderness of glass-
> No swellings tell that winds may be
> Upon some far-off happier sea-
> No heavings hint that winds have been
> On seas less hideously serene.

The extract features several parallelisms. To avoid exact repetition, Poe uses synonyms. You should have noticed two sets. Firstly, 'tell' and 'hint'; secondly, 'ripples', 'swellings', and 'heavings', which are used to signify waves (earlier in the stanza, Poe also uses the noun phrase 'luminous waves').

Lexical relations can be used for poetic effect. In the opening stanza to 'The City in the Sea' (1992 [1831]: 963), Poe uses both synonyms and antonyms. **Antonyms** are words with opposite meanings and often come in pairs:

> Lo! Death has reared himself a throne
> In a strange city lying alone
> Far down within the dim West,
> Where the good and the bad and the worst and the best
> Have gone to their eternal rest.

In the fourth line of this first stanza, Poe uses two sets of antonyms: the evaluative adjectives 'good'/'bad' and the superlatives 'worst'/'best'. He also juxtaposes the ordering of the pairs, presenting the positive adjective first in 'good and bad' but second in 'worst and best'. *Good/bad* and *worst/best* are examples of **gradable antonyms** which, whilst expressing interdependent meanings, represent two opposing positions on a scale. Thus, just because something isn't *good*, it isn't necessarily *bad*; it could be *alright*, for instance. Other gradable pairs include: *dark/light*, *hot/cold*, *fast/slow*, *happy/sad*. In 'The City in the Sea', Poe uses these two related pairs of gradable antonyms to demonstrate that the dead represent all types of man. Thus, Poe suggests that death does not distinguish virtue but is inescapable for all mortal souls.

In addition to gradable antonyms, there are other forms of antonymic pairings. **Mutually exclusive complementaries** are pairs in which if one of the antonyms is applicable, the possibility of the other is excluded. Some examples of mutually exclusive complementaries are: *dead/alive*, *true/false*, *present/absent*, *awake/asleep*, *pass/fail*. Another category of antonyms is **relational opposites** (including mutually dependent converses and directional/reversive opposites) which display symmetry in meaning. Some examples are: *give/receive*, *buy/sell*, *teacher/pupil*, *employer/employee*.

Considering the lexical semantic relationships in texts can be revealing both in terms of uncovering the meaning-making strategies of a text and in terms of understanding writing processes. In relation to the latter, for instance, scholars exploring the poetry of Emily Dickinson have suggested that Dickinson drew heavily on synonyms and antonyms in her writing, often consulting her 1844 edition of Noah Webster's *American Dictionary of the English Language* (Hallen 2007). More recently, the poet Matthew Welton used *Roget's Thesaurus* to create thirty-nine variations of the title poem in his collection *The Book of Matthew* (2003).

6.3 Equivalence and opposition

Synonymic and antonymic relations can also be created through textual structures. Equivalence and opposition can be generated by syntax. Jeffries (2010b: 58–9) summarises the most common syntactic triggers of equivalence and opposition. As can be seen from Table 6.1, X and Y can be occupied by lexemes that are semantically related. Words that are specific instances of a particular semantic category or field are called **hyponyms**. Thus, 'orange' and 'black' in the first example are both hyponyms of 'colour'. The general class (in this case 'colour') is known as a **hypernym** or superordinate. Because the syntactic structure generates equivalence or opposition though, X and Y need not have much in common.

We've already seen an example of syntactically triggered opposition in Chapter 2 when we considered parallelism in Lynne Tillman's short

Table 6.1 Syntactic triggers of equivalence and opposition (adapted from Jeffries 2010b: 58–9)

Syntactic triggers of equivalence		Examples
Intensive relational equivalence	X is Y; X seems Y; X became Y; X appears Y; Z thinks X Y; etc.	Orange is the new black. The conference became a pantomime.
Appositional equivalence (using apposition)	X, Y, (Z); X and Y; etc.	Women, fire, and dangerous things.
Metaphorical equivalence (e.g. using metaphors, similes)	X is Y (relational); The X of Y; X is like Y; etc.	The quiet of the dark. Life is like a box of chocolates.
Syntactic triggers of opposition		**Examples**
Negated opposition	X not Y; Not X, Y (plesionymic) Some X, no Y; etc.	Cars, not babies. It's not a tool, it's an idea.
Transitional opposition	Turn X into Y; X becomes Y; From X to Y; etc.	Turn water into wine.
Comparative opposition (using comparative adjectives)	More X than Y; Less X than Y; etc.	More ignorant than happy.
Replacive opposition (conjunctions of alternatives)	X instead of Y; X rather than Y; etc.	Sad instead of bereft.
Concessive opposition (using concessive conjunctions)	Despite X, Y; X, yet Y; etc.	Despite rain, the sun shone. Fearful, yet excited.
Explicit opposition	X by contrast with Y; X, as opposed to Y; etc.	Comfortable rather than wealthy.
Syntactic triggers of equivalence and/ or opposition (these require interpretation in context)		**Examples**
Syntactic parallelism	He liked X. She liked Y; Your house is X, mine is Y; etc.	He liked words. She liked gymnastics.
Contrastives (using contrastive conjunctions)	X, but Y; etc.	She felt tired, but happy.

story 'Living with Contradictions': 'He didn't want to fight in any war and she didn't want to have a child' (2002: 81). '[W]ar' and 'a child' are not opposites, but the parallelism constructs them as the conflicting desires of the two characters. Jonathan Safran Foer's (2010) short story 'Here We Aren't, So Quickly' is also constructed using parallel structures. It begins (2010: 72/139; sentences numbered for analysis):

> (1) I was not good at drawing faces. (2) I was just joking most of the time. (3) I was not decisive in changing rooms or anywhere. (4) I was so late because I was looking for flowers. (5) I was just going through a tunnel whenever my mother called. (6) I was not able to tell if compliments were back-handed. (7) I was not as tired as I said.

Together, S1 and S2 form an example of negated opposition by giving the impression that the reason the narrator is 'not good at drawing faces' is because he 'was just joking most of the time'. S3 creates a contrastive opposition between 'rooms' and 'anywhere' through the contrastive conjunction 'or'. S4 does not create equivalence as such but the subordinating conjunction 'because' sets up a causal relationship between the narrator's act of 'looking for flowers' and their lateness. S5, S6, and S7 do not feature equivalence or opposition, but their repetition of similar structures (using the adverb 'just' and the syntactic negator 'not') could be said to create the illusion of continuing the pattern through foregrounding.

The entirety of 'Here We Aren't, So Quickly' relies upon syntactic structures such as those discussed above. In the second paragraph, the perceptual address changes from 'I' to 'you', but negated oppositions are still used to create contrast between unconnected facts (2010: 72/139): 'You were not able to ignore furniture imperfections. You were too light to arm the airbag.' In the third paragraph, Foer starts to interchange 'I' and 'you' so that the oppositions appear to occur between the different characters as well as between their individual acts (2010: 72/139):

> (8) I was not able to run distances. (9) You were so kind to my sister when I didn't know how to be kind. (10) I was just trying to remove a stain; I made a bigger stain. (11) You were just asking a simple question. (12) I was almost always at home, but I was not always at home at home. (13) You were not able to cope with a stack of more than three books on my bedside table, or mixed currencies in the change dish, or plastic. (14) I was not afraid of being alone; I just hated it. (15) You were just admiring the progress of someone else's garden. (16) I was so tired of food.

This third paragraph relies on syntactic parallelisms throughout, using copulative constructions: *I was X. You were Y.* Because every sentence begins in this way, Foer creates the effect of frequent contrastive parallelisms. This is the case in S8 and S9 as well as S11 and S12. In both instances, the latter sentence – S9 and S12 – contains two clauses. While the first clause initially appears to contrast the former sentence through parallelism, the subordinating conjunction 'when' in S9 and the coordinating conjunction 'but' in S12 work with the latter clauses' negations to in fact contrast the parallel structures *within* S9 and S12. S10 is an example of comparative opposition using the adverb 'just' in the first clause, asyndetic coordination of the semicolon, and the comparative adjective 'bigger'. S13 creates contrastive oppositions between noun phrases using 'or', and S14 is another negated opposition. S15 and S16 invite contrast simply through their parallelism.

Not many literary texts use syntactic structures of equivalence and opposition to the same extent as Foer's short story. Nevertheless, 'Here We Aren't, So Quickly' shows some of the syntactic triggers of equivalence and opposition in a literary context. Moreover, the prevalence of these structures is important to the narrative. 'Here We Aren't, So Quickly' narrates the story of a relationship between 'I' and 'you'. Towards the end, the narrator claims (2010: 73/143):

> And here we aren't, so quickly. I'm not twenty-six and you're not sixty. I'm not forty-five or eighty-three . . .

The negated ages denote that the characters are no longer young nor are they old. Rather, they've reached some indeterminate middle point, both in years and in terms of their relationship. Foer's use of the syntactic structures of equivalence and opposition ultimately suggests that their relationship and its history has been defined as much by what they have done as by what they haven't, as much by their individual acts as by how those acts do or do not fit together.

6.4 Cohesion

Cohesion is described by Halliday and Hasan as 'relations of meaning that exist within the text, and that define it as a text' (1976: 4). Thus, texts are not merely random combinations of clauses or sentences; there are textual devices which create the sense of those clauses and sentences functioning as an integrated text. Halliday and Hasan outline five central forms of cohesion:

Reference: Using a grammatical word to reference a word or phrase used elsewhere in the text; most often personal pronouns (though other pronouns and comparative constructions also fulfil this function). There are two types:

- **Exophora**: referring outside of the text (situational).
- **Endophora**: reference within the text (textual):
    - **anaphora** refers to preceding text
    - **cataphora** refers to succeeding text.

Substitution: Using grammatical function words to replace words or phrases; most often, demonstrative pronouns such as *this*, *that*, *these*, *those*, impersonal pronouns such as 'one', and forms of the dummy auxiliary verb *do*.
Ellipsis: Leaving out words or phrases, because the missing content is predictable and/or to avoid unnecessary repetition.
Conjunction: Using conjunctions to join textual elements.
Lexical Cohesion: Repeating linguistic items. There are three forms:

- **Repetition**: repeating similar or identical words, phrases, or clauses (thus, including parallelism and related to foregrounding).
- **Lexical Relations**: using semantic forms such as synonyms, antonyms, hyponyms, etc.
- **Collocations**: using words or phrases that tend to co-occur together.

Some of these devices have already been discussed in this chapter. For our analysis, we'll consider how cohesion works and how it can help to shed light on the meanings of difficult texts.

American poet Dean Young is often described as a neo-surrealist (*neo-* meaning new), and openly cites surrealism as an important influence. As such, many of his poems often bring together seemingly contradictory elements. A good example is his poem 'Facet' (2005), which can be read in full online (a link is provided in the reference list). Read the poem and consider what it might be about. It is a short poem, consisting of twelve lines, but might seem somewhat incomprehensible. Did you find it hard to understand when you read it? Looking at its cohesive strategies will enable us to open up its meaning.

An initial observation is that the poem is written in the first person and addressed to a second-person 'you'. There is, however, no endophoric reference to a proper name for either character. As a result, the use of the interpersonal pronouns makes the poem seem personalised: it suggests an intimacy between the 'I' and the 'you' who does not need naming because of their importance to the poetic voice. We can also note the repetition of the negative prefix *un-* in the words 'unbroken' and 'unpunished' (L1 and L2), and 'unable' (L9). Added to this is the syntactic negation of 'not' (L2), the clitic 'n't' (L5 and L6), and syntactic 'no' (L10). The repeated negation here creates the impression of the poetic voice feeling debilitated, perhaps even depressed. Looking more closely at the cluster of three negations in L1–2, we might wonder what is being communicated: 'I've gone unbroken / but not unpunished'. To be 'unbroken' is a way to express being fine – not broken – whilst drawing on the negative meaning of the noun; the double negative construction 'not unpunished' suggests that the 'I' *has been* punished. Young applies the negative prefix to words that describe unpleasant states ('broken', 'punished') in a way that obscures those meanings whilst expressing a deep despondence.

Thinking about the lexical sets and semantic fields in the poem, readers might connect lexemes such as 'stars', 'afterlife', 'monk', and 'scorpion'. These words fit together only tangentially, but the strong association of 'afterlife' with death might trigger readers to link the meaning of the poem to death and a grief felt by the poetic voice who may have lost a loved one – 'you'. Following this reading, the end of 'Facet' is rather heart-breaking: the poetic voice expresses concern that their emotional connection to the 'you' will become more 'detached' using the simile 'like a monk / for a scorpion' (L11–12). The semantic relations between 'monk' and 'scorpion' are far from obvious. Thus, the equivalence created by the simile suggests that the poetic voice fears that their feelings for 'you' could become as disconnected as the semantic connections between 'monk' and 'scorpion'. In the context of our analysis of the poem's cohesion, the poetic voice is concerned that if they let go of their deep emotional connection to 'you', let go of their grief, they will also lose their only remaining attachment with 'you'.

Dean Young's poem 'Facet' is a surreal and initially confusing poem. The analysis presented here demonstrates the value of a semantic analysis – considering semantic fields, structures of equivalence and opposition, and forms of cohesion – for making sense of difficult texts and uncovering concealed meanings.

Keywords and summary

Antonym (gradable, mutually exclusive complementaries, relational opposites), cohesion, collocation, ellipsis, equivalence, hypernym, hyponym, lexical set, mode/medium, opposition, reference (anaphoric, cataphoric, endophoric, exophoric), register (-mixing, re-registration), semantic field, substitution, superordinate, synonym, tenor/tone.

This chapter has demonstrated the ways in which register, lexical semantics, syntactic structures of equivalence and opposition, and cohesion can be useful for stylistic analysis. Exploring contextual and semantic features can reveal the meaningful relationships between words and clauses, as well as across larger spans of text. Semantic analysis can expose the initially incomprehensible meaning of difficult texts and show how certain meanings are constructed.

Activities

1. Choose a relatively short poem or a single stanza from a larger poem (around ten lines) and replace the content words with either synonyms or antonyms. What effect does your rewrite have on the meaning of the poem?
2. Find the text for a political speech. Thinking of the three variables (mode, tenor, field), what is the register of the text? Are there any syntactic structures that create equivalence and contrast? Finally, based on your answers to the previous questions, decide if you think the speech is successful.
3. Pick a poem or prose extract that you find difficult to understand; perhaps something surrealist. Read through it carefully and list any cohesive features. When you have done so, consider these cohesive features (and look at how they are working in the original literary context). Do you have a better understanding of the text as a result of your analysis?

Further reading and references

The mode–tenor–field framework for the context-dependent study of language and register can be found initially in Halliday et al. (1964) and is later developed in Halliday (1978: 61–4) and Halliday and Hasan (1989 [1985]: 12–43) where the authors analyse a line from Ben Jonson's poem 'To Celia'. For further work on register in stylistics, see: Leech (1969: 49–51), Short (1996: 80–105), and Wright and Hope (1996: 203–33). Semino (2002b) offers an excellent analysis of register mixing in Carol Ann Duffy's poem 'Poet for Our Times'. Biber and Conrad (2009) offer a corpus linguistic approach to the study of register and genre in texts (including literary texts).

See Cruse (1986) for a comprehensive discussion of lexical semantics including the various sub-categories of synonyms (265–94) and antonyms (197–264). Our discussion of types of antonym stems from Jeffries and McIntyre (2010: 93) and Jeffries (2010b: 51–65) who also discusses opposition (see also Davies 2007, 2013; Jeffries 2010a). Stockwell (2000b) also explores syntactically constructed equivalence, focusing on plesionymy in a poem by Hugh Sykes Davies. Harrison (2017: 114–28) offers an analysis of Foer's 'Here We Aren't, So Quickly', but from the perspective of cognitive grammar.

The text-driven study of cohesion stems from Halliday and Hasan (1976). For linguistic and stylistic analyses of cohesion, see: Emmott (1999), Fairley (1981), Gutwinski (1976), Heoy (1991, 2005), Jeffries and McIntyre (2010: 84–7), Simpson (1992; 1997: 101–27), Stoddard (1991), Thompson (1994), Toolan (1990: 131–43; 1998: 23–45), Wales (1998), Werth (1984), and Wright and Hope (1996: 163–201). Flowerdew and Mahlberg (2009) offer a corpus linguistic exploration of lexical cohesion.

For a stylistic approach to surrealist literature, see Stockwell (2016).

Part III

Literature as discourse

7 Dialogue and spoken discourse

7.1 Meaning and context in spoken discourse

In Chapter 1, we noted that stylistics has always been influenced by developments in the field of linguistics. In the 1970s and 80s, more linguists began studying language as it is used in everyday situations, rather than as an abstract grammatical system. This focus on the meanings and functions of language when used *in a particular context* is at the heart of the fields of pragmatics, sociolinguistics, and discourse analysis. These fields have developed influential frameworks for the analysis of *spoken* interaction which form our focus in this chapter. We will consider how frameworks derived from the study of spoken interaction can be applied in the analysis of literary language, to examine the representation of characters' conversational interaction. This entails a shift from thinking about language in terms of sentences to thinking about language in terms of *utterances*.

Pragmatics differs from semantics (see Chapter 6) since, in Trask's words, pragmatics is 'the branch of linguistics which studies those aspects of meaning which derive from the context of an utterance, rather than being intrinsic to the material itself' (1997: 174). In order to understand the significance of context in determining meaning, it is helpful to consider a specific example. Let's consider the utterance 'I'm sorry'. 'I'm sorry' could have a number of different meanings depending on when it is uttered. In response to an exclamation like 'Someone's nicked my drink!', it could function as an admission of guilt and/or as an apology. When addressed to worried relatives by a doctor emerging from a hospital operating room, it functions as a way of informing those relatives of a bad outcome (at least, in TV dramas!). When uttered with a questioning intonation ('I'm sorry?'), it functions as a request, asking another speaker to repeat something they have just said which has not been fully apprehended. When uttered as an exclamation, it can function to express someone's outrage or indignation at a perceived insult. This example demonstrates that context is crucially important in meaning creation.

Work in sociolinguistics and discourse analysis has demonstrated that, as well as playing a central role in pragmatic meaning, context also influences the structural properties of spoken interaction. Despite seeming free-flowing and unconstrained, even informal spoken interaction proceeds according to certain rules and conventions. When we converse, we take turns to contribute and different speakers 'hold the floor' at different moments. The tacit rules about when we can speak, and what it means if we overlap with or interrupt each other, can differ for interactional contexts. A key idea here is that the structure which a conversation takes both reflects and constructs the context in which it occurs. For example, consider a traditional university lecture. The turn-taking rules here are quite clear: the lecturer holds the floor for the majority of the time, and other participants are expected to listen. The lecturer can nominate other people to speak, but it is highly dispreferred to speak without such sanction. This conversational structure both reflects the relative power of the lecturer in the institutional context (they have the role of 'teacher' addressing 'students') and constructs that power as they are not interrupted or challenged. An informal conversation between a group of friends in a café looks quite different. The floor is theoretically open to everyone and the turn-taking rules are more complex. Whoever holds the floor can nominate another person to take a turn. Otherwise, when they finish speaking, the floor is open for competing speakers. If no one else begins to speak, the original speaker will usually continue. In this context, turn-taking will likely reflect and construct existing and developing relationships between the participants.

The point in a conversation where a change of speaker could occur is called a **transition relevance place** (**TRP**). A TRP can be indicated by a number of factors, including intonation and syntax. We are good at predicting TRPs, and as such it is normal in real conversation for speakers' turns to overlap slightly at TRPs. This kind of partial overlapping is very hard to achieve in scripted dialogue delivered by actors, and as a result scripted speech tends to involve fewer overlaps than everyday speech. In both real and fictional conversations though, the negotiation of turn-taking can be revealing. If TRPs are met with long **silences**, or if there is substantial **overlap** between the turns of participants, for instance if one speaker **interrupts** another by starting their turn outside of a TRP, this can suggest a number of things about the speakers' relationships. Silence can signal familiarity and comfort, or awkwardness. Overlaps can be supportive and cooperative, or challenging.

Table 7.1 Tendencies of 'powerful' and 'powerless' speakers (adapted from Short 1996: 206)

Powerful speakers . . .	Powerless speakers . . .
• Have the most turns*	• Have the fewest turns
• Have the longest turns	• Have the shortest turns
• Initiate conversational exchanges	• Respond to the initiation of others
• Control the conversational topic	• Follow the topics of others
• Interrupt	• Are interrupted
• Allocate turns to others	• Respond to allocated turns
• Use informal terms of address	• Use formal terms of address

* In interaction between two people it is normal for the amount of turns to be roughly equal, and so this indicator usually better applies to multi-party interaction.

Conversational structure is often related in some way to the relative **power** of the participants involved in an interaction. As noted above, the structure of a traditional lecture reflects the institutional power of the teacher in relation to their students. Even in informal café chat, power relations are being enacted between friends, and some speakers can dominate more than others. Think, for example, about the group conversations of your immediate family: does one speaker tend to dominate? Are there overlaps or silences? What does this tell you about the family structure and relationships?

There are different types of power (such as physical, personal, social, institutional) which are manifest in every human interaction and can be reflected in conversational structure. Table 7.1 offers a general sketch of some of the tendencies of 'powerful' and 'powerless' speakers. We've used the word 'tendencies' here deliberately, because these tendencies do not always hold true. For example, a speaker who has short conversational turns and says very little might, in fact, hold the most power. It is therefore always vital to consider the context in which fictional dialogue and conversation takes place. Sections 7.2 to 7.4 below develop these insights into the context-dependency of linguistic meaning and structure with reference to examples from literary texts.

7.2 Speech acts

The 'I'm sorry' example discussed in section 7.1 illustrates how the same words can function to admit or apologise, to describe a situation, to express an emotion or to ask a question. Our words have specific effects on other people and an impact on the world in which they are uttered. Therefore, speech utterances are more than words: they are also a type of action. **Speech act theory** (Austin 1962; Searle 1969, 1991 [1965]) provides terminology to enable the analysis of pragmatic meaning and the types of actions which utterances perform. It distinguishes between a **locutionary act** (what is literally said) and its **illocutionary force** (the speech act it performs; that is, its function in the context of the conversation). For example, consider the following utterance, and imagine it being spoken by a student as they poke their head around the door of their tutor's office, shortly after having a meeting with the tutor:

> 'It's me again.'

Literally, these words describe the student's return to a place they have already been. Uttered in this context, however, this expression also has the illocutionary force of an apology. It expresses the speaker's recognition that they are intruding upon the tutor's time once again.

Of course, in any communicative interaction there is the possibility that the speech act you intend to perform is not received in the way intended by hearers and therefore does not have the desired effect. To reflect this, speech act theory also makes a distinction between the **intended perlocutionary effect** and the **actual perlocutionary effect** of utterances. The intended perlocutionary effect of the apology expressed by 'It's me again' might be to mollify the tutor, to make them more amenable to the request for further help which will inevitably follow. There is no way of guaranteeing the actual perlocutionary effect, though – there is always a chance that this kind of indirect apology could be received with irritation rather than acceptance.

Speech act theorists have categorised different types of speech act (see Table 7.2). Although these categories are not always clear-cut, these terms can be useful when describing and analysing speech acts in stylistic analysis. The 'It's me again' example discussed above looks like a representative (stating or describing some state in the world) but in this context, it has the illocutionary force of an expressive (the student is apologising for an intrusion by expressing an awareness that they are disturbing the tutor again).

Thinking of utterances as actions highlights the potential discrepancy between the actual words uttered and their meaning or function. This taps into the notion that utterances can perform speech acts in **direct** or **indirect** ways. 'It's me again' is an indirect apology, because the action being performed isn't explicitly stated. Instead, the hearer has to **infer** the meaning and intent of the utterance. 'I'm sorry to bother you again' would be a more direct way of performing the same expressive speech

Table 7.2 Types of speech act

Type of speech act	Description
Representatives	Commit the speaker (in varying degrees) to something's being the case, e.g. stating, claiming, describing, alleging, announcing
Directives	Attempts by the speaker (with varying strengths of commitment) to get the hearer to do something, e.g. requesting, commanding, suggesting, forbidding, urging
Commissives	Commit the speaker (in varying degrees) to some future course of action, e.g. promising, threatening, vowing
Expressives	Express a psychological state about a state of affairs, e.g. thanking, congratulating, apologising, deploring, welcoming, offering condolence
Verdictives	Deliver a finding, official or unofficial, upon evidence or reasons, e.g. assessing, ranking, estimating
Performatives	Bring about some change of state through their performance; usually occur in official discourse, e.g. blessing, firing, baptising, marrying

act. Directness and indirectness are also part of the politeness strategies used in communication, which are discussed further in section 7.3.

Speech acts are generally performed during an interaction between two or more people and as such are performed as part of a **conversational turn** in that interaction. Some types of utterance strongly predict particular utterances in response: a greeting is usually reciprocated with another greeting; directive speech acts such as questions are usually followed by an answer; a request or offer by acceptance/refusal. These expected initiation and response sequences are known as **adjacency pairs**, and an initiating turn can be met with either a **preferred** or **dispreferred response**. For instance, failing to respond when someone greets you is a dispreferred response, and may cause the person greeting you to think you are purposefully ignoring them.

When analysing dialogue in literature it can be interesting to consider the speech acts which are performed by respective characters' utterances. The extract below from the novel *American Psycho* (Ellis 1991: 117–18) represents a telephone conversation between the main character-narrator, Patrick Bateman, and his girlfriend Evelyn. The previous night, Evelyn's neighbour was murdered and although she tried to call Patrick, she could not get hold of him. Now, too scared to remain at home alone, she is staying in the Carlyle Hotel. Patrick narrates whilst Evelyn quizzes him on his whereabouts. The conversational turns in the extract have been numbered for analysis.

> She says, before I can make up a plausible lie, an acceptable excuse, (1) "Where *were* you last night Patrick?"
>
> I pause. (2) "Why? Where were *you*?" I ask, while guzzling from a liter of Evian, still slightly sweaty from this afternoon's workout.
>
> (3) "Arguing with the concierge at the Carlyle," she says, sounding *rather* pissed off. (4) "Now tell me Patrick, where *were* you?"
>
> (5) "Why were you arguing with him?" I ask.
>
> (6) "Patrick," she says – a declarative statement.
>
> (7) "I'm here," I say after a minute.

Evelyn begins by asking Patrick a question: a directive speech act, which requires an answer. Instead of answering in turn (2), Patrick responds to Evelyn's question with another question. This dispreferred response suggests he is trying to avoid having to answer Evelyn. In turn (3), Evelyn answers Patrick's question (the preferred response) with a representative speech act describing where she was. Then in turn (4) she reiterates her previous directive, this time issuing a strong command ('Now tell me'). Once again, in (5) Patrick responds with a question. When Evelyn utters Patrick's name in turn (6), the narrator tells us that it is expressed as 'a declarative statement' rather than a question. Yet this statement has the illocutionary force of a directive, with the intended perlocutionary effect of prompting Patrick to answer her. This time, Patrick responds to the directive in turn (7) with 'I'm here', choosing to respond as though Evelyn were asking a question about whether he can hear her, rather than responding to her command for him to tell her where he was last night.

In terms of the tendencies of powerful and powerless speakers outlined in Table 7.1, it is clear that this extract features a power struggle rather than a single dominant speaker. This struggle is evident in the way Patrick and Evelyn compete to control the conversational topic. Both use directive speech acts to try and initiate topics of discussion: Evelyn wants to talk about where Patrick was last night, and Patrick wants to talk about anything but his whereabouts. In this exchange, Patrick proves to be a highly uncooperative speaker, evading the question which Evelyn is asking him and deliberately misinterpreting her speech acts. Evelyn, on the other hand, is more cooperative: she responds to Patrick's questions in turn (3) and repeats her request for information when she does not receive the response she desires in (4) and (7). Although Evelyn has no idea about Patrick's psychopathic tendencies, the reader of *American Psycho* does. Thus, Patrick's evasive behaviour may lead readers to infer that he has had some involvement in her neighbour's murder.

Studying speech acts and conversational structure can offer illuminating insights into characters' social relationships. Section 7.3 introduces politeness as another aspect of language which impacts upon our social relationships.

7.3 Politeness

The academic study of politeness considers the way speakers' language use is influenced by the social relationships which exist between them, and how speakers use language to 'create, maintain or repair' positive and effective social relationships (Bousfield 2015). Brown and Levinson's (1987) influential work on politeness proceeds from the notion that humans have a sense of social value or self-esteem, known as **face**, which they seek to maintain during interactions with others. In addition to maintaining their own face, speakers will also seek to maintain the face of their interlocutors. There are two aspects to face: positive and negative. **Positive face** is 'the want of every member that his[/her] wants be desirable to at least some others' (Brown and Levinson 1987: 62). In other words, our positive face represents our desire to be liked and approved of by others. **Negative face** is 'the want of every "competent adult member" that his[/her] action be unimpeded by others' (Brown and Levinson 1987: 61). Negative face represents our desire to be free to act as we please and without being inconvenienced by others.

Every act of communication with others has the potential to threaten one or both aspects of a person's face. Such threats are called **face-threatening acts (FTAs)**. For example, giving critical feedback (rather than praise) on someone's performance of a task is a threat to their positive face, whilst asking someone to do something for you is a threat to their negative face. Politeness is an attempt to reduce the threat or damage to face that is inherent within linguistic interaction. There are a range of **politeness strategies** that speakers can employ in order to be attentive to, and reduce their threat towards, another person's face. The particular strategies used are dependent upon the parameters of power between the speaker and hearer, the social distance between them and the perceived seriousness of the FTA, which is influenced by the cultural context in which they are interacting.

When performing a face-threatening act, speakers have a choice about how to present it. They could do the act baldly, without any mitigation or redress, in the 'most direct, clear, unambiguous and concise way possible' (Brown and Levinson 1987: 69). Or, they could use linguistic strategies oriented towards the person's positive or negative face in order to mitigate the threat to various degrees. For instance, when asking a workmate if you can borrow some lunch money, a **bald, on-record** FTA would be 'Lend me some lunch money.' In order to perform the same FTA in a way which reduces threat to an addressee's positive face, you would have to claim some common ground between yourself and your workmate, present yourselves as co-operators, or somehow fulfil things they might want. For instance, the same request with positive politeness redress could be phrased as: 'Jane, could I borrow some lunch money? I wouldn't ask if I wasn't desperate, and you're the only person I feel comfortable asking!' Alternatively, in order to reduce threat to your addressee's negative face, you might perform the act indirectly, making an effort to reduce coercion and not to presume/assume the acts of another. Negative politeness might also involve the communication of your desire not to impinge upon your addressee, and recognition of things they might want. For instance, 'I don't suppose you have any money you could lend me for lunch, do you? I'm really sorry, I can pay you back tomorrow morning.' This is much more indirect, hedging the request with modals such as 'suppose' and 'could'. The speaker apologises for their imposition, and points out when the money will be returned. Speakers could also choose to perform the FTA **off-record**; for instance, saying: 'Oh no, I've left my lunch money at home!' This is even more indirect and requires your addressee to infer possible meanings.

Examining the politeness strategies employed by literary characters can provide further insight into the relationships being portrayed by a text.

7.4 Power play in dialogue

Our next analysis considers our transcription of a scene from the TV drama series *House of Cards* (Netflix Originals 2014). *House of Cards* is a political drama set in Washington DC following the career trajectories of congressman Frank Underwood and his political lobbyist wife Claire Underwood as they work their way towards greater influence in the American government. The scene portrays a meeting between Claire and two military representatives. Claire is trying to implement legislation that will change the way the military deal with sexual assault cases involving their personnel. She thinks the military need to change the advice they issue about sexual assault, and allow civilians to become involved in their legal procedures. The military representatives are very resistant to Claire's proposals: they do not want to change their existing procedures. Claire is supported by a congresswoman who has previously raised issues about sexual assault with the military but to little effect. Half-way through the scene, Claire also receives support from Mrs. Walker, the wife of the President of the United States (the First Lady). As you read through the extract, consider who appears to be the most powerful speaker, and why. Multiple dashes in the transcript mark interruptions.

[Military Representatives 1 and 2 walk into the Vice President's large, grand office in White House and shake hands with Mrs. Underwood and the Congresswoman. After exchanging greetings, the participants sit. Claire and the Congresswoman are on one sofa and military commanders on an opposite sofa, coffee table in the middle.]

1 Claire: I know this isn't the first conversation you've had about sexual assault
2 Military 2: We've had a very open dialogue with the congresswoman for quite some time
3 CongressW: "Open" is one way to put it, I think the Joint Chiefs have tolerated my concerns---
4 Military 1: ---To be fair, we've been quite responsive. Over the past two years alone we---
5 Claire: ---The congresswoman has expressed her frustration to me that there's still room for improvement
6 Military 2: Mrs. Underwood, if I may
7 Claire: [*nods*] Please
8 Military 2: This is an issue we've grappled with seriously. Increased education and prevention measures, restructuring the reporting process, insulating courts-martial from abuse of power
9 Claire: It's still not enough
10 Military 2: Civilian jurisdiction is not gonna happen. We're all aware that's what the congresswoman would prefer, but we won't allow our chain---

[The First Lady, Mrs. Walker, is shown in, all participants stand. After a brief exchange about why Mrs. Walker is late, everyone is seated. Mrs. Walker takes an armchair at the head of the coffee table.]

11 Military 2: We didn't know you'd be attending, Mrs. Walker
12 First Lady: I'm sorry for interrupting. Continue
13 Military 2: As I was saying [*swallows*] putting sexual assault cases entirely in the hands of civilian courts fundamentally erodes the military's ability to self-discipline

14 Claire:	What about civilian oversight instead of civilian courts?
15 Military 1:	That's a slippery slope
16 CongressW:	There were those who said the same of racial integration
17 Military 2:	Integration didn't change the core operational nature of the---
18 Claire:	---But it did prove that the military could shape its own evolution
19 Military 2:	Absolutely. But in this case, civilian oversight is not the answer
20 First Lady:	My husband is a civilian who oversees the military *[Pause]* Are you suggesting that civilians can offer no guidance in matters like this?
21 Military 2:	Forgive me, Mrs. Walker. I didn't mean to suggest that at all
22 First Lady:	Then maybe you should listen to the civilian sitting across from you [*Pause*]
23 Military 2:	Yes, ma'am
24 Claire:	This is from your own sexual assault prevention literature. And in it, it says in some cases it may be advisable to submit than to resist. I think it's quite clear that there's still room for improvement

In terms of politeness, there is a lot of face-work going on in this meeting, as participants orient to each other's positive and negative face. As the discussion becomes more heated, however, there are more bald, on-record face-threatening acts.

Across turns (T) 1–10, Claire and Military 2 exhibit positive politeness by recognising the contributions of others to the ongoing issues they have met to discuss (T2) and the seriousness of the issue to which Claire and the Congresswoman are dedicated (T8). Military 2 also exhibits positive politeness when he requests permission to speak (T6) and Claire reciprocates by granting this permission (T7). This politeness is not evident in the contributions of the Congresswoman or Military 1, however. In T3, the Congresswoman contradicts Military 2 by suggesting that he is misrepresenting their previous interactions, which threatens his positive face. Military 1 responds by contradicting the Congresswoman, threatening her positive face by suggesting that *she* is not being fair and is misrepresenting things (T4). The face-threatening nature of their interaction suggests that there is animosity between the Congresswoman and military representatives. As the extract progresses, however, Claire and Military 2 also become increasingly impolite. This begins in T9 when Claire makes a bald, on-record statement criticising the military's actions: 'It's still not enough.' Military 2 responds by asserting that they will not do anything more – and again, this is expressed as a bald, on-record face-threatening act directed at the Congresswoman: 'Civilian jurisdiction is not gonna happen . . . we won't allow [it]' (T10).

At this point, the First Lady joins the meeting. The First Lady's association with the President endows her with institutional power which exceeds that of other speakers. This institutional power is reflected in her contributions to the discourse, and in the way other participants interact with her. After apologising for being late and her imposition on the speakers – an example of negative politeness – she asks them to continue (T12). Interestingly, in her presence Military 2 rephrases the bald, on-record face-threatening statement he made in T10 as an indirect statement which adds negative politeness redress (T13): 'putting sexual assault cases . . . in the hands of civilian courts . . . erodes the military's ability to self-discipline'. The First Lady's presence has not, however, influenced his views. In T19, he reiterates his disagreement with Claire and the Congresswoman: 'civilian oversight is not the answer', this time with some positive politeness redress through his initial agreement with Claire's previous utterance ('Absolutely', T19).

The First Lady then contributes to the debate, by outlining the face-threatening implications of Military 2's refusal to consider civilians. She points out that her husband, the President, is also a civilian, and therefore implies that the military are disrespecting her husband (threatening her positive face). In pointing this out, she also threatens the positive face of Military 2. Military 2 apologises to the First Lady in order to repair his FTA (T21). The First Lady then suggests that he ought to listen to Claire, using indirectness to mitigate the threat of her order to his negative face: '<u>Maybe</u> you should listen to . . .' (T22). In responding to her suggestion with obedience, the military representative acknowledges her institutional power.

Structural aspects of this conversation also contribute to the relative power of the participants. There are several instances of interruption in the dialogue which have a challenging rather than cooperative effect. Significantly, Claire interrupts the most, cutting across Military representatives 1 and 2, and is not interrupted herself. Claire also has the power to allocate turns in this interaction (e.g. T7). However, when she joins the conversation the First Lady allocates the most turns: she asks Military 2 to continue (T12), asks him a direct question (T20), and allocates the floor to Claire (T22). At first, the meeting is essentially a power struggle between Claire (who called the meeting, controls the topic, and interrupts) and Military 2 (who has the most turns). However, when the First Lady joins the meeting she backs Claire and allocates turns in a way that overpowers Military 2. There is an interaction here between conversational power and institutional power: the First Lady's association with the President makes her the most powerful speaker institutionally speaking, and her stature is reflected in the effect of her contributions to the discourse. Close analysis of the turn-taking and politeness in this scene helps to account for the tension created by the dialogue, and the impressions which a viewer might develop of the characters and their relationships.

Keywords and summary

Adjacency pairs, bald on-record, conversational turn, direct/indirect communication, dispreferred response, face (positive, negative), face-threatening act (FTA), illocutionary force, inference, interruption, overlap, perlocutionary effect (intended, actual), preferred response, silence, speech act, speech act theory, transition relevance place (TRP), turn-taking.

Linguistic frameworks for the study of spoken discourse offer a useful means for describing the structure, meanings, and social effects of dialogue in literature. They provide rich insight into the portrayal of character relationships and individual characterisation. Of course, it is important to remember that many literary texts represent *fictional* dialogue, which is scripted rather than real conversation! Nevertheless, readers and viewers are likely to use their experience of spoken communication in order to interpret these textual representations.

Activities

1. Look again at the extract from *House of Cards* in section 7.4. This time, with reference to the speech act categories outlined in Table 7.2, categorise as many speech acts as you can. What kinds of speech acts are used by the participants? Are there any patterns? How do they interact with the politeness strategies and power dynamics we have already examined?
2. Are there any problems with applying linguistic frameworks designed to analyse real spoken interaction (such as conversation analysis, speech act theory, and politeness theory) to fictional or literary texts? What might these frameworks miss?
3. Find an extract of dialogue in a novel or a dramatic script. Analyse the conversational structure, speech acts, and politeness of the

interaction. What does your analysis suggest about the characters and their relationships? How do the things you have noticed contribute to your understanding of the scene and its effects?

Further reading and references

For further introduction to pragmatics, see: Cutting (2002) and Grundy (2000). Levinson (1983) is an influential and readable advanced textbook in the field. Simpson (1993: ch. 5) discusses pragmatics and point of view. Some of the key principles of conversation analysis are set out in Sacks et al. (1974). Cameron (2001) and Schiffrin (1994) are useful practical introductions to discourse analysis. The categorisation of powerful and powerless speakers is elaborated in Short (1996: 206; see also chs 6–8). The speech act categories in Table 7.2 are adapted from publications by Austin (1962), Searle (1969, 1991 [1965]), and Short (1996) and their presentation in this chapter is designed to provide descriptive labels for stylistic analysis. See the original publications for further debate over the categories. Bousfield (2015) provides a comprehensive introduction to politeness theory. See Brown and Levinson (1978, 1987) for key foundational work in this field. Further examples of stylistic analysis which draw upon the frameworks covered in this chapter include: Buck and Austin (1995), Culpeper et al. (1998), Hurst (1987), Nash (1989), Short (2014), and Toolan (1985). For cognitive stylistic work on dialogue and characterisation, see: Culpeper (2001) and McIntyre (2006).

8 Speech, thought, and narration

8.1 Speech and thought (and writing)

As we saw in Chapter 7, who speaks, how much they speak, and what they say is an important consideration in stylistic analysis, particularly when considering the implied meaning of speech and the social relations between characters. The stylistic presentation of characters' speech and thought can also affect readers' felt sense of the immediacy of the narrative, their judgements about the reliability of characters and narrators, and their interpretation of character and/or narrative voice.

Leech and Short first developed a model of the various forms of speech and thought presentation in their seminal book *Style in Fiction* (2007 [1981]: 255–81). Their model has since been developed to include the presentation of writing, to understand the effect of grammatical elements (such as connectives and parentheticals), and to account for representations of collective consciousness. This section introduces the model and its applications. The different types of speech, thought, and writing presentation are categorised based on how they are presented linguistically.

The following example of fictional speech comes from the young adult novel *Why We Broke Up* (2011: 343) by Daniel Handler. The narrator, Min, is in a restaurant discussing her recent break-up from high school jock Ed with her two best friends Lauren and Al:

> "Have some dignity," Lauren said to me, and Al nodded in agreement over the cheese grater. "You don't want to be that sad ex-girlfriend in the stands."
>
> "I am that sad ex-girlfriend in the stands," I said.
>
> "No, you're here with us," Al said firmly.
>
> "That's all I am," I said, "or having dinner with my mother all sullen, or crying on my bed, or staring at the phone–"

Every instance of speech in the extract is presented as **direct speech**. There are several linguistic indicators of this. Firstly, we find a **reporting clause** (e.g. 'I said') and a **reported clause** (representing the words that were spoken) in **inverted commas**. Secondly, these are examples of *direct* speech because they present the exact words a character has spoken. The extract continues (2011: 344):

> "Oh, Min."
> "–or listening to Hawk Davies and throwing him away and fishing him out of the trash and listening to him more and going through the box again. There's nothing else. I'm–"
> "The box?" Al said. "What's the box?"

Al's last conversational turn is also direct speech, as it uses inverted commas and a reporting clause. However, at the start of this extract, a different type of speech presentation is used. Look at the first two conversational turns: how are they presented differently compared with the previous examples?

The key difference is that the reporting clause has been omitted. These are therefore **free direct speech**. Free direct speech comes in three forms:

"Oh, Min."	*Reporting clause omitted.*
Oh, Min. said Lauren.	*Inverted commas omitted.*
Oh, Min.	*Reporting clause <u>and</u> inverted commas omitted.*

What makes these three examples *free* is that they are less anchored or grounded in the narration by reporting clauses and inverted commas. The characters' words are represented verbatim, and the presence of the narrator (or the distinction between the narrator and characters' voices) is diminished. The final example – without reporting clause and without inverted commas – is the **free-est form of free direct speech**.

There are four more categories of speech presentation, as shown in Table 8.1, which uses a transformative exercise to demonstrate the linguistic markers of the various forms. We've already discussed the first two categories: direct and free direct speech including the free-est form. **Indirect speech** differs from direct forms in three central ways. Firstly, whilst direct speech is marked by first- and second-person pronouns, indirect speech uses the third person. Secondly, the tense appears 'backshifted' which means that it is pushed into the past. Simpson (2014 [2004]: 31) explains that in direct forms, verbs that appear as simple present tense (e.g. 'I am . . .') would appear as simple past in indirect presentation (e.g. 'I was . . .'); similarly, if a direct form contained simple past, the indirect form would shift this further into

Table 8.1 Speech presentation categories

Speech presentation category	Examples
Direct Speech (DS)	'I am that sad ex-girlfriend,' I said.
Free Direct Speech (FDS)	'I am that sad ex-girlfriend.' *or* I am that sad ex-girlfriend, I said.
Free-est form of FDS	I am that sad ex-girlfriend.
Free Indirect Speech (FIS)	She was that sad ex-girlfriend.
Indirect Speech (IS)	She said that she was that sad ex-girlfriend.
Narrative Presentation of Speech Act (NPSA)	She spoke of her sadness.
Narrative Presentation of Voice (NPV)	She moaned sadly.

past perfect (a change from 'was' to 'had been'). Thirdly, any references to time, place, or person are shifted away from the character. Thus, adverbs such as 'now' and 'here' might become 'then' or 'there', moving them from being proximal to being distal (we'll learn more about these forms of reference in Chapter 13 on deixis).

In terms of literary effect, the distal composition of IS detaches the discourse from the character. That is, while direct presentation appears to present a character's exact words, IS seems instead to be set at a remove. Thus, instead, the discourse appears to stem from a **narrator** or **narratorial voice**. The same is true of the last two categories of speech presentation shown in Table 8.1: Narrative Presentation of Speech Act (NPSA) and Narrative Presentation of Voice (NPV), so named because a narrative voice informs readers that speech takes place with only minimal information about what is actually said. NPV is the most vague in terms of speech content, stating only that speech has occurred; NPSA provides some information about the nature of the speech act, but again without exact details of the words spoken.

The final category, **free indirect speech**, will be discussed in more detail in the next section. For now, it suffices to say that since it is free, the reporting clause is removed. 'She said that she was that sad ex-girlfriend' (IS) becomes 'She was that sad ex-girlfriend.' Because it is indirect, we would expect FIS to retain distal linguistic composition. To some extent it does; the above example features third person and past tense. In free indirect forms, however, some proximal markers – such as adverbs of time and place – retain their proximity to the speaker. This is reflected by the presence of 'now' in the free indirect forms shown in Table 8.2.

Table 8.2 Speech, thought, and writing presentation categories

Presentation category	Speech	Thought	Writing
Direct	'I love you now,' she said. (DS)	'I love you now,' she thought. (DT)	'I love you now,' she wrote. (DW)
Free-est form of FD	I love you now. (FDS)	I love you now. (FDT)	I love you now. (FDW)
Free Indirect	She loved him now. (FIS)	She loved him now. (FIT)	She loved him now. (FIW)
Indirect	She said that she loved him then. (IS)	She thought that she loved him then. (IT)	She wrote that she loved him then. (IW)
Narrative Presentation of ____ Act	She told him how she felt. (NPSA)	She wondered about the strength of her feelings for him. (NPTA)	She wrote about how much he meant to her. (NPWA)
Narrative Presentation of Voice (NPV)	She spoke softly. (NPV)	She thought to herself. (NPT)	She wrote to him. (NPW)

Having discussed the forms of speech presentation, we must briefly explain how these forms work in relation to thought and writing. The answer is simple: the linguistic features of free, direct, and indirect presentation work in the same way across the three categories (see Table 8.2).

8.2 Narrators and free indirect discourse

You'll have noticed, in Table 8.2, that the free indirect forms of speech, thought, and writing look identical. For this reason, they are often simply referred to as **free indirect discourse** (FID) or free indirect style. As such, whether speech, thought, or writing occurs is often a matter of reader interpretation, based on narrative context. FID has attracted the attention of stylisticians and narratologists because of its diverse effects, and is therefore the focus of this section.

Before discussing FID in more detail, it is useful to introduce the concept of **point of view**, or in other words the perspective from which a story is written. In order to determine point of view, it is necessary to make two key distinctions. The first, following our discussion of speech and thought presentation, is to distinguish *who speaks* by examining a text's use of pronouns. Is the narrative written in first person ('I', 'we'), second person ('you'; which is more rare), or third person ('he', 'she', 'they')? Answer this question about the following extract, taken from the opening to Ali Smith's short story 'Astute Fiery Luxurious' (2008: 169):

> A parcel arrived. It looked really creepy. There was nobody in the house but me. I phoned you. You were still at work and very busy.
> Uh huh, what now? you said.
> A weird parcel came, I said.

This is written in first-person singular 'I'. As such, we can say that we have a first-person narrator. It also contains two instances of FDS; did you notice them? Narrators that are internal to, that is involved in, the action of the story are called **homodiegetic** narrators. Thus, the narrator of 'Astute Fiery Luxurious' is a first-person homodiegetic narrator. When narrators are seen to be external to the story they tell, this is called **heterodiegetic** narration. Such externality is usually signalled by the use of third-person pronouns.

Consider the following extract from American writer Emily Holmes Coleman's (1997 [1930]: 5) modernist and somewhat autobiographical novel, *The Shutter of Snow*. Using the categories discussed above, identify what type of narrator the extract has:

> How could they expect her to sleep when she was going through all of it? They didn't know. She had swung about the room from the ceiling and it was a swinging from the cross. There had been a burial. She was lying quietly in the bed and being covered over her face. She was carried quietly out and put in the casket. Down, down she went in the rectangle that had been made for her. Down and the dirt fell in above. Down and the worms began to tremble in and out. Always she had kept telling of it, not one word of it must be forgotten. It must all be recorded in sound and after that she could sleep.

How did you get on? The extract is written in third-person heterodiegetic narration.

The second distinction concerns who *sees*, that is **focalisation**. This can remain consistent or can shift throughout a literary text. First theorised in narratology by Genette (1980, 1988), focalisation can be external or internal. **External focalisation** is focalisation that is separate from the character. Thus, it encapsulates omniscient, all-knowing narrators as well as objective narrators who appear to have little insight into the characters of the story. On the other hand, **internal focalisation** occurs when the point of view is linked directly to a character; what the narrator says and knows is restricted to what a given character sees and knows. This is fairly straightforward in first-person narration because events are focalised through that speaking character. In the extract from *The Shutter of Snow*, however, despite third-person narration, the narrative is focalised through the female character's perspective (for instance, her delusional burial). Thus, internal focalisation is present. This is free indirect discourse.

FID does not feature reporting clauses or inverted commas (because it is free) but is presented in third person with generally distal linguistic composition (because it is indirect). Its indirectness, on the one hand, creates the impression of a narratorial voice while its freeness, on the other, appears to align the discourse with a particular character's viewpoint. For this reason, FID (e.g. heterodiegetic narration with internal focalisation) has been said to create 'a dual voice *effect*' (Fludernik 1993: 348; original emphasis).

The Shutter of Snow contains additional linguistic features that are typical of FID. The extract opens with a question that the main character, Marthe Gail, appears to be asking herself. Although not present in the extract, exclamations function similarly to questions in FID: both express the impassioned consciousness of a character. We can also see a frequent use of modal auxiliaries like 'could' and 'must' (modality is the focus of the next chapter), repetition – of the adverb 'down' which has both a cohesive and emphatic function – and what appears to be idiomatic phrasing suggestive of a subjective point of view ('the worms began to tremble in and out'). In *The Shutter of Snow*, Marthe has been committed to a mental asylum with psychosis after giving birth. The above extract blends Marthe's experience in the asylum with her psychological delusions (that she died and was resurrected). Whilst there are other forms of speech and thought presentation in the novel (often free direct speech), it matters that Coleman predominantly wrote *The Shutter of Snow* using FID. FID holds readers at a distance from the character. In *The Shutter of Snow*, this distancing has the added effect of suggesting that Marthe observes herself; her psyche is seemingly split as she is distanced from herself in these delusions. Moreover, because of the duality of voice, FID allows readers not only to imagine and witness Marthe's madness but to simultaneously experience her pain and confusion. Traditional analyses of FID have demonstrated its function in providing deep psychological insight into the consciousness of a single (usually central) character.

8.3 Shifting viewpoints

Forms of speech and thought presentation – and the viewpoints they entail – shift throughout literary texts. Take the following example from B. S. Johnson's novel *Albert Angelo* (2004 [1964]: 163). Albert works as a teacher but his real ambition is to be an architect:

> Albert lazed at his drawingboard before the great window. Nearly seven weeks' summer holiday lay ahead of him in which to work; and he could not work today, always tomorrow was the day he was going to work. Part of the trouble, he thought, was that he lived and loved to live in an area of absolute architectural rightness, which inhibited his own originality, and resulted in him being--- OH, FUCK ALL THIS LYING!

The first sentence describes Albert's actions – no speech, thought, or writing is represented and therefore this is an instance of narration. This narration appears to continue into the second sentence, though the phrase 'lay ahead of him' portrays the future summer holiday spatially in relation to Albert and might therefore suggest internal focalisation and a subtle shift into FID. FID is undoubtedly present after the semi-colon in the second sentence, with its emphatic reiteration of Albert's procrastination: 'and he could not work today, always tomorrow was the day he was going to work'. The third sentence shifts again into IT, adding more narratorial control with the inclusion of the reporting clause 'he thought'. The final sentence creates a shocking rupture, in the form of a stylistic shift from IT to a Free Direct form. There is no reporting clause, which makes it difficult to interpret whose exclamation this is, although their rage is evident through the use of an expletive and the typographical foregrounding through capitalisation.

In *Albert Angelo*, this passage is placed at the end of a chapter. The next chapter begins: '---fuck all this lying look what im really trying to write about is writing not all this stuff about architecture trying to say something about writing about my writing im my hero' (Johnson 2004 [1964]: 167). The lack of punctuation implies the agitation of the speaker, whilst the use of first person and the repeated references to writing and to 'my hero' imply that this should be interpreted as the voice of the author. This is FDW in which the extra-textual authorial voice of Johnson reveals that the novel uses Albert's ambition and feelings about architecture as a metaphor for Johnson's own opinions about writing. In stylistic terms, the analysis demonstrates that literary texts are not composed consistently in one form of narration or speech and thought presentation but can fluctuate between modes (see section 20.4 for more on the roles of author/narrator/characters in narrative).

Recent studies have demonstrated that as well as shifts at sentence breaks (as in *Albert Angelo* above), grammatical features such as conjunctions (e.g. 'and', 'but', 'for') and parentheticals (text set apart from surrounding content by hyphenation or parenthesis like this) can work either to reinforce a single character's view or to shift viewpoints to another character. This type of shifting occurs in the following scene from D. H. Lawrence's (1995 [1915]: 214) novel *The Rainbow*. The scene focuses on Will Brangwen, whose wife Anna no longer accepts his sexual advances. Subsequently, when Will meets a young girl named Jennie in Nottingham, he attempts to seduce her. Sentences are numbered for ease of analysis:

> (1) But he was patiently working for her relaxation, patiently, his whole being fixed in the smile of latent gratification, his whole body electric with a subtle, powerful, reducing force upon her. (2) So he came at length to kiss her, and she was almost betrayed by his insidious kiss. (3) Her open mouth was too helpless and unguarded. (4) He knew this, and his first kiss was gentle, and soft, and assuring, so assuring. (5) So that her soft, defenceless mouth became assured, even bold, seeking upon his mouth. (6) And he answered her gradually, gradually, his soft kiss sinking in softly, softly, but ever more heavily, more heavily yet, till it was too heavy for her to meet, and she began to sink under it. (7) She was sinking, sinking, his smile of latent gratification was becoming more tense, he was sure of her. (8) He let the whole force of his will sink upon her to sweep her away. (9) But it was too great a shock for her.
>
> (10) With a sudden horrible movement she ruptured the state that contained them both.
>
> (11) "Don't-don't!"

The majority of the extract is FID. S1 presents Will's perspective, shown particularly through his awareness of his own bodily sensations. However, S2 instigates a shift into the girl's perspective as she observes Will's initial advance and frets over her nearly spoiled chastity. Using the connective in sentence initial position, this example fits with existing research into how connectives can signal viewpoint shifts. However, rather than simply showing the girl's experience in contrast to Will's, because 'so' is an illative connective it suggests causal reference. Thus, Jennie's experience also appears to result from Will's action and intentions. This is in line with Sotirova's study of connectives in Lawrence's work in which she states that connectives are able to link 'two viewpoints, which are incompatible with each other, but its presence signals their relatedness and the intention to make them sound as two sides of a whole; two angles from which the same problem is focussed' (2004: 226).

S3 is a continuation of Jennie's anxiety, whilst S4 returns to Will's knowledge and careful coaxing. S5 is more ambiguous and could potentially be either her experience of aroused passion or his interpretation of her growing boldness. This ambiguity, which continues into S6, appears deliberate: Lawrence uses FID to fuse not only a narrative voice with character consciousness but in a moment of physical passion, the perspectives of the two characters also seem to merge. It is only when, midway through S6 with 'till it was too heavy for her to meet . . .', does the blurring of perspectives start to refocus. Starting with the subordinating conjunction 'till', the placement of this also seems significant in Lawrence's writing since it is at this point that Jennie begins to reject Will's embrace. Nevertheless, the separation of character viewpoints is not entirely clear-cut since the repetition of 'sinking, sinking' in S7 resonates with the various repetitions in S6 such as 'gradually, gradually', 'softly, softly', and 'more heavily, more heavily'. We see Will's expression through Jennie's eyes in S7 whilst S8 gives Will's perspective on his final attempt to overwhelm Jennie. Even so, since throughout S6–8 'sink' and 'sinking' continue to be repeated (a total of five times), any disentanglement of the two characters' perspectives is complicated by the dialogic quality created by the shared lexis. Thus, it is only in S9 with the sentence initial 'But' that the joint consciousness is completely ruptured. Finally, the heterodiegetic narration of S10 details Jennie's physical rejection of Will, a rejection confirmed by her FDS in S11: '"Don't-don't!"'.

8.4 *We*-narration

Joshua Ferris is a contemporary American author, whose (2007) debut novel *Then We Came to the End* has a distinctive narrative style. It is written in first person but unusually, rather than singular 'I', the narration uses first-person plural 'we'. It opens (2007: 3):

> We were fractious and overpaid. Our mornings lacked promise. At least those of us who smoked had something to look forward to at ten-fifteen. Most of us liked most everyone, a few of us hated specific individuals, one or two people loved everyone and everything. Those who loved everyone were unanimously reviled.

This is homodiegetic narration but the effect of this somewhat unnatural first-person plural 'we' is that it creates the sense of a collective consciousness. This consciousness belongs to the employees of an advertising agency and therefore presents the communal tedium of office work. There are slight divisions in the consensus, intimated by the noun phrases 'those of us', '[m]ost of us', 'a few of us', and 'one or two people'. With the exception of the latter, these represent some of the workers as the grammatical head of the phrase ('those', '[m]ost', 'few'), only to subsume them as part of the larger group – 'us'. There is also a paradoxical and witty tension to the final statement that 'those who loved everyone were unanimously reviled', that is, hated by their colleagues. Because it is first person, it appears to bypass a narratorial presence to tell the story. This becomes more explicit a little later, when after describing aspects of their daily work, 'we' directly addresses the reader in second person (Ferris 2007: 4): 'Is this boring you yet? It bored us every day. Our boredom was ongoing, a collective boredom, and it would never die because we would never die.'

In order to give insight into the minds of individual characters, Ferris uses FID to switch perspectives. This is the case, for instance, as 'we' discusses the office gossip mill (Ferris 2007: 5–6):

> Karen Woo always had something new to tell us and we hated her guts for it. She would start talking and our eye would glaze over. Might it be true, as we sometimes feared on the commute home, that we were callous, unfeeling individuals, incapable of sympathy, and full of spite toward other people for no reason other than their proximity and familiarity? We had these sudden revelations that employment, the daily nine-to-five, was driving us far from our better selves. Should we quit? Would that solve it? Or were those qualities innate, dooming us to nastiness and paucity of spirit? We hoped not.
>
> Marcia Dwyer became famous for sending an e-mail to Genevieve Latko-Devine. Marcia often wrote to Genevieve after meetings. "It is really irritating to work with irritating people," she once wrote. There she ended it and waited for Genevieve's response. [. . .] The only thing bearable about the irritating event and the irritating person was the thought of telling it all to Genevieve, who would understand better than anyone else. Marcia could have called her mother, her mother would have listened. She could have called one of her four brothers, any one of those South Side pipe-ends would have been more than happy to beat up the irritating person. But they would not have understood. They would have sympathized, but that was not the same thing. [. . .] But the e-mail Marcia got back was not from Genevieve. It was from Jim Jackers. "Are you talking about me?" he wrote. Amber Ludwig wrote, "I'm not Genevieve." Benny Shassbryger wrote, "I think you goofed." Tom Mota wrote, "Ha!" Marcia was mortified. She got sixty-five e-mails in two minutes. One from HR cautioned her against sending personal e-mails. Jim wrote a second time. "Can you please tell me – is it me, Marcia? Am I the irritating person you're talking about?"

The first paragraph in the extract maintains *we*-narration. There is a shift, though, in the second paragraph, with the introduction of Marcia

Dwyer in third person. Marcia's email to Genevieve is realised as Direct Writing (note the reporting clause 'she once wrote'). The following sentence ('There she ended it . . .') returns to a narrative perspective external to Marcia. However, there is a definite shift into Marcia's internal focalisation with FID, beginning 'The only thing bearable about the irritating event . . .' and continuing with consideration of the relationships in Marcia's personal life. FID is indicated here by the persistent presence of modal auxiliaries ('could', 'would'), the repetition of 'irritating', and colloquial language such as 'pipe-ends' that suggests Marcia's personal idiolect. 'But the e-mail Marcia got back was not from Genevieve' moves back into the narratorial voice, after which another string of DW occurs. Including the narratorial report about the email from HR, these suggest that Marcia has, albeit accidentally, sent her email to all her colleagues rather than only to Genevieve, whilst the exact content of the emails shows up the confusion, scorn, and insecurities of Marcia's colleagues.

As a form, *we*-narration is quite constraining since it subsumes the viewpoints of many individuals into a singular collective consciousness. However, as this brief analysis shows, by using DW alongside FID, Ferris is able to reveal the opinions and perspectives of particular characters too.

Keywords and summary

Connectives, focalisation, free indirect discourse, narration (heterodiegetic, homodiegetic), point of view, reported clause, reporting clause, shifting viewpoints, speech, thought and writing presentation (direct, free direct, free indirect, indirect).

This chapter has introduced the forms of speech and thought presentation, paying particular attention to FID. This has been connected with forms of narration and focalisation: the distinction between *who speaks* and *who sees*. The analyses presented in this chapter demonstrate the effects of different types of speech and thought presentation, and the way they offer insights into character consciousness and the amount of narratorial intervention that seems to be present.

Activities

1. Pick a novel at random from your bookshelf and turn to the first page. Read the first few paragraphs and decide what type of narrator the novel has in terms of *who speaks* (pronoun use and narration type) and *who sees* (focalisation).

2. Below is an extract from another Joshua Ferris novel, *To Rise Again at a Decent Hour*, in which the narrator, a dentist, is interacting with his receptionist Betty (2014: 23):

> "What exactly have you been doing?" I'd tell her, and she'd say, "Why do you feel the need to lie to me?" I'd tell her, and she'd say, "Scrutiny does not kill people. Smoking kills people. What kind of example do you think you're setting for your patients by sneaking off to smoke cigarettes?" I'd tell her, she'd say, "They do not need a reminder of 'the futility of it all' from their dental professional. When did you take up smoking again?" I'd tell her, she'd say, "Oh, for heaven's sake. Then why did you tell everyone you quit?" I'd tell her, she'd say, "I do not see how the occasional show of concern is 'utterly strangulating.' I would like to see you live up to your potential, that is all. Don't you wish you had more self-control?" I'd tell her, she'd say, "Of course I will not join you. What are you doing? Do not light that cigarette!"

What forms of speech presentation are used? What is the effect of this in terms of your experience of reading this conversation?

3. The extract below is from *Passing* by Nella Larsen (2004 [1929]: 45), in which two characters, Brian and Irene, are discussing Brian's son:

> "We-ll, I s'pose you're right. You're expected to know about things like that, and I'm sure you wouldn't make a mistake about your own boy." (Now, why had she said that?) "But that isn't all. I'm terribly afraid he's picked up some queer ideas about things – some things – from the older boys, you know."
>
> Her manner was consciously light. Apparently she was intent on the maze of traffic, but she was still watching Brian's face closely. On it was a peculiar expression. Was it, could it possibly be, a mixture of scorn and distaste?
>
> "Queer ideas?" he repeated. "D'you mean ideas about sex, Irene?"

Analyse the extract in terms of forms of speech and thought presentation. Are there any shifts in perspective and if so, what causes them? Are there any points of ambiguity? What is the effect of the way in which this is written?

Further reading and references

The stylistic categorisation of forms of speech and thought presentation was developed by Leech and Short (2007 [1981]). Additional accounts are: Banfield (1982), Chapman (2002), Erlich (1990), Fludernik

(1993), McHale (1978), Page (1987), Short (1996: 288–325), Simpson (1993: 21–30; 2014 [2004]), and Toolan (1998: 105–35). The addition of writing presentation was developed through corpus study in the Lancaster speech, writing, and thought presentation research projects, whose work is explained in: Semino and Short (2004), Short (2003), and Short et al. (1996); it is further discussed in Short (2012) and applied to the epistolary novel by Bray (2010). In this chapter we use the term 'presentation' throughout, and category abbreviations such as NPSA, NPV, and NPA, following Short's (2012) recommendation, though it is worth noting that 'representation' and 'report' are also used (e.g. NRA).

Free indirect discourse has been studied variously by Adamson (2001; who calls it 'empathetic narrative'), Bray (2003, 2007a), Cohn (1966; under the term 'narrated monologue'), Dry (1995), Fludernik (1996), Ikeo (2007), and Pascal (1977). Bray (2007b) and Sotirova (2006) have conducted reading experiments to test the dual voice effect of FID, though the results have been somewhat inconclusive. Rundquist (2014) has sought to categorise FID as an umbrella term encapsulating three further sub-categories to the representation of character consciousness. Shifting viewpoints using connectives and parentheticals in FID have been analysed by Cui (2014), Ikeo (2014), and Sotirova (2004, 2005, 2010, 2011, 2013), all of whom focus on modernist texts. Bray (2014b) considers how FID can be used to present forms of collective consciousness in contemporary experimental fiction. The passage from *Albert Angelo* discussed in this chapter is also analysed by Hucklesby (2016: 105–6), who identifies the capitalised outburst as free direct discourse.

Finally, the distinction between *who speaks* and *who sees* (including homodiegetic and heterodiegetic narratives and forms of focalisation) stems from Genette's work in narrative theory (1980, 1988).

9 Modality and point of view

9.1 Types of modality

Chapter 8 introduced the concept of **point of view** in texts and the importance of considering *who speaks* and *who sees* when analysing the perspective from which a story is told. We noted that narratives can be told in the first, second, or third person by narrators who exist within (homodiegetic) or outside of (heterodiegetic) the story. Furthermore, in third-person narration, as well as representing the point of view of a heterodiegetic narrator (external focalisation), narratives can be focalised through the viewpoints of characters (internal focalisation). The analyses in Chapter 8 provided examples of the representation of speech, thought, and writing in narrative and the way such representations intersect with the creation and manipulation of point of view. This chapter focuses on the ways in which the representation of *attitudes* in a text intersect with the study of point of view.

Language is often imbued with the attitudes of a speaker: indeed, language is one of the central resources which we use to communicate our opinions and feelings. **Modality** is one of the major systems involved in the communication of attitudes through language. Imagine the happy occasion on which you might utter the following words:

(a) I have a day off.

This is a simple sentence which presents a categorical assertion about a state of affairs: that the speaker has a day away from work or school or other service. **Categorical assertions** have no markers of modality: they are statements of fact. Consider the transformations of this sentence in the examples below:

(b) I should have a day off.
(c) I want a day off.
(d) I might have a day off.

The statement of fact in (a) has been changed into a statement of opinion or belief, so sentences (b)–(d) indicate the speaker's *attitude* towards having a day off. These sentences are not categorical; they *do* contain markers of modality. Modal auxiliary verbs 'should' or 'might' modify the verb 'have' in (b) and (d), and a lexical verb that indicates desire ('want') is used in (c).

As Fowler (1986: 131–2) notes, modality can be expressed linguistically in several ways, such as:

- **modal auxiliary verbs** (so named because they act as an auxiliary to the main verb in a verb phrase) including 'must', 'might', 'may', 'shall', 'should', 'will', 'needs to', 'ought to'
- **modal or sentence adverbs** such as 'probably', 'maybe', 'perhaps', 'certainly'
- **lexical verbs of knowledge, prediction or evaluation**, such as 'know', 'think', 'believe', 'seem', 'like/dislike', 'approve', 'guess', 'foresee'
- **evaluative adjectives and adverbs** such as 'regrettably', 'luckily', 'fortunate', and many others
- **generic sentences** which claim generalised, universal truths. A classic example of a generic sentence is the opening line of *Pride and Prejudice* (Austen 1992 [1813]): 'It is a truth universally acknowledged, that a single man in possession of a good fortune, must be in want of a wife.' Note the use of a modal auxiliary ('must') in this sentence too.

These linguistic resources can be used to express three main types of attitude. In example (b), having a day off is represented as something the speaker feels obliged or compelled to do. In (c), a day off is represented as something the speaker desires or values. Lastly in (d), a day off is represented as a possibility, something the speaker is not completely sure will happen. In English, these three types of attitude are represented via four modal systems, known as: deontic, boulomaic, epistemic, and perception modality.

Simpson (1993: 47) describes **deontic modality** as the modal system of 'duty' which is used to indicate a 'continuum of commitment' from permission, to obligation, to requirement. Deontic modality expresses a speaker's perception of the degree of obligation attached to a particular proposition, and as such is a regular feature in persuasive discourse and social interaction. Deontic modality can be indicated through modal auxiliary verbs such as 'should', 'must', and 'may'; and also 'BE . . . THAT' constructions such as 'it is necessary/possible that'; and 'BE . . . TO' constructions such as 'is permitted/allowed/obliged/

forbidden to'. We saw an example of deontic modality in the extract from *The Shutter of Snow* in section 8.2 (Coleman 1997 [1930]: 5; our emphasis):

> Always she had kept telling of it, not one word of it **must** be forgotten. It **must** all be recorded in sound and after that she could sleep.

Deontic modality here suggests that the character feels obliged and committed to tell her story.

Boulomaic modality is the modal system of 'desire', used to indicate the extent to which a speaker finds a particular proposition desirable or undesirable. Modal lexical verbs such as 'hope', 'wish', 'regret', 'love', 'hate', 'like', 'dislike', 'want', and so on are central in expressing this type of modality. 'BE . . . TO' and 'BE . . . THAT' constructions such as 'it is hoped/good that' are also used, as well as modal adverbs such as 'regrettably', 'hopefully', and so on. This extract from *The Narrow Road to the Deep North* exhibits boulomaic modality (Flanagan 2014: 131; our emphasis):

> Suddenly she **wished** he would just disappear. She **wanted** to push him away, and would have but she was terrified of what might happen if she touched him.

These boulomaic lexical verbs provide an insight into the female character's attitude towards the male protagonist.

Epistemic modality represents a speaker's degree of confidence or lack of confidence in the truth of a proposition. It is the modal system involved in communicating concepts of knowledge, belief, and cognition. Epistemic modality is expressed by modal auxiliaries including 'could', 'may', 'might', 'must', 'shall', 'should', and 'will'. Note that modal auxiliaries can express more than one type of modality, so 'must' could express deontic modality in a sentence like 'You must stop!' or epistemic modality in a sentence such as 'It must be raining': the context of their use is key in determining the type of modality expressed. Epistemic modality is also indicated by modal adverbs such as 'allegedly', 'arguably', 'certainly', 'maybe', 'perhaps', 'possibly', 'probably', 'surely', 'supposedly', and by adjectives in 'BE . . . TO' and 'BE . . . THAT' constructions such as 'sure to' and 'doubtful that'. Lexical verbs such as 'think', 'believe', 'know' also communicate epistemic modality.

A continuum from weak to strong commitment can be expressed. Compare, for instance, the degree of commitment expressed by 'I will have a day off' and 'I might have a day off': in the former a speaker appears much more certain. Can you identify the epistemic modality in the extract below, from Adam Thirlwell's novel *Lurid & Cute* (2015: 341)?:

> Beside me, kids were in trucks smoking weed while in a more compact sports thing a probably coked-up girl was probably going to see her orthodontist who was probably superhot.

The modal adverb 'probably' indicates the speaker's medium degree of confidence in his assumptions about the people around him. From his ready guesses we get an insight into the stereotypes he perceives in his surroundings. Epistemic modality is, in fact, also present in the extracts above from *The Shutter of Snow* ('after that she *could* sleep') and *The Narrow Road to the Deep North* ('*would* have', 'what *might* happen').

The final category, **perception modality**, is actually a sub-category of epistemic modality. In this type of modality, the speaker's confidence in the truth of a proposition is based not on their own knowledge but on their faculties of perception, usually visual but also auditory perception. Modal adverbs such as 'obviously', 'clearly', 'evidently', and 'apparently' express perception modality, as do adjectives in 'BE ... THAT' constructions such as 'obvious that', 'clear that', 'apparent that' and verbs such as 'seem', 'see', and 'hear'. Not all verbs which represent perception processes are necessarily modal. Sentences such as 'I saw the show' or 'I heard the phone' are just categorical assertions that represent a speaker's observations. In contrast, in statements such as 'I hear you got a promotion' or 'I see you've got a new dress', 'hear' and 'see' additionally indicate the speaker's belief about something. Perception modality refers to external signs in order to indicate a speaker's commitment to the truth of a proposition. In the extract from *The Bone Clocks* below (Mitchell 2014: 82; our emphasis), it is the narrator's first day in her new job as a fruit picker and she is describing her assumptions about the people around her:

> Once we get going, it's **pretty obvious** who's used to field-working: Stuart and Gina move up their rows twice as fast as the rest of us, and Alan Wall's even faster.

The narrator expresses a high degree of confidence in her assessment of her workmates' experience through the use of the adjective 'obvious'. Her assumptions about others are grounded in her perception of external signs (the speed with which they work).

Whilst setting out these four modal systems, reference has been made to very short sentence-level examples, but in stylistics attention is usually paid to the distribution of modality across longer stretches of text. This is the focus of the next two sections.

9.2 Modal shading

Stylisticians such as Fowler (1986, 1996) and Simpson (1993) have studied the role modality plays in the construction of point of view in narrative. Both note that the frequent use of particular types of modality creates specific effects, having a significant impact on the 'feel' of a text, including the impressions which readers develop of particular characters and the atmosphere or tone established by a piece. Simpson (1993) argues that it is possible to classify narrative texts not only in terms of their narrative perspective (e.g. first person, third person, internal/external focalisation), but also based on their dominant type of modality, known as **modal shading**. Simpson (1993: 75) analysed a range of texts to arrive at a definition of three types of modal shading. Table 9.1 summarises the central features and effects of different types of modal shading.

Narratives which have a predominance of deontic and boulomaic modality (to do with duties and desire) and very little epistemic modality, as well as words that denote thoughts, feelings, and perceptions (***verba sentiendi***) and evaluative lexis have what Simpson calls **positive shading**. In positively shaded texts, the narrator's/focaliser's 'desires, duties, obligations and opinions *vis-à-vis* events and other characters are most prominent' (Simpson 1993: 56), and the modality contributes to the sense of an opinionated narrator who is communicating cooperatively with an addressee.

On the other hand, some narratives feature little deontic or boulomaic modality, and instead the epistemic and perception modal systems (to do with truth, knowledge, belief, and cognition) dominate. Simpson describes these as **negatively shaded**. Negatively shaded passages often feature '**words of estrangement**' which emphasise a narrator's/focaliser's interpretative effort and (often) lack of understanding or insight into other characters or situations: expressions such as 'apparently', 'evidently', 'perhaps', 'it seemed', and 'as if'. Texts with negative modal shading may create the impression of an alienated, bewildered, distanced, or estranged narrator/focaliser.

A final type of narrative text is that which features little or no modality, and is comprised for the most part of categorical assertions. Simpson describes this type as having **neutral shading**. Narratives with neutral shading are associated with a journalistic 'feeling of reportage' (Nash 1990: 134) and might create the impression of a 'flat', unreflective narrator or a passive focaliser.

Simpson's (1993) work on modal shading emphasises the influence which modality can have on the 'feel' of a particular passage and

Table 9.1 Types of modal shading

Type of shading	Linguistic indicators	Possible effects	Canonical examples
Positive	• Dominance of boulomaic and deontic modal systems • Presence of words denoting thoughts, feelings, and perceptions (*verba sentiendi*) • Use of evaluative lexis (adjectives and adverbs) and generic sentences	Impression of a 'co-operative' or opinionated character or narrator	• Jane Austen • Charlotte Brontë's *Jane Eyre* • Henry Fielding • Henry James' *The Ambassadors*
Negative	• Dominance of epistemic and/or perception modality • Presence of words emphasising an act of interpretation from external observation ('words of estrangement')	Impression of a less 'co-operative', distanced, bewildered, or estranged narrator or character	• Samuel Beckett's *Molloy* • Franz Kafka's *The Trial*
Neutral	• Dominance of categorical assertions, overall lack of modality • Few *verba sentiendi* or evaluative adjectives/ adverbs	Impression of a 'flat', unreflective, or passive narrator or character	• Detective fiction • Ernest Hemingway • Gustave Flaubert

provides a useful catalogue of potential effects. However, as Simpson notes, although some texts have a discernibly dominant modal shading, many texts involve fluctuation between modal systems to achieve their effects.

9.3 Analysing modal shading

This section will examine the role of modality in the point of view of two first-person narratives. Consider the opening paragraph of *What Is the What* by Dave Eggers (2006: 9–10). The novel is based on the true story of Valentino Achak Deng, a Sudanese refugee in America, and is written in first person from the perspective of Valentino. Can you spot any modality in this extract? What kind of modal shading is present?:

> I have no reason not to answer the door so I answer the door. I have no tiny round window to inspect visitors so I open the door and before me is a tall, sturdily built African-American woman, a few years older than me, wearing a red nylon sweatsuit. She speaks to me loudly. "You have a phone, sir?"
>
> She looks familiar. I am almost certain that I saw her in the parking lot an hour ago, when I returned from the convenience store. I saw her standing by the stairs, and I smiled at her. I tell her I do have a phone.
>
> "My car broke down on the street," she says. Behind her, it is nearly night. I have been studying most of the afternoon. "Can you let me use your phone to call the police?" she asks.
>
> I do not know why she wants to call the police for a car in need of repair, but I consent. She steps inside. I begin to close the door but she holds it open. "I'll just be a second," she says. It does not make sense to me to leave the door open but I do so because she desires it. This is her country and not yet mine.
>
> "Where's the phone?" she asks.
>
> I tell her my cell phone is in my bedroom. Before I finish the sentence, she has rushed past me and down the hall, a hulk of swishing nylon. The door to my room closes, then clicks. She has locked herself in my bedroom. I start to follow her when I hear a voice behind me.
>
> "Stay here, Africa." I turn and see a man, African-American, wearing a vast powder-blue baseball jacket and jeans. His face is not discernible beneath his baseball cap but he has his hand on something near his waist as if needing to hold up his pants.
>
> "Are you with that woman?" I ask him. I don't understand anything yet and am angry.
>
> "Just sit down, Africa," he says, nodding to my couch.
>
> I stand. "What is she doing in my bedroom?"
>
> "Just sit your ass down," he says, now with venom.
>
> I sit and now he shows me the handle of the gun. He has been holding it all along, and I was supposed to know. But I know nothing; I never know the things I am supposed to know. I do know, now, that I am being robbed, and that I want to be elsewhere.

The majority of this extract is comprised of unmodalised categorical assertions, such as those in the first three sentences. As such, sections of the passage are neutrally shaded, and consist of the unreflective description of events with little indication of the narrator's views or feelings. From L5, however, there is some perception modality in the sentence 'She looks familiar': the verb 'looks' refers to visual perception in order to express the narrator's possible recognition of the woman. There is also epistemic modality expressed by the modal adjective 'certain' in the 'BE . . . THAT' construction: 'I am almost certain that'. As it progresses, the passage shifts between neutral and negative shading.

At first the neutral shading places readers in a similar position to the narrator; viewing the actions of the criminals without comprehending their intent. However, as the passage progresses, the epistemic modality begins to indicate the narrator's confusion. Readers may infer that something fishy is going on several lines before Valentino himself realises he is the victim of a crime. The 'flat', unemotional style created by the neutral shading takes on a different effect when it becomes evident that Valentino is narrating a traumatic experience (robbery in his own home), and it begins to signal things about his character and mindset. In L8–9 we learn that Valentino has been studying all afternoon, and may be distracted or preoccupied when opening the door, but the neutral style also seems to contribute to a sense of his apparently trusting or unstreetwise nature. The neutral shading also communicates something about the narrator's response to trauma: as the rest of the novel shows, this is not the first horrible thing that has happened to Valentino.

Negative shading is evident in the epistemic modal lexical verbs 'understand' and 'know' (used with both negative and positive polarity): 'I do not know' (L11), 'I don't understand' (L24), 'I know nothing', 'I never know' (L28) and 'I do know' (L29). Along with these epistemic and perception modals, there are also other words of estrangement which emphasise the narrator's act of interpretation, such as when he describes the male intruder's face as 'not discernible' and his hand position '*as if* needing to hold up his pants' (L21–2). The negative shading creates a sense of distance or estrangement between the narrator and the situations he perceives and experiences. Such estrangement and alienation are thematically significant, as Valentino explicitly refers to his position as a refugee in a strange country ('This is her country and not yet mine', L14) and is acutely aware of the things he does not know (L28–9).

Although the modal shading of this passage is mostly neutral and negative, there are some instances of features associated with positive shading, particularly towards the second half of the extract, as we gain further sense of the character's opinions. For instance, the narrator uses evaluative lexis to describe the size of the intruders, as 'a hulk' (L17) and 'vast' (L20). There is an instance of *verba sentiendi* when the narrator describes himself as 'angry' (L23). Deontic modality is evident in the sentences about what the narrator 'was supposed to know' (L28–9) with the verb 'supposed' indicating duty or obligation. Finally, there is boulomaic modality in the statement of desire: 'I want to be elsewhere' (L29). This extract demonstrates that shifts in modality types can influence the 'feel' and impression of a text.

Another example can be seen in this extract from the opening of Ethan Hawke's novel *Ash Wednesday* (2002: 3). It is a romantic drama set in the USA, which establishes the first-person narration of one of the novel's main characters, Jimmy Heartsock. Again, consider the modality of the extract as you read it:

> I was driving a '69 Chevy Nova four-barrel with mag wheels and a dual exhaust. It's a kick-ass car. I took the muffler out so it sounds like a Harley. People love it. I was staring at myself through the window into the driver's-side mirror; I do that all the time. I'll stare into anything that reflects. That's not a flattering quality, and I wish I didn't do it, but I do. I'm vain as hell. It's revolting. Most of the time when I'm looking in the mirror, I'm checking to see if I'm still here or else I'm wishing I was somebody else, a Mexican bandito or somebody like that. I have a mustache. Most guys with mustaches look like fags, but I don't. I touch mine too much, though. I touch it all the time. I don't even know why I am telling you about it now. I just stare at myself constantly and I wish I didn't. It brings me absolutely no pleasure at all.
>
> My fingers were frozen around the steering wheel. Albany in February is a black sooty slab of ice. The woman on the radio announced the time and temperature: eight forty-two and twenty-three degrees. Christy and I had broken up fifteen hours earlier, and I was in a tailspin. I had my uniform on, the dress one; it's awesome. Military uniforms make you feel like somebody, like you have a purpose, even if you don't. You feel special, connected to the past. You're not just an ordinary person, a *civilian* – you're noble. The downside of this Walk of Pride is, it's a lie.

Boulomaic modality (to do with desire) is the most prominent type of modality in this passage, evident in the repeated use of the modal lexical verb 'wish': 'I wish I didn't' (L4–5 and L9–10), 'I'm wishing I was somebody else' (L6). There is also a high frequency of evaluative lexis, including evaluative adverb phrases such as 'too much' (L8) and evaluative adjectives in copulative clauses such as 'it's a kick-ass car' (L2) 'That's not a flattering quality' (L4), 'I'm vain as hell', 'It's revolting' (L5), 'it's awesome' (L14), 'you're noble' (L17–18). *Verba sentiendi* is also present as the narrator tells us how he feels: 'you feel like somebody' (L15), 'absolutely no pleasure at all' (L10), 'you feel special' (L15–16). This combination of boulomaic modality, evaluative lexis, and *verba sentiendi* is indicative of a positively shaded narrative, in which the narrator's opinions about his surroundings and himself are foregrounded. The narrator seems to have a rather low opinion of himself (he describes himself as 'vain', 'revolting', etc.), yet because we get such a clear sense of his opinions and evaluations through the text's language, we describe the narrative as positively shaded (the evaluations themselves do not need to be positive!).

Although the modal shading is positive overall, there are instances of epistemic modality towards the end of each paragraph: the modal lexical verb 'know' in 'I don't even know why I am telling you about it now' (L8–9) and in the assertion 'it's a lie' (L17). This appearance of epistemic modality in an otherwise positively shaded narrative has an interesting effect. Whilst the positive shading makes Jimmy appear confident and opinionated, the epistemic modality undermines this by revealing Jimmy's lack of understanding or lack of belief in his own words. Combined, they begin to signal things about Jimmy's character, for instance that he may appear gregarious but is also insecure.

The analyses in this section demonstrate the ways in which modal shading can contribute to the 'feel' of a passage and affect readers' interpretations of characters and events.

9.4 Modal shading and point of view

In third-person narratives, the intersection between modality and point of view can be slightly more complicated. It is important to consider whether the attitudes represented by the modality belong to the narrator outside of the consciousness of any of the characters (external focalisation) or a character (internal focalisation). In the extract below from David Lodge's *Changing Places* (1993 [1975]: 6; our emphasis), a third-person narrator is describing the differences between the main characters, and there is a shift from external to internal focalisation. The passage also features some negative modal shading, evident in bold:

> One of these differences we can take in at a glance from our privileged narrative altitude (higher than any jet). It is **obvious**, from his stiff, upright posture, [. . .] that Philip Swallow, flying westward, is unaccustomed to air travel; while to Morris Zapp, slouched in the seat of his eastbound aircraft, [. . .] the experience of long-distance air travel is tediously familiar.
>
> Philip Swallow has, in fact, flown before; but so seldom, and at such long intervals, that on each occasion he suffers the same trauma, an alternating current of fear and reassurance that charges and relaxes his system in a persistent and exhausting rhythm. While he is on the ground, preparing for his journey, he thinks of flying with exhilaration – soaring up, up and away into the blue empyrean, cradled in aircraft that **seem**, from a distance, effortlessly at home in that element, **as though** sculpted from the sky itself. This confidence begins to fade a little when he arrives at the airport [. . .] In the sky the planes look very small. On the runways they look very big. Therefore, close up they **should look** even bigger – but in fact they don't. His own plane **doesn't look** quite big enough for all the people who are going to get into it.

The perception modality in the first paragraph ('it is obvious that') reflects the attitude of the third-person narrator, who is describing the characters' appearances from a point outside of the characters' minds, at a 'privileged narrative altitude'. This is an example of external focalisation. The modality expresses the narrator's confidence in their inferences regarding the characters' relative experience of air travel, and emphasises the narrator's distanced, disembodied perspective on the characters.

The perception modality in the second paragraph reflects the attitudes of the character Philip Swallow when he travels by air. This is because the second paragraph shifts to internal focalisation, evident in the way the narrator has insight into Swallow's thoughts and feelings (the 'alternating current of fear and reassurance'). The character's thoughts are initially relayed as a Narrative Presentation of a Thought Act (NPTA): 'he thinks of flying with exhilaration', before the passage shifts into Free Indirect Thought (after the hyphen '– soaring up, up and away …') and provides further insight into Swallow's reasoning. Perception modality such as 'seem', 'should look', and 'don't look', and words of estrangement such as 'as though', function here to indicate *the character's* discomfiting lack of certainty about aeroplane safety.

Although there are indicators of negative shading in this passage, one instance represents the attitudes of the narrator, and the others that of the character. They therefore contribute to the effect of the passage in different ways. Discerning the source of modal expressions in third-person narrative requires close attention to other indicators of point of view, such as speech and thought presentation (Chapter 8) and deixis (Chapter 13).

Keywords and summary

Categorical assertion, modal auxiliary verbs, modality (boulomaic, deontic, epistemic, perception), modal shading (negative, neutral, positive), verba sentiendi, words of estrangement.

Modality is one of the ways in which speakers indicate their attitudes through language. The four modal systems in English (boulomaic, deontic, and epistemic including perception) communicate a speaker's sense of duty, desire, or certainty in relation to specific propositions. In literary narrative, modality intersects with the study of point of view. Concentrations of particular types of modality and associated stylistic features can have a significant impact on the 'feel' of a narrative and the effects it creates.

Activities

1. Identify the modal shading of the following third-person narrative extract from Avery Corman's (1977: 7) *Kramer versus Kramer*. How does the modality contribute to the passage's effect?:

> Joanna Kramer was nearly professional in her looks, too slight at five-three to be taken for a model, possibly an actress, a striking, slender woman with long black hair, a thin, elegant nose, large brown eyes and somewhat chesty for her frame. 'The prettiest girl around', Ted called her. His image of himself was less secure. A reasonably attractive man of five-ten with brown eyes and light-brown hair, he was self-conscious about his nose, which he felt was too long, and his hair, which had begun to thin. An indication of his self-image was that he felt most attractive when Joanna was on his arm. His hope was that the child would not, by some unfortunate irony, have his looks.

2. Pick one of the extracts used in this chapter and rewrite it using a different modal shading (if it is in negative or neutral, change it to positive, and vice versa). What did you change? How did it impact upon the passage's effects?
3. Pick a passage from a novel that you are familiar with, and try to identify the modal shading. What types of modality are present? Is the shading consistent or does it shift? What is the effect? The opening paragraphs of novels, or pivotal/dramatic scenes, are often good places to look.

Further reading and references

Simpson (1993: chs 2–3) is essential further reading on modality and point of view, including a detailed discussion of modal shading across canonical texts with different points of view. Our chapter is based on Simpson's modal grammar, which reviews and contributes to the work of Fowler (1986, 1996) and Uspensky (1973). Neary (2014) provides a useful overview of stylistic approaches to modality. See Gavins (2005) for a cognitive stylistic perspective; and for traditional linguistic work on modality, see: Coates (1983), Palmer (1986), and Perkins (1983).

10 Transitivity and ideology

10.1 Transitivity and choice

When we speak or write we have a choice about the words we use. In this chapter, we pay particular attention to the verbs which speakers and writers choose to use in order to form clauses and sentences (clauses and sentences were discussed in Chapter 5). This analysis of verbs and their accompanying words is known as **transitivity** analysis. In Chapter 5, we learnt that the terms 'transitive' and 'intransitive' refer, in traditional grammar, to whether a verb is followed by an object (transitive) or not (intransitive) in order to produce a grammatical sentence. In the 1970s, M. A. K. Halliday devised a new grammar called **Systemic Functional Grammar** which highlights the connection between the grammatical structure of a linguistic expression and the *function* which the expression performs, for instance the way it represents the world by portraying an event or thing in a certain way. Rather than simply describing verbs as transitive or intransitive, a **Systemic Functional Linguistic** approach to transitivity provides a new set of terms (introduced in section 10.2) for describing types of verbs and their accompanying participants in a clause. The study of transitivity in stylistics has its roots in Halliday's approach.

The effects of transitivity are most noticeable when you compare different linguistic representations of the same event. Consider, for instance, the quotes below which we have transcribed from a British TV sitcom about student life, *Fresh Meat* (first aired 2011–16). In this series, a first-year dentistry student called Josie takes part in a clinic session whilst very hungover and accidentally cuts her patient's face with her drill. She is, of course, expelled from her dentistry course, but (this being a sitcom) the accident is capitalised upon for comic effect. In this scene, Josie's housemates – Heather, Kingsley, and Vod – find out about what has happened. Josie was keeping the accident and her expulsion a secret, but Heather decides it is time everyone knew:

Heather: She's been kicked off her course. She put an implement through a woman's cheek and she's got a hole.
[. . .]
Kingsley: Josie, this is really bad.
Josie: It's a challenge. It's a mountain I must climb to clear my name of my so-called offence.
Vod: You disfigured a human woman.
Josie: 'Disfigured' is a very emotive word, Vod.

(*Fresh Meat* Series 2, Episode 7)

In this exchange, Heather and Vod represent the event as an action, using the verbs 'put' and 'disfigured' to describe Josie's physical acts. In both cases, Josie is represented as an actor carrying out deliberate actions. Heather uses the ditransitive verb 'put', which takes two objects: here the direct object is the 'implement' and the indirect object is the 'woman's cheek' ('She put an implement through a woman's cheek'). Heather's representation of the event seems slightly less accusatory than Vod's, because Josie is represented as acting directly upon the implement, and thus only indirectly on the woman's cheek. In 'You disfigured a human woman', Vod, however, uses 'disfigured': a transitive verb requiring a direct object. As Josie points out, 'disfigure' is an emotive verb, and Vod also emphasises the action's effect on the unwitting victim by describing the recipient of the action as a 'human woman' (rather than just a part of her body: 'a woman's cheek').

By contrast, Josie and Kingsley (who is Josie's on-off boyfriend) represent the event as a state, using the present tense of the copula verb 'to be' (is) to describe its features:

This is really bad. (Kingsley)
It's a challenge. (Josie)

By describing the event in this way, as something which just happened, or just exists, and focusing on its challenging or negative attributes, Josie and her actions are removed from the picture. Clearly, Josie represents the event this way because she is trying to avoid responsibility for it, and Kingsley's utterance appears supportive of Josie because (unlike Heather's and Vod's descriptions) it avoids attributing blame to her.

The following academic year, Josie decides that she wants to return to the university and study for a different degree. Her older housemate Sabine, who works in student registration, reveals that she will need a reference from her dentistry course before she can apply, and questions:

Sabine: Wasn't that the one that they asked you to leave because you were drunk and you cut a hole in a woman's face?

Josie: It was an incident of a particular nature, the nature of which I cannot recall the details of.

(*Fresh Meat* Series 3, Episode 2)

Again, there is a contrast between the way Josie and others represent the event. Sabine represents the event as a physical action performed by Josie ('you cut a hole in a woman's face') whereas Josie still represents it as a state ('It was an incident of a particular nature'). Josie's vague yet formal register makes her description euphemistic, and her flustered state of mind is suggested by non-standard grammar ('the nature of which I cannot recall the details of'). It turns out that Sabine could provide Josie with a reference herself, but she refuses to do so until, finally, when trying to persuade Sabine to help her, Josie says:

Josie: I know I fucked up last year, I can admit that now, I drank too much and I drilled a hole in a woman's face which let's face it in most people's view is wrong, but isn't that why we go to University, to grow up?

(*Fresh Meat* Series 3, Episode 2)

As Josie finally comes to terms with what she has done she represents herself as an active participant in the event, performing actions ('I drank too much', 'I drilled a hole in a woman's face') rather than being caught up in an unavoidable state of affairs. It is at this point that Sabine agrees to help her get a place on another course.

In these extracts, each of the characters is referring to the same event, but they make different linguistic choices which are motivated by the extent to which they assign blame or responsibility to Josie. Indeed, some of the humour in the scenes comes from the distinction between the way Josie and other people talk about what happened. Josie's changing perception of herself and her situation is reflected in the changes in her transitivity choices. This example shows how the verbs (and related noun phrases) chosen to describe particular situations reflect how a speaker sees or wishes to represent the world. These kinds of transitivity choices are a fundamental part of using language and we make them (often effortlessly) every time we construct a clause. Longer texts are comprised of a series of such choices, and stylistic analysis can help us to systematically notice and consider their effects. A set of terminology derived from Halliday's work adds further analytical rigour to the study of transitivity.

10.2 Transitivity categories

This section introduces the terminology which forms the basis of a transitivity analysis. This analytical framework can illuminate patterns

Table 10.1 Typical clause elements in transitivity analysis

Transitivity components	Lexical group
Process	Verb Phrases
Participants	Noun Phrases
Circumstances	Adverbial and Prepositional Phrases

of representation in a chosen text and 'facilitate debate on the consequences of those choices' (Jeffries 2010b: 38). There are quite a lot of new terms here, so it might be useful to remember that transitivity analysis builds upon your knowledge of phrases and clauses in Chapters 4 and 5. For instance, there are three typical components of a clause in transitivity analysis and these take the form of specific lexical groups, as shown in Table 10.1.

The transitivity framework classifies verbs into one of five main categories which reflect the type of **process** being represented by the verb, and the participants involved. These are:

1. Material processes (involving an actor and a goal).
2. Mental processes (involving sensor and phenomenon).
3. Behavioural process (including behaver and circumstance).
4. Verbalisation processes (involving sayer, verbiage, and target).
5. Relational processes (involving a carrier and attributes).

Material processes are those in which something is done or happens, often physical actions or events. They are processes which can include at least two participants: an ACTOR and a GOAL (though the participants may not always be represented in the clause). The ACTOR is the person or thing carrying out the material process, and the GOAL is the thing which is receiving the process or being changed by it. There are three sub-categories of material processes. ***Material action intention*** processes are those which are performed by an animate actor (i.e. a living or conscious being). For instance:

(a) Olga kicked the ball.
(b) The snake bit the keeper.

Sometimes animate actors perform material actions without doing so deliberately, and these processes are known as ***material action supervention*** processes. Material action supervention processes are unintentional actions of conscious beings, which are beyond their control. For instance:

(c) Sheila dropped the pot plant.
(d) The skater fell over.

A third type of material process is ***material action events***, which differ from intention and supervention processes because they involve *inanimate* actors. In material action event processes, animate actors are missing or played down. For instance:

(e) The storm raged.
(f) The protest shut down roads and public transport in the area.

Mental processes are those which represent happenings within the minds or brains of human beings (often in interaction with their environment). They are processes which can involve at least two participants: a SENSOR and a PHENOMENON. Because it is not really possible to observe these processes in the same way as material or verbalisation processes, they can be particularly tricky to classify. Nevertheless, there are three sub-categories of mental processes to consider. ***Mental cognition*** processes are those which are related to thinking, knowing, reasoning, remembering, and understanding. For instance:

(g) She remembered the last time she visited the place.
(h) The reporter realised the interviewee was drunk.
(i) I thought it was the right thing to do.

Mental reaction processes are those which represent the experience of emotions or preferences such as liking and hating. For instance:

(j) She felt sad.
(k) I love going to gigs.

Mental perception processes are those which represent the experience of senses such as hearing, feeling, seeing, tasting, and so on. For instance:

(l) Stacey heard the ice cream van approaching.
(m) We saw the sunset.

Behavioural processes represent physiological and psychological behaviour and are therefore a process type that sits somewhere between the material and the mental. The BEHAVER is typically a conscious human who experiences states such as breathing, coughing, laughing, shivering, and so on. Usually, the clause only consists of behaver and process but sometimes CIRCUMSTANCE can also be included. Circumstances are optional elements that can occur in relation to any type of process. They are usually represented by adverbial or prepositional phrases. For instance:

(n) He smiled.
(o) She fainted into his arms.
(p) I exhaled deeply.

Behavioural processes can represent vocal responses too, such as 'She gasped at his touch.' Representations of language use, however, are categorised as **verbalisation processes**. Verbalisations are processes which can involve three participants: the SAYER who speaks, the VERBIAGE which is what they say, and the TARGET which is who the verbal process is directed at (it is not necessary to represent all of these participants in the clause). Verbal processes usually have an animate human actor. For instance:

(q) I keep telling her that she should leave him.
(r) The government minister claimed he had done nothing wrong.
(s) 'Keep going!' she said.

So far, we have considered processes which represent happenings, including performing actions and saying/thinking/feeling things. **Relational processes** are the final category of process, and are those which perform identifying and classifying functions. The copulative verbs 'to be' and 'to have' are often used in relational processes. Relational processes can involve two participants: a CARRIER and its ATTRIBUTES. There are three sub-categories of relational processes. ***Relational intensive*** processes link a person or a thing with a particular attribute or quality in an 'X is Y' relationship. For instance:

(t) She is the worst housemate in the world.
(u) This book is the best novel ever written.
(v) He's the manager.

Relational possessive processes link a person or a thing with a possessor in an 'X has Y' relationship. For instance:

(w) That is my book.
(x) They have an enormous house.

Lastly, ***relational circumstantial*** processes link a person or thing with a location, place, or timing, in an 'X is on/at/with Y' relationship. For instance:

(y) The meeting is at 2 p.m.
(z) The party is upstairs.
(aa) The main sights are to the East of the city.

The transitivity model is summarised in Table 10.2. It is important to note that not every linguistic expression you find will fit neatly into these categories, and indeed many found in real texts might be difficult to classify straightforwardly, seeming to fall at the boundaries between processes, or encompass more than one process. Even if this is the case,

Table 10.2 A summary of the transitivity model (adapted from Jeffries 2010b: 43)

Transitivity category	Participants	Sub-categories
Material Action	Actor, Goal	• Intention • Supervention • Event
Mental Cognition	Sensor, Phenomenon	• Cognition • Reaction • Perception
Behavioural	Behaver, Circumstance	
Verbalisation	Sayer, Verbiage, Target	
Relational Processes	Carrier, Attribute	• Intensive • Possessive • Circumstantial

the transitivity framework is useful as a typology or tool which you can use to consider and reflect upon representation choices in a text.

Here are some useful tips for applying the transitivity framework:

1. First, locate the verbs in each clause of the text you are analysing. Focus on the main clauses first, then consider subordinate clauses. Try to find as many verbs as you can, but if you're unsure of some then make a note of them to check.
    - If your text contains direct speech, focus on the text outside of inverted commas first. If you wish, you can consider the transitivity within the direct speech too, but it is best to do this separately as direct speech typically represents another voice in the text.
2. Once you have identified all the verbs you can, consider each one and its participant roles and try to categorise the verb using the transitivity model.
3. If you find examples which are hard to categorise (which is likely!), make a note of why they are difficult and move on to the next one.
4. Once you have a list of the different types of processes being represented in the clauses of your text, you can do a number of things depending on the kind of text you are analysing and the kind of questions you are asking. It is often useful to make a note of *who* is taking part in the scene you are analysing, and then consider which processes they are most associated with. Who does what to whom? Does a particular character predominantly perform one type of process?

Why might this be? Who is portrayed as most active/passive in the scene? What effect do the processes have on your impressions of what is going on, or the message of the text? Is it what you would expect?
5. Do your problematic cases tell you anything about the way the text is representing things? Do they tell you anything about the shortcomings or issues with the transitivity framework?
6. Using a table to organise your observations (e.g. participants down one side, transitivity categories across the top) can sometimes help.

We will put this into action as we start to undertake transitivity analysis in the next section.

10.3 Transitivity patterns in longer texts

So far we have considered the transitivity of individual clauses, but usually transitivity analysis is applied to longer texts. As Halliday and Matthiessen note, 'part of the "flavour" of a particular text, and also of the register it belongs to, lies in its mixture of process types' (2014: 219). In literary fiction, transitivity choices can contribute to the representation of characters' points of view (see also Chapters 8–9). Consider the extract below, which comes from the opening of the novel *The Finkler Question* by Howard Jacobson (2010: 3; our sentence numbering):

> (1) He should have seen it coming.
>
> (2) His life had been one mishap after another. (3) So he should have been prepared for this one.
>
> (4) He was a man who saw things coming. (5) Not shadowy premonitions before and after sleep, but real and present dangers in the daylit world. (6) Lamp posts and trees reared up at him, splintering his shins. (7) Speeding cars lost control and rode on to the footpath leaving him lying in a pile of torn tissue and mangled bones. (8) Sharp objects dropped from scaffolding and pierced his skull.
>
> (9) Women worst of all. (10) When a woman of the sort Julian Treslove found beautiful crossed his path it wasn't his body that took the force but his mind. (11) She shattered his calm.
>
> (12) True, he had no calm, but she shattered whatever calm there was to look forward to in the future. (13) She *was* the future.

This paragraph features a third-person narrator describing the mindset of the protagonist Julian Treslove. It creates the impression that Treslove is a worrier, a pessimist, and has little control over the way he feels. This impression of Julian's character is created in part by the transitivity patterns in the text.

For instance, in this extract Julian Treslove performs mostly mental processes: 'he should have seen it' (S1) (mental perception); 'he should have been prepared' (S3) (mental cognition). Note that a transitivity analysis focuses on the main lexical verbs in a clause (which are underlined in these examples). The verb phrases in these sentences also contain deontic modals (e.g. 'should') and auxiliary verbs which create the past perfect tense (e.g. 'have been'). Treslove is also described through relational processes, for instance: 'He was a man who saw things coming' (S4) (relational intensive), 'he had no calm' (S12) (relational possessive).

So far, we have focused on the lexical verbs in main clauses, but similar transitivity is also apparent in the subordinate clauses. The relative clause 'who saw things coming' (S4) is a mental perception process, and the subordinate clause in (S10) 'of the sort Julian Treslove found beautiful' is a mental reaction process because it represents the experience of an emotion or preference. Transitivity analysis is always context-dependent. In S10 the verb 'found' represents a mental reaction process, but in a different context the same verb could also be used to represent a material action intention process (for instance, 'He found the accelerator'). Applying the transitivity categories involves making interpretative decisions about the process being represented by a particular clause.

In stark contrast to the mental and relational processes associated with Treslove, almost all the other entities or objects represented in the passage perform material processes, which have Treslove as their goal. For instance, the woman that 'crossed his path' (S10) is an actor in a material action intention process while 'She shattered his calm' (S11) is either an intention or supervention process depending on your interpretation of her intentionality. Inanimate actors are the grammatical subjects of material processes in 'Lamp posts and trees reared up at him' (S6), 'Speeding cars lost control and rode onto the footpath' (S7), and 'Sharp objects dropped from scaffolding' (S8). The latter is likely to be interpreted as a material event processes. However, the verb 'lost' in S7 appears to function more like a material action supervention process, whilst 'reared' and 'rode' function like material action intention processes. Attributing material action intention or supervention processes to inanimate objects has the effect of **personifying** the object and making it seem more animate. Ultimately, the transitivity in this passage gives the reader an impression of how Julian Treslove sees the world: he is represented as a victim who is affected by the world and women rather than acting upon them.

10.4 Gender representation in romance fiction

Because of its influence upon the way language represents the world, transitivity plays a significant role in the communication of ideologies in discourse. An **ideology** is a set of beliefs or attitudes about the world which can be consciously or unconsciously held by members of a particular social community. Work in **Critical Discourse Analysis** (CDA) examines the ideologies encoded within the language of a wide range of discourse types, including newspaper reports, advertisements, and literary texts. Feminist stylistic studies of romance literature have found that sexist ideologies are often encoded in the representation of men and women in such works. In intimate or sexual scenes in particular, women are often portrayed as passive and acted upon by a male agent. Such literary representations reproduce and sustain dominant ideologies about the differences between men and women and their roles in heteronormative relationships. Some critics argue that romance literature promotes gender inequality and reinforces passivity and subservience in its mainly female readers, though other theorists argue that readers are able to resist the ideological messages in such texts. Applying transitivity analysis to romantic fiction can provide interesting insights into the way characters of different genders are represented, feeding in to wider debates about the effects of such works.

E. L. James' adult romance trilogy *Fifty Shades of Grey* achieved enormous international success in 2012, topping bestseller lists in the US and UK. *Fifty Shades of Grey* tells the story of the inexperienced twenty-one-year-old virgin Anastasia Steele and her romantic and sexual relationship with the wealthy businessman Christian Grey. They first meet and recognise their mutual attraction when Anastasia interviews Grey for a student newspaper. The extract below describes events towards the end of their second meeting as they leave a coffee shop near Grey's workplace. Anastasia has become increasingly flustered by her feelings for Grey throughout the meeting. As they walk out of the coffee shop she decides it is time for her to leave (James 2012: 48):

> I have to go. I have to try and reassemble my thoughts. I have to get away from him. I walk forward, and I trip, stumbling headlong into the road.
>
> "Shit, Ana!" Grey cries. He tugs the hand that he's holding so hard that I fall back against him just as a cyclist whips past, narrowly missing me, heading the wrong way up this one-way street.
>
> It all happens so fast – one minute I'm falling, the next I'm in his arms and he's holding me tightly against his chest. I inhale his clean, wholesome scent. He smells of freshly laundered linen and some expensive body wash. It's

intoxicating. I inhale deeply.

"Are you okay?" he whispers. He has one arm around me, clasping me to him, while the fingers of his other hand softly trace my face, gently probing, examining me. His thumb brushes my lower lip, and his breath hitches. He's staring into my eyes, and I hold his anxious, burning gaze for a moment, or maybe its forever . . . but eventually, my attention is drawn to his beautiful mouth. And for the first time in twenty-one years, I want to be kissed. I want to feel his mouth on mine.

The scene begins with Anastasia expressing a desire to get away from Grey. She imagines carrying out a number of material action intention processes (e.g. 'to go', 'to get away') but only actually performs one such process in this scene: when she walks forward (L2). Otherwise, Anastasia is the actor in four material action supervention processes beyond her control as she trips, stumbles, and falls into Grey's arms (L2, L4, and L6) and the behaver in two behavioural processes when she inhales twice in order to experience Grey's scent (L7 and L9).

In contrast, Grey is represented as the actor in five material action intention processes ('tugs', L3; 'holding', L3 and L7; 'clasping', L10; 'staring', L13) which have Anastasia's hands, eyes, and body as their goals. Grey is also the sayer in two verbalisation processes ('cries', L3; 'whispers', L10). Overall, he is represented as being more active and competent than Anastasia, and she is often the object of his actions. The only other human actor in the scene is the cyclist who nearly hits Anastasia, who performs three material action intention processes (L4–5).

Interestingly, once Grey has rescued Anastasia from the immediate danger, Grey's body parts are represented as the actors in a series of material processes (from L10): his fingers trace, probe, and examine her face (L11–12), his thumb brushes her lip (L12). Whilst his fingers seem to be performing action intention processes, it is hard to decide whether his thumb brushing her face is an intention or supervention process. His breath hitching (L12) is a behavioural process, a physiological reaction that appears to be beyond his control. This shift from intentional to less intentional actions in L10–12 reflects a brief loss of control from Grey and implies that Anastasia's proximity has a powerful effect on him. However, Anastasia's body parts (her face and lower lip) remain the goal of Grey's material processes.

Anastasia's relative passivity is also reflected in the phrasing of her mental reaction processes in the final lines: 'I want to be kissed. I want to feel his mouth on mine' (L15–16). **Active sentences** are those in which the grammatical subject is the actor in the process. For instance:

Active sentences:

	She	kissed	him.
	Steve	kicked	the ball.
	Police	shot	a boy.
Sentence structure:	***Subject***	***Verb***	***Object***
Transitivity labels:	***Actor***	***Process***	***Goal***

Passive sentences are formed when the Subject of the sentence is the *Goal* of the process, achieved by altering the verb phrase to: 'be/get + past participle'. For instance:

Passive sentences:

	He	was kissed	(by her).
	The ball	was kicked	(by Steve).
	A boy	was shot	(by the police).
Sentence structure:	***Subject***	***Verb***	***(Adjunct)***
Transitivity labels:	***Goal***	***Process***	***(Actor)***

Passive sentences foreground the recipient of a particular process by making them the subject of the sentence. They also background or allow for the deletion of the Actor, who can either appear after the verb or not be mentioned at all (indicated by the bracketed optional phrases).

In the example from *Fifty Shades of Grey*, Anastasia expresses her desire in the main clause using a mental reaction process 'I want'. However, the desire itself, expressed in the subordinate clause 'to be kissed', is passive: she wants to be kissed by Grey rather than kiss him herself. Constructed as an active sentence, Anastasia would say:

	I	want	to kiss	him.
Sentence structure:	***Subject***	***Verb***	***Verb***	***Object***
Transitivity labels:	***Actor***	***Process***	***Process***	***Goal***

But instead, Anastasia uses a passive construction, representing herself as something to be acted upon by Grey:

	I	want	to be kissed	(by him.)
Sentence structure:	***Subject***	***Verb***	***Verb***	***(Adjunct)***
Transitivity labels:	***Goal***	***Process***	***Process***	***(Actor)***

Analysing the transitivity processes in this scene offers evidence to support the idea that *Fifty Shades of Grey* represents the leading female character as relatively passive in relation to the dominant male. However, there is also some evidence that Grey's power, although overwhelming, is not absolute. Furthermore, larger themes in the novel, such as Anastasia's inexperience and submission, and Grey's dominance and attempt to maintain control, are reflected in this transitivity of this scene.

Keywords and summary

Active sentence, Critical Discourse Analysis, feminist stylistics, ideology, participant roles (actor, attribute, behaver, circumstance, carrier, goal, phenomenon, sayer, sensor, target, verbiage), passive sentence, personification/personify, process (behavioural, material, mental, relational, verbal), Systemic Functional Grammar/ Linguistics, transitivity.

Transitivity analysis is the study of verb choice and the accompanying noun phrases in a clause. Transitivity choices play a significant role in the way linguistic expressions represent the world: for instance, how they apportion blame and responsibility and how they represent the activities of characters or classes of people in the situation being described. Therefore, transitivity can be both indicative of point of view in a text and revealing of a text's ideological positioning.

Activities

1. Find a picture of a busy scene involving multiple people and, focusing on different aspects of the scene, write ten sentences to describe what is happening. Use the transitivity model to analyse the transitivity in each of your sentences. Turn some of your active sentences into passives. What effect does the passive version have?
2. Look at the extract from *Fifty Shades of Grey* again and consider what effect different transitivity choices would have in the representation of characters in this passage. Pick one or two sentences and rewrite them using a different configuration of transitivity. How could Anastasia and Grey be represented differently?
3. Find two newspaper reports of the same event, preferably from the same date. It may be useful if you compare broadsheet and tabloid newspapers, or newspapers with different types of readerships. Analyse and compare the transitivity choices in each report. Pay particular attention to the headline, bylines, and first few paragraphs. What are the differences in the way the event is represented? What does this suggest about the ideological position of the author and/or the publication?

Further reading and references

Halliday's work on transitivity is introduced in Halliday and Matthiessen (2014). Thompson (2004) is an alternative introduction to Systemic Functional Grammar. For stylistic applications of transitivity, see: Birch (1989), Carter (1993), Fowler (1991), Halliday (1973), Kennedy (1982), Simpson (1993), and Simpson and Canning (2014). Jeffries (2010b) covers the combination of Critical Discourse Analysis (CDA) and stylistics. Other reading in CDA includes Bloor (2007) and Fairclough (2010). For examples of feminist text analysis, see: Burton (1982), Wareing (1994), and Mills (1995a, 1995b) which includes transitivity analysis. Jones and Mills (2014) engage with the question of whether readers can resist the ideological messages in *Fifty Shades of Grey*.

11 Varieties and invented languages

11.1 Language varieties

This chapter considers the representation of different styles of voice in literature. We all speak in a slightly different style and this style is likely to vary depending upon the context and purpose of an interaction. Linguistic styles also vary across regional and social groupings, so an individual's speech style tends to be influenced by the place(s) where they live, the nature of their education, and the communities of which they are a part. Distinctive languages and linguistic styles are referred to in linguistics as **varieties** (this is a general, overarching term). Linguistic varieties associated with a particular region and/or social class are known as **dialects**. A dialect is characterised by particular vocabulary and grammatical patterns. Some particularly recognisable English dialects include Cockney English (from parts of London), Geordie English (from the North East of England), and West Country English (from the South West of England). Certain pronunciations are associated with dialects, and these are known as **accents**.

In England and other English-speaking countries, the dialect most used in public life is **Standard English**. This variety is taught in schools and used in media, publishing, law, and government. Because it is associated with authority and education, Standard English is a **prestige** dialect in the British Isles. It is important to note that there is nothing inherently superior about Standard English as a linguistic variety; the prestige is a result of social and cultural factors. Most literary works are written in Standard English, as this is the dominant written dialect. However, in spoken English, dialectal variety is much more common.

The accent most associated with Standard English dialect is **Received Pronunciation (RP)**; it is sometimes known as the 'Queen's English' and is linked with higher social classes rather than a particular geographical area. Nevertheless, Standard English dialect is also often spoken with a regional accent. Thus, it is possible for someone with a Cockney accent, for example, to speak in a Cockney English dialect (using the grammar and vocabulary of this variety) or in a Standard English dialect (using the grammar and vocabulary of that variety). Indeed, it is not uncommon for speakers to be **bidialectal** and use different varieties in different situations.

The dominance of Standard English in written contexts poses particular challenges for writers who wish to represent regional or non-standard dialects in their work. There are many reasons why a writer may wish to do this. In everyday life, we infer things about others based upon the way they speak, and these deductive processes can also be applied to characters. Thus, dialect representation in literature can contribute to characterisation or the creation of social realism. It can also contribute to a writer's representation of different worldviews and the construction of political and moral themes. The **Standard English ideology** – an ideology which holds Standard English up as the valued 'norm' and marginalises other varieties – has a significant impact on communities who do not speak in that dialect. Representing non-Standard English dialects in literature can be a way of questioning and undermining this Standard English ideology. However, representing non-standard dialects in literature can also reinforce the Standard English ideology if the characters who speak Standard English are represented as authoritative and educated, and those who do not are represented negatively or **stereotypically**. Representations of language varieties in literature, therefore, can be highly controversial and can have different effects. As Hodson (2014: 239) points out, key questions to ask of a work are: (1) *what dialect is represented?* (2) *How is it represented?* (3) *And what purpose does it serve?* As Hodson's questions suggest, the study of dialect representation and its purposes can encompass both text-internal and text-external concerns (2014: 3–14). A stylistic examination of dialect representation can provide insights into characterisation, inter-character relationships, and the thematic concerns of literary works. It also assists in considering the way such representations interact with the social context in which they appear and the interpretations of readers.

11.2 Strategies for representing linguistic varieties in writing

Linguistic varieties are usually represented in literature through the manipulation of spelling and punctuation, and the inclusion of specific lexis, morphology, and syntax. Consider the extract below from Emily Brontë's *Wuthering Heights* (1995 [1847]: 21). The passage comes from

Catherine Earnshaw's diary, in which she describes a Sunday's activity in Wuthering Heights after her father's death. Catherine and the other children want to play quietly, but Joseph, their deeply religious servant, wishes them to read instead:

> On Sunday evenings we used to be permitted to play, if we did not make much noise; now a mere titter is sufficient to send us into corners. [. . .] I had just fastened our pinafores together, and hung them up for a curtain, when in comes Joseph, on an errand from the stables. He tears down my handiwork, boxes my ears, and croaks:
>
> "T' maister nobbut just buried, and Sabbath not o'ered, und t' sound o' t' gospel still i' yer lugs, and ye darr be laiking! Shame on ye! sit ye down, ill childer! there's good books eneugh if ye'll read 'em: sit ye down, and think o' yer sowls!"

Hodson (2014) notes that dialect representation can appear in various locations in literary texts: in direct speech, with a contrast between the represented speech and the narrative voice; in the narrative voice itself; and in free indirect discourse in which the voices of the narrator and character are blended (see sections 8.2 and 11.3). In this example, dialect representation appears in the direct speech of Joseph while the Catherine (the narrative voice in the first paragraph) uses Standard English.

A number of techniques are used to represent Joseph's Yorkshire dialect. The direct speech features **semi-phonetic respelling** of words in order to communicate aspects of Joseph's regional accent to the reader, such as 'maister' for 'master' and 'sowls' for 'souls'. Hodson (2014: 91) describes the manipulation of spelling to indicate accent as 'an inexact art' because it is liable to be interpreted differently by different readers. One interpretation might be to view the respelling 'maister' as indicative of a shift from the initial [ɑː] vowel of RP 'master' to [eɪ] (IPA symbols are used in the stylistic discussion of phonetics – see Chapter 3). The spelling of 'sowls' could indicate a shift from RP vowel [əʊ] or [ɒ] to [aʊ]. Often, semi-phonetic respelling works best if readers have some familiarity with the variety being represented. Did you recognise a Yorkshire accent when reading Joseph's utterance? Punctuation also contributes to the representation of Joseph's accent. Apostrophes after 't'' and 'o'' appear to represent glottal stops [ʔ] (where airflow is obstructed by the glottis, for instance in the middle of the phrase 'uh-oh'), a common feature of a Yorkshire accent.

Sometimes respellings represent natural phonetic processes which ordinarily occur in informal speech in *any* accent (including RP):

these are known as **allegro speech respellings** and there is an example in Joseph's speech in the spelling of an unstressed 'your' as 'yer' and the contraction of 'them' to ''em'. The use of an apostrophe in 'em helps readers to fill in the omitted letters. Although these pronunciations are widespread across all accents, in literature they only tend to be marked for characters who speak a dialect other than Standard English.

Joseph's speech also makes extensive use of **regionalisms**: the vocabulary and grammar associated with his dialect. There are a number of Yorkshire dialect words such as 'nobbut' for 'only', 'laiking' for 'playing', 'childer' for 'children', and 'lugs' for 'ears' and 'ye' is used as a second-person pronoun.

In *Wuthering Heights*, dialect representation serves various purposes. It evokes the setting of the novel in rural Yorkshire, and represents Joseph as a native of that area. The dialect representation also marks a contrast between the characters: Catherine (in the first paragraph), for instance, narrates in Standard English, despite also being a native of rural Yorkshire. The contrast evoked is therefore one of class: Joseph is the servant and thus his dialect is marked. Consequently, dialect representation contributes to the construction of a hierarchy of voices in the novel, with Standard English voices used for the most prestigious and central characters (as was conventional in Victorian novels). In the context of Catherine's journal, the choice to mark Joseph's dialect also seems to indicate stereotyped ideas about non-standard speakers, representing Joseph as rather backwards and something of a 'caricature', deserving of less respect (indeed, Mr Lockwood, who is reading Catherine's diary, describes her rendering of Joseph as 'an excellent caricature . . . rudely yet powerfully sketched' (Brontë 1995 [1847]: 20)).

Although the respellings in this extract from *Wuthering Heights* seem designed to represent specific linguistic features of the Yorkshire dialect or speech more generally, it is worth watching out for literary respellings which 'reflect no phonetic facts whatsoever' (Preston 2000: 615). Examples might include spelling 'was' as 'woz', or 'sez' for 'says', or 'ennything' for 'anything'. These respellings *look* dialectal on the page, but upon closer consideration do not seem to indicate a particularly different *sound* at all, and are therefore examples of **eye dialect**. Eye dialect may be used when an author wants to influence readerly assumptions about a character's class or intelligence, drawing on social stigmas and stereotypes, without attempting a more detailed rendering of a particular linguistic variety.

11.3 Style switching in poetry

The representation of linguistic varieties can also be used to great effect in poetry. Consider this piece by Sheffield-based poet Sally Goldsmith (2012):

Received Pronunciation

As a boy, my Sussex granddad could
spot the runty dillin in a pig's litter,
play the fool down the pleached twittern,
cry fainits when he wanted out of the game,
make jokes about the daglets on a sheep's bum
comparing them to his own number two's.

From the Warwickshire lot I got
the blart of waltzers at Stratford Mop,
learned to swill the sink after washing up,
to call down the jutty at the side of the 'us –
loud enough to wake the diddikais about whom
my mother said I never should.

In rural Oxfordshire, I wuz moi duck
to aunts who let me tiffle biddy hens
off their eggs, bring in pecked bottles
of miwk off of the step, nudged me
out of looking a sawney, warned me
to avoid the bunt of boys or even a cow.

In Sheffield now with you, flower,
I look after us tranklements, crozzle
me bacon and modge me pudding,
put t' door on t' sneck, go to t' foot
of our stairs, let da into t' entry, talk
clarty at neet, laik and love da till ah dee.

The title of this poem plays with the phrase 'received pronunciation'. When describing the accent most associated with Standard English, the adjective 'received' means that which is generally adopted or approved (cf. 'received wisdom'). The poem puns on the other meaning of the adjective 'received': 'that which has been bestowed, accepted, taken in' (OED). In the poem, then, the poetic voice describes the dialects they have 'received' from their family and loved ones and which contribute to their linguistic repertoire and sense of identity, listing four regional varieties of English: the Sussex dialect (a region on the south east coast of England), Warwickshire and Oxfordshire dialects (regions in central

England), and the Sheffield dialect (a city in Yorkshire in the north of England).

As well as representing these varieties, each stanza also represents different times in the poetic voice's history, beginning with the speech of their grandfather in his youth (stanza 1) before referring to the origins of the poetic voice's family in Warwickshire (stanza 2) and the aunts they used to visit 'in rural Oxfordshire' (stanza 3). In these stanzas, dialect representation occurs through free indirect discourse, as the poetic voice represents the voices of family members alongside their own. The representation of other voices ceases in the final stanza, which shifts to the present and represents the speaker's own voice 'in Sheffield now'. Each stanza combines Standard English with dialectical aspects of each region, represented for the most part through regionalisms and semi-phonetic respellings.

Regional lexis in the poem includes 'dillin' (weakling of a litter), 'twittern' (path or alleyway), 'fainits' (truce), and 'daglets' in stanza 1; 'blart' (cry), 'jutty' (narrow walkway), and 'didikais' (gypsies) in stanza 2; 'tiffle' (to disorder or disarrange), 'sawney' (fool), and 'bunt' (knock or push) in stanza 3; and 'tranklements' (ornaments/trinkets), 'crozzle' (to burn or char), 'modge' (to hoard or steal), 'sneck' (latch), 'clarty' (dirty), 'neet' (night), 'lake' (play), and 'dee' (die) in stanza 4. The regional use of the words 'duck' and 'flower' as informal terms of address is also evident in stanzas 2 and 4.

Respelling is used to indicate features of pronunciation. The spelling of 'dillin' (L2) without the final letter 'g' is suggestive of g-dropping, a common phonetic feature in colloquial speech. The representation of the word 'house' ([haʊs]) as ''us' ([ʊs]) (L10) seems to reflect h-dropping, another non-region-specific aspect of joined-up speech. These allegro speech respellings contribute to the evocation of the characters' spoken voices.

Elsewhere, semi-phonetic respelling reflects features of specific regional accents. The spelling of 'was my' as 'wuz moi' (L13) seems to represent the vowel sounds of an Oxfordshire accent, where RP 'my' [mʌɪ] or [maɪ] becomes [mɔɪ] or [mɑɪ]. The potential pitfalls of using semi-phonetic respelling are evident here, as readers without prior knowledge of the Oxfordshire dialect could reasonably interpret 'moi' as a representation of the French borrowing for 'me' [mwa:]. The respelling of 'wuz' also appears to indicate a different vowel sound, from RP [wɒz] to [wʌz], although the replacement of the letter 's' with 'z' is eye dialect because it does not represent a different sound, and still reads as the voiced alveolar fricative [z]. The respelling of 'milk' as 'miwk' seems to indicate L-vocalisation in which the lateral approximant [l] sound is replaced by a vowel or semi-vowel. This is another feature of the Oxfordshire accent. The letter 'w' could be interpreted as representing a pronunciation like [mɪʊk]. Features of a Yorkshire accent are indicated by the apostrophes in L22–3, which represent glottal stops [ʔ] (as in *Wuthering Heights*), and the respelling of 'I' [aɪ] as 'ah', could represent the vowel sound [a:] (L24). Finally, the spelling of 'da' (L24) seems to represent th-stopping in the pronunciation of the Yorkshire second-person pronoun 'tha/thou', where [ð] becomes [d].

When considering how readers might respond to dialect representations, Hodson (2014: 155) identifies two contextual factors that often come into play: 'the identity of the intended audience and the identity of the writer'. Studies of dialect representation distinguish between **dialect literature**, which is aimed essentially (though not exclusively) at an audience who are familiar with a particular non-standard dialect, and **literary dialect**, which is aimed at national or international audiences. Dialect literature tends to make extensive use of non-standard dialect representation, whereas literary dialect tends to represent non-standard speech in work which is otherwise written in Standard English. The boundaries between literary dialect and dialect literature are not rigid, but highlight the role of intended readership in any assessment of the purposes and effects of dialect representation. A further important reader-related issue is the tendency for dialect representations that depart noticeably from standard colloquial speech to be met with a degree of what Toolan (1992b) terms '**reader resistance**'. This is because they demand more effort of a reader, and have the potential to negatively impact reader comprehension and motivation.

The identity of the writer can also impact upon the effects of dialect representation in their works. Writers who are not authentic speakers of the dialect(s) they choose to represent can be accused of linguistic **stereotyping** more readily than those who are. As Hodson (2014: 117) points out, any published writer will be literate by virtue of an education in Standard English; they are therefore likely to be bidialectal with Standard English and have 'mixed attitudes towards the variety they are trying to represent'. Even writers who are authentic speakers of a variety face the problem of how to represent that variety without evoking negative responses in their audience.

The poem 'Received Pronunciation' is a good example of the fluid boundaries between literary dialect and dialect literature. The poem is published in an anthology of poems about Sheffield, produced by a local press (Lehoczky et al. 2012). The intended readership of the poem in this context is relatively local, and the representation of the Yorkshire dialect in particular appears designed to be read by people who are familiar with that variety (there are more regionalisms in the final stanza). The poem is also available more widely though, for instance on the Poetry Society website. Although it contains dialect representation, it is still written for the most part in Standard English, with regionalisms (particularly in the first three stanzas) contextualised in some way to aid the interpretation of readers, for instance 'cry fainits when he wanted out of the game' (L5). It is unlikely that many readers will share the poetic voice's specific hybrid regional identity, thus the use of Standard English and contextualising devices function to mitigate reader resistance.

The identity of the author is also a factor in the potential effects of this poem. Sally Goldsmith is a Sheffield-based writer whose biography overlaps with that of the poetic voice. When she reads the poem aloud, she performs stronger forms of all four represented dialects, particularly the Yorkshire accent of the final stanza. This performance could risk being perceived as 'inauthentic' caricature, even though the author has a personal relationship with the varieties being portrayed. At the same time, the poetic voice's ability to **style switch** and adopt the different dialects is central to the poem's meaning: it cleverly raises questions about what 'authenticity' means for speakers with mixed regional identities. The poem is a demonstration of **linguistic accommodation**: the ability to adjust one's speech style or dialect depending on the situation and intended audience. Its form also enacts the stylistic repertoires that we acquire through our family history, upbringing, travel, and relationships.

11.4 Invented dialects

Sometimes, rather than representing existing linguistic varieties, authors invent new dialects or languages as part of the fictional worlds they create. This might involve the use of **neologisms** (new words) or **neosemes** (existing words which are given new meaning). It could also feature more extensive **dialectal extrapolation** in which grammatical or phonological features as well as new vocabulary are created, or even the construction of entire languages (conlangs or **neographies**) with their own comprehensive grammars and histories (such as J. R. R. Tolkien's Elvish language Sindarin).

Stockwell points out that invented languages in literary fiction function to 'delineate the distance and connections between the reader's world and the world imagined in the text' (2006: 3). Invented dialects can contribute to the evocation of a particular world and/or take on a central thematic purpose (such as 'Newspeak' in Orwell's *1984*, which is a method of oppression used by the state). As such, the representation of an invented variety has a similar function to the representation of existing varieties, in that they contribute to the creation of believable fictional worlds and the construction of political or moral commentary.

David Mitchell's (2004) novel *Cloud Atlas* comprises six narratives each told in different styles (including a journal, a series of letters, a novel-within-the-novel, and an interview transcript, as well as some more conventional first-person narration) by characters from vastly different spatio-temporal locations in the past, present, and future. There is no overarching narrative voice linking the stories together or introducing them. Instead, it is largely up to the reader to make connections between the narrative threads. The following extract comes from a chapter titled: 'Sloosha's Crossin' an' Ev'rythin' After' which is narrated in the first person by a goatherd called Zachary. It gradually emerges that Zachary is part of a future post-apocalyptic generation living after a 'Fall' which has wiped out the rest of civilisation. The opening paragraphs of the chapter read (Mitchell 2004: 249):

> Old Georgie's path an' mine crossed more time'n I'm comfy mem'ryin', an' after I'm died, no sayin' what the fangy devil won't try an' do to me . . . so gimme some mutton an' I'll tell you 'bout our first meetin'. A fat joocesome slice, nay, none o'your burnt wafery off'rin's . . .
>
> Adam, my bro, an' Pa'n'me was trekkin' back from Honokaa Market on miry roads with a busted cart-axle in draggly clothesies. Evenin' catched us up early so we tented on the southly bank o' Sloosha's Crossin', 'cos Waipio river was furyin' with days o' hard rain an' swollen by a spring tide.

At first glance, the narrative seems somewhat deviant from Standard English due to the frequent use of apostrophes. However, despite *appearing* deviant, it is surprisingly easy to read. Closer inspection of the punctuation reveals that the passage makes extensive use of allegro speech respellings, such as: the use of 'an'' and 'n' for 'and'; ''bout' for 'about'; 'o'your' for 'of your', 'gimme' for 'give me'; ''cos' for 'because'; 'off'rin's' for 'offerings'; and g-dropping in 'trekkin'' and 'meetin''. These respellings represent very conventional pronunciation features of spoken Standard English, but add an oral quality and colloquial register to the narrative voice.

There are still a number of unfamiliar vocabulary items in the passage, which suggest some differences between the reader's world and the world of the text. Words such as 'fangy', 'wafery', 'draggly', and 'southly' are formed by adding the +(l)y suffix to existing nouns or verbs to create adjectives. Similarly, 'furying' turns the noun 'fury' into a verb by adding a progressive '-ing' ending. Interestingly, all of these words are listed in the *Oxford English Dictionary*, and are recorded as occurring in the mid-1800s or early 1900s (except 'southly', which is much older). The OED identifies these words as 'not part of normal discourse' and 'unknown to most people', so they are likely to be interpreted as neologisms by readers. There are other genuine neologisms in the passage too. Familiar English nouns such as 'memory' and 'tent' appear as verbs formed by the addition of conventional verb endings ('-ing' and '-ed') to form 'memorying' (instead of 'remembering') and 'tented' (to refer to setting up a camp).

Further morphological change is evident in the adjective 'joocesome', formed by adding the suffix '-some' instead of '-y' to the noun 'juice'. The spelling of 'jooce' is also unfamiliar, although notice how the pronunciation of the word remains unchanged. In the context of this invented dialect, eye dialect such as 'jooce' makes a common Standard English word appear less familiar, perhaps indicating that changes in the spelling system have occurred in this future world. The plural noun 'clothes' also appears with an '-ies' suffix, which could also indicate morphological change.

This combination of rare, old-fashioned, and new words makes it difficult to identify whether the narrative is located in the past or the future, representing an archaic or new dialect. At first, the unfamiliar vocabulary, combined with reference to a rural environment and the use of old-fashioned carts, for instance, suggests a historic setting. Yet, morphological and grammatical elements could also be intended to suggest language development in the future.

Grammatically, the narrator's language also deviates in some instances from Standard English, such as in the use of a verb ('died') instead of the adjective ('dead') in 'after I am *died*'; the use of the singular rather than plural form of the past-tense copula verb 'to be' in: 'Adam, my bro, an' Pa'n'me *was* trekkin'; and the use of a regular '-ed' verb ending instead of the irregular 'caught' in 'Evenin' *catched* us up'. These deviations, along with the mention of bedraggled clothing and primitive vehicles, could be suggestive of the narrator's lack of formal education or could indicate language development in this fictional future world. Dialect representation does not have to be consistent in order for it to have an effect on readers' impressions of a character or fictional world. It is only through further contextual information that readers are able to infer the futuristic setting of this story. The narrator's linguistic style indicates both the distance and the connections between his world and that of a twenty-first-century reader.

Keywords and summary

Accent, accommodation, allegro speech respellings, bidialectal, borrowings, dialect, dialect literature, dialectical extrapolation, eye dialect, literary dialect, neography, neologism, neosemy, prestige, reader resistance, Received Pronunciation, regionalisms, semi-phonetic respelling, Standard English ideology, stereotyping, style-switching, varieties.

Authors may choose to write all or part of their work in a dialect other than Standard English, in order to represent dialects associated with particular regional and social groupings, or to invent dialects representative of a particular fictional world. Stylistic analysis is concerned with the linguistic description of *how* these dialects are represented (for instance, through respellings, punctuation, vocabulary, morphology, and grammar) and also, crucially, the meanings and effects of such representations for readers, which are influenced by factors including intended audience, reader resistance, and author identity.

Activities

1. The greetings below are featured on the front of birthday cards produced by the company 'Dialectables' (www.dialectable.co.uk). Marketed as 'giftware that talks like you', they represent the generic greeting 'HAPPY BIRTHDAY [AFFECTIONATE NAME]' in a selection of British dialects:

   (a) APPY BIRFDAY MY LUVVER!
   (b) APPY BIRTHDOY BAB!
   (c) APPY BIRTHDEE AAR KID!
   (d) APPY BUTHDY OUR LASS
   (e) HAPPY BIRTHDAY MA WEE DARLIN'

   Can you identify the regional dialect being represented in each case? Does your own experience of English dialects seem to play a role here? What linguistic choices have been made in order to represent the dialects? What are the effects of these representations?
   Try to write the greeting in another dialect, such as your own (if it is not represented here). What linguistic changes have you made?
   (Answers: (a) Bristolian, (b) Birmingham, (c) Liverpool, (d) Yorkshire, (e) Scots.)

2. Discuss your responses to the poem 'Received Pronunciation' with others. Did you experience 'reader resistance' to the non-standard dialect in the poem? To what extent do you agree with our reading

of the poem? If you had to write a poem about your own regional identity or style switching, which varieties would it include?

3. Find examples of written representations of dialect in literature. The poem 'Six O'Clock News' by Tom Leonard (1995 [1976]) or 'Dis Poetry' by Benjamin Zephaniah (1995) are good places to start. Describe the linguistic strategies used to represent the dialect, and consider how the dialect representation contributes to the piece's effects.

Further reading and references

Hodson (2014) is a comprehensive introduction to the stylistic techniques and effects of dialect representation introduced in this chapter. For a concise overview, see Beal (2006). For more stylistic work on invented languages in literature, see Stockwell (2000a) and, more concisely (2006). Toolan (1992b) discusses the implications of dialect representation in literature. More on the origin of Standard English and the Standard English ideology can be found in: Crowley (2003), Crystal (1995: 110–11), and Labov (1969). Books about modern language varieties include: Crystal (1995: part V), Davies (2005), Hughes et al. (2012), Kortmann and Upton (2008), and Lippi-Green (1997). Information about the Oxfordshire dialect discussed in section 10.3 comes from Altendorf and Watt (2008) and Wells (1982: 258–60), and insights into the Yorkshire dialect from Beal (2008) and Stoddart et al. (1999: 79). On respelling and the effect of representations of speech, see Preston (1985, 2000). Other stylistic work on literary dialect includes: Blake (1981), Fowler (1981), Hodson (2016), Hodson and Broadhead (2013), Mey (1998), Page (1987), Scott (2009), and Traugott and Pratt (1980: chs 8–9). For more on hierarchies of textual voices, see Bakhtin (1981 [1934–5]). Our focus has been on poetry and prose, but see Hodson (2014) on dialect in film and McIntyre (2004) on plays. A recording of Sally Goldsmith reading 'Received Pronunciation' is available at: <https://soundcloud.com/sally-goldsmith/poems-the-bird-doubletake-in#t=3:02> (last accessed April 2016).

Part IV

Text as cognition

12 Figure and ground

12.1 Cognitive stylistics

As Parts II and III of this book have already demonstrated, stylistics has a long history of adapting models and theories from linguistics to a literary context. Part II introduced stylistic work that draws on the linguistic sub-disciplines of phonetics, morphology, syntax, and semantics; Part III covered the influence of pragmatics, sociolinguistics, discourse analysis, and functional linguistics. In Parts IV and V of this book, we turn our attention to the influence of another linguistic sub-discipline: **cognitive linguistics**. Cognitive linguistics aligns the study of language with the study of the mind and brain (the word 'cognitive' indicates this focus on mental faculties, such as perception and knowledge, as part of the study of language). Cognitive linguistics first emerged in the 1970s with some radical new ideas, which have had a lasting impact and increasing traction in linguistics, and are hence referred to as part of 'the cognitive turn' in the discipline. Some basic tenets of a cognitive linguistic approach are:

1. Language is dependent upon the cognitive mechanisms which are used in other areas of human experience: such as the way we perceive, categorise, and imagine/represent the world.
2. Human minds work in fundamentally similar ways because they possess these cognitive mechanisms.
3. An account of language should accord with what is generally known about the mind and brain in other scientific and psychological disciplines.

The insights of cognitive linguistics span across linguistic levels and encompass both grammatical/structural and functional approaches to language. Stylisticians have been quick to notice the potential of ideas in cognitive linguistics for the study of literature.

Stylistics is centrally concerned with the *interactions* between the language of a text and a reader of that text. Combining the study of language with the study of the mind suggests that more can be understood about how that interaction between text and reader occurs, and why particular effects are produced. A series of frameworks which adapt cognitive linguistic research for the study of literary reading have now been developed, and will be introduced in the coming chapters. Each chapter considers the role of particular cognitive mechanisms in our understanding and appreciation of literature. This chapter begins by applying ideas from the psychology of perception to the language of literature.

12.2 Figure and ground

Human sensory input is organised in terms of prominence: **figures** are the things we pay most attention to, and **ground** is everything else we perceive but pay less attention to. This basic distinction underpins human sensory perception and therefore is a powerful concept. For instance, when watching a tennis match, our eyes will follow the movements of the tennis ball rather than rest on the grass or the net. Similarly, when listening to a piece of pop music, the vocal melody will tend to appear more prominent than the rest of the musical accompaniment. Right now, the letters on this page are figures in your visual perception, they have **prominence** and everything else you can see – the white page, anything around the edges of the book (or screen) – is probably a bit blurry or indistinct; it is backgrounded. Once you have finished reading this sentence, make a conscious effort to shift your attention away from the writing on this page and instead to the whole object (the book or device) that you are viewing it on (then come back!). When you did this, you altered the configuration of elements in your perceptual field: the book/device became the prominent figure, and everything else (including the writing on it) became ground.

The optical illusion shown in Figure 12.1 plays with figure and ground for its effect. There are two possibilities when looking at it: you could see two faces in white, or a vase in black. When you see the vase, it becomes the figure and the white spaces become the ground. When you see the faces, they become the figure and the black space is ground. This is a **bistable illusion**, so you can't see both the vase and the faces at the same time. This segregation between figure and ground is integral to the way human perception works.

Furthermore, human perception automatically finds some things more attractive of attention than others (as in the tennis and

Figure 12.1 Rubin's vase. For original, see Rubin (1958 [1915]: 201) (from Gibbons 2012a: 43; see also Stockwell 2002a: 14)

music example above). Figures usually attract our attention because they:

- have form or shape – being self-contained objects or features with well-defined edges that stand out from the ground
- are moving in relation to a static ground
- precede the ground in time or space – being on top of, in front of, or above the ground
- are more detailed or brighter than the ground
- are an object or entity we might interact with.

Research in cognitive linguistics and stylistics is concerned with how these cognitive 'norms' of attraction, which form the bedrock of human sensory perception, are manifest in language. For instance, how might distinctions between figures and grounds be rendered in words? And how do speakers/writers use language to direct the attention of hearers/ readers in particular ways? Consider the sentences below (from Talmy 2000: 311–12). What is the figure and ground in each sentence?:

(a) The pen lay on the table.
(b) The pen fell off the table.

Both sentences represent the pen as figure and the table as ground. The pen is a self-contained object in front of the ground: in (a), its position is given using the preposition 'on', it is also the subject of the sentence and performs the verb 'lay'; in (b), the pen is represented as moving ('fell') in relation to a static ground. When reading (a) and (b), you momentarily imagine the pen and the table and their relationship in order to process the meaning of the sentences. As Stockwell notes, 'All linguistic representations are *simulations* either of an actual reality or of a fictional, imagined putative reality' (Stockwell 2014b: 30; citing Langacker 2008: 536–7). These imagined simulations have figures and grounds just like other areas of human perception. Linguistic cues contribute to the figuring and grounding of represented objects in language.

Stockwell (2002a, 2009a) has pioneered the investigation of figures and grounds in literary language and the act of reading. He modified the features of good figures listed above for application in a written, literary context. Objects and entities that attract attention, and are therefore figures, are known as **attractors**. Stockwell argues that, during reading, stylistic features can work to direct reader attention towards particular attractors, sustain this attention, or distract reader attention to other newly attractive elements. Analysing the direction of attention during reading, then, involves paying close attention to the stylistic features of a text and the way they might work to confer prominence on particular elements, and background others. Backgrounded elements that are no longer the focus of attention are described as being **neglected** and will eventually **decay** (or disappear) from attentional prominence. Table 12.1 lists properties of attractors in written literary language.

This list incorporates traditional, grammatical features such as the ordering of constituents in sentences (agency, topicality) and the use of articles (definiteness), verbs (activeness), and noun phrases (largeness), along with more experiential features such as the progression of the act of reading (newness), the perception of particular properties (e.g. brightness, noisiness), and the relationship with a reader's sense of what is 'normal' (aesthetic distance from the norm). This connection between grammar and experience is characteristic of a cognitive stylistic approach. Attractiveness in one dimension of the table is often paralleled by attractiveness in other dimensions, so that figures are created (Stockwell 2009a: 32).

Reading is a dynamic process, and as such the figure/ground distinction during reading is not a binary segregation, but a gradable one which represents a cline from most attractive to least attractive. Objects and entities represented in a text move up and down this cline as reading progresses, and this shifting of attention is the result of both textual features and readers' motivation and expectations. Stockwell regards this nuanced shifting of attention as responsible for the felt **texture** of reading, and the source of many literary works' effects (2009b: 31).

Before demonstrating how these ideas work in literary analysis, it is worth pointing out the connections between the cognitive stylistic

Table 12.1 Stockwell's list of features of good textual attractors (based on Stockwell 2009a: 25)

Features of good textual attractors	Explanation
Newness	Currency: the present moment of reading is more attractive than the previous moment. A reader's attention is continually shifting as they move through a text.
Agency	Noun phrases in active position are better attractors than in passive position. *Compare: (a) 'Herbert broke the door handle' / (b) 'The door handle was broken by Herbert'. In (a) the noun phrase 'Herbert' attracts more attention than in (b), where the passive construction reduces focus on Herbert's agency.* (See Section 10.4.)
Topicality	In a sentence, grammatical subject position confers attraction over object position. *In: 'The man shot the boy', the man is a better attractor than the boy, because he appears in the subject position of the sentence (featured first, and performing the action of shooting); the boy (the recipient of the action in the object position) is less attractive.* (See Chapter 5.)
Empathic recognisability	Animate entities attract more attention than objects or abstractions. There is a scale of attraction, as follows (> = is more attractive than): human speaker > human hearer > animal > object > abstraction.
Definiteness	Definite noun phrases attract more attention than indefinites. There is a cline, as follows (> = is more attractive than): definite ('the man') > specific indefinite ('a certain man') > nonspecific indefinite ('any man').
Activeness	Verbs denoting action, violence, passion, wilfulness, motivation, or strength.
Brightness	Lightness or vivid colours being denoted over dimness or drabness.
Fullness	Richness, density, intensity, or nutrition being denoted.
Largeness	Large objects being denoted or very long elaborated noun phrase used to denote.
Height	Objects that are above others, are higher than the perceiver, or which dominate.
Noisiness	Denoted phenomenon which are audibly voluminous.
Aesthetic distance from the norm	Referents attract attention if they are denoted as beautiful or ugly, dangerous or alien, and the creation of dissonance.

notion of figure and ground, and the notion of foregrounding in stylistics (introduced in Chapter 2). Foregrounding also refers to the ways in which certain aspects of a text can be made to attract attention through forms of textual patterning. In stylistics, foregrounding is thought to be created by repetition, parallelism, and deviation at different linguistic levels of a text. The study of figure and ground contributes to this existing research area, and expands our inventory of the kinds of textual cues that might direct and reduce attention by drawing analogies between reading and other forms of human perception.

12.3 Attraction and neglect

This poem, 'The House Is Not the Same since You Left', by Henry Normal (1993) is a good example of how the language of a text works to foreground and background aspects of its content:

The house is not the same since you left
the cooker is angry – it blames me
The TV tries desperately to stay busy
but occasionally I catch it staring out of the window
The washing-up's feeling sorry for itself again
it just sits there saying 'What's the point, what's the
point?'
The curtains count the days
Nothing in the house will talk to me
I think your armchair's dead
The kettle tried to comfort me at first
but you know what its attention span's like
I've not told the plants yet
they think you're on holiday
The bathroom misses you
I hardly see it these days
It still can't believe you didn't take it with you
The bedroom won't even look at me
since you left it keeps its eyes closed
all it wants to do is sleep, remembering better times
trying to lose itself in dreams
it seems like it's taken the easy way out
but at night I hear the pillows
weeping into the sheets.

Let's track the process of figuring and grounding in the first lines of the poem. This analysis assumes that you are familiar with the grammatical concepts of subject and object in a sentence, which are covered in Chapter 5.

The first line presents two main attractors: the house and the person who left it. The noun phrase 'the house' is a good attractor because it denotes a large object and has topicality: it appears in the subject position of the main clause of the sentence. The 'you' has empathic recognisability and activeness ('you left'). However, the syntax of this line works to promote the house as an attractor over the 'you' because 'you' appears in a subordinate clause ('since you left').

The second line shifts attention to a new attractor, 'the cooker', which is the subject of a new sentence. By personifying the cooker and describing it as 'angry', the poem shifts the cooker up the scale of empathic recognisability (from inanimate to animate object) and renders it a better attractor. The attractiveness of the cooker is sustained in the second clause of this line as the pronoun 'it' refers anaphorically to this animate object. The personification also continues, as the cooker 'blames' the poetic voice ('me'). The referent 'me' is also an attractor due to its empathic recognisability. Once again though, the syntax of this line functions to promote the cooker as more attractive than the human, because the 'me' appears in the object rather than subject position.

L3–4 shift attention once again by presenting a new attractor in subject position: the TV. This inanimate object is personified by the verb phrases it is associated with, and this functions to make it a better attractor. Thus far, the stylistic features of the poem repeatedly confer attention on inanimate objects rather than human participants.

In L4 the poetic voice is promoted as an attractor for the first time, as the pronoun 'I' is represented in the subject position of the clause, with topicality, empathic recognisability, and activeness over the TV. L5, however, shifts attention from poetic voice to another new, personified attractor: 'the washing-up'. The washing-up is sustained as an attractor over L5–7 in several ways: it repeatedly appears in the subject position, it has empathic recognisability as it is capable of emotion and speech, and the representation of its direct speech confers noisiness.

Notice how at this point in reading the poem, the lack of reference to attractors which were present in earlier lines, such as 'the house' (L1) or 'the cooker' (L2), means that these items begin to fall into neglect, and fade out of perceptual prominence. Instead, the poem presents a succession of new attractors that continually distract attention.

The poetic voice is sustained as an attractor throughout the poem through repetition of the referents 'I' and 'me', although with fluctuating prominence. The poetic voice moves into prominence in L10, L13, L16, and L23 when 'I' appears in the subject position. The 'you' addressee is also sustained as an attractor throughout the poem, but with less prominence: it is only the subject in L12 'but you know . . .'. Elsewhere, as we have seen, objects in the house are significantly better attractors than the human participants in the scene: they are continually presented as topical, animate, active, and noisy. Yet they tend not to be sustained as attractors for more than a few lines, so they fall into neglect when another household object takes prominence.

The language of the poem seems designed to continually distract attention from one attractor to the next and, in the context of a poem about a break-up, this distraction serves to iconically communicate the poetic voice's means of coping with the situation through deflection. Rather than describing their feelings directly, the poetic voice portrays the reactions of the couple's shared household possessions.

The poem plays with cognitive norms of attraction by promoting these inanimate objects as attractors. In a poem about a break-up, we might expect the actions of the human participants to be figured and their environments grounded. The configuration of attractors presented by the text deviates from these expectations, and this goes some way to explaining the poem's defamiliarising quality.

12.4 Attention and atmosphere

Figure and ground analysis is also useful for examining particularly evocative or atmospheric texts. Below are the opening paragraphs of the first chapter of *The Lives of Others* by Neel Mukherjee (2014: 5; sentences numbered for analysis). The novel is set in Calcutta in the 1960s and tells the story of the Ghosh family. It features a heterodiegetic, omniscient third-person narrator with variable focalisation: sometimes the narrative world is represented from the narrator's external point of view, and at others the narrator moves in and out of the perspectives of multiple character (see Chapter 8 on point of view). In this opening passage, the narrative is focalised through the character Purnima as she wakes up, but as well as representing her perceptions, this passage also functions to introduce the reader to the narrative world and evoke the sounds and activities of a typical Calcutta morning:

> (1) Around six, the zoo starts to shake itself up from its brief sleep. (2) Lying in bed, wide awake, Purnima hears the stirrings of life, each animal, each part of each animal, becoming animated in slow succession. (3) Under the mosquito net the September humidity is already beginning to congeal into the suffocating blanket it will soon become. (4) The fan, running at its top speed of five, battles away, unmindful of its futility.

(5) The only thing it circulates around the room is the sound of the fluttery pages of the Ghosh Gold Palace calendar hanging from a nail on the cream-painted walls. (6) That calendar is a sign of her defiance; by some silent understanding reached a long time before she arrived in this house, all tokens of Ghosh Gold Palace are forbidden here, so she has made a point of having their calendar on the wall in her room.

(7) Beside her, Priyo sleeps the sleep of the sinless. (8) His early-morning snore has a three-toned sound to it – a snarly growl in the inhalation, then a hissing during part of the exhalation, completed by a final high-pitched insect whine. (9) She hears the scouring sound of a broom sluicing out with water some drain or courtyard. (10) Someone is cleaning his teeth in the bathroom of a neighbouring house – there is the usual accompaniment of loud hawking, coughing and a brief, one-note retch. (11) A juddering car goes down Basanta Bose Road with the unmistakeable sound of every loose vibrating component about to come off – a taxi. (12) A rickshaw cycles by, the driver relentlessly squeezing its bellows-horn. (13) Another starts up, as if in response. (14) Soon an entire fleet of rickshaws rackets past, their continuous horn shredding what little sleepiness remains of the morning.

(15) Now she can hear other vehicles: the toot of a scooter-horn, the bell of a bicycle. (16) This is how the world begins every day; noise is the way it signals that it is alive, indomitable.

This descriptive passage intuitively feels atmospheric – it creates a sense of the quality of the literary world and attempts to draw the reader into that world. Although this world forms the focus of the passage, we are also afforded glimpses into the character Purnima, the focaliser. Examining the patterns of attraction across the text can help to account for the sense of **atmosphere** and characterisation which are achieved.

The passage begins by conferring attention on 'the zoo', through topicality and through personification, which makes this uncountable noun more empathically recognisable. The ground is indicated syntactically by the prepositional phrase 'Around six' (S1). The narrative perspective in this first sentence is unclear: it could reflect the floating point of view of an omniscient narrator, or that of a character. The second sentence, however, moves more clearly into focalised narration through the presentation of a human character and her perceptions: 'Purnima hears . . .' (S2). Purnima is figured in this sentence because of her empathic recognisability and topicality. However, once her existence and perception are established, aspects of her sensed environment are presented as attractors. The animals distract attention due to their activeness ('becoming animated', S2) and the repetition in the noun phrase 'each animal, each part of each animal' which iconically represents the slowness of their awakening. S3–5 present the humidity, the fan, and the wall calendar as attractors through various stylistic techniques. The humidity is represented as a blanket, which moves it up the empathic recognisability scale from abstraction to object. Personification is evident again in the representation of the fan performing mental and physical actions ('battles', 'running', 'unmindful'). S5 presents the sound of the calendar (an abstraction) as an object, a 'thing' which is circulated by the fan, a noisy and active attractor. Then, the calendar making this sound gains prominence due to the convergence of a number of properties. It is noisy, active ('fluttery'), it is denoted in a deviantly long noun phrase ('the sound of the fluttery pages . . . cream-painted walls') and it has brightness through the connotations of the word 'Gold' (making it prominent against the 'cream-painted' walls). Thus, across S3–5, Purnima gradually moves down the cline of attractiveness as elements in her auditory perception become attractors instead. Rather than readers' attention being continually drawn to Purnima's *act* of perception, the perceptions are presented directly, and this has the effect of drawing the reader in to the narrative world: her perceptions are our perceptions too.

S6 interrupts the account of Purnima's perceptions to provide more information about the calendar and its significance for her character. Interestingly, this sentence promotes objects and abstractions as attractors in a way that generates mystery and intrigue, and therefore also acts to draw readers in to the story. The calendar is sustained as a strong attractor through definiteness and topicality in the first clause ('That calendar') and its attractiveness is maintained by repeated reference in both subject ('all tokens of Ghosh Gold Palace') and object position ('their calendar'). Across S6, Purnima moves up the cline of attractiveness through the repeated use of pronouns 'her' and 'she', although she is not the subject of main clauses – only a referent in the object position ('sign of her defiance') or the subject in subordinate clauses ('before she arrived . . .', 'so she has . . .'), which reduces her relative prominence. Individual human agency is also minimised in the passive construction in the middle of S6, which is reordered below for clarity:

> all tokens of Ghosh Gold Palace are forbidden here [by some silent understanding reached a long time before she arrived in this house]

As we saw in section 10.4, passive constructions foreground the recipient of an action and background the agent who carried out that action. The agent can be deleted completely, or appear after the main verb, usually preceded with the preposition 'by' (e.g. 'A boy was shot [by the police]'). Notice how human agency is absent from this representation: the act of forbidding is not attributed to an individual human agent here, but an abstraction: 'some silent understanding'. We later learn than Purnima married in to the Ghosh family and is resentful of her lack of influence. This perception of herself in relation to the family is already reflected in the configuration of attractors in this sentence. In the final clause of the sentence ('so she has made a point of . . .'), Purnima is represented as a stronger attractor than the abstractions that govern the Ghosh family home, due to her topicality, empathic recognisability, and her wilfulness.

The remaining sentences shift attention back to Purnima's auditory perception. She is backgrounded syntactically in S7 and her husband Priyo introduced as a figure through topicality: 'Beside her, Priyo . . .', before his snore becomes the focus of attention, and its noisiness is described at some length (S8). After S9, which represents her act of perception ('She hears . . .'), Purnima once again gradually moves down the cline of attractiveness as elements in her auditory perception are presented as attractors through their topicality and noisiness: the sound of a broom (S9); someone cleaning their teeth (S10); cars, rickshaws, and vehicles moving down Basanta Bose Road (S11–15). Purnima's perception is evident across these sentences by reference to their familiarity ('the usual accompaniment', S10); some indefiniteness which reflects her lack of visual perception ('some drain or courtyard' (S9), 'Someone' (S10); and her inferences ('unmistakeable sound . . . – a taxi', S11). Her prominence fades across S12–14, which figure the rickshaws (through topicality, activeness, and noisiness), and once again momentarily create the impression that readers are perceiving the fictional world directly. Purnima's act of perception is returned to prominence again in S15: 'Now she can hear . . .'.

Analysis of patterns of attraction across a text can provide fine-grained insights into the texture of a piece of writing. Cognitive stylistic work on figure and ground demonstrates how grammatical choices influence reader perception and sensation during the dynamic process of reading.

Keywords and summary

Atmosphere, attractor, bistable illusion, cognitive linguistics, decay, figure, ground, neglect, prominence, texture.

The study of figure and ground in language is based upon the segregation of figure and ground which naturally occurs in human sensory perception and attention. Cognitive stylistic approaches are interested in how linguistic features combine to place, maintain, or neglect attractors across a text, and how this figuring and grounding of textual elements interacts with readerly attention during the dynamic process of reading. Figure and ground relations are thought to contribute to the felt texture of reading, and have been linked to the creation of literary atmosphere, tone, resonance, and ambience.

Activities

1. Rewrite sentences 1–5 in the extract from *The Lives of Others* in section 12.4 in order to alter the configuration of attractors in the scene. Your sentences should still include the objects and entities that are represented in the novel, but you can make as many additions and alterations as you like in order to focus attention on them differently. A good place to start might be to think about how you could make Purnima the most attractive entity across the whole excerpt. What changes did you make? How did they alter the attentional focus in the passage?
2. Track the attractors in this passage from *The Memory Keeper's Daughter* (Edwards 2005: 3). How does the configuration of attractors contribute to the passage's effects?:

   > The snow started to fall several hours before her labour began. A few flakes first, in the dull gray late-afternoon sky, and then wind-driven swirls and eddies around the edges of their wide front porch. He stood by her side at the window, watching sharp gusts of snow billow, then swirl and drift to the ground. All around the neighbourhood, lights came on, and the naked branches of the trees turned white.

3. Cognitive stylistic analyses of figure and ground, such as those in this chapter, model close, attentive reading based on *the analyst's own* close, attentive study of a short excerpt of literary language. Do we always read with such close attention? What impacts upon the level of attention you pay to a text? What are the implications of your answers for cognitive stylistics?

Further reading and references

Stockwell (2002a: ch. 2; 2002b, 2003, 2009a, 2009b, 2013, 2014a, 2014b) sets out the stylistic approach to figure and ground, and its role in the creation of atmosphere, tone, and resonance. Other stylistic work on figure and ground includes: Emmott and Alexander (2010), Nuttall

(2014), Päivärinta (2014), and Whiteley (2016). Sanford and Emmott (2012: ch. 4) present empirical stylistic studies of attention and reading, and provide a useful review of empirical research into linguistic foregrounding (see also Emmott et al. 2007, 2010). For narratological work on narrated perception such as that in the extract in 12.4, see Brinton (1980) and Fludernik (1993: 299). Evans and Green (2006: ch. 2) introduce the core assumptions of cognitive linguistics; Ungerer and Schmidt (1996: ch. 4) discuss the cognitive linguistics of figure and ground; see also Evans and Green (2006: 69–70), and Haber and Hershenson (1980). On the difference between cognitive stylistics and stylistics, see Stockwell (2005b). Note that 'cognitive stylistics' is also called 'cognitive poetics': the names are interchangeable. The principles of figure and ground are also fundamental in cognitive grammar, which is discussed in more detail in Chapter 15.

13 Deixis and deictic shift

13.1 Cognitive deixis

In Chapter 12, we explored the cognitive poetic framework of figure and ground, which depends on processes of sensory perception. In this chapter, we consider 'deixis', which Green refers to as 'a fundamental element of human discourse' (1995: 11). **Deixis** is a Greek term meaning 'pointing', and refers to a subset of words that are dependent on their contexts of usage for meaning. Our understanding of deictic words is underpinned by our **embodied cognition**. This is an important idea in cognitive linguistics, highlighting that our cognition of language is grounded in our bodily experiences within the world. Pronouns, demonstratives, and adverbs are typical deictic elements, though deixis is not restricted to any particular word class.

Deictic expressions encode a language user's embodied position in the world. The **origo** or **deictic centre** is the conceptual position from which the speaker cognises the world. The deictic expressions 'I', 'here', and 'now' encode a central point in relation to perceptual, spatial, and temporal fields. 'I', 'here', and 'now' also show up the contextually bound nature of deictic expressions. For instance, in conversation, you refer to yourself using the first person yet when somebody else uses 'I', you have no problem understanding that the first person now refers to the new speaker. This is because deictic terms shift their reference in the context of usage and we reorient our interpretive cognition in relation to the deictic centre of the discourse (in this case, the speaking 'I').

There are six **deictic fields** or dimensions. The first three are rather straightforward: **spatial deixis** provides spatial orientation, **temporal deixis** anchors the text in time, and **perceptual deixis** involves the subjective participants as represented by personal pronouns and characters (including proper names as well as noun phrases such as 'the woman'). The fourth, **relational deixis**, is linked to perceptual deixis: it relates to participants by encoding social relations. Thus, relational deictic items include naming and address conventions such as social titles (e.g. 'Mr', 'Ms', 'Dr') and social roles (seen, for instance, in nouns like 'soldier', 'father', 'daughter'). The last two dimensions, textual and compositional deixis, are forms of what has traditionally been called **discourse deixis**, where a deictic expression refers metatextually to the utterance or discourse in which it occurs. For instance, in the statement 'This sentence is composed of seven words', the demonstrative 'this' refers to the sentence itself. In developing a cognitive poetic analysis of deixis in literary texts, Stockwell (2002a) outlines two related dimensions of discourse deixis: **textual deixis**, which foregrounds the text itself through devices such as metatextual reference and explicit 'signposting' (e.g. chapter titles); and **compositional deixis**, such as expressions that encode literary genres (e.g. 'Once upon a time').

The notion that we take a cognitive stance in relation to language is fundamental to the cognitive stylistic account of deixis. Humans have the imaginative and interpretive capacities to cognitively relocate into deictic stances other than their own. This is known as **deictic projection**. With this in mind, read the opening to Margaret Forster's novel *How to Measure a Cow* (2016: 1) and reflect on how you imagine the scene:

> The first day, free. She walked in a public park, her legs heavy, and yet she felt untethered, floating, waiting for a wind to blow her along. All the green of the trees ahead made her eyes feel muzzy. She blinked constantly, to clear the shimmering. There were groups of people about, sitting on the grass having picnics, or sauntering along the pathways in the full sun. She came to a pond. She took in a woman throwing sticks for a dog, and another, watched by a child in a buggy, feeding ducks. She swayed slightly, and wondered which path she should take. Then she registered a man, all in black, standing on a hillock above the pond.

In terms of perceptual deixis, the extract is written in third person primarily using 'she' and 'her' to refer to a central character. However, it is also focalised because the spatio-temporal deixis encodes the character's perspective. This is evident from adverbs such as 'along', 'ahead', and 'about' which represent the space of the park from the character's standpoint. Her viewpoint is also clear in the verb and prepositional phrase 'came to a pond' and the two prepositional phrases that locate the man 'on a hillock above the pond'. Temporal deixis further works to enhance the reader's imaginative experience of the text from the third-person character's focalised viewpoint: although the extract begins in past tense, her visions of other people are presented in continuous tense ('sitting', 'sauntering', 'throwing', 'feeding', 'standing') to make them appear more immediate in her experience. Finally, other participants are presented in a rather vague way as 'groups of people' or with the indefinite article 'a' ('a woman', 'a man') suggesting they aren't known to the main character. Consequently, the deictic expressions in the opening of *How to Measure a Cow* not only help us to build a mental image of the world of the text but the spatial and temporal points of view encourage us to project into the text in order to view it from the focalising character's perspective.

13.2 Deictic shifts

When you first start reading a novel, such as the above extract from *How to Measure a Cow*, you might project into the world of the story, but such projection is by no means stable. You may be distracted by something in the real world and thus your attention will shift back to reality; alternatively, the deictic parameters of the narrative might change, for instance if the character were to experience a flashback. Both scenarios would involve a **deictic shift**, a term which describes our ability to shift our cognitive stance across deictic coordinates, such as those of other speakers in conversation or into a fictional world. Within fictional worlds, when the parameters of a deictic field change (especially along the perceptual, spatial, and temporal dimensions), a deictic shift occurs and readers must subsequently reorient their projected deictic centre.

Borrowing from computer science, Galbraith (1995) and Stockwell (2002a) described the directionality of deictic shifts using the terms 'push' and 'pop': a **push** involves a cognitive shift to a deictic plane further away from the reader's reality, for instance when we first start reading, whilst a **pop** is a shift to a deictic level closer to a reader's reality (including reality itself). Although McIntyre (2006: 111) has been critical of these terms, we can consider them useful at least when describing deictic shifting across the ontological boundary between fiction and reality.

To illustrate **Deictic Shift Theory**, let's consider another fictional extract: the opening to *My Name Is Lucy Barton* by Elizabeth Strout (2016: 3–4; sentences numbered for analysis):

> (1) There was a time, and it was many years ago now, when I had to stay in a hospital for almost nine weeks. (2) This was in New York City, and at night a view of the Chrysler Building, with its geometric brilliance of lights, was directly visible from my bed. (3) During the day, the building's beauty receded, and gradually it became simply one more large structure against a blue sky, and all the city's buildings seemed remote,

> silent, far away. (4) It was May, and then June, and I remember how I would stand and look out the window at the sidewalk below and watch the young women – my age – in their spring clothes, out on their lunch breaks; I could see their heads moving in conversation, their blouses rippling in the breeze. (5) I thought how when I got out of the hospital I would never again walk down the sidewalk without giving thanks for being one of those people, and for many years I did that – (6) I would remember the view from the hospital window and be glad for the sidewalk I was walking on.

The passage shifts between different time zones and represents the character's thoughts and perceptions in the past and present. The opening clause 'There was a time' is an example of compositional deixis since it suggests that a story or anecdote is about to be told. It uses the spatial adverb 'there' as a dummy subject (although 'there' is in grammatical subject position, it has no concrete point of reference). The copulative construction of the clause equates 'there' with 'a time' using the copula verb in past tense ('was'). This opening clause therefore initiates a temporal deictic shift to a previous moment. Continuing in past tense, the second clause in S1, 'and it was many years ago now', includes the noun phrase 'many years' and post-modifying adverb 'ago' which serve to provide further specificity about how far into the past the story will be set. The following adverb 'now', though, foregrounds the present moment from which the narrative is being relayed. Consequently, 'now' creates a **toggle**, where a reader's imaginative attention and deictic orientation shift quickly between two distinct deictic realms. Here, the toggle occurs between the **story-now** (when the narrative events occur) set up by the first clause and a **speaker-now** (the moment in which the narrative is being told) initiated by the adverb 'now'. The toggle is completed with the return to story-now through the subordinating conjunction 'when'. In this subordinate clause, more detail is given about the space and time of the story using the stacked prepositional phrases 'in a hospital' and 'for almost nine weeks'. The first-person pronoun 'I' in S1 introduces the speaker and the perceptual deictic centre of the discourse. Reading the first sentence of *My Name Is Lucy Barton*, then, involves a push into the fictional world, projecting into Lucy's perceptual deictic centre ('I') as well as into her past.

S2 spatially locates the hospital in 'New York City' and gives the narrator's viewpoint 'from her bed' looking 'directly' at 'the Chrysler Building'. Between S2 and S3, there is a temporal shift from 'night' to 'day'. Over the course of S3, the temporal preposition 'during' and adverb 'gradually' emphasise the slow passing of time. The spatial references to 'all the city's buildings' as 'remote' and 'far away' encode spatial separation and thus serve to imply the narrator's felt sense of isolation from the outside world whilst in hospital. The first clause in S4 'It was May' is another copulative construction with dummy subject. It pinpoints the month in which the narrator went to hospital before a temporal shift to 'June'.

As S4 continues, the narrator states, 'I remember . . .'. The lexical verb 'remember' is interesting in terms of temporal deixis: although it is used here in present tense, semantically it looks back to the past. It thus generates another toggle, implicitly referencing the narrator's act of remembrance in speaker-now whilst also introducing the recalled memory. In the verb phrase 'would stand', the past tense of the modal 'will' with an infinitive verb form references the narrator's past behaviour. The narrator's spatial viewpoint is encoded in the prepositional phrases 'out the window at the sidewalk' and succeeding adverb 'below'. The description of what she sees introduces additional participants (perceptual deixis) and a social viewpoint is communicated (relational deixis) with the noun phrase 'the young women'. The relational aspect of this phrase is implied by the adjective 'young' and emphasised by the subsequent parenthetical noun phrase 'my age' which also causes a toggle because although the women seem *young* to the narrator in speaker-now, her interjection clarifies that, at the time of story-now, she was herself around the same age as these women.

There is a perceptual and temporal deictic shift in S5: 'I thought how when I got out of the hospital I would . . .'. The perceptual shift is the product of 'I thought' as a reporting clause, suggesting a push into the consciousness of the narrator's past self. This is combined with a temporal shift triggered by the subordinating conjunction 'when' and the conditional use of the past-tense modal 'would' in the verb phrase 'would never again walk' which suggest that getting 'out of hospital' is, at this point in the story-now, a hypothetical fantasy. The prepositional phrase in 'and *for many years* I did that' later in S5 evokes another temporal shift to a point in time that is in the future of the story-now, although the past tense verb 'did' indicates the action remains in the past of the speaker-now. In S6, another toggle occurs with the second use of the verb 'remember'. The grammatical object of the act of remembering – 'the view from the hospital' – locates the deictic centre firmly in story-now. However, the succeeding clauses 'and be glad for the sidewalk I was walking on' (S6) generate a spatial shift – using the infinitive form of the copula verb 'be' and past-continuous tense in 'was walking' – to the street outside the hospital and a temporal shift to the years after the narrator's hospital stay.

This analysis suggests that, when reading the opening to *My Name Is Lucy Barton*, we quickly push into a story-now that has past temporality. Strout develops the spatial and temporal parameters of the story-now to guide our imaginative projection so that we experience New York from Lucy's deictic position, in her hospital bed detached from the people and action of the city. The toggles, however, serve to remind readers that the narrator is telling the story from a different point in time (speaker-now) to the depicted events (story-now). Additionally, they highlight the fact that, as readers, our imaginative experience of the events is projected through Lucy's memories.

13.3 Perceptual deixis and projection relations

We have so far described the way in which readers shift their deictic centre into fictional worlds. In Forster's *How to Measure a Cow*, the deictic centre was perceptually located somewhat outside of the third-person character but nevertheless shared the temporal and spatial experiences of that character. In contrast, because Strout's *My Name Is Lucy Barton* has a first-person narrator, a shift into the character's perceptual deictic centre was possible.

It is possible, then, for a reader to project not only into the narrator's or focaliser's perspective, but also into the roles presented by other pronouns, particularly the second-person 'you'. As you read the opening to Dave Eggers' (2007) short story 'The New Rules', consider whether you take the cognitive stance of 'I' or 'you' (sentences numbered for analysis):

> (1) I don't know why it came down to me to tell you about this, but anyway, here goes: (2) if you don't buy at least ten books a year, you'll be struck by lightning, or maybe a bus. (3) It's the new rule. (4) Yeah. (5) You'll probably be sent a more official notice in the mail pretty soon, but for now, you're hearing it from me. (6) Ten books a year, or the bus or lightning, each of them very painful and likely deadly.

In S1, there is textual deictic foregrounding of the act of communication between an 'I' and a 'you', through the infinitive verb phrase 'to tell' and the metatextual use of the demonstrative 'this'. Consequently, the first sentence quickly establishes a discourse situation in which the narrating 'I' addresses 'you'. The spatial adverb 'here' in 'here goes' also works metatextually, insinuating that, after the colon, the narrator is delivering the message in question. In what follows, 'you' is given increasing prominence, becoming the grammatical subject of the clauses in S2 as well as S5 where the narrator is backgrounded in the prepositional phrase 'from me'. In terms of content, the reference to buying 'tens book a year' activates a semantic field related to books and reading, and therefore implies through association that the 'you' is a reader of books. As such, readers are likely to feel addressed by second-person 'you'. Did this fit with your experience? Readers do not necessarily project into the 'you' role just because the second-person pronoun is used. However, this is probable in 'The New Rules' due to the combination of its foregrounding of an interpersonal communicative situation, textual deictic language which suggests that the communicative situation relates to the act of reading, and prominent second-person address.

Readers' perceptual deictic shifts are therefore influenced by the pronouns used in the text as well as by other factors such as the length of a given narrative, its linguistic composition in relation to other deictic fields, and the discursive context.

13.4 Double deixis

Not only can deictic projection be inconsistent and unstable, but pronouns shift their reference in context. This was discussed in section 13.1, when we said that 'I' changes its referent depending on who is speaking. Second-person *you* is even more complex, since in English the second-person pronoun can be used to designate a number of referents. Herman (1994: 381; 2002: 345) categorises the use of 'you' into five types:

1. **Generalised *you*:** indefinite plural 'you' to address a group of people.
2. **Fictional reference:** 'you' is used to designate a character and therefore functions more like third-person 's/he'.
3. **Fictionalised (= horizontal) address:** when 'you' is used by a character to address another character.
4. **Apostrophic (= vertical) address:** where direct address to readers in the real world transcends the boundaries of fiction.
5. **Doubly deictic *you*:** when 'you' appears to have two reference points – one within the fiction and one outside of the fiction.

Herman describes this final category as a 'superimposition of deictic roles, a blended or double form of person deixis' (2002: 349). What he means is that sometimes in literary texts, the second person can appear to designate two referents simultaneously with neither context seeming primary or more important. For 'you' to be functioning doubly, one of the referents exists within the fictional world ('you' points to a character) and the other referent is situated in the actual world ('you' addresses a reader).

Our next analysis explores the dynamics of the second-person pronoun in Mohsin Hamid's (2013) novel *How to Get Filthy Rich in Rising Asia*. Although a work of fiction, the title uses the adverb 'how' + infinitive verb phrase construction to parody the genre of 'how-to . . .' self-help manuals. Before readers even open the book then, there is some compositional deixis, with the title aligning itself (albeit mockingly) with this genre. The novel begins (2013: 3):

> Look, unless you're writing one, a self-help book is an oxymoron. You read a self-help book so someone who isn't yourself can help you, that someone being the author. This is true of the whole self-help genre. It's true of how-to books, for example.

It starts with an imperative verb 'Look'. As an imperative, the subject is not linguistically explicit, it is implied: because imperatives function to direct an addressee to perform the action of the verb, 'Look' suggests apostrophic address. However, the second-person pronouns that follow appear to be self-reflexive and generalised. Nevertheless, both apostrophic and generalised 'you' point to the real-world context in this case – to a reader or generalised readers.

The first chapter continues (2013: 4):

> This book is a self-help book. Its objective, as it says on the cover, is to show you how to get filthy rich in rising Asia.

The spatial demonstrative 'this' works metatextually and along with the prepositional phrase 'on the cover' serves to foreground the book itself. This textual deixis additionally emphasises the context of the real reader, reading the novel, and consequently supports an interpretation of the second-person pronoun in the verb phrase 'to show you how to get filthy rich in rising Asia' as apostrophic address. Despite the apostrophic address, readers might struggle to fully align themselves with the deictic centre of 'you' if they find the insistent spatial reference to 'rising Asia' jarring: Asia probably does not match the reader's own spatio-temporal setting – for instance, reading the book in bed. And why Asia? This becomes clear in the next sentence (2013: 4).

> And to do that it has to find you, huddled, shivering, on the packed earth under your mother's cot one cold, dewy morning.

At first, the second-person pronoun appears to maintain apostrophic address, but as the sentence continues it becomes clear that this is not possible. Not only is the spatio-temporal narrative context at odds with the reader's reality, but the location 'you' occupies – 'under your mother's cot' – suggests that this character is a child. If details such as this do not match a reader's reality, their projection into the perceptual deictic centre of 'you' is likely to falter. In *How to Get Filthy Rich in Rising Asia*, 'you' subsequently becomes fictionalised and is used to designate a character in the story.

How to Get Filthy Rich in Rising Asia is a second-person fiction throughout, and as the first chapter progresses it becomes clear that 'you' is the central fictional protagonist of the novel, a male born and living in an indeterminate part of Asia. The book follows him from birth and youth (as in this first chapter) to death in the final chapter. Each chapter begins with apostrophic 'you' and prominent textual or compositional deixis before shifting the designation of 'you' to fictionalised reference. Occasionally, though, 'you' may appear to blend both referents thus becoming doubly deictic. Read the next extract from *How to Get Filthy Rich in Rising Asia* (2013: 77), thinking about the second-person pronoun as you read:

> To be effective, a self-help book requires two things. First, the help it suggests should be helpful. And second, without which the first is impossible, the self it's trying to help should have some idea of what help is needed. For our collaboration to work, in other words, you must know yourself well enough to understand what you want and where you want to go with it. Self-help books are two-way streets, after all. Relationships. So be honest here, and ask yourself the following question. Is getting filthy rich still your goal above all goals, your be-all and end-all, the mist-shrouded high-altitude spawning pond to your inner salmon?
>
> In your case, fortunately, it seems to be. Because you have spent the last few years taking the next essential step, learning from a master. [. . .]
>
> The master at whose feet you metaphorically squat is a middle-aged man with the long fingers of an artist [. . .]

Initially, several factors contribute to making 'you' appear apostrophic. Firstly, compositional deixis features prominently, through references to the book's parodied genre. Perceptually, the first-person plural possessive is used in '*our* collaboration' and, along with the proximal spatial adverb 'here', this suggests a shared space occupied by the narrative voice and the 'you' it addresses. It is, though, a little harder to pinpoint whom 'you' refers to in the question: 'Is getting filthy rich still your goal above all goals, your be-all and end-all, the mist-shrouded high-altitude spawning pond to your inner salmon?' On the one hand, as a reader, you have engaged with this book, at least to this point – page 77 – and therefore you are invested, through reading, in the goal of 'getting filthy rich'. On the other, at this point in the novel, readers have become familiar with the conceit of the novel: they know it is not actually a self-help book and that the desire to get rich belongs to the main character. This instance of 'you' is therefore doubly deictic since it seems to involve both the apostrophic reader and fictionalised character. This ambiguity continues in 'In your case, fortunately, it seems to be', and is only resolved in the final sentence of the extract when the narrative context clearly returns to the fictional world.

This analysis demonstrates that because the reference of personal pronouns can shift according to context, literary works can use them to create multiple effects. This is particularly true of second-person pronouns. In Hamid's *How to Get Filthy Rich in Rising Asia*, the use of second person and the occasional uncertainty and duplicity of double deixis is important. Hamid deliberately involves readers at the start of each chapter with apostrophic address and exploits fleeting moments of double deixis to capture their attention, so that when 'you' does turn to fictionalised reference, readers are engaged enough to project into the fictional world of the character.

Keywords and summary

Deictic centre, deictic field, deictic shift (pop, push), Deictic Shift Theory, deixis (compositional, discourse, perceptual, relational, spatial, temporal, textual), double deixis, embodied cognition, identification, origo, speaker-now, story-now, textual 'you' (apostrophic, fictional, fictionalised, generalised), toggle.

The analyses in this chapter demonstrate our advanced capacity to project and shift our deictic centre when we cognitively process language. Deictic language emphasises that cognition is not only psychological but also embodied and social (projection is returned to in our discussion of reader emotion in Chapter 20). Additionally, interpretation of deictic language is always dependent on context. Table 13.1 summarises the five deictic fields and provides representative (but not exhaustive) examples of corresponding linguistic markers.

Activities

1. Deictic terms often come in pairs, such as 'this'/'that', 'here'/'there', 'I'/'you'. Write pairs of sentences that are identical except in terms of which word in a pair is used. What is the difference between these pairs in terms of interpretation and effect?

Table 13.1 Deictic fields and linguistic markers

Deictic field		Representative lexis/Linguistic markers
Spatial		• Demonstratives: 'this', 'that', 'those', etc. • Adverbs: 'here', 'there', 'away', 'ahead', 'above', 'below', etc. • Prepositional phrases: 'on the hill', 'under the window', etc. • Proper names: 'New York', 'Chrysler Building', etc. • Noun phrases: 'the city', 'the park', 'a building', etc. • Verbs of motion: 'come/go', 'arrive/leave', etc.
Temporal		• Adverbs: 'today', 'now', 'then', 'later', 'gradually', etc. • Prepositional phrases: 'in my youth', etc. • Noun phrases: 'many hours', 'a time', 'May', '2 p.m.', etc. • Tense and aspect
Perceptual		• Pronouns: 'I', 'you', 'she/he', 'we', 'they', 'it', etc. • Proper names: 'Sally Barton', 'Mary', etc. • Noun phrases: 'the girl', 'a woman', 'many people', etc. • Verb markers of character cognition: 'think', 'remember', etc.
Relational		• Titles: 'Ms', 'Reverend', 'Baron', 'Duchess', etc. • Forms of address: 'Your royal highness', etc. • Noun phrases indicating social role: 'nurse', 'mentor', 'Dad', etc. • Evaluative word-choices including adjectives: 'the *young* woman', etc.
Discourse:	Textual	• Metatextual references to writing, textual production, authorship • Metatextual use of spatial demonstrative 'this': e.g. 'this book' • Explicit signposts, such as chapter titles, directives (e.g. 'See page . . .') or co-reference to other parts of the text ('in chapter 2 . . .'), etc.
	Compositional	• Expressions that cue literary conventions and/or genres such as: 'I'm going to tell you a story' (narrative, fiction), 'Once upon a time' (fairy tale), 'spaceship' (science fiction genre), etc.

2. Consider the opening to Chris Cleave's novel *Everybody Brave Is Forgiven* (2016: 3):

> War was declared at 11.15 and Mary North signed up at noon. She did it at lunch, before telegrams came, in case her mother said no. She left finishing school unfinished. Skiing down from Mont-Choisi, she ditched her equipment at the foot of the slope and telegraphed the War Office from Lausanne. Nineteen hours later she reached St Pancras, in clouds of steam, still wearing her alpine sweater. The train's whistle screamed. London, then. It was a city in love with beginnings.

   Mark all instances of spatial, temporal, perceptual, and relational deixis. How is the opening constructed? What does it require of you as a reader in terms of deictic projection? Are there any instances of deictic shift; if so, what linguistic features trigger the shift?

3. Read the opening of *Memory Palace* by Hari Kunzru (2013):

> Here is how to remember. First you must choose a place. It should be somewhere you know very well. Most people pick somewhere spacious and grand – a great hall, one of the ruined towers of the city. You get to know this place as well as you can. You walk around it, impressing every detail into your memory, until you can tour it in your mind when you are not there. Then you place the things you need to remember around the building in the form of pictures. These pictures must be startling enough to trigger your imagination.

   What type(s) of 'you' is Kunzru using? What other deictic elements influence your interpretation of 'you'? Does the reference of 'you' shift at any point(s)? Are there any instances of double deixis?

Further reading and references

Cognitive deixis and Deictic Shift Theory were initially presented in an edited volume by Duchan et al. (1995). Green's (1995) collection followed soon after. Stockwell (2002a: 41–57) develops a cognitive poetic account of deixis in literary texts, including the introduction of discourse, textual, and compositional deixis. Discourse deixis has been further developed by Macrae (2010). Literary stylistic analyses of deixis include: Jeffries (2008), Kennedy (2010, 2012), McIntyre (2006, 2007), and Warner (2009). Important studies of deixis from a traditional linguistic standpoint are: Bühler (1982 [1932]), Dry (1988), Levinson (1983: 54–96), Lyons (1982), and Rauh (1983).

Wales (1996) considers the referential value of personal pronouns. Pronouns are also the focus of edited collections such as Gardelle and Sorlin (2015) and Gibbons and Macrae (2018). The effect of pronouns in literary contexts is an extensive area of research in stylistics and narratology. For example, see: Cornis-Pope (1994), Fludernik (1994a, 1994b), Kacandes (1994, 2001), Macrae (2012, 2016b), Margolin (2001), and Richardson (1991, 1994, 2006). The concept of double deixis comes from Herman (1994, 2002).

14 Schemas, scripts, and prototypes

14.1 Knowledge: Schemas and scripts

In our day-to-day interactions with the world, we constantly and automatically draw on our stores of knowledge about the people, places, situations, and things we encounter. Our knowledge is organised into **Idealised Cognitive Models (ICMs)**. ICMs are relatively stable knowledge structures that represent given experiences. They are considered 'idealised' because, rather than relating to any one specific experience, they incorporate knowledge from various related experiences in order to form a more generalisable (and sometimes over-simplified) abstract representation. Stores of knowledge are built up over time and through repeated exposure to particular experiences. When you go to a restaurant, for example, you expect there to be food, tables, chairs, a menu, and waiting staff. You have, through various trips to restaurants, built up a restaurant **schema**: a cognitive structure which supplies information about your generic understanding of a particular phenomenon. You apply that schema in order to navigate the specifics of each particular restaurant visit.

Schemas are large knowledge structures that incorporate scripts. **Scripts** provide information about temporally ordered sequences of events. As part of the restaurant schema, your restaurant script is characterised by a number of **slots** which detail the entry conditions (being hungry, going into a restaurant), participant roles (diners and waiting staff), props (menus, cutlery, money, etc.), results (diners get fed, restaurant is paid), and sequence of events (viewing the menu, ordering, being served, paying the bill). Of course, there are different tracks through the restaurant script, depending on the type of restaurant: at a drive-through restaurant, it is necessary to order and pay before you are given the food; in a pub restaurant, you might have to order at the bar, and so on.

The notions of schemas and scripts received particular development in Artificial Intelligence (AI) research after World War II. AI researchers aim to replicate the cognitive functions of the human mind (such as human learning, problem solving, and language processing skills) using computers. They quickly found that even basic language processing requires vast stores of knowledge, and developed schema theory to describe those knowledge structures. Whilst AI research is ongoing, their early models of knowledge structure have been influential in cognitive studies and applied to literary reading by cognitive stylisticians. We deploy schematic knowledge when we read, in order to 'fill gaps' in a text and supply more information than is explicitly stated. Take, for instance, the following sentence:

(a) Alison got into the car and drove away.

When we interpret this sentence, we know that Alison must have opened the car door to get in, closed it, and started the engine before she drove away. This information is part of our background knowledge about cars and informs our interpretation of the text. Consequently, we'd have no problem also understanding the next sentence:

(b) The engine stalled as she stopped at the traffic lights.

Thanks to our knowledge schemas, we already know that the car has an engine. The definite article 'the' can be used to refer to the engine because it is already a given part of our concept of a car.

Schemas (and scripts) are dynamic structures, created through experience but also altered with new experiences. The experiences that form and alter schemas do not need to be direct: for instance, even if you have never visited the USA, you are still likely to have a schema for the United States based on things you have heard, read, or watched. As well as being deployed during reading, schemas can also be affected when we read. Indeed, readers' schematic knowledge is something that authors (via texts) can subvert, exploit, alter, or violate in order to create particular effects (Emmott et al. 2015: 261). Firstly, it is worth noting that schemas can be altered through three main processes:

1. **Accretion**, in which new information is added to existing schemas.
2. **Tuning**, in which information or relations within a schema are modified in some way.
3. **Restructuring** or **refreshment**, in which new schemas are created (based on existing templates).

Accretion and tuning are relatively minor schema alterations, whilst schema restructuring is more major. Secondly, discourses can be categorised in terms of the ways they affect readers' schemas, as shown in Table 14.1.

Table 14.1 Ways in which discourses can affect schemas

Type of discourse	Effect	Examples
Schema preserving discourses	Simply maintain a reader's existing schemas (no new information added), or add information to existing schemas through schema accretion	• Reading a review of a new film release • Reading an instruction manual for a replacement TV
Schema reinforcing discourses	Present new information but strengthen and confirm existing schemas – often those that represent stereotypes	• An advertisement for a new train set that only represents boys playing with it • A romance novel that ends with the heroine marrying the hero
Schema disrupting discourses	Create some conceptual deviance, and offer a potential challenge to existing schemas; likely to result in schema accretion, tuning or restructuring	• Reading something that surprises you, or seems wrong to you, or is unlike your previous experiences

The consequences of schema disruption are discussed in section 14.3. First, we introduce another central, and related, concept in cognitive psychology: the prototype.

14.2 Categorisation: Prototypes

Work in cognitive psychology has also generated insights into the way humans categorise the people, places, situations, and things they encounter in the world. Our cognitive system for categorisation does not promote clear-cut, in-or-out categories, but instead organises elements in a radial structure: from core, central examples outwards to poorer, more peripheral ones. The core examples of a particular category are the **prototypes**, which possess features considered central to that category. More peripheral examples are less prototypical and possess fewer of the central features, yet can still be conceptualised as part of the category. Consider, for instance, the category of 'bird'. Prototypical items are those you'd be most likely to name first if asked to give an example of a specific category, such as robins, blackbirds, sparrows, magpies, and pigeons. Creatures such as pheasants, hawks, peacocks, penguins, ostriches, and pterodactyls can be seen as progressively less typical examples of the 'bird' category, and are therefore positioned further out from the centre of the radial prototype structure.

Categories have **fuzzy boundaries** rather than fixed edges. It is not possible to determine where the category 'bird' ends and the category 'dinosaur' begins, for instance, and one item may have membership of several different conceptual categories. If you were asked: 'which is a better example of a bird: an anteater or an aeroplane?', it is likely that you'd be able to pick one of these and give reasons (e.g. an anteater because it is a living creature which eats insects, or an aeroplane because it has wings and can fly) even though neither is a good example of a 'bird'. The boundaries of your 'bird' category are flexible and determined by the features of your prototype.

As is clear from the examples above, prototypes are structured based on our experience and are greatly influenced by socio-cultural factors. The configuration of items in our 'bird' category is dependent on our location in Northern Europe: people living in New Zealand or Bolivia, for instance, would probably categorise different creatures as prototypical birds. Moreover, people with specialist knowledge of 'birds' or 'dinosaurs' would also be likely to configure the categories differently. Recent research suggests that the way we apply our conceptual categories is also highly influenced by the context in which we are situated and our goals. Prototype organisation is present throughout our knowledge schemas. For example, consider your schema for the literary romance genre. If you were asked to name texts that are examples of this genre (e.g. *Romeo and Juliet*, *Love Actually*), or things-that-happen-in-a-romance (e.g. boy meets girl, they fall in love, there is a problem but ultimately they reach a happy ending in which they stay together), the things that most readily come to mind are your prototypes for those particular concepts. Less prototypical examples of the romance genre depart in some way from these more central examples. Prototype theory has particular explanatory power when it comes to the discussion of literary genres, which are also in themselves categories that exhibit a radial prototype structure (see Activity 2 at the end of this chapter).

14.3 Responding to schema disruption

Schemas and scripts are instantiated by **headers** in our surroundings or, when reading, by the language of the text. Headers are references to slots: the entry conditions, objects, participants, or actions that are associated with the schema. Stockwell (2002a: 78) suggests that at least two headers are required for a particular schema to be activated. For instance, the opening sentences of *The Unconsoled* by Kazuo Ishiguro (2005 [1995]: 1; our sentence numbering) enable readers to infer that the protagonist (called Ryder) has arrived at a hotel even though the text does not explicitly state this:

> (1) The taxi driver seemed embarrassed to find there was no one – not even a clerk behind the reception desk – waiting to welcome me. (2) He wandered across the deserted lobby, perhaps hoping to discover a staff member concealed behind one of the plants or armchairs. (3) Eventually he put my suitcases down beside the elevator doors and, mumbling some excuse, took his leave of me.

Mention of the 'clerk behind the reception desk' in S1 is not enough to instantiate the HOTEL schema on its own – for instance, many businesses and leisure centres have reception desks. However, when reference is made to the 'lobby' in S2, and later 'plants', 'armchairs', 'suitcases', and 'elevator', the HOTEL schema becomes more clearly instantiated. Here, a reader's knowledge of hotels provides a fairly recognisable context to Ryder's and the taxi driver's actions, and enables a number of gap-filling inferences. From the application of our schema, we can infer that Ryder is a new guest to the hotel, and that he needs to check in and be allocated a room. The taxi driver's embarrassment can be explained by our knowledge that it is good practice for hotel receptionists to greet new guests upon arrival. Note that the names of schemas/scripts (such as the HOTEL or RESTAURANT schemas) are typically presented using small capitals, to indicate that they refer to a knowledge structure.

Narrative theorists suggest that readers make inferences about fictional worlds based, at least initially, on a '**principle of minimal departure**' (Ryan 1991), meaning that readers will assume that the world represented by a text operates in the same way as the real world unless it is indicated otherwise. As well as applying their schematic knowledge about hotels in these opening lines, readers will therefore also assume, for instance, that the physical laws of the actual world – including things like gravity, time, and the subjective nature of human perception – remain the same.

As Ishiguro's opening chapter progresses, a hotel receptionist appears and Ryder is checked in to the hotel. The receptionist indicates that Ryder should follow the porter, named Gustav, to his room. The 'porter' participant role is typically only a feature in upmarket hotels, and this knowledge feeds into inferences about the type of establishment depicted in the text (we imagine it as rather swanky). The sequence of events in the text fits the checking-in script that forms part of our UPMARKET HOTEL schema (a porter carries your bags and guides you to your room). The text at this point, then, can be regarded as schema preserving. However, as Ryder joins the porter and proceeds to his room, the novel begins to challenge the principle of minimal departure and deviate from readers' schematic expectations. First, this sequence of events is narrated (Ishiguro 2005 [1995]: 4–5):

> an elderly porter was waiting across the lobby. He was standing in front of the open elevator, staring into its interior with a preoccupied air. He gave a start as I came walking up to him. He then picked up my suitcases and hurried into the elevator after me [. . .] As we began our ascent [. . .]

The headers in this extract (specifically the reference to an 'open elevator' and going 'into the elevator') instantiate an ELEVATOR schema and related scripts that enable readers to predict the sequence of events to follow. For instance, an ELEVATOR script enables the assumption that the elevator doors closed before Ryder and the porter began their ascent, even though this is not explicitly stated in the text. Other aspects of our ELEVATOR schema include the fact that elevators are generally small, enclosed spaces only suitable for small groups of people, and that elevator journeys are typically short in duration. Although we have encountered other types of elevators (e.g. elevators with manual doors, paternosters, enormous elevators which accommodate larger amounts of people), the information presented here characterises our elevator prototype. This is obviously culturally determined: for example, people who are used to living and working in high-rise buildings may be more accustomed to lengthy elevator rides, and as such may respond differently to what happens next.

Once they are in the elevator, Gustav the porter insists on holding both of Ryder's heavy suitcases, despite Ryder's concerns that he is dangerously over-exerting himself. Gustav explains that they are 'not going up far' – an assertion which matches with our schematic knowledge about the short duration of elevator journeys. The two characters enter into dialogue about Gustav's life as a porter, but Gustav's utterances are extremely long and enter into repetitive detail (Ishiguro 2005 [1995]: 4–11). The elevator ride finishes seven pages later, going on for much longer than our ELEVATOR schema (and cues in the text) would lead us to expect.

Taken alone, this temporal deviation may seem a rather minor issue. However, the spatial elements of the elevator are also rather strange. During the last of his lengthy monologues, Gustav makes reference to a 'Miss Hilde', who he claims will be able to 'vouch for what I'm saying'.

As Ryder asks who Miss Hilde is, he suddenly realises that there is another person in the elevator (Ishiguro 2005 [1995]: 9):

> 'Pardon me,' I said, 'but who is this Miss Hilde you keep referring to?' No sooner had I said this, I noticed that the porter was gazing past my shoulder at some spot behind me. Turning, I saw with a start that we were not alone in the elevator. A small young woman in a neat business suit was standing pressed into the corner behind me. Perceiving that I had at last noticed her, she smiled and took a step forward.

Some aspects of this new information preserve our schematic knowledge about elevators as being small, enclosed spaces: Miss Hilde is 'pressed into the corner', for instance. A related assumption, however, based on the understanding of human perception which applies to this narrative (due to the principle of minimal departure) is that upon entering a small, enclosed space like an elevator, one would easily be able to perceive whether there were other people inside of it. The adverbial 'at last' in the penultimate line of the extract suggests that Miss Hilde has been present in the elevator since the beginning of their journey, and this is further supported by the fact that she goes on to offer her opinion on Gustav's speech. The sudden appearance of Miss Hilde is surprising both for Ryder and for readers. It presents conceptual deviance that potentially challenges the existing schemas that were being applied in our comprehension of the text.

When faced with potential schema disruption, readers are motivated to find explanations that will downgrade the challenge (Stockwell 2002a: 80). Beaugrande (1980) provides a useful way of describing the relative unexpectedness of information in a text (referred to as 'informativity'), as shown in Table 14.2.

Beaugrande suggests that most texts include some second-order informativity, as this is what makes them interesting. When faced with the higher levels of informativity, there are a number of strategies readers can use in order to resolve the schema disruption: by looking backwards to the memory of the previous text, forwards to anticipate what will happen, or outwards beyond the text (e.g. if the informativity is attributed to a reader's misunderstanding, for instance).

In the extract from *The Unconsoled*, the lengthy elevator journey has second-order informativity, as it seems strange but not wholly unexplainable. It might be possible to resolve this schema disruption through forward downgrading, by presuming that you'll be provided with some reason why your assumptions about the duration of elevator journeys did not apply in this context. Another possible resolution might be through outward downgrading, assuming that your ELEVATOR schema doesn't apply in this circumstance.

Table 14.2 Orders of informativity (adapted from Beaugrande 1980: 103–14 and Stockwell 2002a: 80)

Order of informativity	Description	Examples
First-order informativity	Normal, unremarkable things which are schema preserving or reinforcing.	Presence of reference to 'trunk' in a description of a tree.
Second-order informativity	Unusual or less likely things which are non-typical but still conceivable. Can develop schematic knowledge by accretion or tuning.	If a tree is described as having several trunks.
Third-order informativity	Impossible or highly unlikely things which can cause schema disruption. In such cases, readers will expect an explanation or assume that they are dealing with a highly fictional world. Can result in schema accretion, tuning or restructuring.	If a tree is described as having no trunk at all, with its branches simply hovering in mid-air.

The sudden appearance of Miss Hilde, however, is more of a third-order incident. Ryder's failure to perceive her in the elevator is strange and unexpected. However, even this third-order occurrence can be backwardly downgraded through inferences about Ryder's state of mind. Earlier in the text, Ryder mentions his lack of energy, and the hotel receptionist tells him 'you must be tired after such a long journey' (Ishiguro 2005 [1995]: 4). His failure to perceive a character in such close quarters could be attributed to his severe jet lag or exhaustion. In this case, the schema disruption prompts the accretion of new information about the mind of the narrator and his unreliability as a focaliser, but extensive schema restructuring is not required.

This example shows that schema theory and the notion of schema disruption can be useful to help track readers' reactions to texts which are unusual or challenging in some way.

14.4 Schemas and humour

A major approach in the study of humour regards the production and comprehension of humorous language to involve **incongruity**. Several researchers have applied schema theory in the study of the workings of humorous texts. Raskin (1985) proposes that texts can be characterised as humorous if they are compatible with two different schemas/scripts that are opposed in some way. Thus, a joke typically 'describes a certain "real" situation and evokes another "unreal" situation which does not take place and is fully or partially incompatible with the former' (Raskin 1985: 108). Similarly, Semino (1997) suggests that humour can be created by the switching between schemas involved in jokes and sketches.

Consider the following transcription of the first minute of a comedy sketch ('My Blackberry Is Not Working'). This sketch was performed by the comedians Ronnie Corbett and Harry Enfield on a BBC TV show *The One Ronnie* (2010). What kinds of schemas are activated in the comprehension of this text?:

A customer walks into greengrocer's shop brandishing a carrier bag. The greengrocer stands behind a counter. Boxes of fruit are displayed behind him and around the walls.

[1] **Customer:** I bought something from you last week and I'm very disappointed
[2] **Greengrocer:** Oh yeah, what's the problem?
[3] **Customer:** Yeah, well, my blackberry is not working

Customer removes something from carrier bag and places on the counter. Camera zooms out and then cuts to a close-up to reveal a small piece of fruit.
[Audience Laughter]

[4] **Greengrocer:** What's the matter, has it run out of juice?
[Audience Laughter]
[5] **Customer:** No, no, it's completely frozen
[Audience Laughter]

Greengrocer picks up blackberry and bashes it on the counter top. It makes a hard knocking sound.

[6] **Greengrocer:** Oh yeah, I can see that. I tell you what, let's try it on orange

Reaches behind him to pick up an orange, and places it on the counter top. Puts the blackberry on top of the orange.
[Audience Laughter]
Customer leans in and looks at the skin of the orange.

[7] **Customer:** That's got a few black spots you see there
[8] **Greengrocer:** Oh dear, yeah, sorry about that

Greengrocer picks up blackberry and throws orange behind him.

This excerpt evokes a number of schemas and scripts. For instance, a SHOP RETURN/COMPLAINT script is instantiated when the customer approaches the counter holding a carrier bag and delivers their first line. This script is preserved in the sketch: as expected, the shop assistant enquires about the problem (2, 4), tries to find solutions which appease the customer (6), and apologises (8). The sketch also evokes a GREENGROCER schema, so the setting is instantly recognisable as a specialist fruit and vegetable shop. In many English cities, the advent of large supermarkets and convenience stores means that it is relatively rare to shop for fruit and veg in a dedicated greengrocer's shop. Our GREENGROCER schema, then, includes the sense that these shops are somewhat old-fashioned.

The main thrust of the humour in the sketch arises from the opposition of two schemas. In (3) the line 'my blackberry is not working' instantiates a MOBILE PHONE schema through the co-presence of the headers 'blackberry' and 'not working': a Blackberry (with a capital 'B') is a popular mobile device. The header 'B/blackberry' is compatible with two different schemas, however. When line 3 is delivered, the customer could be referring to a mobile phone, but the visual context of the greengrocer's shop also suggests that a FRUIT schema could be relevant. When the customer goes on to produce a small piece of fruit, the FRUIT schema is visually instantiated, and the first burst of audience laughter appears. Consequently, the text is compatible with two different schemas, and it continually uses language that plays on the overlap between these schemas, summarised in Table 14.3.

The FRUIT schema applies to the 'real' situation being presented to the viewer, and the MOBILE PHONE schema supplies the 'unreal' situation, which is partially incompatible with the 'real' one. The FRUIT and MOBILE PHONE schemas are semantically opposed in that the former characterises natural objects whilst the latter is a form of man-made technology. When the FRUIT schema is associated with the

Table 14.3 FRUIT and MOBILE PHONE schemas in *The One Ronnie*

Header	FRUIT schema	MOBILE PHONE schema
'blackberry not working'	blackberry = fruit	Blackberry = device name
'run out of juice'	juice = fruit juice	juice = battery life
'completely frozen'	frozen = frozen fruit	frozen = stopped responding
'try it on orange'	orange = fruit	Orange = mobile phone network provider
'got a few black spots'	black spots = discoloured skin on fruit	black spots = areas of poor signal in mobile phone network

GREENGROCER schema, an opposition between old-fashioned practices and the new-technological practices is also established. The sketch plays in particular on the way concepts from the domain of FRUIT are used metaphorically to talk about mobile phones.

Schema theory offers great potential for explaining variation in reader response and discussing both the similarities and the differences across responses. At the time of writing this analysis, the mobile phone network provider called Orange has been taken over and is in the process of being phased out, and Blackberry devices are becoming less popular. Thus, it may be that, by the time you read this, some of the humour in this sketch no longer fires because audiences do not possess the schema overlap which it plays upon.

For viewers familiar with the comedian Ronnie Corbett, their schemas about his previous work and biography may add an additional level of meaning which affects their responses to the text. Ronnie Corbett was part of a comedy duo 'The Two Ronnies' who starred in a TV show that ran from 1971 to 1987. One of their most well-known sketches is set in a hardware shop and plays on puns and mispronunciations (the customer orders 'fork handles' and is presented with 'four candles', for instance). The sketch analysed above was performed as part of a celebration of Ronnie Corbett's eightieth birthday, and was the first time he had performed since the death of co-star Ronnie Barker. For some viewers, then, in possession of particular knowledge about the wider context of the show, the sketch has **intertextual** links. These supply an additional level of meaning and reinforce the opposition between old-fashioned and new-technological references.

Keywords and summary

Headers, informativity (first, second, and third order), principle of minimal departure, prototype (fuzzy boundaries), schema, schema alteration (accretion, refreshment, restructuring, tuning), schema effects (disruption, preservation, reinforcement), script, slots.

This chapter has introduced two big ideas about the way human knowledge and categorisation works, and discussed their application to literature. Firstly, humans use schemas and scripts derived from their previous experience in order to process new experiences. Secondly, human categorisation is organised on the basis of prototypes. We discussed how literary texts interact with readers' schemas to produce different effects, including presenting information which causes schema disruption and creating humour through schema opposition. The prototype concept can also provide insights into the workings of literary genre classifications.

One of the main problems you may encounter as you apply schema theory to texts will likely revolve around the naming of the schemas/scripts you feel are instantiated during reading. Our knowledge structures are intricately interrelated networks and operate on multiple levels of detail/abstraction. For instance, how can we be sure that the HOTEL schema isn't actually part of a RETAIL schema, or a DWELLING PLACE schema? Like all analytical decisions in stylistics, you need to be able to explain and justify your naming choice, and add clarity and retrievability to your discussion with specific textual evidence. If you provide detailed information about the headers which instantiated the schema, then even if your reader disagrees with your precise naming choices, they should still be able to follow your analysis.

Several sub-disciplines of cognitive linguistics are concerned with the study of knowledge structures or ICMs, and therefore knowledge structures are often referred to using different terms. The role of knowledge in language processing is also discussed in Chapter 15 'Cognitive grammar and construal', which discusses conceptual bases, knowledge domains, and dominions; in Chapter 16 on metaphor, which discusses conceptual domains and image-schemas; and in Chapter 17, which discusses schemas or frames in Text World Theory.

Activities

1. The passage below is the opening of a short story by Christine Kieser called 'Completely Overloaded' (1997). Read it, and identify the headers which instantiate particular schemas in your interpretation of it. How did you identify and label the schemas involved in your comprehension of the text? Compare your analysis with a partner. How does your schema identification compare with theirs? Are there similarities or differences in your interpretations? Can these be accounted for using schema theory?:

> Saturday is the day to see and be seen at the record shop and the hordes have descended upon the Platter Palace. Punks with their hair done up in dangerous cone spikes come perilously close to poking each others' eyes out as they peruse the 45 rack, looking for hardcore favourites. Gangs of straight-edgers with big black Xs on their hands yell at each other across the store and hold up records for their buddies to see. Other shoppers – who could be their parents – dig through the blues section. Our newest employee, Darlene, sits on one of the shoddy stools behind the counter,

rocking violently back and forth in time to the Godbullies record that is playing far louder than necessary.

2. (a) Choose a genre you know well: this could be a literary genre, or a genre of film/TV/theatre, etc. Make a list of texts that you feel are good examples of this genre. From this, make a list of what, in your view, are the central and peripheral features of this genre. In doing so, you are tapping into your prototypes for your chosen genre.
(b) Now consider texts you are familiar with from the list below:

   Pride and Prejudice
   Harry Potter series
   Marvel comics
   Back to the Future films
   Eastenders soap opera
   the Bible
   Lord of the Flies
   A Christmas Carol

   To what extent do they fit your chosen genre prototype? If they are not a central member of the genre as you see it, is it still possible to argue that they have links to your chosen genre in some respects? Here, you are experimenting with the fuzzy boundaries of your prototype.

3. Find a text you found surprising or funny in some way, or which seems to deliberately manipulate you. Consider the schematic knowledge involved in your understanding of the text. Can schema theory offer an account of your response to the text?

Further reading and references

Lakoff (1987) outlines the forms of idealised cognitive models (ICMs) including Barsalou's (1983) argument for ICMs being constructed online for 'ad hoc' categories. For recent cognitive psychological work on the context-dependency of knowledge structures, see Barsalou (2003). Work in schema theory began with Bartlett (1995 [1932]) and was developed by Artificial Intelligence researchers in the 1970s (e.g. see Minsky (1975) on 'frames'; Schank and Abelson (1977) on 'scripts'). Work on prototypes began with Rosch (1975, 1977, 1978) and see Lakoff (1987: 5–153) for an overview. Cook (1994) discusses literariness using the notion of schema refreshment (see Semino (1997) and Jeffries (2001) for critique and expansion of these ideas). Stockwell (2002a: 27–40, 75–90) provides a pioneering overview of the application of schema theory to literature, drawing on Cook (1994) and connecting schema disruption with Beaugrande's (1980) work on informativity. Emmott et al. (2015) provide another useful overview of schema theory in stylistics, including more examples of its applications. See Walsh (2007) for an analysis of crossover fiction using schema theory. Prototype theory and schema theory are adopted to explore genre by: Gavins (2013), Gibbons (2016b), and Steen (2003, 2011). Ryan (1991) discusses the 'principle of minimal departure'. For more on incongruity in humour, see Raskin (1985) and Simpson (1998, 2000, 2003). For more on schema theory and intertextuality, see Mason (forthcoming).

15 Cognitive grammar and construal

15.1 What's cognitive about grammar?

In Chapters 5 and 10, we considered two approaches to analysing the grammar of texts: the way phrase and sentence structure influences literary meaning, and the system of transitivity in which verb choice affects the representation of entities and events. This chapter introduces some ideas from the cognitive study of grammar, which differs from other linguistic approaches to grammar because of its emphasis on the psychological components of language. Langacker argues: 'grammatical structure can only be understood in relation to the conceptual organization it embodies and expresses' (2008: 405). Conceptualisation is central to cognitive grammar, which emphasises the mental activity involved in producing and comprehending language.

This chapter will focus on one aspect of cognitive grammar, the study of construal. Langacker argues that linguistic meaning consists of both conceptual content and a particular way of construing that content. **Construal** refers to our 'ability to conceive and portray the same situation in different ways' (Langacker 2008: 43). For example, the image on the far left of Figure 15.1 represents some conceptual content – the conception of a glass containing liquid. In order to form a linguistic expression about that conceptual content, we necessarily impose a certain construal, designating or referring to particular aspects of it. Compare these construals:

(a) The glass with water in it.
(b) The water in the glass.
(c) The glass is half full.
(d) The glass is half empty.

The differences between these construals are indicated by emboldened lines in Figure 15.1. Construal (a) is a noun phrase, designating the container; Construal (b), another noun phrase, designates the liquid it

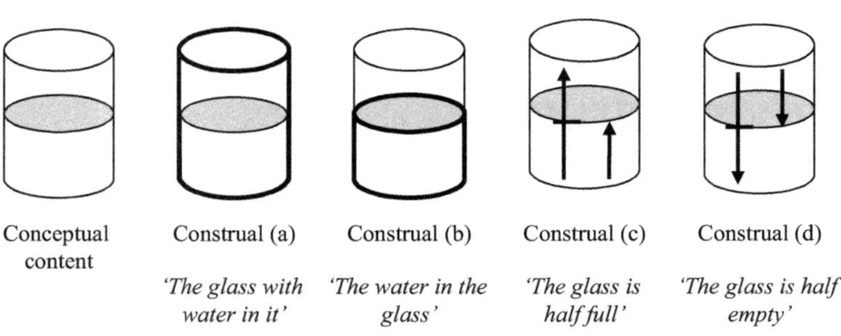

Figure 15.1 Linguistic construals of conceptual content (adapted from Langacker 2008: 43–4)

contains; Construals (c) and (d), both simple sentences, designate either the relationship between the liquid and the potential volume of the glass, or the void and the potential volume of the glass.

Another example of construal was discussed in Chapter 10 when we considered different descriptions of the same event provided by characters in the sitcom *Fresh Meat*. These descriptions differed in the amount of blame they attributed to Josie. These are all examples of different construals of the same event, with different linguistic choices representing the conceptual content differently. Construal reflects the mental activity of the speaker, but it also affects how the hearer/reader conceptualises the content.

15.2 Dimensions of construal

Cognitive grammar provides several, interrelated labels for discussing different dimensions of construal, which fall under four main headings:

- specificity
- prominence
- dynamicity
- perspective.

These dimensions of construal will be introduced below with short examples, before they are applied in literary analysis in sections 15.3 and 15.4.

Specificity refers to the level of detail in linguistic construal. The inverse of specificity is **schematicity**. Speakers make choices about the level of specificity: the options can be thought of as a cline – from the most schematic to the most detailed. For example, an electric guitar could be referred to with a high level of specificity as 'that beautiful honey-coloured Gibson Les Paul', or more schematically as 'that thing'. Specificity can be discussed across linguistic levels, from phrases to sentences to larger stretches of text. This is illustrated below with possible clines of specificity in choices of adverbial phrases, noun phrases, and clauses:

> ← schematic specific →
>
> ages ago – last year – last April – on 4 February 2016
>
> thing – instrument – musical instrument – electric guitar – that beautiful honey-coloured Gibson Les Paul
>
> Somebody saw something – A person perceived an instrument – A girl saw an electric guitar – A tired little girl wearing a bobble hat stood staring at that beautiful honey-coloured Gibson Les Paul with the expensive price tag

A combination of schematic and specific construal is common.

Another dimension of construal is prominence. **Prominence** refers to the way linguistic expressions direct attention to particular aspects of the conceptual content. This aspect of construal draws upon the figure/ground distinction (introduced in Chapter 12). Langacker uses a stage metaphor to help describe the study of prominence: imagine sitting in a theatre looking at a stage, and consider what you can see and how you direct your attention. The **maximal scope** of your field of view would be everything you can see from your position – that might include other audience members, the architecture of the theatre, as well as the stage itself and the actors and props upon it. During your average theatre performance, however, your attention will be primarily directed at the stage itself – the 'onstage region'. This is the **immediate scope** of your perception. Furthermore, you will be paying attention to specific foci of attention in this onstage region, such as the actor who is currently speaking or moving. These specific foci are most prominent – they are the figure or the thing which is **profiled** while the immediate and maximal scope forms the ground.

These different levels of perceptual attention can be considered in the study of linguistic expressions too. For instance, at the lexical level, word choices profile particular aspects of a broader **conceptual base** (or knowledge domain) that is part of a word's meaning. The word 'elbow' profiles (i.e. refers to) part of an arm, which in turn is a part of a human body. Thus, the immediate scope of the expression 'elbow' is ARM, and the maximal scope is the human BODY. Similarly, reference to 'eyes', 'nose', 'cheek', or 'chin' all profile a different aspect of the same conceptual base: FACE. The word 'mouth' is polysemous and can profile aspects of several conceptual bases – including BODY, RIVER, BOTTLE, or CAVE. During reading, words profile particular elements of the conceptual content they evoke.

At the clausal level, linguistic expressions profile relationships. When relationships are profiled, another type of prominence comes into play: **trajector/landmark alignment**. This is another manifestation of the figure/ground distinction. A **trajector** is the most prominent entity or object in a relationship, and the **landmark** is the secondary or background focus. Consider the sentences below:

(a) The lights are above the dancefloor.
(b) The dancefloor is below the lights.

Both (a) and (b) construe the same relationship, with the same conceptual base, but profile different trajector and landmark alignments. In (a), the lights are the trajector; in (b), the dancefloor.

Grammatical prominence is related to the embodied nature of human perception. Imagine, for instance, the balls on a snooker table. The balls are static until some force is applied to them by a snooker cue. Once hit, the balls ricochet across the table, hitting each other and having knock-on effects until the initial force is spent. This 'billiard ball model' (Langacker 2008: 103) provides an example of some of the basic interactions we perceive between objects in the world, and these interactions can be represented in clauses. Transitive clauses, such as 'Alison chopped the wood with her axe', can be thought of as portraying an **action chain** in which energy is transmitted from an energy source (the agent) to other participants (e.g. a patient, sometimes via an instrument). The grammatical roles of entities in a sentence are related to these **archetypal roles**, summarised in Table 15.1.

Prototypical transitive clauses such as (c) below profile a full action chain with the agent as the subject and trajector of the clause, the patient as the object or landmark, and the energy transfer profiled by the verb:

(c)	Jake	smashed	the window	with a tennis ball
	Subject	Verb	Object	Adjunct
	Agent		Patient	Instrument
	Trajector		Landmark	

In prototypical active clauses such as (c), the agent of the action chain is given most prominence.

Different clause structures can create different construals of this event by profiling different aspects of the action chain. Sometimes, the full action chain is not profiled in the clause, and instead forms part

Table 15.1 Archetypal roles in cognitive grammar (adapted from Langacker 2008: 356)

Archetypal role	Explanation/Examples
Agent	Individual who initiates and carries out an action, typically a physical action affecting other entities; an 'energy source' in an action chain, e.g. '*Alison chopped the wood with her axe*': 'Alison' is the agent
Patient	Something that undergoes a change of state, usually as the result of being affected by outside sources; an 'energy sink' in the action chain, e.g. '*Alison chopped the wood with her axe*': 'wood' is the patient
Instrument	Used by an agent to affect another entity in an action chain, e.g. '*Alison chopped wood with her axe*': 'the axe' is the instrument
Experiencer	Sentient, normally human, location of mental experience, e.g. '*Sara enjoys the disco*': Sara is the experiencer
Mover	Anything that moves, animate or inanimate, e.g. '*The lights flash across the dancefloor*': 'the lights' are a mover
Zero	Neutral or baseline role of participants that merely exist, occupy some location, or exhibit a static property, e.g. '*The lights are above the dancefloor*': 'the lights' and 'the dancefloor' are zeroes

of its conceptual base. In (d), a passive sentence, only the patient and the energy transfer is profiled. Most prominence is conferred upon the patient (the window) in this construal. The agent is not profiled, yet is still part of the conceptual base (because we know that an action chain requires an agent to instigate the energy transfer):

(d)	The window	was	smashed
	Subject	Verb	Complement
	Patient		

In (e), only the instrument and patient are profiled, and therefore represented as the most prominent in this construal:

(e)	A tennis ball	smashed	the window
	Subject	Verb	Object
	Instrument		Patient
	Trajector		Landmark

Example (f) uses 'smashed' as an intransitive verb, so profiles only the patient and end-state of the action chain. The omitted agent and the instrument of the action chain are therefore not part of the immediate scope of the construal, but they are part of the maximal scope of the clause:

(f)	The window	smashed
	Subject	Verb
	Patient	

Not all clauses represent action chains, and therefore the grammatical roles of 'experiencer', 'mover', and 'zero' (from Table 15.1) construe mental experiences, agent-less movement, or static properties.

Because language both represents time and is conceptualised through time, construal also affects the way a situation or event is mentally 'scanned'. Using the term **dynamicity**, Langacker likens language processing to a movement between successive stimuli. **Sequential scanning** represents a dynamic process or series of processes that develop through time, whereas **summary scanning** offers a cumulative representation, giving rise to a more static cognitive representation. The difference between sequential and summary scanning is evident in (g) and (h) below:

(g) Simon organised the house efficiently.
(h) His organisation of the house was efficient.

(g) represents a dynamic process using a finite verb ('organised') to denote an action while the adverb 'efficiently' describes the act of organising. Because it gives rise to a dynamic mental representation involving a process occurring through time, (g) is an example of **sequential scanning**. In (h), the scene is construed as a state through nominalisation: the verb 'organised' becomes the noun 'organisation', which has a property expressed by the adjective 'efficient'. Although a finite verb is also used ('was'), it represents a state not a process. This is an example of **summary scanning** which represents the scene in a cumulative fashion.

The dynamicity of language processing also impacts upon the way knowledge is activated during conceptualisation. Another type of scanning is the **reference point relationship**, which refers to 'our ability to invoke the conception of one entity in order to establish mental contact with another' (Langacker 2008: 83). During reading, we scan along a chain of successive reference points, both across a sentence and across larger stretches of text. Each reference point provides access to a number of activated knowledge domains, known as **targets**, which collectively make up the referent's **dominion**. The workings of reference point relationships can be illustrated by removing words from a sentence and considering what could fill the gap. Which word would you place in the gap below?:

> Alison got in the car and _________ away.

The reference point 'car' affords access to a number of potential targets, primarily a motor vehicle. More peripheral potential targets include rollercoasters or fairground rides, which also have 'cars'. For the primary target to be activated in the sentence, the missing word would be 'drove', which is conceptually associated with motor vehicles. The more peripheral targets could be activated with the verb 'rode'. Because of the dominion activated by the reference point 'car', you are unlikely to fill the gap with 'swam' or 'flew'. Once one possible target is activated, the others fade from attention and a fresh dominion is activated for the next reference point. This demonstrates the network of associations which develop as we read and which form part of a particular construal.

The final dimension of construal is **perspective**. Because all linguistic expressions are produced by a particular conceptualiser in a specific spatio-temporal context, they encode a particular **vantage point** which can be made more or less prominent. If a speaker profiles themselves in a clause, using pronouns or other deictic markers, for instance, the vantage point is more explicit. If the focus is instead on what is being conceptualised, the vantage point is less prominent. There are a wealth of terms which can be used to describe perspective in cognitive grammar but, as Harrison et al. (2014: 10) note, vantage point is broadly comparable with the notion of point of view in stylistics (see Chapters 8 and 9), so here we discuss perspective using stylistic frameworks.

The terms introduced above are not hierarchical, and are best thought of as sets of interrelated descriptors that tap into different aspects of construal. Although it is good to consider each of these dimensions when analysing construal, it is not obligatory to use all the terms in any one analysis: they can be applied where relevant to the specific text under study.

15.3 Construal and narrative point of view

Cognitive grammar can provide added nuance to a discussion of narrative point of view. Consider the opening paragraph of the popular thriller *The Girl on the Train* (Hawkins 2015; sentences numbered for analysis). This chapter is titled 'Rachel' and dated 'Friday 5th July 2013, Morning':

> (1) There is a pile of clothing on the side of the train tracks. (2) Light-blue cloth – a shirt, perhaps – jumbled up with something dirty white. (3) It's

> probably rubbish, part of a load fly-tipped into the scrubby little wood up the bank. (4) It could have been left behind by the engineers who work this part of the track, they're here often enough. (5) Or it could be something else.

Interestingly, the first five sentences of the paragraph involve the narrator making repeated construals of the same scene, which is at first described as: 'a pile of clothing on the side of the train tracks'.

The first two sentences confer prominence on the 'pile of clothing' in different ways. In S1, 'There' is in subject position, placing emphasis on the abstract, unspecified setting. The rest of the sentence offers more information about what 'There' consists of, and profiles the 'pile of clothing' as the trajector in relation to the landmark of 'the train tracks' through the prepositional phrase 'on the side of'. No actions are profiled here, so the elements have the archetypal role of zero. The noun phrase 'pile of clothing' is quite schematic as it profiles a number of objects collectively.

In S2, the 'pile of clothing' becomes part of the conceptual base of the noun phrases 'light-blue cloth', 'a shirt', and 'something dirty white', which thus construes the 'pile of clothing' with greater specificity. S2 profiles the 'light-blue cloth' as the trajector by placing it in subject position, in relation to the less specific landmark 'something dirty white'. Again, no actions are profiled, just the state of being 'jumbled', so the elements have the archetypal role of zero. In S2, the vantage point of the construal also becomes more visible through the use of the modal 'perhaps' which indicates attitude. The first-person narrator is not directly referenced until S6 when the first-person pronoun appears, yet from S2 onwards they are brought to our attention through the use of modality. In particular, the negative modal shading of this passage contributes to this effect (see Chapter 9).

The opening sentences direct and maintain attention on the pile of clothing. This object is a reference point with a dominion that includes knowledge about fashion, retail, household storage, rubbish, lost property, and nudity (amongst others). In S3 and S4, the narrator begins to ponder the origin of the clothing, and in doing so activates certain targets within this dominion. S3 construes the pile of clothing as rubbish, and more specifically as 'part of a load fly-tipped into the scrubby little wood up the bank'. The post-modification in this noun phrase consists of an embedded clause, since the past participle 'fly-tipped' is a verb. The embedded clause is a passive construction, as only the patient (the load of rubbish) and the energy transfer (the act of fly-tipping) is profiled. The agent of the fly-tipping is omitted and is only part of the inferred conceptual base. Because of its passivity and embedment within a noun phrase, the clause offers a summary scan of the end-state of an action chain. This maintains focus on the mysterious pile of clothing.

S4 also profiles the clothing as a patient in an action chain: as an object 'left behind' by the railway engineers (who are the agents). S4 activates an alternative domain as the target of the reference point: the clothing is now interpreted as lost property. The passive construction profiles the clothing 'It' as the trajector (rather than the engineers) by placing it in subject position. Although the engineers are profiled in the clause as agents, they are shown as part of the landmark. Their backgrounding continues in the second clause ('they're here often enough'): although referred to again, the engineers are not performing any action and instead simply occupy a location on multiple occasions, which are summary scanned. Attention thus still remains focused primarily on the clothing. S3 and S4 offer possible hypothetical explanations for the pile of clothing on the side of the train tracks: it is construed as the patient in two action chains.

S5 attributes a further property to the pile of clothing, but is interesting for its marked schematicity: the clothing ('It') is simply described as 'something else'. This sentence invites the reader to supply other potential explanations for these discarded objects. Drawing on the dominions established by reference points in the text (as well as wider schematic knowledge, for instance about the thriller genre), readers are likely to infer more sinister possibilities. Clothing has the human body as part of its conceptual base, and also plays a role in several domains. Could the clothing be discarded evidence of a crime? Of a missing person? A dead body? The profiling in this sentence implicates the reader in making construals of the scene.

From S6, the vantage point of the narrative becomes more explicit, as the narrator tells us more about herself.

> (6) My mother used to tell me that I had an overactive imagination: Tom said that too. (7) I can't help it, I catch sight of these discarded scraps, a dirty T-shirt or a lonesome shoe, and all I can think of is the other shoe, and the feet that fitted into them.

In S6, the narrator's mother and Tom are agents in action chains with the narrator ('me') as patient. The fact that two other people, at different points in time, have accused the narrator of being overly imaginative, raises some questions about her reliability. In S7, the narrator is portrayed as the experiencer in a series of clauses ('I can't help it', 'I catch sight of', and 'all I can think of'). As well as suggesting that she ponders the significance of discarded clothing fairly often, this sentence reveals some of the reasoning behind her interest in these objects. In a similar way to S1–2 above, there is a shift from a fairly schematic noun phrase 'discarded scraps' to more specific noun phrases 'a dirty T-shirt' or 'a lonesome shoe'. Later in the clause, elements of the conceptual base of 'lonesome shoe', that is that shoes come in pairs and exist to be worn on feet, are also profiled as the narrator traces her inferences and explains her rather macabre interpretation of their significance.

If, like us, you had already considered the more macabre implications of discarded clothing when prompted by the text in S5, then S7 could function to promote affinity between the reader and the narrator. This might counteract the effect of the narrator's self-confessed overactive imagination. Either way, the repeated construals of discarded clothing are intriguing and likely to draw readers in to this thriller's plot. Grammatical choices in the narrative both reflect the narrator's preoccupations (her mind style – see Chapter 2) and involve the reader in the evaluation of her point of view.

15.4 Construal and conceptual deviance

Cognitive grammar can also provide insights into texts that subvert usual processes of perception and cognition in order to achieve defamiliarising effects (see also Chapter 2). Consider this nine-line poem 'I Am the Song' by Charles Causley (2000):

1 I am the song that sings the bird.
2 I am the leaf that grows the land.
3 I am the tide that moves the moon.
4 I am the stream that halts the sand.

5 I am the cloud that drives the storm.
6 I am the earth that lights the sun.
7 I am the fire that strikes the stone.
8 I am the clay that shapes the hand.
9 I am the word that speaks the man.

Each line of the poem has the same syntactic structure, containing one main clause ('I am the X') and one embedded subordinate relative clause 'that Y the Z'. The first clause construes an attribute of the speaker using a copulative construction ('I am') and the embedded clauses profile action chains. Across the poem a static image of the speaker is built up alongside more dynamic portrayals of the actions of which they are part. The nouns and verbs that comprise the subordinate clauses vary across each line. These lexical items are all fairly simple, short vocabulary items; there is little variation in their specificity or schematicity. However, despite this simple-looking, repetitive structure, this poem creates a peculiar effect.

Each line profiles elements which share a conceptual base; for instance, 'bird' and 'song', 'tide' and 'moon'. However, the construal of the relationships between these natural objects is deviant. Entities that are usually agents are construed as patients, whilst entities that are usually patients are construed as agents. For instance, normally birds sing songs; but here songs sing birds. The reversal in agent/patient relationship results in a reversal of trajector/landmark alignment that creates the sense of conceptual deviance.

There are differences in the prototypicality of the profiled action chains too. The patterns of causality which are reversed in L1 and L3 (birds singing songs, tides moving the moon) are more prototypical because, in their normal conception, they involve a clearer transfer of energy between agent and patient. L2 and L4, however, construe action chains in which this energy transfer is more convoluted. It would be unusual, for instance, to say that 'the land grows the leaf'. The noun 'leaf' profiles a highly specific part of the conceptual base of 'plant' or 'tree', thus appears to be used metonymically to stand for plant life in general. Even then, the growth of plants/trees is not entirely due to the agency of the land: land is not a prototypical agent. Similarly, 'sand' in L4 is not a prototypical agent, despite being construed here as involved in a dynamic process of 'halting'. Despite their apparent similarities on the page, there are nuanced differences in the conceptualisations prompted by each line, which creates internal deviation and interest. You can continue the analysis of L5–9 of the poem in Activity 2 at the end of this chapter.

The familiar natural objects portrayed in the poem are represented as attributes of the poetic voice, who furthermore appears capable of surpassing conventional worldly relationships. This may lead readers to interpret the 'I' of the poem as a deity or spiritual being. Reference to 'the word' in the final line, sometimes used as a metonym for religious texts, adds further weight to this religious reading. The defamiliarising construals of the poem refresh our perceptions of the organisation of the world, and in a religious reading could serve to highlight the presence and power of this deity.

Keywords and summary

Action chain, archetypal roles (agent, patient, instrument, experiencer, mover, zero), construal, dynamicity, mental scanning, perspective, profiling, prominence, reference point relationship (target, dominion), schematicity, sequential scanning, specificity, summary scanning, trajector/landmark alignment, vantage point.

Cognitive grammar is a practical and theoretical approach to language. The study of construal in cognitive grammar offers a suite of terms emphasising the connections between grammar and conceptualisation. When a speaker or writer formulates a linguistic expression, they impose a particular construal of conceptual content. The construals encoded in language by speakers/writers also influence the construals produced by hearers/readers. This chapter has considered the construals of a first-person narrator, and the deviant construals of a poem, discussing the way grammatical choices influence these texts' effects on readers.

Activities

1. Find a picture of a scene that involves lots of different actions. Generate ten simple sentences to describe aspects of the picture. In doing so, you are generating construals. Now examine the construals you have made using the terms in section 15.2. Which aspects have you chosen to profile in your sentences? What have you established as the trajector and landmark? What archetypal roles are present?
2. Continue our discussion of Charles Causley's 'I Am the Song' in section 15.4, by analysing L5–9 of the poem. What construals are generated by these lines? Do they involve the reversal of prototypical action chains (as in L1 and L3), or do they create less prototypical construals? Can concepts from cognitive grammar help you to describe the deviance of the poem?
3. Harrison et al. (2014: 8) suggest that the archetypal roles in cognitive grammar and the transitivity framework (introduced in Chapter 10) are 'complementary in terms of their different merits'. What are the similarities and differences between the two frameworks? What are their respective advantages or disadvantages for stylisticians like yourself? For comparison, you could label the extracts from *Fresh Meat* in section 10.1 using cognitive grammatical and transitivity terms.

Further reading and references

The most well-established and developed framework of cognitive grammar is set out by Langacker: see his 2008 introduction (especially chapter 3 on Construal); and also Langacker (1987, 1991a, 1991b, 2002, 2007, 2009). Other linguistic work in cognitive grammar includes: Croft (2001), Goldberg (1995), and Talmy (2000). Evans and Green (2006) provide excellent introductions to the different aspects of cognitive grammar (use the index); see also Croft and Cruse (2004) and Ungerer and Schmidt (2006).

Cognitive stylisticians have been working on 'scaling up' cognitive grammatical ideas and using these concepts in literary analysis. Harrison et al. (2014: 1–18) offer a concise overview of cognitive grammar in literature, as does Stockwell (2002a: 59–74). For books on the topic, see Giovanelli and Harrison (forthcoming) and Harrison (2017). Stylistic applications of cognitive grammar can be found in: Browse (2018), Burke (2011b: 203–30), Hamilton (2003), Harrison et al. (2014), Nuttall (2015, 2017), and Stockwell (2002a, 2009a, 2009b, 2014a, 2014b).

Part V

Reading as mental spaces

16 Conceptual metaphor and conceptual integration

16.1 Metaphorical cognition and conceptual mapping

The chapters in this Part of the book continue the study of conceptualisation, focusing on the way readers create and manipulate mental representations or mental spaces. These can be understood as assemblies of knowledge and information which are created during reading and used in processes of interpretation and imagination.

Figurative expressions such as metaphor have traditionally been studied as predominantly linguistic phenomena. Cognitive linguists, however, revolutionised the study of metaphor by establishing that metaphor is, in fact, a way of thinking, not just an ornamental patterning of words on a page. Rather, metaphor has a conceptual basis which is reflected in metaphorical language. This view of metaphor is known as **Conceptual Metaphor Theory**.

Conceptual metaphors make use of knowledge structures known as conceptual domains. A **conceptual domain** is 'a body of knowledge within our conceptual system that contains and organises related ideas and experiences' (Evans and Green 2006: 14). The creation and interpretation of metaphor involves the transfer or **conceptual mapping** of features from one domain to another. Consider the following, anonymously attributed lines:

(a) My love for you is a journey; starting at forever and ending at never.

This expression makes a comparison between the speaker's love and a journey, each of which functions as a domain within the conceptual metaphor: LOVE is the **target domain** – the idea being described by the metaphor; JOURNEY is the **source domain** – the concept being drawn upon in order to describe the target. To interpret the metaphor, correspondences between the two domains are identified and then the relevant features from the source LOVE are transferred or mapped onto the target JOURNEY. The latter half of the above expression guides interpretation by highlighting which features are relevant to the mapping: namely the notion that a journey has a start and end point, and is an experience with a duration through time. Interestingly, the expression also suggests how the target LOVE is *not* like its source through the use of negation ('never'): in contrast to a JOURNEY, the speaker's love is unending.

Like other knowledge structures in cognitive linguistics, domains are represented using small capitals. Conceptual metaphors are expressed as a capitalised sentence using a copula verb (IS, ARE) to connect the target in subject position with the source: [TARGET] IS/ARE [SOURCE]. Thus, the conceptual metaphor articulated in (a) is LOVE IS A JOURNEY. Target domains tend to be abstract concepts, such as LOVE or LIFE, whilst source domains are generally more concrete and often grounded in bodily and/or everyday experience, such as JOURNEY or CONTAINER.

Metaphor is often (wrongly) thought to be a special property of creative, poetic, and literary texts, but cognitive linguists have shown that metaphor is pervasive in everyday language and thought. Indeed, we commonly map from more basic, familiar domains in order to understand abstract or unfamiliar domains of knowledge. Furthermore, while the linguistic expression in (a) realises both the metaphor and the mappings quite explicitly using the copula (X IS Y), metaphor is not always expressed in language is such a visible manner. Look at the following colloquial expressions found in everyday language (from Lakoff and Johnson 1980: 44–5; see also Evans and Green 2006: 294):

(b) Look *how far* we've *come.*
(c) We're *at a crossroads.*
(d) We'll just have to *go our own separate ways.*
(e) We can't *turn back* now.
(f) I don't think this relationship is *going anywhere.*
(g) *Where* are we?
(h) We're *stuck.*
(i) It's been a *long, bumpy road.*
(j) This relationship is a *dead-end street.*
(k) Our marriage is *on the rocks.*

These expressions might not initially appear to be metaphorical. However, when used to describe a romantic relationship, they are all linguistic realisations of the same conceptual metaphor we saw in (a): LOVE IS A JOURNEY (Lakoff and Johnson 1980: 44–5). The italicised lexis all draw from the JOURNEY source as a means of comprehending the abstract target LOVE. Although these linguistic expressions do not name the source or target domains nor use copular constructions, on

Table 16.1 Conceptual mappings in LOVE IS A JOURNEY (Kövecses 2002: 6; Evans and Green 2006: 295)

Source: JOURNEY		Target: LOVE
the travellers	→	the lovers
the vehicle	→	the love relationship
the journey	→	events in the relationship
the distance covered	→	the progress made
obstacles encountered	→	difficulties experienced
decisions about which way to go	→	choices about what to do
the destination of the journey	→	the goal(s) of the relationship

a conceptual level their interpretation nevertheless involves mapping between the domains LOVE and JOURNEY.

Expressions (b)–(k) involve the mapping of a number of properties from the source onto properties in the target domain. For instance, the couple are cast in the role of travellers, the distance travelled is symbolic of the progress of the relationship, while the destination of the journey relates to the goals of the relationship. Such mappings, as shown in Table 16.1, help to comprehend the abstract target LOVE.

Because it appears regularly in everyday language, LOVE IS A JOURNEY can be considered to be a **conventional metaphor**, often used (in certain cultural contexts) to structure our understanding of LOVE. In such conventional metaphors, the mappings between domains are well established. The mapping process is also thought to be unidirectional (shown diagrammatically in Figure 16.1). This is because the physical, experiential basis of a source is used to explain an intangible target, but the process is not reciprocated. The source therefore remains unchanged. This unidirectionality is known as the **invariance hypothesis**.

This section has introduced conceptual metaphor. Sections 16.2

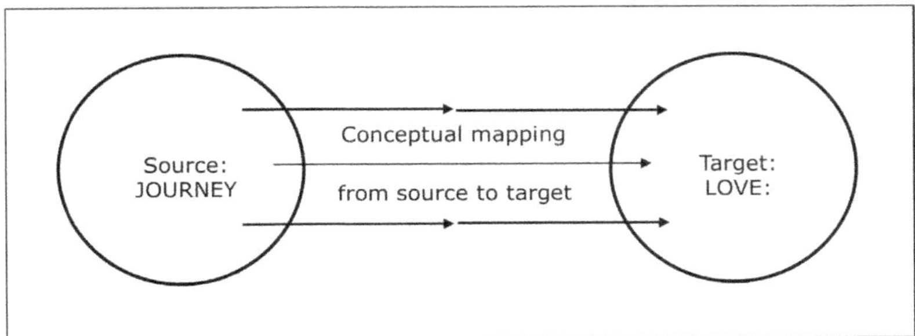

Figure 16.1 Unidirectional conceptual mapping in conceptual metaphor

and 16.3 offer further discussion of mapping and source domains, whilst section 16.4 introduces another model of metaphor: conceptual integration.

16.2 Conceptual metaphor and conceptual metonymy in literature

Processes of conceptual mapping underpin the comprehension of a number of literary devices which are referred to in traditional literary scholarship and rhetoric as 'figures of speech'. Table 16.2 shows four figures of speech: metaphor, simile, synecdoche, and metonymy. These four devices involve two models of conceptual mapping: conceptual metaphor and conceptual metonymy.

As discussed above, conceptual metaphor involves a mapping between two conceptual domains, a source and a target. In Shakespeare's lines in Table 16.2, the noun phrase 'The course of true love' creates a mapping between the source domain JOURNEY ('The course') and the target domain LOVE ('true love'): LOVE IS A JOURNEY. Likewise, the simile 'O my luve's like a red, red rose' (Burns 1953 [1794]) entails a mapping between LOVE and A PLANT, but makes the mapping explicit by using 'like'. The conceptual metaphor underlying this simile is LOVE IS A PLANT.

The figures of speech synecdoche and metonymy are also underwritten by conceptual mappings. However, whilst conceptual metaphor involves mapping between two distinct domains (source and target), in contrast both synecdoche and metonymy create mappings within a

Table 16.2 Metaphorical figures of speech

Figure of speech	Examples	Conceptual model
Metaphor	'The course of true love never did run smooth' (*A Midsummer Night's Dream* – William Shakespeare)	Conceptual Metaphor
Simile	'O my luve's like a red, red rose, That's newly sprung in June' ('A Red, Red Rose' – Robert Burns)	
Synecdoche	'My heart has made its mind up And I'm afraid it's you' ('Valentine' – Wendy Cope)	Conceptual Metonymy
Metonymy	'My true love hath my heart, and I have his' (Sir Philip Sidney)	

single conceptual domain. We can think of this as a sub-domain taking the role of source and its overarching domain acting as the target. This form of single-domain mapping is known as **conceptual metonymy** and it involves a *stands-for* relationship between the source and target. In **metonymy**, this relationship is one of association whilst **synecdoche** relies on a part–whole relationship between the source and its overarching target domain. In the example from Sidney's (1994 [1580]) poem, it is through association that HEART stands for emotions of love; thus, the conceptual metonymy is HEART FOR LOCUS OF EMOTION. In Cope's (1992) poem, the 'heart' is personified: by attributing decision-making to the heart, 'heart' – as part of the human body – is used to represent the whole person. Thus, in 'My heart has made its mind up', HEART stands for PERSON (HEART FOR PERSON). Like conceptual metaphors, conceptual metonyms are also presented in capitals but using 'FOR' to signal the *stands-for* relationship: [SOURCE] FOR [TARGET].

It can be useful to think about the expression of metaphors as a cline in terms of their visibility. **Visible metaphors** are realised linguistically (for instance, using 'is' or 'like'). **Invisible metaphors** – such as Shakespeare's noun phrase 'The course of true love' – require more creative, interpretive work from readers. Other forms of invisible metaphor include pre-modification, compounds, grammatical metaphor (e.g. personification), and allegory.

Lakoff and Turner (1989: 67–72) have argued that conventional metaphors are often used in novel, creative ways – particularly in literary contexts – through four central devices: elaboration, extension, combining, and questioning. **Elaboration** develops a conceptual metaphor by elaborating an existing property of the source in a novel way. For instance, when Shakespeare first wrote the line 'The course of true love never did run smooth', he elaborated LOVE IS A JOURNEY by suggesting a journey that was difficult (that is, not 'smooth').

Extension refers to a new linguistic expression of a conceptual metaphor that introduces a new conceptual element from the source domain. Consider the following lines from D. H. Lawrence's unfinished novel *Mr. Noon* (1985: 152), written sometime between 1920 and 1921 (at which point Lawrence abandoned it):

> The course of true love is said never to run true. But never did the course of any love run so jagged as that of Johanna and Mr Noon. The wonder is, it ever got there at all.

Lawrence intertextually cites Shakespeare's noun phrase 'The course of true love' and therefore also draws on LOVE IS A JOURNEY. Many of the properties typically associated with LOVE IS A JOURNEY are present.

For instance, the closing phrase 'it ever got there at all' uses the spatial adverb 'there' as reference to the destination of the journey which we understand metaphorically to be the successful achievement of the relationship. However, Lawrence alters the linguistic realisation of the metaphor, most notably by using a different adverb: 'run smooth' becomes 'run true'. In the second sentence, Lawrence extends LOVE IS A JOURNEY by introducing the troublesome nature of Johanna and Mr Noon's relationship. He does this by using 'jagged', an antonym of Shakespeare's original adverb 'smooth'. This 'antonymic replacement', Naciscione argues (2010: 87), 'creates associations of contrast: things differing from each other in compelling ways'. Thus, whilst Shakespeare originally used 'smooth' as a synonym of 'easy', Lawrence's antonymic play implies that the journey is not only the opposite of easy – difficult; it is also a route that is jagged, that is – not straight.

Combining is the process of combining more than one conceptual metaphor. Returning to *Mr. Noon,* Lawrence continues (1985: 152):

> And yet, perhaps, a jagged, twisty, water-fally, harassed stream is the most fascinating to follow. It has a thousand unexpected thrills and adventures in it.

Lawrence develops LOVE IS A JOURNEY by combining it with another conceptual metaphor, LOVE IS A FLOWING RIVER. Lawrence's repetition of the lexeme 'jagged' makes the combination clear.

Finally, **questioning** involves interrogating the accuracy, appropriateness, or use-value of a conceptual metaphor (an example of which is given in the next section).

16.3 Image-schema metaphors

Image-schemas are kinaesthetic knowledge structures, based on bodily experiences in space. They are called image-schemas because they are said to be 'imagistic', meaning that they are developed through our sensory experiences in the world from infancy. The 'image' in 'image-schema' thus refers to all the senses, not just the visual. Think about the prepositions in these three descriptions of morning activities (from Johnson 1987: 30–1):

(l) I get *out* of bed.
(m) I walk *into* the bathroom.
(n) I look *in* the mirror.

Locative expressions, such as prepositions, often reflect underlying image-schemas. Diagrams can be used to represent image-schemas

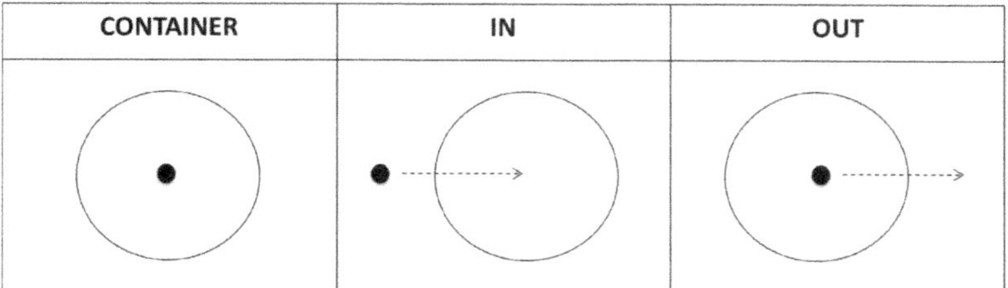

Figure 16.2 Image-schemas for IN, OUT, and CONTAINER

as shown in Figure 16.2. Prepositions such as 'in' and 'out' are reliant on our ICM of CONTAINER. We therefore have a basic CONTAINER image-schema. The container is represented in Figure 16.2 as a circle; it doesn't resemble any specific form of container (e.g. a cup) as this is a schematic representation. The container consists of three essential structural elements: interior, boundary, and exterior. The contained object is represented by the black dot inside the circle. As the diagrams show, IN and OUT are dynamic extensions of the CONTAINMENT image-schema which involve motion, as represented by the dashed arrows: *in to* or *out of* the container.

We often use prepositions such as 'in' and out' to express metaphorical meanings and when we do, we draw on image-schemas as source domains in metaphorical thought. For instance, consider the following three expressions:

(o) Alison wanted to get the most *out* of life.
(p) Let *out* your anger
(q) Sara is *in* love.

'Life', 'anger', and 'love' are all abstract emotions. Thus, in the three expressions, the prepositions use our image-schematic knowledge metaphorically. In (o) LIFE is the target of the conceptual metaphor LIFE IS A CONTAINER; in (p) emotions such as 'anger' appear to be held inside our bodies, thus the metaphor is THE BODY IS A CONTAINER; finally, in (q) LOVE IS A CONTAINER. In each case, the CONTAINER image-schema functions as source because, typical of source domains, image-schemas are based on bodily experience.

We have a great many image-schemas, some of which are shown in Table 16.3. Image-schema metaphors do not have to be realised using prepositions. For instance, THE BODY IS A CONTAINER can be expressed in phrases such as 'She felt *full* of life.' Similarly, an expression such as 'I'm feeling really *low*' is dependent on the spatial UP-DOWN image-schema. Here, it forms part of an **orientational metaphor**, which relies

Table 16.3 Partial list of image-schemas (from Evans and Green 2006: 190)

Experiential grounding	Related image-schemas
SPACE	UP-DOWN, FRONT-BACK, LEFT-RIGHT, NEAR-FAR
CONTAINMENT	CONTAINER, IN-OUT, SURFACE, FULL-EMPTY, CONTENT
LOCOMOTION	MOMENTUM, SOURCE-PATH-GOAL
BALANCE	AXIS-BALANCE, TWIN-PAN BALANCE, POINT BALANCE, EQUILIBRIUM
FORCE	COMPULSION, BLOCKAGE, COUNTERFORCE, DIVERSION, REMOVAL OF RESTRAINT, ENABLEMENT, ATTRACTION
UNITY/MULTIPLICITY	MERGING, COLLECTION, SPLITTING, ITERATION, PART-WHOLE, COUNT-MASS, LINK(AGE)
IDENTITY	MATCHING, SUPERIMPOSITION
EXISTENCE	REMOVAL, BOUNDED SPACE, CYCLE, OBJECT, PROCESS

on spatial orientation as source. 'I'm feeling really *low*' or 'I'm on a high' are underwritten by HAPPY IS UP/SAD IS DOWN.

Continuing to focus on the CONTAINER metaphor, we'll now turn to a literary example, Julia Copus' poem (2003) 'In Defence of Adultery'. The poem consists of twenty-four lines and begins:

1 We don't fall in love: it rises through us
2 the way that certain music does –

Using the familiar collocation 'fall in love', these opening words are underwritten by the image-schematic conceptual metaphor: LOVE IS A CONTAINER. However, because the phrase is negated using 'not' ('don't'), the poetic voice in fact questions the accuracy of the conceptual metaphor. In L1's second clause 'it rises through us', an alternative understanding of love – anaphorically referred to using 'it' – is offered by recasting it as a substance contained within the human body (THE BODY IS A CONTAINER). Moreover, the verb 'rising' suggests that if love is a substance, it takes liquid form. These opening lines therefore combine the conceptual metaphor THE BODY IS A CONTAINER with LOVE IS FLOWING LIQUID. In L2, the movement of 'love' in the body is redefined again by comparison to music, introducing another conceptual metaphor: LOVE IS MUSIC.

As the poem continues, it fluctuates between the conceptual metaphors LOVE IS A CONTAINER and THE BODY IS A CONTAINER. On the one hand, LOVE is a CONTAINER that 'part of us dips into' (L11); on the other,

LOVE is contained in our bodies again as a liquid substance that 'seeps / through our capillaries' (L13). As the poem reaches its end, the poetic voice refers to humans as the 'victims' of love, as 'mere vessels' (L15). Again, 'vessels' instantiates the image-schematic conceptual metaphor THE BODY IS A CONTAINER. The noun 'victims' has very different semantic associations though and, in combination with lexis in the poem relating to the human body, triggers another conceptual metaphor LOVE IS A DISEASE. The penultimate sentence of the poem features a visible metaphor 'love is an autocrat' (L21). An 'autocrat' is a tyrannical ruler with absolute power, and this one – love – must not be 'disobeyed' (L21). The opposition Copus has set up – between love as 'autocrat' and lovers as 'victims' – therefore entails a further conceptual metaphor: LOVE IS A BATTLE.

Despite being titled 'In Defence of Adultery', Copus' poem does not explicitly discuss adultery; rather, it explores the feeling of falling in love. It does this using a number of conceptual metaphors. First, it questions the conceptual metaphor LOVE IS A CONTAINER, then contrasts it with another CONTAINER metaphor, THE BODY IS A CONTAINER, in which LOVE becomes the contained substance (LOVE IS FLOWING LIQUID). The poem combines several conceptual metaphors of love: LOVE IS FLOWING LIQUID, LOVE IS MUSIC, LOVE IS A DISEASE, and LOVE IS A BATTLE. As these metaphors accumulate over the course of the poem, love is increasingly characterised not only as a powerful force but also as a negative or destructive enemy. The final, visible metaphor – 'love is an autocrat'– takes this even further by suggesting that love is unstoppable. If love is unstoppable, lovers are helpless; and herein is the connection to the poem's title, 'In Defence of Adultery'. Copus' poem addresses the guilt of committing adultery. The poetic voice, represented by the first-person plural 'we' and 'our', tries to reframe their actions and ease their conscience by conceiving of love not as something they entered (hence, the questioning of LOVE IS A CONTAINER) but as an unwinnable battle in which they are 'victims'.

16.4 Interanimation and conceptual integration

As noted in section 16.2, Conceptual Metaphor Theory hypothesises conceptual mapping as unidirectional from source to target (the invariance hypothesis). Thus, while the source impacts our understanding of the target, the source itself is unaffected. Expressions such as 'this relationship isn't going anywhere' therefore use the JOURNEY source domain to structure our understanding of LOVE, but our understanding of JOURNEY is not revised to necessarily include the development of a relationship. Although Conceptual Metaphor Theory works well for conventional metaphors like LOVE IS A JOURNEY, unconventional metaphors seem to involve more complex conceptual mapping. Consider the following phrase:

(r) The bullet was a dream.

The copulative construction signalled by the past-tense verb 'was' prompts a conceptual mapping between the two nouns and therefore also between the conceptual structures the nouns represent: BULLET and DREAM. It is less clear, though, which domain functions as source and which functions as target. Arguably, DREAM is the more abstract domain so it might be tempting to interpret it as the target. However, in our interpretation of this phrase, 'the bullet' takes on a dream-like quality (perhaps, for instance, 'the bullet' isn't real but has been dreamt). Furthermore, the inverse is also true: we cannot say that BULLET is the target because, in our interpretation, 'the dream' is a bad one – it is nightmarish – because of its association with BULLET. Rather than unidirectional conceptual mapping, conceptual properties appear to be mapped dual-directionally between both BULLET and DREAM. Stockwell (1999) has called this **interanimation**.

The unidirectional mapping in Conceptual Metaphor Theory does not therefore adequately account for the dynamic nature of interanimation in unconventional metaphors. **Conceptual Blending** or **Conceptual Integration Theory** developed from Conceptual Metaphor Theory and Mental Spaces Theory. It considers domains as **mental spaces**, conceptual 'packets' of knowledge, structured by ICMs (which we introduced in Chapter 14). These mental spaces are constructed online (or 'in the moment') as we think and talk and we draw upon them to infer meaning. Conceptual Integration Theory offers a different model of the way that we process metaphors and is a very flexible framework that can account for complex conceptual mappings between multiple domains.

A conceptual integration network involves at least four mental spaces, as shown in Figure 16.3. The **input spaces** are independent mental spaces. If we were interested in considering the integration network for the phrase 'this relationship isn't going anywhere', these input spaces would encapsulate LOVE and JOURNEY respectively; in 'the bullet was a dream', they would capture BULLET and DREAM. **Cross-space mapping** occurs between the input spaces, and this can be dual-directional. The input spaces are linked by a **generic space** containing information that the two input spaces have in common. The fourth space is the **blended space**. Properties from the input spaces are **projected** into the blended space from which the **emergent structure** develops; within the emer-

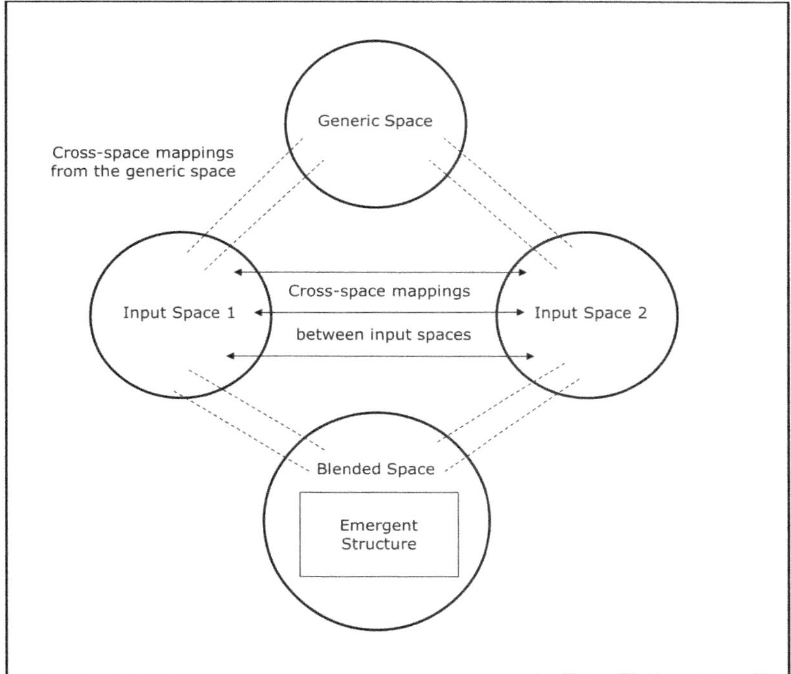

Figure 16.3 A conceptual integration network

gent structure are properties projected from the original input spaces as well as new meanings arising from the entire conceptual integration network.

In conceptual integration, a **single-scope network** accounts for conventional source-target metaphors where only one input space (source) is projected to structure the blend (e.g. LOVE IS A JOURNEY). In contrast, a novel or innovative metaphor, such as in 'the bullet was a dream', will involve a **double-scope network** in which, as Fauconnier and Turner (2002: 131) explain, both input spaces 'make central contributions to the blend, and their sharp differences offer the possibility of rich clashes. Far from blocking the construction of the network, such clashes offer challenges to the imagination; indeed, the resulting blends can be highly creative.' The conceptual mappings in the double-scope network for 'the bullet was a dream' account both for the conceptualisation of a blended DREAM-BULLET as well as for the way in which our interpretations of BULLET and DREAM change as a result of the blend.

The phrase 'the bullet was a dream' is, in fact, from the first line of Ross Gay's (2011: 17) poem 'The Lion and the Gazelle'. Here it is in the context of the poem's first four lines:

> Because the bullet was a dream before it was a bird.
> Because the bullet was a dream before
> it alighted in the child's body while he looked
> at a pigeon wobbling through the air.

As already discussed, 'the bullet was a dream' in L1 prompts us to run a blend with BULLET as one input space and DREAM as another. These input spaces clash; it is difficult to recognise shared properties and they are therefore input spaces in a double-scope network. Both input spaces are transformed: the bullet takes on a dream-like quality (is it real?) while the dream becomes dangerous, nightmarish. The life-threatening danger of the bullet and the irreality of dreams must therefore be salient properties projected from the input spaces into the blended space of the DREAM-BULLET.

The subordinate clause that begins with 'before' introduces a second copulative construction in which the blended DREAM-BULLET becomes 'a bird'. BIRD subsequently becomes a third input space. Although the shared properties between BIRD and DREAM aren't obvious, there are potential shared properties between BIRD and BULLET: the bullet's propulsion through the air and the bird's flight can be cross-mapped. We now have a blended DREAM-BULLET-BIRD. L2 is a repetition but doesn't include the reference to the 'bird'. When the relations between blended elements are tightened or loosened, it is called **compression** and **decompression**. The omission of the bird in L2 means that we decompress the second blend, **disintegrating** it in order to revisit our original DREAM-BULLET blend.

In L3, 'it' anaphorically refers back to the 'bullet' of L2 (now blended as DREAM-BULLET), and it enters 'the child's body'. Because of the nature of the DREAM-BULLET blend, it is unclear at this point whether a bullet has actually been shot into a child's body (perhaps this is occurring in a dream; perhaps it's children's make-believe). Furthermore, when we read about the 'pigeon' in L4, our interpretation is influenced by the resonance of the earlier DREAM-BULLET-BIRD blend: If the bullet is real, perhaps it went through the child and into the bird.

These questions remain unresolved though since the poem continues:

> Because the child has moved into photographs
> on mantles and the dreamer's hands
> are folded in his lap and have not felt

a dead child's face as the blood empties from it.
Because this is not a dream. [. . .]

In L5–6, the repositioning of the child as an image in 'photographs / on mantles' suggests that the child was shot and has died. The 'dreamer', however, is described as having 'not felt / a dead child's face as the blood empties from it'. Even though this situation is negated using 'not', its emotive force is strong in our interpretation and the naming strategy (e.g. 'the dreamer' rather than 'the man') implies that it is only in dreams (rather than reality) that the child is alive. This interpretation – of the child's death and the grieving man – is reinforced by 'this is not a dream' in L9. L9's assertion that 'this is not a dream' prompts a further decompression, this time of the original DREAM-BULLET blend. At this point in reading the poem, then, the bullet is reinterpreted as having been 'real' all along; the child is therefore dead. The properties of DREAM nevertheless remain meaningful in relation to the bullet: for the grieving 'dreamer', the bullet is dream-like, a nightmarish event that resulted in the child's death and which continues to haunt him.

The opening nine lines to Ross Gay's poem 'The Lion and the Gazelle' involve at least three mental spaces: DREAM, BULLET, and BIRD. These are used as inputs in double-scope conceptual integration networks. The conceptual relationships between these input spaces are complex, due to the rich semantic clashes between input spaces and to the dynamic process of reading whereby new information can compress or decompress blends. Interpreting 'The Lion and the Gazelle' immediately involves running DREAM and BULLET into a blend, then blending the emergent meaning of the DREAM-BULLET blend with the BIRD input space (L1). Subsequently in L2, the DREAM-BULLET-BIRD is decompressed and disintegrated (extracting BIRD). In the succeeding lines, the poem features lexis related to the three input spaces – BIRD: 'pigeon' (L4); DREAM: 'dreamer' (L6), 'dream' (L9); BULLET: 'dead' (L8), 'blood' (L8). These resonances mean that we develop an interpretation influenced by the various, accumulating input spaces and blends, even after a blend has been disintegrated.

Keywords and summary

Conceptual integration, conceptual mapping, conceptual metaphor, domains (source, target), idealised cognitive models, image-schema, interanimation, invariance, mental spaces (blended space, emergent structure, generic space, input space), metaphor, metonymy, simile, synecdoche.

Cognitive linguistics revolutionised the study of metaphor by establishing that metaphor is not just a rhetorical flourish; rather, metaphor is fundamental to the way we think. Conceptual metaphors involve mapping between a source and target domain, whilst conceptual metonymy involves a *stands-for* relation with conceptual mapping occurring between a sub-domain and its over-arching domain. Although conceptual metaphors can draw on any domains of knowledge, conventional metaphors – which reoccur regularly in our everyday language and interactions in the world – typically involve conceptual mapping from a concrete source to an abstract target. Source domains have an experiential basis because they draw on embodied experience. This is particularly the case when image-schemas are used as source domains. Conceptual Metaphor Theory is useful for considering conventional metaphors that involve two domains. However, many metaphors are more complex and integrate features from several domains. Conceptual Integration Theory is better suited for considering these instances of multi-domain mapping and the dynamic nature of metaphorical patterning across a text.

Like any cognitive approach that involves the identification of knowledge domains, one problem you might run into when identifying metaphors or blends in your own analyses is how to name conceptual domains. It is worth consulting existing work on metaphor and integration to get a sense of the domains that have already been identified and named.

Activities

1. Read the following phrases and consider what domains or mental spaces are involved in the process of conceptual mapping or projection:

    She could feel the anger building up inside her.
    The surgeon is a butcher.
    The commuters arrived in swarms.
    It's raining cats and dogs
    George Orwell's *Animal Farm.*
    Alcoholism sniggered at me.

    'Now the dream that used to turn in your sleep,
    sails into the year's coldest night.' ('Tomorrow' – Mark Strand (2014 [1970]))

    In each case, do you think conceptual metaphor or conceptual integration is the most useful in explaining your interpretations?

2. Read the following extract from Jeannette Winterson's (1992: 15) novel *Written on the Body*:

   It's flattering to believe that you and only you, the great lover, could have done this. That without you, the marriage, incomplete though it is, pathetic in many ways, would have thrived on its meagre diet and if not thrived at least not shrivelled. It has shrivelled, lies limp and unused, the shell of a marriage, its inhabitants both fled. People collect shells though don't they? They spend money on them and display them on their window ledges. Other people admire them. I've seen some very famous shells and blown into the hollows of many more. Where I've left cracking too severe to mend the owners have simply turned the bad part to the shade.

   What conceptual metaphors does the narrator use in her description of love and this relationship? If there is more than one, are they used in combination? Are any of the conceptual metaphors elaborated, extended, or questioned?
3. Read the opening lines from Simon Armitage's poem 'Meanwhile, Somewhere in the State of Colorado' (2001 [1999]: 153). How do you imagine this scene? Is conceptual integration at work? If so, what lexis triggers the blend and what properties are mapped? What is the emergent meaning?:

   Meanwhile, somewhere in the state of Colorado, armed to the teeth
   with thousands of flowers,
   two boys entered the front door of their own high school
   and for almost two hours
   gave floral tributes to fellow students and members of staff
   beginning with red roses
   strewn amongst unsuspecting pupils during their lunch hour,
   followed by posies
   of peace lilies and wild orchids. Most thought the whole show
   was one elaborate hoax
   using silk replicas of the real thing, plastic imitations,
   exquisite practical jokes,
   but the flowers were no more fake than you or I,
   and were handed out
   as compliments returned, favours repaid, in good faith,
   straight from the heart.

   Now that you've read the extract, it might also be useful for you to know that Armitage's poem was written in response to the 1999 Columbine High School massacre. Does this real-world knowledge affect your reception and experience of the poem? What impact does it have on your conceptual integration network?

Further reading and references

Conceptual Metaphor Theory was developed by: Lakoff and Johnson (1980), Johnson (1987), Lakoff (1987), Lakoff and Turner (1989), and Turner (1991). For subsequent discussions, see: Browse (2014, 2016a, 2016b), Crisp (2003), Gibbs (2008), Gibbs and Steen (1999), Goatly (1997), Kövecses (1988, 1990, 2002), Ortony (1993), Punter (2007), Steen (1994), Stockwell (2002a, 2004). The invariance hypothesis is interrogated by Stockwell (1999).

Mental spaces are defined by Fauconnier (1994 [1985]) and developed in Conceptual Blending/Conceptual Integration Theory by Fauconnier and Turner (2002). Dancygier (2006) is also an excellent introduction to Conceptual Integration Theory; for further accounts, see: Brandt (2004), Brandt and Brandt (2005), Coulson (2001), Coulson and Oakley (2000), and Grady et al. (1999). Contemporary stylistic applications of conceptual integration include: Canning (2008), Canovas and Jenson (2013), Crisp (2008), Dancygier (2005), Freeman (2005, 2006), Hamilton (2002), McAlister (2006), Semino (2006), Sweetser (2006b), Tobin (2006), and Turner (2006).

17 Text-worlds

17.1 Language, conceptualisation, and Text World Theory

As we have seen in Parts IV and V of this book, the production and comprehension of language involves processes of conceptualisation, including the creation of mental representations. Text World Theory is a cognitive linguistic framework which seeks to examine conceptualisation as it occurs in discourse. Imagine having a conversation with a friend and telling them about what you did the previous night. First, you'd have to remember what you did last night and represent it mentally, then somehow put this conceptualisation into words. Your friend has to use the linguistic cues you provide (along with other communicative modes, such as gesture and intonation) to build their own conceptualisation of what you are describing. Language is a system of symbols that provides prompts for the construction of these potentially rich, elaborate conceptualisations (Evans and Green 2006: 8). The conceptualisations, produced by both you and your friend, are also influenced by your understanding of the discourse context: the situation and purpose of the conversation, and the knowledge which you have of each other and the events being described. The mental activity involved in linguistic communication is indivisible from this wider discourse context. Because Text World Theory has an interest in both the linguistic cues which inform our conceptualisations and also their wider communicative context, it is often described as a 'holistic' framework.

In Text World Theory the mental representations produced during communication are referred to as 'worlds'. Every communicative event involves at least two levels of world. The **discourse-world** is the conceptualisation of the *context* of a particular interaction (the actual circumstances in which the discourse takes place). Discourse-worlds always involve two or more human **participants** in communication, and incorporate their spatio-temporal location, the objects and entities that surround them, and also the relevant personal and cultural knowledge they bring to the interaction.

Text-worlds are the conceptualisations that are evoked by the *language* that is used in the interaction. Sometimes, language is used to refer to elements of the discourse-world: for instance, if one participant points out something the other participant can see, such as: 'Look at that dog over there!' Very often, though, language is used to evoke remote situations (real or imaginary) that occur in different spatio-temporal locations: for instance, when one participant describes to another what they did last night, or might do later. Language provides cues for text-world creation.

The brief examples mentioned so far have referred to face-to-face conversation, which text-world theorists regard as the prototypical form of discourse. Text World Theory was designed for application to any form of spoken or written linguistic communication (the word 'text' in 'text-world' simply refers to 'the linguistic part of discourse'). The rest of the chapter will focus on Text World Theory's application to written, literary discourse.

17.2 Building and switching text-worlds

The human participants involved in written communication are an author and a reader. These participants typically occupy separate spatial and temporal locations. Dickens, for instance, wrote *Great Expectations* in the early 1860s but subsequent readers of his text have engaged with it at different moments in space and time (initially, it was published in weekly instalments, so it was read several weeks after he penned it; now, of course, centuries separate contemporary readers and Dickens). In written discourse, then, the discourse-world is typically **split** and the words of the written text form the main point of contact between participants. As a result, a literary reader's discourse-world is centrally comprised of the personal and cultural knowledge schemas which they use in order to comprehend the text (see Chapter 14 for more on schemas. Some text-world theorists refer to schemas as 'knowledge frames'). We all possess vast stores of personal and cultural knowledge, but only relevant aspects of this are **incremented** into the discourse-world in order to facilitate our comprehension and involvement in the discourse. The areas of knowledge and experience which are deemed relevant are dependent on the text; thus, they are **text-driven**. When reading *Great Expectations*, for instance, your knowledge of romantic relationships and blacksmithery is likely to be incremented in to the discourse-world, whilst your knowledge of how to use a mobile phone or your memories of the 2016 Olympics are unlikely to be needed.

In literary discourse, language tends to be used to create remote, often fictional, text-worlds in the minds of readers. These text-worlds are formed through the combination of linguistic cues in the text and a reader's inferences (drawn from their discourse-world knowledge). Below is the opening to Alifa Rifaat's short story 'An Incident in the Ghobashi Household' (1985: 86). As you read it, pay attention to the linguistic cues that help you to imagine the represented world, and the kind of knowledge you're drawing on to do so:

> Zeinat woke to the strident call of the red cockerel from the rooftop above where she was sleeping. The Ghobashi house stood on the outskirts of the village and in front of it the fields stretched out to the river and the railway track.
>
> The call of the red cockerel released answering calls from neighbouring rooftops. Then they were silenced by the voice of the muezzin from the lofty minaret among the mulberry trees calling: 'Prayer is better than sleep'.
>
> She stretched out her arm to the pile of children sleeping alongside her and tucked the end of the old rag-woven kilim round their bodies, then shook her eldest daughter's shoulder.

Text-worlds are created by two types of linguistic cues, known as world-builders and function-advancers. **World-builders** are cues that specify the building blocks of a text-world. They are typically deictic elements, indicating the time, location, entities, objects, and relationships being represented. The world-builders in this passage can be summarised thus:

- **time:** past tense, unspecified (can infer that it is morning due to entity's actions)
- **location:** unspecified (but inferrable from the entities/objects present)
- **entities:** Zeinat, her children, the red cockerel, the muezzin
- **objects:** rooftops, the Ghobashi house, surrounding landmarks such as the village, fields, river, railway track, minaret, and mulberry trees, the calls of the cockerels, the voice of the muezzin, and the characters' body parts (arm, shoulder) and possessions (kilim).

The passage is narrated in the past tense (e.g. 'woke', 'stood', 'stretched') and thus describes a scenario that exists at a temporal distance from the reader's discourse-world. The exact temporal location of the text-world is unspecified, but the passage clearly represents a span of time in the morning between Zeinat waking up and deciding to move. The spatial location is also not explicitly defined, but can be inferred from the world-building elements. The passage refers to a number of entities and objects (listed above) and also the relationships between them (e.g. the cockerel is on the rooftops above the characters' heads, the house is on the outskirts of the village in front of the fields, Zeinat is mother to the children). These world-builders activate fields of knowledge relevant to the text's interpretation. Readers' knowledge about cockerels, minarets, mornings, mother–daughter relationships, and so on is incremented into the discourse-world. Based on the presence of minarets and the muezzin call, readers may be able to infer that the text-world represents an Islamic country. The references to farmyard animals, villages, and natural landmarks (river, trees, etc.) also suggest a rural location.

Function-advancers are propositions which propel the narrative forward in some way, for instance by representing actions or providing description. Function-advancers are typically verb phrases indicating the activities or properties of the text-world entities and objects. Text World Theory imports descriptive terms from the study of transitivity (see Chapter 10) in order to specify different types of function-advancer. The passage above is dominated by material action processes (in which physical actions or events occur). Initially, the passage represents unintentional events performed by animate entities ('Zeinat woke'), or actions performed by inanimate objects which are personified (e.g. 'the house stood', 'the fields stretched'). Towards the end of the passage, human entities perform intentional actions ('She stretched . . . tucked . . . shook'). Material processes are represented in text-world notation using vertical arrows, as shown in Figure 17.1.

The cumulative effect of all these material action processes is the impression of a busy and active text-world representing an unfolding situation. First, the reader is provided with information about the setting of the world but towards the end of the passage, human action begins to take centre stage. These opening lines set out the normality of the day and establish the ground upon which narrative events involving the characters are set to figure.

Whilst the opening to 'An Incident in the Ghobashi Household' describes events occurring in the same location, it is also very common for discourses to create multiple switches between different locations in time and space (these were referred to as 'deictic shifts' in Chapter 13). Consider the opening lines from Hanif Kureshi's novel *Intimacy* (1998: 3; sentences numbered for analysis) below:

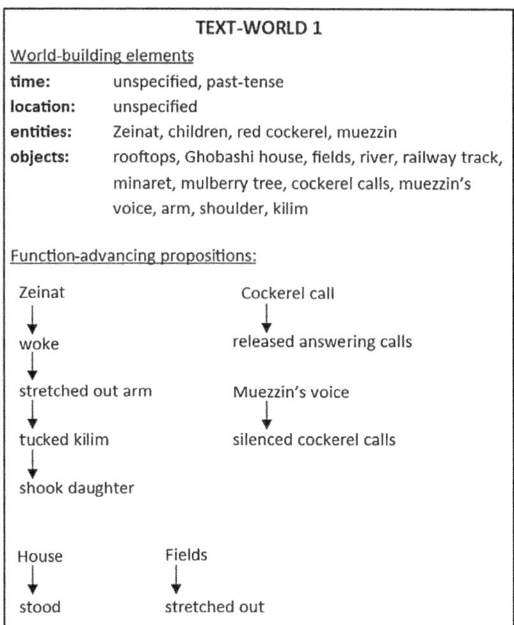

Figure 17.1 Text-world diagram representing the world-builders and function-advancers in the passage from 'An Incident in the Ghobashi Household' (Rifaat 1985). Vertical arrows represent material action processes

> (1) It is the saddest night, for I am leaving and not coming back. (2) Tomorrow morning, when the woman I have lived with for six years has gone to work on her bicycle, and our children have been taken to the park with their ball, I will pack some things into a suitcase, slip out of my house hoping that no one will see me, and take the tube to Victor's place. (3) There, for an unspecified period, I will sleep on the floor in the tiny room [. . .] next to the kitchen.

Even across these few opening sentences, the narrator represents multiple moments in time. The extract begins in the present tense with a first-person narrator describing their immediate situation: 'it is the saddest night', 'I am leaving' (S1). This immediate narrative situation forms Text-World 1. The world-building locative 'Tomorrow morning' in S2 indicates a temporal shift and therefore cues a **world-switch** to a new text-world, shown in Figure 17.2 as Text-World 2. Later in S2, the narrator fleshes out Text-World 2 with a series of actions he will perform tomorrow morning: 'I will pack . . . slip out . . . take the tube'.

S2 also creates a series of other world-switches because it represents events that have occurred or will occur *before* the narrator packs and takes the tube. These world-switches are indicated by the use of the present perfect tense: 'have lived', 'has left', 'have been taken' and the representation of distinct spatial locations. First, the narrator represents the actions of his wife in the morning, when she 'has gone to work on her bicycle'. The narrator's description of her as 'the woman I have lived with for six years' creates a brief flashback (indicated by the temporal locative 'for six years') which provides details about the couple's prior relationship. A third world-switch represents the actions of his children in the morning, when they 'have been taken to the park'. Finally, in S3 the narrator turns his attention to what will happen *after* he arrives at Victor's place. World-builders indicating a shift in temporal focus ('for an unspecified period') and spatial location ('There') cue a further world-switch representing this future scenario.

These six text-worlds are represented in the text-world diagram in Figure 17.2. Text-world diagrams can provide a useful way of visualising the basic elements involved in the text-worlds of a particular passage (they are not essential, though). Here, the diagram illustrates the multiple spatio-temporally distinct scenarios represented in the opening lines of *Intimacy*. Although these world-switches may look rather complex when diagrammed this way, our minds can cope effortlessly with the creation of multiple text-worlds, and do so all the time in everyday communication.

Figure 17.2 also nicely illustrates the presence of the narrator in the text-worlds. The reader is presented with multiple representations of the narrator: in the present (Text-World 1), the past (Text-World 5), and in the future (Text-Worlds 2 and 6). Text-world entities are called **enactors** rather than characters because this term better reflects the way that the same character can appear across multiple worlds. Rather than viewing the narrator simply as a stable character, a Text World Theory analysis demonstrates the distinct, multiple conceptualisations through which a character is represented.

17.3 Modal-worlds: Attitudes and ontology

As well as using language to evoke situations that occur in different spatio-temporal locations, we also use language to represent our *attitudes* to those situations. As discussed in Chapter 9, modality is one of the major systems involved in the communication of attitudes through language. Table 17.1 provides a summary of the main types of modality (see Chapter 9 for further discussion of modality).

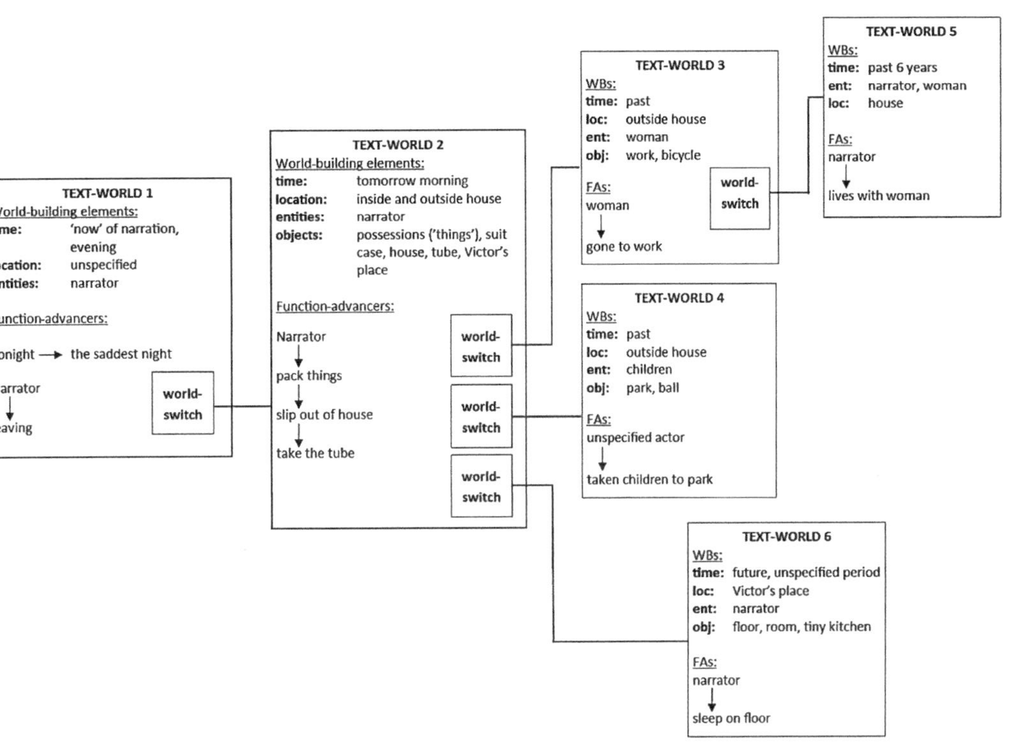

Figure 17.2 Text-world diagram showing multiple world-switches in the opening sentences of *Intimacy* (Kureshi 1998). Horizontal arrows indicate relational processes (e.g. of 'being' or 'having')

Table 17.1 A reminder of different types of modality (based on Simpson 1993)

Type of modality	Explanation	Examples of modal-world cues (not exhaustive!)
Boulomaic modality	The expression of degrees of desire	• hope, wish, regret, love, hate, like, dislike, etc.
Deontic modality	The expression of degrees of obligation	• should, must, may, it is necessary that, it is permitted/allowed/obliged/forbidden to, etc.
Epistemic modality	The expression of degrees of personal knowledge or belief	• could, may, might, must, shall, should, will, allegedly, perhaps, possibly, surely, clearly, obviously, etc. • the representation of hypothetical scenarios (e.g. 'If X, then Y') • uses of focalisation in narrative • representations of thought

Gavins explains that in order to understand instances of modality, discourse participants must 'conceptualise both the propositions being modalised and, separately, the speaker's attitude towards them' (2005: 13). Uses of modality therefore cue the construction of **modal-worlds** which represent scenarios that are separate from their originating text-world, either because they are unrealised or because they are being held up for comment by the speaker. Consider the different attitudes expressed by the first-person narrator in this extract from James Frey's novel-memoir *A Million Little Pieces* (2003: 119; sentences numbered for analysis), which is a fictionalised account of the author's experiences as a drug addict. During a meal at his rehabilitation centre, the narrator begins reflecting upon how his addiction has affected his family relationships:

> (1) We were a family, a happy Family, and we stayed that way until I stopped showing up. (2) It would be nice to have my Family here with me now. (3) It would be nice [. . .] to have a final dinner with them. (4) Though I doubt we would talk much, it would be nice to look each of them in the eye and say goodbye to them. (5) Though I doubt we would talk much, it would be nice to hold each of their hands, tell them that I'm sorry, that me being who I am wasn't their fault. (6) Though I doubt we would talk much, I would like to tell them to forget me.

This extract is underpinned by a text-world located in the present moment of the narration (speaker-now), in which the narrator is seated at a table in the rehabilitation centre refectory, eating a meal.

This text-world is only referenced briefly in the extract shown above, with the temporal locative 'now' (S2), but it has been established by the previous narrative.

When the narrator describes his family in S1 of the extract, it cues a world-switch to a text-world located in the past (signalled by past simple verb tense: 'were', 'stopped'), which contains an enactor of the narrator and his family. In the following sentences, the narrator goes on to express various desires and expectations regarding his family. In doing so, he represents a number of scenarios that are hypothetical and unrealised at text-world level (i.e. they do not actually happen). The representations of these scenarios are modalised in order to reflect the narrator's attitudes towards them. The narrator uses boulomaic modality evident in the expressions 'it would be nice' and 'I would like' in order to represent his desires. He also uses epistemic modality when he represents his beliefs about how the interaction would play out: 'I doubt we would talk much'. These uses of modality cue both boulomaic and epistemic modal-worlds that represent imagined scenarios. Through repetition of the modal phrases 'I doubt' and 'It would be nice', the narrator toggles back and forth between these modal-worlds. Each time the narrator switches to the boulomaic modal-world, he fleshes it out with more world-building and function-advancing information about his wishful interactions with his family. The epistemic modal-world is less elaborately developed, and this reinforces the contrast between his idealistic and more realistic assessments of what would happen if his family were really there. The text-worlds and modal-worlds created by this extract are represented in Figure 17.3.

Text World Theory provides insights into the ontological status of the different worlds that make up a discourse. **Ontology** is a philosophical term used to describe the study of being and existence. Participants in communication at the discourse-world level (even if it is split) are real people, belonging to the real world (e.g. authors, readers, speakers, hearers). Enactors at the text-world level belong to a different domain of existence: they exist in the minds of participants, and can be fictional. Because Text World Theory is fundamentally a spatial model of mental representation, the ontological relationships between worlds are discussed in terms of proximity (closeness/remoteness). When text-world enactors create world-switches or modal-worlds in their narration, those worlds belong to an even more remote domain of existence. For instance, in the extract from Frey (2003: 119), the text-world representing the immediate moment of the narration feels conceptually 'closer' to the reader, whereas the modal-worlds representing the hypothetical and unrealised contents of the narrator's imagination feel conceptually

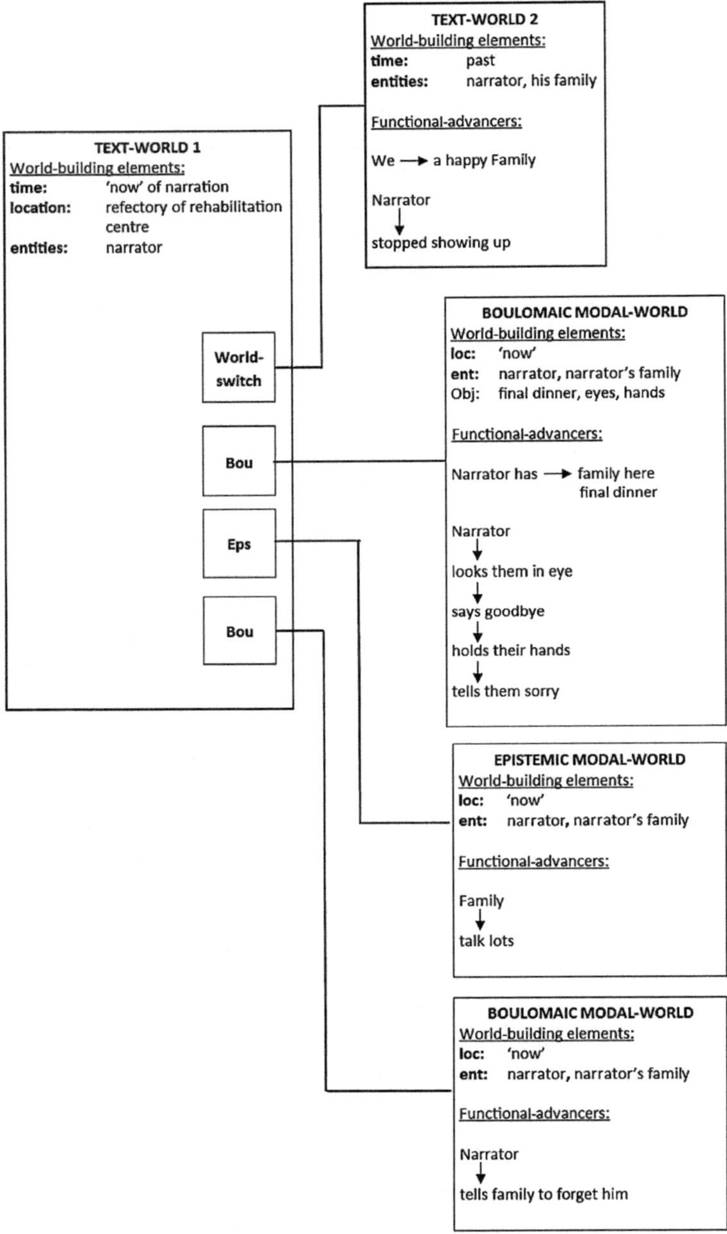

Figure 17.3 Text-worlds and modal-worlds in an extract from *A Million Little Pieces* (Frey 2003)

'further away'. These ontological properties of discourse are often used to great effect in literary writing, as demonstrated by the poem discussed in the next section.

17.4 Play with worlds

Readers are, generally, motivated to construct coherent text-worlds which possess some internal logic. Following the principle of minimal departure (introduced in Chapter 14), readers tend to assume that text-worlds function in the same way as the real world, unless they are notified otherwise. Some literary works create text-worlds which are designed to resemble the materiality of the real world, but others play with ontology and the interpretative tendencies that underpin text-world construction in order to create different effects. The poem 'Hypothetical' by Maria Taylor (2014: 45–6) plays with multiple representations of hypotheticality in order to capture something of the wildness of human imagination, with humorous results:

Hypothetical

A friend of mine asked me if I'd sleep with Daniel Craig,
would I make love to him or kick him out of bed?
Before I have time to answer, I'm in bed with Daniel Craig.
He's stirring out of sleep, smelling of Tobacco Vanille,
he flatters my performance, asks if I'd like coffee.
'Hang on,' I say, 'I did not sleep with you, Daniel Craig,
this is just a conversational frolic.' My friend stands
in the corner of my bedroom, 'You've gone too far,' she says.
I'm pulling the duvet away from his Hollywood body
at exactly the moment my husband enters the room.
I say, 'Yes, this is exactly what it looks like, darling,
but it's hypothetical, a mere conversational frolic.'
He's threatening me. There are lawyers in the room.
My children begin to cry. I don't even like Daniel Craig.

It's too late. The sheets are full of secreted evidence.
There are forensics in the room, covering my body
in blue powder, checking my skin for finger prints:
they match Daniel Craig's. He doesn't even know
he's slept with me. My marriage is a dead gull.
My neighbours come into the room shaking heads
oh dear oh dear oh dear. My husband has drawn lists
of all the things he wants to keep: a plasma screen,
an Xbox, a collection of muesli-coloured pebbles

from our holidays in Truro, 'When you loved me!'
he snaps. My children will see a therapist after school.
Daniel Craig is naked in a hypothetical sense,
telling me we can make this work. My friend smirks
behind a celebrity magazine featuring lurid details
of our affair. There are photos. We are on a beach
in the Dominican Republic, healthy and tanned
both kicking sand at a playful Joan Collins.
'I don't even like Daniel Craig,' I tell the ceiling.

The poem begins with an unidentified poetic voice creating a text-world located in the past ('asked'). This text-world contains an enactor of the poetic voice and her friend in conversation. The poetic voice's report of her friend's speech creates a series of fleeting epistemic modal-worlds representing unrealised hypothetical scenarios ('if I'd', 'would I') from which the poetic voice is asked to choose. The scenarios relate to whether the poetic voice would engage in sexual relations with the Hollywood actor Daniel Craig (most famous for playing James Bond) if she were given the chance.

The subordinate clause in L3, 'Before I have time to answer', suggests that the conversational situation evoked at the beginning of the poem remains ongoing, though the shift to present tense cues a new text-world with greater proximity to the reader. However, instead of continuing to describe the conversation, the main clause includes some unexpected world-building elements: 'I am in bed with Daniel Craig'. World-builders from the hypothetical worlds evoked in L1–2 are suddenly represented as part of this new text-world, creating an unexpected blurring of the ontological boundary between realised and unrealised situations in the text. In order to process the logical inconsistency this introduces, readers are likely to assume that rather than representing the conversation between friends, the text has shifted, now representing the fantasies of the poetic voice as she decides how to respond.

The use of progressive tense in L4 ('He's stirring') cues a world-switch with even greater temporal proximity to the reader, as interactions between the poetic voice and Daniel Craig are represented as unfolding as we read. This draws us into the fantasy being created by the poetic voice. Even though it is declared to be 'just a conversational frolic' (L7), this text-world – located in the poetic voice's bedroom – is fleshed out across the rest of the poem with the addition of further world-building and function-advancing information, which becomes increasingly serious! First, her friend appears within the room (L7), then her husband (L10), then lawyers (L13), her crying children (L14), forensics (L16), and her neighbours (L20). Some of the humour in the poem is created by the insertion of these domestic and legal enactors into this fantasy. Despite the poetic voice's assertion that the situation is 'hypothetical', other text-world entities respond as though it were not, with anger, disapproval, and upset.

The second stanza involves some further world-switching, although it repeatedly toggles back to the unfolding situation in the bedroom. The use of the present perfect 'has drawn' (L21) cues a temporal world-switch containing her husband itemising the possessions he wants to keep during their divorce. The use of 'will' (L25) cues a brief world-switch to the future and the treatment her children will receive in order to deal with their parents' split. These text-worlds represent the ramifications of the situation beyond the immediate bedroom scene.

The lines 'He [Daniel Craig] doesn't even know / he's slept with me' (L18–19) are particularly interesting, as they cue a text-world containing a different enactor of Daniel Craig. This version of Daniel Craig is oblivious to his sexual relationship with the poetic voice, and stands in direct contrast to the Daniel Craig who 'flatter[ed] [her] performance' in an earlier text-world. This Daniel Craig exists at a different ontological level, presumably closer to the real world. Meanwhile, the Daniel Craig in the bedroom remains 'naked in a hypothetical sense' (L26), and his relationship with the poetic voice has upgraded to an all-out 'affair' (L29). The images from a celebrity magazine which show the poetic voice and Daniel Craig 'on a beach / in the Dominican Republic' (L29–30) cue a spatial world-switch – rather than representing Daniel Craig in the poetic voice's family home, the poetic voice is inserted in to Daniel Craig's glamorous A-list lifestyle.

L32 cues a final spatio-temporal world-switch, featuring the poetic voice addressing the ceiling. The initial text-world, featuring the poetic voice in conversation with her friend, is never returned to. This is evocative of the disorientation that might be experienced when you emerge from an elaborate daydream. Overall, the poem creates a number of text-worlds and modal-worlds that reflect the inherently compelling and contradictory nature of fantasy and imagination. The poetic voice tells her husband and Daniel Craig that the modal-worlds they inhabit reflect a 'mere conversational frolic' (L7), whilst at the same time these worlds become richly detailed scenarios. It is this contrast – between the hypotheticality of the text-worlds on the one hand and their meticulous realisation on the other – that creates the humour of this poem.

Keywords and summary

Discourse-world, enactors, function-advancers/function-advancing elements, incremented, modal-world, ontology, participants, split discourse-world, text-driven, text-world, Text World Theory, world-building elements/world-builders, world-switch.

Text World Theory provides a framework for the analysis of both the content and context of discourse. Discourse context is represented by the discourse-world, which consists of real human participants in communication, and the relevant knowledge they draw upon to comprehend the discourse. Discourse content is represented by text-worlds, which are mental representations created within the participants' minds. Text-worlds occur through time and space, and are populated by entities called enactors. It is common for discourses to create multiple text-worlds. Shifts in time and space cue world-switches to new text-worlds. Expressions of attitude using modality cue modal-worlds, which are held at a greater conceptual distance from the discourse-world. Text World Theory incorporates and combines elements of some of the other stylistic approaches we have considered so far, including cognitive deixis, schema theory, modality, and transitivity. It also provides useful underpinning to other areas of research in stylistics: Chapter 18 discusses the use of negation from a Text World Theory perspective, and Chapter 20 draws on Text World Theory to discuss readers' emotional experiences.

Activities

1. Consider this extract from the opening of David Lodge's novel *Changing Places* (1993 [1975]), which creates a number of text-worlds and modal-worlds. What are the world-building elements? Can you identify any world-switches? Can you spot any instances of modality which cue modal-worlds? Once you have identified some text-worlds and modal-worlds, consider the function-advancing elements, which represent the actions or events within them. What do the text-worlds of this passage suggest about the narrator?:

    High, high above the North Pole, on the first day of 1969, two professors of English Literature approached each other at a combined velocity of 1200 miles per hour. They were protected from the thin, cold air by the pressurised cabins of two Boeing 707s, and from the risk of collision by the prudent arrangement of the international air corridors. Although they had never met, the two men were known to each other by name. They

> were, in fact, in process of exchanging posts for the next six months, and in an age of more leisurely transportation the intersection of their respective routes might have been marked by some interesting human gesture: had they waved, for example, from the decks of two ocean liners crossing in the mid-Atlantic, each man simultaneously focusing a telescope, by chance, on the other, with his free hand; or, more plausibly, a little mime of mutual appraisal might have been played our through the windows of two railway compartments halted side by side at the same station somewhere in Hampshire or the Mid-West, the more self-conscious part relieved to feel himself, at last, moving off, only to discover that it is the other man's train that is moving first.

If you feel it will help, you could try to diagram the text-worlds that you identify (diagramming is not a compulsory part of text-world analysis, but is useful to work out and/or illustrate small sections of an analysis).

2. Consider the discourse-world level of your own reading of the poem 'Hypothetical' by Maria Taylor (2014). What kinds of personal and cultural knowledge do you increment into your discourse-world? What elements in the text evoke this knowledge? What inferences did you make in order to comprehend the poem? How does this knowledge influence your reaction to the poem or your interpretation of its meaning?
3. Find a text that plays with fictionality or ontology in some way. Can Text World Theory help you to explain how it creates its effects?

Further reading and references

For a comprehensive introduction to Text World Theory, see Gavins (2006, 2007). Text World Theory was pioneered in the late 1990s by Paul Werth (e.g. 1995a, 1995b, 1997a, 1997b, 1999). Note that older accounts of Text World Theory in Werth (1999) and Stockwell (2002a) refer to world-switches and modal-worlds as 'sub-worlds', but that following Gavins (2005, 2007) this terminology has been adjusted. Examples of Text World Theory analyses include: Gavins (2000, 2003, 2006, 2007, 2010), Gavins and Lahey (2016), Lahey (2003, 2004, 2006, 2014), and Stockwell (2009a). Lugea (2013) applies Text World Theory to film; Cruikshank and Lahey (2010) and Gibbons (2014a, 2016a) to theatre and performance; and Gibbons (2012a) to multimodal discourse.

18 Negation and lacuna

18.1 Negation

As a linguistic variable, negation is usually understood in contrast to affirmative constructions. As such, it is sometimes referred to as negative polarity (in contrast to positive polarity). For instance, the copula verb *to be* can be seen in positive and negative forms: *is*/*isn't*. The negative case is said to be marked because extra linguistic matter is required to bring about the negation. In the case of *is*, the contraction *n't* is added. Negation can occur on a number of linguistic levels, which can be broadly grouped into three central categories: syntactic, morphological, and semantic.

Syntactic negation is principally realised by the negative particle *not* and its contracted form *n't*. These are seen as prototypical forms of negation (Jeffries and McIntyre 2010: 94). (We classify *n't* as a form of syntactic negation here because it is a clitic. This means that although it is a morpheme, it possesses syntactic characteristics – so *n't* fulfils the same grammatical function as *not* – but in this contracted form it is morphologically and phonologically bound to another lexeme, *is*.) This type of syntactic negation most often modifies verbs or verb phrases. For example, Jane Rule's novel *This Is Not for You* features syntactic negation in its title and in the opening sentence: 'This is not a letter' (1970: 1). In both, 'not' negates the primary auxiliary 'is' to declare that the novel is neither 'a letter' nor intended for the second-person recipient. Later, the narrator says, 'You don't need to be called anything by me because I don't intend to call you' (Rule 1970: 2). Here, negations occur in the verb phrases 'don't need' and 'don't intend', attaching 'n't' to the dummy auxiliary 'do' to negate it along with the main lexical verbs 'need' and 'intend'.

Another form of syntactic negation occurs through the adjectival use of *no* to pre-modify nouns or noun phrases. For instance, in his fictional memoir, Dave Eggers struggles to make sense of the tragedies of his life, writing: 'There is no logic to that' (2000: 236). Other explicitly negative words are also forms of syntactic negation. These include nouns (*none*, *nothing*, *naught*, *nowhere*), pronouns (*nobody*, *no one*), adverbs (*never*), and conjunctions (*nor*). Although these negative words can be grouped according to lexical categories, they are examples of syntactic negation because they are linguistically derived from *not* and *no*. In the case of nouns and pronouns, they also fulfil functional syntactic roles in the context of a clause, such as subjects and objects.

Morphological negation occurs at the lexical level, whereby negative morphemes affix to other morphemes or words; for instance, negative prefixes such as *un-*, *in-*, *dis-*, *de-*, or a negative suffix like *-less*. If we think of these negative affixes as typical, Nahajec (2012: 129) claims that there are also peripheral examples, such as *anti-* and *counter-*. In Chapter 4, we discussed e. e. cummings' use of morphological deviation, in which he used the negative affixes *un-* ('unlove') and *-less* ('heavenless') (see section 4.2). Another example is the title to Michel Faber's (2016) poetry collection *Undying* which adds the negative prefix 'un-' to the continuous verb 'dying'. The collection functions as an elegy to Faber's wife who died after suffering from cancer for six years. Thus, the deviant morphological negation is representative of the way in which the poems keep the memory of Faber's wife and Faber's love for her alive.

The final category of negation is **semantic negation**, which focuses on words that are negative in meaning. Givón (1979: 133) refers to this category as 'inherent negation'. However, since meaning is not inherent to a word but rather an act of interpretation in context, semantic negation is a more accurate label. Semantic negation can manifest across lexical classes. Thus, we can identify semantically negative nouns (*absence*, *error*, *death*, *hole*), verbs (*fail*, *forget*, *miss*, *remove*), adjectives (*empty*, *lost*, *scarce*), and adverbs (*almost*, *nearly*). The examples given here are representative rather than exhaustive. Because semantic negation is largely interpretive, Nahajec (2012: 128) argues that it should be understood as 'open ended' in contrast to syntactic and morphological negators, which are 'a closed category'. Susanna Moore's novel *In the Cut* opens with the following two sentences: 'I don't usually go to a bar with one of my students. It is almost always a mistake' (1995: 3). Both sentences feature negation: the first contains syntactic negation in the verb phrase 'do<u>n't</u> usually go' while the second includes semantic negation in the noun 'mistake'. Together, the negations create a sense of uneasiness: they raise questions about the outcome of the opening scene of the novel, in which the female narrator *does* go to a bar with her student, encouraging us to read on.

This section has introduced the linguistic forms of negation and, in discussing brief examples of their use, we have begun to suggest how negation creates certain literary effects. The next section discusses these effects in more detail, using concepts from cognitive stylistics.

18.2 Negation and cognition

In cognitive terms, negation is recognised as a foregrounding device that makes certain aspects of a text more prominent (see Chapters 2 and 12). George Lakoff makes the foregrounding capacity of negation clear in the title to his (2004) analysis of American politics, *Don't Think of an Elephant*. Now, when you read that, did you think of an elephant? It's hard not to, because the negated instruction 'Do<u>n't</u> think' serves to foreground the very object it negates: 'an elephant'.

The following extract, from the opening of Rick Moody's (2003: 267) short story 'Circulation', illustrates the foregrounding capacity of negation in a literary context. As you read it, think about which images or narrative details become prominent:

> Bern Lewis, divorce lawyer, opened the file folder before him and removed the offending paper clip from a portion of the materials relating to Westman v. Westman. He pursed his lips thoughtfully as he dropped it, dropped the paper clip – it inappropriately bound together pages of two separate documents – carelessly onto the surface of his rolltop desk. [. . .] He was rushing to get the last details in order.
>
> This story however does not concern Bern whose successful practice is its own reward. It does not concern his convertible Alfa Romeo nor his house in East Hampton nor his daughter (at the Spence School) nor his wife – the first Jewish person to be admitted to the Junior League of Westport. Nor, in fact, does this story concern the Westmans themselves and their divorce or recent unscientific theories (no control group in the landmark study) of developmental problems in young adults who have suffered through the agonies of a broken home. No, this story is about something else entirely. It's about the paper clip.

There is a cluster of syntactic negation in the second paragraph: 'not' occurs twice followed by four iterations of the negative conjunction 'nor'. Pre-modifying 'no' is also present in the phrase 'no control group' while 'unscientific' contains the morphologically negative prefix 'un-'. These negations foreground the things they negate: the character Bern Lewis, his Alfa Romeo, house, daughter, and wife, as well as the Westmans who feature in the divorce case. Although the negation insistently informs readers that these enactors and objects are not central to the story, it nevertheless forces readers to imagine them. Thus, while the paper clip is mentioned in the first paragraph, it therefore becomes neglected in terms of readers' attention in the second. This serves to add import to the final sentence of the extract which reactivates the paper clip as a figural attractor. Indeed, the positive assertion 'It's about the paper clip' insists that it is the paper clip itself that is most important to the story.

There is scientific support for the foregrounding capacity of negation: psycholinguistic experiments show that it takes longer to process negative assertions (see Clark and Clark 1977: 108, 110). This evidence suggests that processing negation involves a conceptual journey whereby the supposition must first be conceived as positive polarity (e.g. *Think of an elephant*) before being converted into negative polarity – in other words, before being cancelled out (e.g. *Don't think of an elephant*). Sweetser (2006a: 315) explains the foregrounding process of negation in relation to mental spaces (discussed in Chapter 16 as well as in Chapter 17 on Text World Theory):

> negatives evoke a more complex mental space structure than corresponding positive forms: the positive forms regularly evoke one mental space fewer than the negatives. Interestingly, this hypothesis is consistent with another robust finding, namely that negatives take longer to process than equivalent positives, which suggests greater cognitive complexity in negatives.

In other words, a negative assertion triggers at least two mental spaces, one in which the positive counterpart is realised and one in which that positive assertion is negated. In Text World Theory (see Chapter 17), the positive counterpart is imagined by readers in a **negative text-world**. For instance, the negative assertion 'The doors are not bolted' prompts readers to first imagine the corresponding affirmative 'The doors *are* bolted' in a negative text-world before translating it into an *unbolted* door in the positive text-world from which the negation originates. The conceptual route that is modelled by Text World Theory represents the way in which negation is cognitively processed and is shown in Figure 18.1.

The negative text-world is plotted in Figure 18.1 using dashed lines, which represent the liminal status of the negated assertion. That is, the bolted doors imagined in the negative text-world are unrealised in terms of actual linguistic content. The Text World Theory view of negation therefore accounts for its foregrounding capacity as well as the way in which negatives consequently influence readers' imaginative construction of a text and their developing interpretations.

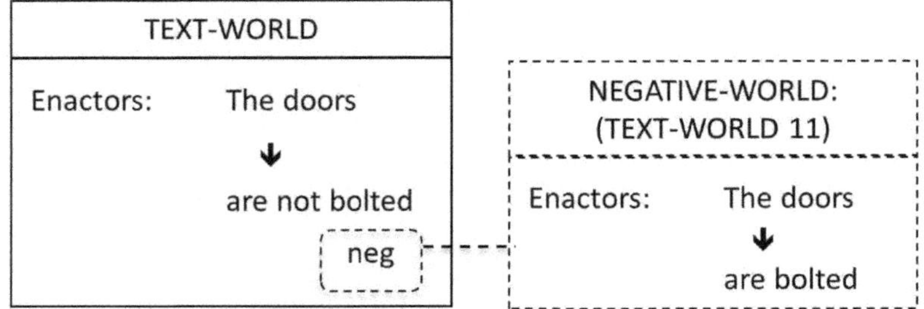

Figure 18.1 Text-world diagram, cognising negation in 'The doors are not bolted'

18.3 Negation and attention

The foregrounding effect of negation is also discussed in Stockwell's (2009a, 2009b) work on figure and ground. He applies research about human visual perception to literature in order to track the shifts of attention involved in reading. In Chapter 12, we explained that figures are the attentional focus, whilst the ground functions like a backdrop that is perceptually neglected. In human perception, good figures are self-contained objects with form or shape and well-defined edges that stand out from the ground. They are gestalt shapes that are perceived and thus cognised as a holistic form (whether they are indeed singular – e.g. a person – or a collection of shapes seen to be connected – e.g. a crowd). Stockwell (2009a) points out that sometimes, however, figures can be nothing but edges. Our attention can be directed at something that ostensibly *isn't* there, as well as something that is. For instance, concepts like 'dent', 'hole', 'fissure', or 'valley' 'can be the focus of attention but they are defined by being *not* something which is in their immediate vicinity' (Stockwell 2009a: 31–2; original emphasis). Stockwell argues that, in literary reading, such absent figures, such as a 'hollow, a shadow, a large crack in the wall', might be perceived as figural *lacunae* (2009a: 32). A lacuna is a gap or an empty space.

Stockwell's model allows us to analyse figures that have negative qualities yet are experienced by readers as a 'felt absence' (Stockwell 2009a: 42). For instance, read the following extract from Joe Meno's (2006: 97) *The Boy Detective Fails*:

> It is then that Billy realizes he is lost. He is lost and now he has no clear sense of where the strange man might be hiding in the darkness around him.
>
> Billy begins to turn, and as he does, he stares directly into the face of the man who is missing his head: There are no features, no eyes nor nose

nor mouth nor any kind of face, only a ghostly blank space from which a hideous voice escapes.

"Why are you following me?" the ghoul asks angrily.

There is negation at the start of the extract, with Billy being described twice as 'lost' (semantic) and having 'no clear sense' (syntactic). There is also, though, a lacuna. What was your experience of the noun phrase 'the face of the man who is missing his head'? It is a strange expression, and hard to imagine because it seems illogical. The post-modifying relative clause 'who is missing his head', which uses the semantic negation of the verb 'missing', is the cause of this. It is a logical impossibility for Billy to look into the face of a man with no head, but this impossible scenario is reinforced by the use of pre-modifying adjectival 'no' and the negative conjunction 'nor' to list all the facial features that Billy cannot see: 'no features, no eyes nor nose nor mouth nor any kind of face'. Instead, there is 'only a ghostly blank space'. Readers must therefore interpret this 'blank space' in place of the villain's face and head as a lacuna. Thus, when reading this passage, the villain's head is experienced precisely as a felt absence: Billy is looking into the space where a face would be if the man did indeed have a head.

This short analysis of lacuna in *The Boy Detective Fails* demonstrates how lacunae function in terms of the experiential dimension of reading. Stockwell's notion of lacuna is in keeping with other cognitive stylistic work that suggests that negation creates multiple mental spaces, in which both positive and negative polarities are conceptualised. The analysis also shows that lacunae, like all negations, are foregrounding devices.

18.4 Negation in poetry

Throughout this chapter, we've offered short examples of the types of negation under discussion. In this section, we analyse the effect of negation in a complete text. As you read the poem below by Julia Copus (2012), highlight any negations you notice:

This Is the Poem in which I Have Not Left You

This is the poem in which I have not left you.
The doors of the Green Dragon are not bolted
behind our backs; the pink-faced landlady
(may she be blessed) has not abandoned us
to the unseasonable cold, that March
evening of your thirty-seventh year.

In the gloom that hangs over South Street, in the quiet
made of the humming of streetlights and the moon,
the horn from a distant freight train does not sound;
I do not turn – my tongue is tied, my hands –
whatever there is left to say is left unsaid.
And since I dare not speak, nothing transpires:
the street, in the moments after, does not shrink
to the slam of a door, the flare of an engine, you
suddenly elsewhere, you imagined, gone,
but seen, still seen (the night stretching between us),
cursing the fog on the Blackdowns, curving, finally,
into the narrow driveway of the cottage.

Our cottage, I meant to say, with its yellow walls,
its broken gate – I might have forgotten those,
and the fields and the light, were it not for the fact
that this is the poem in which we do not part,
but lie like lovers, one of whom is sleeping,
my head, as always, nearest the leaky window
through which the old sounds reach me – rain in the trees,
a gust of wind, a tipper truck, a siren
threading its way through the dark (but you'll not wake;
your ears are shut, you won't admit a thing).
Then further off, after the rain is done,
the voice of the redstart calling *do it, do it!*
calling from the smallest tree in the garden.

The title and first line of the poem feature the negated clause 'I have not left you'. Because of the foregrounding capacity of negation, the syntactic negator 'not' suggests that the poem presents a counterfactual scenario. Consequently, this also suggests that there exists a present reality in which the poetic voice *has* left the 'you' to whom the poem is addressed. As such, from the start readers are likely to interpret this poem as being about a relationship or, more specifically, a break-up. In this analysis, we show that the poem's negations initiate multiple text-worlds: a series of negative text-worlds representing the break-up (e.g. *I have left you*) and also a series of positive text-worlds in which the negations of the text imagine that the couple are still together (*I have not left you*).

The interpretation of the poem as a break-up is reinforced by the specific spatial and temporal references throughout the first stanza: 'the Green Dragon' (L2), 'that March / evening' (L5–6), 'South Street' (L7), 'the Blackdowns' (L17), 'the cottage' (L18). While the specificity of these references places the negated events of the first stanza in the South West of England on an evening in March, they also suggest that the poetic voice is recalling a particular memory. Thus, negation is a way to reimagine the past and rescind the break-up itself. The second sentence of the poem, which spans L2–6, includes four negations: two instances of syntactic 'not' (L2 and L4), semantic negation in the verb 'abandoned' (L4), and morphological (prefix) negation in 'unseasonable' (L5). Thus, the Green Dragon – which due to the reference to the 'pink-faced landlady' can be interpreted as a pub – remains open in the negative text-world, whereas in the positive text-world, at the end of the evening, the pub closed; the couple had to leave, going out onto the street with the landlady locking the door after them.

In L7–9, the scene of the street is set, using the semantically negative nouns 'gloom' and 'quiet'. As semantic negations, these do not trigger world switches to negative text-worlds but rather characterise the positive text-world by provide world-building information. Because of its foregrounding effect, syntactic negation in L9 ('the horn from a distant freight train does not sound') emphasises the sound of the horn against the aforementioned quiet street. In L10–12, the poetic voice considers their own actions with syntactic negation in 'I do not turn' (L10) and 'I dare not speak' (L12). Additionally, there is morphological negation in 'unsaid' (L11) and implied negation in 'my tongue is tied' (L10) where the co-occurrence of 'tongue' and 'tied' is again suggestive of a lack of speech. Consequently, the reader infers from these negations that if the poetic voice did in fact speak to their partner; perhaps there was an argument? This interpretation is part of the negative text-world. The lack of speech means that in the positive text-world 'nothing transpires', the negative noun 'nothing' suggesting that whatever the poetic persona said in reality caused a reaction – *something* – from the partner. From L13 to the end of the first stanza, this reaction is clear: the parallel noun phrases 'the slam of a door, the flare of an engine' in L14 alongside the description of the street that 'does not shrink' (L13) and the semantically negative descriptions of the partner as 'elsewhere' and 'gone' (L15) implies that the partner got into a car and drove away (this is realised in the negative text-world). Furthermore, at this point in the poem, the partner becomes a lacuna: 'you / suddenly elsewhere, you imagined, gone, / but seen, still seen' (L14–16). The partner is physically absent from the street but, certainly for the poetic persona, is a felt absence, and this description – which uses verbs of visual perception ('imagined', 'seen') alongside semantic negations – generates the lacuna for the reader.

In the second stanza, there is a spatial deictic shift from the street to 'the cottage' (L18) which the narrator corrects, changing the definite article of the first stanza to first-person plural possessive in the second: 'Our cottage' (L19). Despite the change of scene, it is clear from the semantically negative verb 'forgotten' (L20) that this is still a memory: it is a memory of a home that the couple shared. Much of the second stanza describes the precarious stability of the cottage 'with its yellow walls, / its broken gate' (L19–20) and 'leaky window' (L24); thus it is perhaps itself a metaphor for the state of the couple's relationship. Nevertheless, the poetic persona is insistent that their poem can somehow reverse the break-up. In L22, there is a poignant repetition of the opening sentence, 'this is the poem in which we do not part', though with a change to the closing verb phrase ('have not left you' becomes 'do not part'). The consonance of the alveolar lateral approximant [l] foregrounds the simile in L23 'lie like lovers' while the adverb 'always' (L24) sits in contrast to the negations in the poem, signifying instead a more hopeful unity between the couple. Tucked away in parenthesis in L27–8 are the last negations of the poem: the poetic voice speaks to their partner 'but you'll not wake; / your ears are shut, you won't admit a thing'. Syntactic negation in 'you'll not wake' and the semantically negative adjective 'shut' clarify to readers that it is the partner who was described as 'sleeping' in L23. The poetic persona seems to will the partner not to wake here since the consequence of doing so is a guilty admission. The content of the admission is not revealed. This privacy, along with the placement of the negative assertion 'you won't admit a thing' in parenthesis implies, in our interpretation, that the confession caused the poem's narrator pain and was at the root of the break-up, a confession the morning after the argument in the street. Significantly, the remaining lines (L29–31) of the poem include only one negation – the verb 'done' to signal the end of the rain. Indeed, these final lines of the poem represent what the poetic voice can hear. In the positive text-world, the break-up does not happen, but rather the poem's narrator remains contented, lying in bed next to a silent sleeping lover, a lover who has not woken and has confessed nothing.

Keywords and summary

Lacuna, negation (morphological, semantic, syntactic), negative polarity, negative text-world.

This chapter has discussed the linguistic categories of negation: syntactic, morphological, and semantic. It has introduced the idea that negative expressions create multiple text-worlds, in which we conceptualise both the negation and the thing it negates. Negation consistently has a foregrounding effect, attracting readerly attention. However, the objects of focus do not have to be positive or solid, but can instead be defined by absence, in the form of lacunae. Ultimately, negation has an impact on the way in which we imagine and experience texts.

Activities

1. Classify the types of negation (syntactic, morphological, semantic) present in the following book titles. Be as specific as possible (e.g. try to specify word class or the type of affix too). Titles may include more than one negation:

   No-one ever has sex on a Tuesday. (Tracy Bloom)
   This is not the end. (Jesse Jordan)
   Without you, there is no us. (Suki Kim)
   All the light we cannot see. (Anthony Doerr)
   Breaking the unbreakable. (Timothy Atunnise)
   All things cease to appear. (Elizabeth Brundage)
   Never let me go. (Kazuo Ishiguro)
   The beautifully worthless. (Ali Liebegott)

2. The (2004) film *Lemony Snicket's A Series of Unfortunate Events* opens with what appears to be the title sequence to a vintage animation called *The Littlest Elf.* This sequence is characterised by bright colours and singing woodland creatures, all typical of carefree children's entertainment. However, this is interrupted and the voice of Lemony Snicket, the film's narrator, announces: 'I'm sorry to say that this is not the movie you will be watching. The movie you are about to see is extremely unpleasant.' What types of negation are present in Lemony Snicket's words? What is their effect in the context of the film so far?
3. Analyse the negation in the opening of Nathan Filer's (2013: 1–2) novel *The Shock of the Fall*:

   I should say that I am not a nice person. Sometimes I try to be, but often I'm not. So when it was my turn to cover my eyes and count to a hundred – I cheated.

   I stood at the spot where you had to stand when it was your turn to count, which was beside the recycling bins, next to the shop selling disposable barbecues and spare tent pegs. And near to there is a small patch of overgrown grass, tucked away behind a water tap.

   Except I don't remember standing there. Not really. You don't always remember the details like that, do you? You don't remember if you were

> beside the recycling bins, or further up the path near to the shower blocks, or whether actually the water tap is up there?
>
> I can't now hear the manic cry of seagulls, or taste the salt in the air. I don't feel the heat of the afternoon sun making me sweat beneath a clean white dressing on my knee, or the itching of suncream in the cracks of my scabs. I can't make myself relive the vague sensation of having been abandoned. And neither – for what it's worth – do I actually remember deciding to cheat, and open my eyes.

What impact does the negation have on your imaginative construal of the story? How do you feel about the narrator?

Further reading and references

Hidalgo Downing's (2000a) *Negation, Text Worlds and Discourse* and Nahajec's (2012) doctoral thesis offer detailed accounts of negation, both in terms of analytical studies as well as explicating the critical categorisations of the various forms of negation. Nahajec (2009, 2014) analyses negation using a pragmatic-stylistic approach, whilst Hidalgo Downing (2000b, 2002, 2003) develops a cognitive approach using Text World Theory. Gavins (2007), Gibbons (2011, 2012a), and Werth (1999: 249–57) also use Text World Theory to analyse negation. McLoughlin (2013) and Nørgaard (2007) provide cognitive stylistic accounts, speaking of negative polarity, while the concept of negative lacuna is developed in Stockwell (2009a, 2009b; see also 2016: 99–102). The concept of polarity is discussed in Halliday and Matthiessen (2014: 172–6). Linguistic negation is categorised by Givón (1979, 1993) while psycholinguistic studies are discussed by: Clark and Clark (1977), Horn (1989), and Wason (1961). Other stylistic discussions of negation include Jeffries (2010b: 106–13) and Watson (1999). Negation is also accounted for in Conceptual Integration Theory, with the concept of the counterfactual space: see Fauconnier and Turner (2002) and Sweetser (2006a).

Part VI

Reading as experience

19 Analysing the multimodal text

19.1 Modes and multimodality

The cognitive stylistic frameworks introduced in Parts IV and V of this book offer different was of examining the role of language and context in the experience of reading. The chapters in this Part of the book draw on stylistic principles to examine two particular aspects of the experience of reading: multimodality (this chapter) and emotion (Chapter 20). To understand multimodality, we must first define a mode: a **mode** is a socio-culturally specific semiotic resource used in meaning-making such as images, writing, layout, music, gesture, speech, moving image, and so on. In a cognitive approach, it may seem to make sense to connect modes to each of the five senses (vision, sound, touch, taste, smell). However, this is an imperfect method because attaching modes one-to-one with a sensory system overlooks crucial differences between modes. For instance, the visual would include written language, photographs, and moving images – both animated and filmic. Thus, defining a mode is by no means clear-cut. Indeed, Page claims, 'what might count as a mode is an open-ended set' (2010: 6). Modes need to be carefully considered by an analyst based on the text-type under consideration. In this chapter, we explore digital and printed fictional narratives and consequently focus on modes within three sensory systems: vision, sound, and touch (see Table 19.1).

Having introduced the idea of a mode, we can now define multimodality. As the prefix *multi-* indicates, **multimodality** is the coexistence of multiple modes within any given context. Everyday conversations are an obvious example of multimodal interaction: when we talk, we rely on the modes of spoken language, intonation, and gesture (amongst others). Strictly speaking, there is no such thing as a monomodal text (a text that uses only one mode). Even a textbook like this one, which looks predominantly monomodal, exploits various semiotic resources of the visual system, including written language,

Table 19.1 Indicative list of modes for vision, sound, and touch

Sensory system	Examples of modes
Vision	Pictorial signs, graphological emphasis, colour, textual layout/composition, written signs, numerical signs, gestures, etc.
Sound	Spoken signs, sounds (such as sound effects), music (including soundtracks), etc.
Touch	Texture, kinaesthetic movement, etc.

numerical signs, graphological emphasis such as bold and italics, diagrams, and the conventions of textual layout. Nevertheless, analysts generally reserve the term 'multimodality' for texts that more noticeably use multiple modes.

A stylistic approach to multimodality considers how multimodal texts are composed and how the various modes interact to produce meaning and influence interpretation.

19.2 Analysing multimodal literature

Digital printing technologies reduced the publication costs of books with visual and coloured elements, and this has spurred a steady rise in the number of works of multimodal printed literature. Building on Gibbons (2012a: 2), some possible features of multimodal printed fictions include:

- unusual textual layouts and page designs
- concrete realisation of text to create images, as in concrete poetry
- varied typography
- images, such as photographs or drawings
- use of colour in type and/or imagistic content
- flipbook sections
- textual deictic devices, drawing attention to the text's materiality
- footnotes and self-interrogative critical voices
- genre-mixing, both in literary terms (such as horror) or in terms of visual effect (such as the inclusion of newspaper clippings or play dialogue).

Note that the presence of illustrations does not necessarily make a literary work multimodal. When illustrations appear in fiction, they should only be classed as part of a multimodal text if they function as 'part of the narrative world': most likely, then, they will be 'produced by the narrator' or a character in the story 'and directly woven into the narrative discourse' (Hallet 2009: 133).

Hallet (2009: 149–50) argues that the difference between a so-called monomodal and a multimodal novel is grounded in five conceptual shifts:

1. *From writing to designing:* creating a multimodal text involves considering the many different semiotic resources (words, image, colour, layout) available to the writer, who must decide how to organise them to achieve the intended effect.
2. *From monomodal (verbal) texts to multimodal, multimedial texts:* The writer's decisions make the text a composite literary product.
3. *From narrator to narrator-presenter:* The narrator no longer delivers the story through only verbal means, but might appear to show and present documents (such as images) to the reader.
4. *From reading to a transmodal construction of narrative meaning:* Readers must construe meaning from the combination of modes.
5. *From reader to user:* The reader not only processes the linguistic content and imagines the worlds of the text but might also be required to interact physically with it, such as moving it or writing on it.

We have arranged Hallet's conceptual shifts in the numerical order above to show that the impact of multimodality spans from writing to the textual artefact itself and to the reading process.

An example of a work of multimodal fiction is *13, rue Thérèse* by Elena Mauli Shapiro (2011). In the opening, the third-person heterodiegetic narrator introduces Josianne, an academic assistant. Josianne is the owner of an enigmatic object, which she plants, as a gift, in the office of visiting academics whom she finds intriguing (Shapiro 2011: 3):

> Josianne's gift is a simple square box, its sides about as long as her forearm. It is about as deep as her hand is wide. The white plastic lid has a quaint red crosshatch pattern on it, like the sort you might see on a tablecloth in a small family-owned restaurant. The box is nothing extraordinary, though its contents have been known to induce fevers.

In these opening lines, the box is described in terms of its size and appearance. The verbal text is not particularly exceptional to readers, but from a stylistic perspective we can note that the box is initially referred to euphemistically as a 'gift'. Additionally, in the first two sentences, its description is less precise because it is identified with the indefinite article as 'a simple square box' and is defined approximately using the two parallel adverbial phrases which begin 'about as . . .'. It subsequently becomes more specific when the definite article appears in the noun phrases 'The white plastic lid' and 'The box'. We might also be intrigued by the use of second-person generalised *you*, and the final sentence which features negation ('nothing extraordinary') and uses the conjunction 'though' to create a concessive opposition (see Chapter 6) which heightens the mystery of the box's contents.

Josianne plans to leave the box in the office she has assigned to a visitor named Trevor Stratton. Through free indirect discourse, readers are given an insight into Josianne's consciousness as she imagines Trevor's curiosity when he finds the box 'tucked all the way into the darkness at the back of the bottom drawer' of the file cabinet (2011: 5): She considers, 'How could one see such a thing and then not take a little peek inside?' (2011: 5). As shown in Figure 19.1, the line 'This is the lid on the box' (2011: 5) appears before an aerial view of the box. Through the transmodal construction of meaning, readers are likely to interpret the proximal demonstrative pronoun 'this' as referring to (the image of) the box-lid. Because *13, rue Thérèse* is written in third person (up until this point at least), these words appear to emanate from the narrative voice, who is therefore showing readers the object at the heart of the story.

The image is then followed by the question 'Would you like to open it?' (2011: 5). The use of second person here is somewhat unsettling. In the context of the narrative, it cannot refer to a character and since the proximal deictics of the previous statement foregrounded the narrator as narrator-presenter, *you* seems to function apostrophically as a direct address to the reader. Since this question is the last piece of text on a recto (front, right-hand) page, the reader must turn the page to carry on reading. What follows is a double-page spread of conventionally typed text, typeset on the page as a letter. Thus, it features a right-aligned location ('Paris') and date ('January 12th') and left-aligned salutation 'Dear Sir' (2011: 6). It continues 'Quite by accident, I have found the most fascinating record' (2011: 6). The letter, it transpires, has been written by Trevor Stratton who is therefore the first-person *I* here. In the letter, Trevor explains that he has found the box and will send the unnamed addressee ('Sir') scans of the documents it contains. Such documents include old letters, photographs, postcards, and a diary amongst other things, all of which later appear in *13, rue Thérèse.*

On the one hand, then, the question 'Would you like to open it?' appears to have been overlooked. On the other, the implication is that the box now also contains Trevor's letter and documentation. Thus, the act of the reader (as user) turning the page after having been asked 'Would you like to open it?' is mapped onto the action of opening the box. As such, readers experience the book not merely as a novel, but as the collected record of the box's contents according to Trevor. Through

13, rue Thérèse

starkly black hair, and his mouth caught in something like the beginning of a smile—whether sheepish or mischievous she isn't quite sure. It must be he is ripe for her gift.

She will give him the office with the tall, useless empty file cabinet in the corner. He will probably not think to open all the drawers and look in them his first day on the premises. But he will, eventually, discover a box tucked all the way into the darkness at the back of the bottom drawer, innocent-looking yet unexpected. How could one see such a thing and then not take a little peek inside?

She wonders what effect it will have on him.

This is the lid on the box:

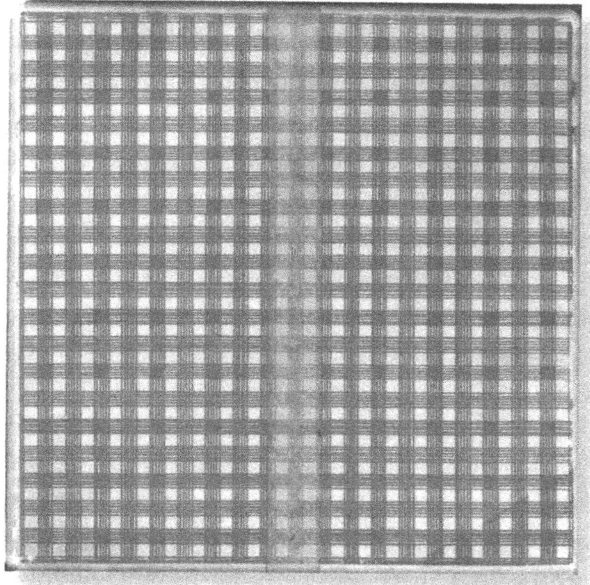

Would you like to open it?

5

Figure 19.1 Page image from *13, rue Thérèse* (Shapiro 2011: 5. Copyright 2011, Elena Mauli Shapiro. Used by permission of the author)

this stylistic analysis, we can see how multimodal literature is characterised by the five conceptual shifts outlined by Hallet. In the next section, we will consider how various modes enable multimodal texts to signal genre.

19.3 Multimodality and genre

Multimodal fiction can exploit modal combinations to play with genre conventions. Gibbons (2016b; building on Bateman 2008) provides a framework that can be used to analyse the various elements that combine to generate an impression of genre. The framework, shown in Figure 19.2, provides a series of steps that examine different levels (or 'bases') of the multimodal text and how they interact. Taken together, these bases comprise a genre (or genres) that is, in turn, produced and interpreted in a wider (interpersonal, spatio-temporal, socio-cultural) context. Genre is understood here as a cognitive construct which is triggered by textual features but identified by readers based on their schematic knowledge (see Chapter 14).

We'll apply the framework in an analysis of the first page of Amie Kaufman and Jay Kristoff's (2015) novel *Illuminae* (shown in Figure 19.3). The analytical process works bottom-up through these bases, starting with the Genre and Multimodality Base. Thus, the first step is to divide the page into base units, which are the smallest semiotic units on the page. Although we could include individual sentences as base units, in this analysis we'll take a slightly broader approach, breaking linguistic content into paragraphs but noting the number of sentences (using *s* =). Base units for the first page of *Illuminae* are shown in Table 19.2. In identifying base units, we have already started to map the relationships between base and embedded units numerically: 1>I>i. Embedded units are also represented visually in the table through indentation.

Continuing to chart the relationship between units, the next step is to consider the Layout base by plotting an area model. The **area model** is a visual representation of the page elements, based on how they cluster together. An area model of the first page of *Illuminae* is shown in Figure 19.3. The entire page is L1, the largest layout unit, and it contains six overarching clusters (L1.1–6). We have identified a top header (L1.1) which features three base units (units 1–3 from Table 19.2). Unit 4 in Table 19.2 (the icon bar) is L1.2 whilst unit 5 is L1.3, the text block in which unit 6 (the paperclip icon) is visually embedded. Finally, units 7, 8, and 9 are shown as L1.4, .5, and .6 respectively. We have mapped all nine base units from Table 19.2 onto the area model, using dashed lines to represent those which are visually embedded within an over-

Multimodal Cognitive Poetic Genre Model
Context Base • Participants (e.g. producers, readers) • Goals and functions of discourse • Spatio-temporal setting • Socio-cultural domain • Medium and its associated role
Genre Base • Content (theme, topic) • Type (narrative, argument, instruction) • Form and Constraint (genre-specific forms and structures) • Structure and Cohesion
Navigation Base • Pointers (continuation, branching, expansion)
Stylistic Base • Typographic: indexical, iconic, discursive including paratypography, dispositive • Linguistic: text-driven (e.g. inc. modality, focalisation, language, register)
Layout Base (clusters) • Layout Structure: Hierarchical XY Trees • Area Model (inc. insets and separators) • Flow (text-, page-, image-) • Microtypography (type face, size, colour) • Mesotypography (alignment, spacing) • Macrotypography (indents, emphasis, image combinations)
Genre & Multimodality Base (base units & embedded units) • Base units: sentences, icons, footnote label, headings table cells, items in menu, floating text, titles, list items, page numbers, headlines, list labels, running heads • Embedded units: sentence fragments, emphasised portions of text, footnotes, images, captions of images, text in images, horizontal or vertical lines, connecting units like lines and arrows

Figure 19.2 The multimodal cognitive poetic framework of genre (Gibbons 2016b)

Table 19.2 Base and embedded units for *Illuminae*, p. 1

Base and embedded units		
1. Planet Earth image	3. Barcode element	6. Paper clip icon
2. Header text	3I. Barcode	7. The Illuminae Group
2I. Para 1	3II. Barcode number	8. Quotation
2Ii. MEMORANDUM FOR:	4. Icon bar	8I. Italicised quote
2Iii. Executive Director Frobisher	4I. Speaker icon	8II. –
2II. Para 2	4II. Down-left arrow icon	8III. –
2IIi: FROM:	4III. Folder icon	9. Page numbers
2IIii: Ghost ID	4IV. Right arrow icon	9I. 1
2IIiii: ([text])	4V. Pencil icon	9II: /
2III. Para 3	5. Text block	9III: 599
2IIIi. INCEPT:	5I. Para 1 (s = 1)	
2IIIii. 01/29/76	5II. Para 2 (s = 3)	
2IV. Para 4	5III. Para 3 (s = 3)	
2IVi. SUBJECT:	5IV. Para 4 (s = 5)	
2IVii. *Alexander* dossier		

arching cluster. We'd expect a more conventional piece of fiction to be composed of only one base unit – a cluster of justified text on the page – or two base units if there is a chapter title. The area model of the first page of *Illuminae* enables us to see how various elements are clustered together in this more complex multimodal fiction, and how they sit on the page in relation to other elements.

We can now build on our mapping of the GeM and Layout bases with stylistic analysis. The first unit, at the top of the page, is L1.1. This features an image (L1.1.1) with the text (L1.1.2) functioning as an inset positioned in front. The image is a view of planet Earth as seen from space. Complementing this, in L1.3 – the central text block – we can find lexis relating to the idea of space exploration, such as the compound noun 'light-years'. Alongside the image, and drawing on our knowledge of register (Chapter 6), such lexis therefore works to suggest to readers that *Illuminae* is a piece of science fiction.

Whilst science fiction is a literary genre, it is not the only generic foundation for *Illuminae*. The largest unit on the first page is L1.3, which is mostly occupied by typed text. The first paragraph (unit 5I) consists of only one sentence and reads, 'So here's the file that almost killed me, Director' (Kaufman and Kristoff 2015: 1). The proximal deictics create a transmodal link: the locative adverb 'here' points to the book itself, suggested to readers that they should also interpret the novel as 'the file' in question. Other markers also point to the book as an official document: the formal address 'Director' implies a professional relationship between the narrative *I* and the addressee, as do other words and phrases in L1.3, such as the pre-modifier in the metaphorical noun

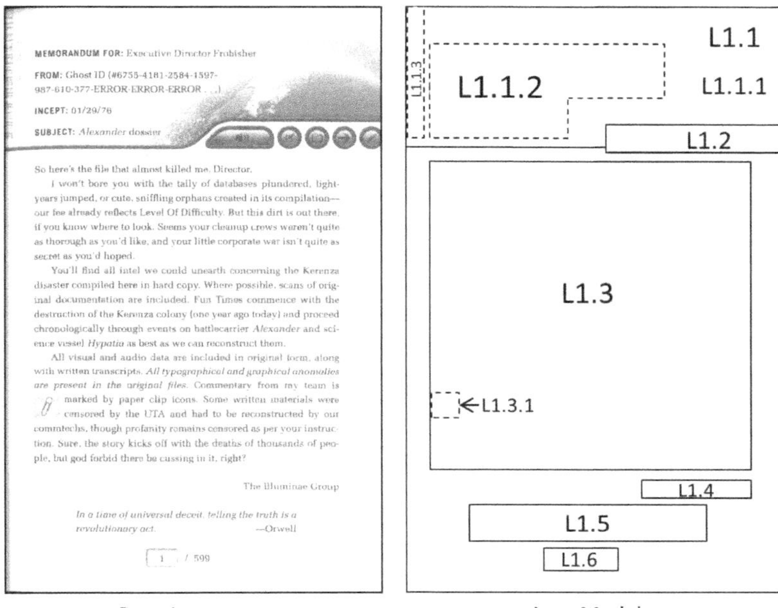

MEMORANDUM FOR: Executive Director Frobisher

FROM: Ghost ID (#6755-4181-2584-1597-987-610-377-ERROR-ERROR-ERROR . . .)

INCEPT: 01/29/76

SUBJECT: *Alexander* dossier

So here's the file that almost killed me, Director.

I won't bore you with the tally of databases plundered, light-years jumped, or cute, sniffling orphans created in its compilation—our fee already reflects Level Of Difficulty. But this dirt is out there, if you know where to look. Seems your cleanup crews weren't quite as thorough as you'd like, and your little corporate war isn't quite as secret as you'd hoped.

You'll find all intel we could unearth concerning the Kerenza disaster compiled here in hard copy. Where possible, scans of original documentation are included. Fun Times commence with the destruction of the Kerenza colony (one year ago today) and proceed chronologically through events on battlecarrier *Alexander* and science vessel *Hypatia* as best as we can reconstruct them.

All visual and audio data are included in original form, along with written transcripts. *All typographical and graphical anomalies are present in the original files.* Commentary from my team is marked by paper clip icons. Some written materials were censored by the UTA and had to be reconstructed by our commtechs, though profanity remains censored as per your instruction. Sure, the story kicks off with the deaths of thousands of people, but god forbid there be cussing in it, right?

The Illuminae Group

In a time of universal deceit, telling the truth is a revolutionary act. —Orwell

1 / 599

Figure 19.3 First page of *Illuminae* (Kaufman and Kristoff 2015: 1) and area model

phrase 'corporate war' and the lexical blend 'commtechs'. Secondly, in L1.1 there is an embedded unit of text (L1.1.2; unit 2) with four further embedded units created by paragraphing (units 2I–IV); within each of these, graphological emphasis further divides the bold from the unboldened type to form two more embedded units. The emboldened text in L1.1.2 (unit 2) also use lexis associated with official, professional documentation, for instance '**MEMORANDUM**' as well as the full name of the addressee, 'Executive Director Frobisher'. This interpretation of the novel as a piece of official documentation is enhanced by the visual layout of the header text and its notation form, which fit with readers' schemas of business memos.

There is another genre evident on the first page of *Illuminae*. Lexis in L1.3, such as the words 'databases', 'scans', and 'data', all trigger the semantic field of digital documentation (which the narrator insists has been 'compiled here in hard copy'). Visual devices also contribute to this semantic field. For instance, the image of the paper clip (L1.3.1) is easily recognised by readers as the 'attachment' icon used in computer-mediated communication. Similarly, the five icons in L1.2 (unit 4 in

Table 19.2) are also evocative of computer keys whilst the graphic realisation of page numbers (L1.6) – themselves navigational devices – suggest that the book was originally a digital document. When one medium – here the printed book – imitates elements from another medium, this is called **intermedial evocation** (Wolf 2005).

Before we conclude our analysis of *Illuminae*, what do you make of the two noun phrases 'battlecarrier *Alexander*', and 'science vessel *Hypatia*'? Do these fit with one of the existing semantic fields and related genres that we have already discussed (science fiction, business documentation, digital technology) or is another semantic field also at play?

In analysing the first page of *Illuminae*, we started by recording its content as base units, which we then mapped onto an area model in our layout analysis. After this, we began analysing *Illuminae* stylistically. In doing so, we focused particularly on how language and images fed into particular semantic fields. These semantic fields trigger genre schemas for readers. The Context base relates to the wider context of the novel: *Illuminae* is aimed at young adult readers. Consequently, we might consider the book's intermedial evocation of the digital to be related to the goal of appealing to a digitally native audience. Another important conceit of the book is the illusion that it is based on documentary evidence, created by the combined effect of the professional/business document and digital textuality genres.

Ultimately, our analysis shows the way in which the novel aligns itself with different genres as well as which modes primarily signal each genre. Thus, this page of *Illuminae* has three central generic foundations: the professional/business document, indicated chiefly through linguistic markers; the intermedial evocation of digital text, signalled both linguistically and using visual elements; and the literary genre of science-fiction, again signified by lexical choice and images. As for the noun phrases 'battlecarrier *Alexander*' and 'science vessel *Hypatia*', you may have decided that they additionally fit with the semantic field of war (which we'd noticed was metaphorically present in 'corporate war'). War in space, it turns out, is a major theme of the story.

19.4 Multimodality and digital fiction

The rise of multimodal fictions has been linked to cultural anxiety about the death of the printed book, in an age of tablet e-readers and smart mobile devices. Printed multimodal fiction adopts creative literary strategies to reinvigorate the novel as a material object. Given the prevalence of the digital in the twenty-first century, it is also important that contemporary stylistics can make sense of digital texts too. Digital fiction is written and designed for a digital device and it is read and experienced by reader-users on that digital device. This means that the 'structure, form, and meaning are dictated by, and in dialogue with, the digital context in which it is produced and received' (Bell et al. 2014b: 4). Digital interfaces may take the form of a computer screen (for instance, as with hypertext fictions), a video or TV screen (computer games), or a tablet or mobile device (apps).

In this section, we analyse the digital work *Karen* (2015) by Blast Theory (produced in partnership with National Theatre Wales). *Karen* is an interactive app, available for both iOS and Android platforms. In the press release, Blast Theory describe it as a 'cross between gaming and storytelling' (2015). The app is named after its central character Karen, who is a life coach. When you first open the app, the screen of your device changes to black with the words 'CALLING KAREN . . .' in white capital letters (see Figure 19.4). A video then appears of a woman walking across a street. This is Karen. She appears to notice the camera, and says 'Oh, great! I've been expecting you.' In her first utterance, then, Karen uses direct address to the reader-user. The interpersonal deictics here ('I' and 'you') along with the visuality of the video medium therefore instantly establish a communicative situation in which the character Karen appears to talk directly to the real reader-user. This is of course impossible; Karen is fictional and this video is pre-recorded. Nevertheless, the introductory 'CALLING KAREN . . .' screen with its present continuous tense, the visual image, and the interpersonal perceptual deictics create the illusion that this is a live video call.

The camera, and thus also the user, moves with Karen as she walks across the street and enters a building. 'I'm looking forward to getting to know you,' she says, 'a bit nervous'. As she walks up the stairs, she mutters, 'There's one or two questionnaires but I'm more of a person-to-person person.' She unlocks a door, enters what appears to be her apartment, and sits on a sofa facing the camera. She says, 'So! I'm knackered. How are you?' As she does this, the video pauses and four boxes appear, overlaying the image. Karen's question appears in a black box on the screen of the device along with three blue boxes that read 'Me too', 'I'm quite excited actually', and 'This feels weird.' These are clearly responses to Karen's question. Moreover, the use of first-person ('I' and 'me') in these responses intimates that the user must select an option by touching the screen. It is in this way that *Karen* is interactive.

When we played this app, we selected the option 'I'm quite excited actually.' The boxes then disappear and the video chat with Karen

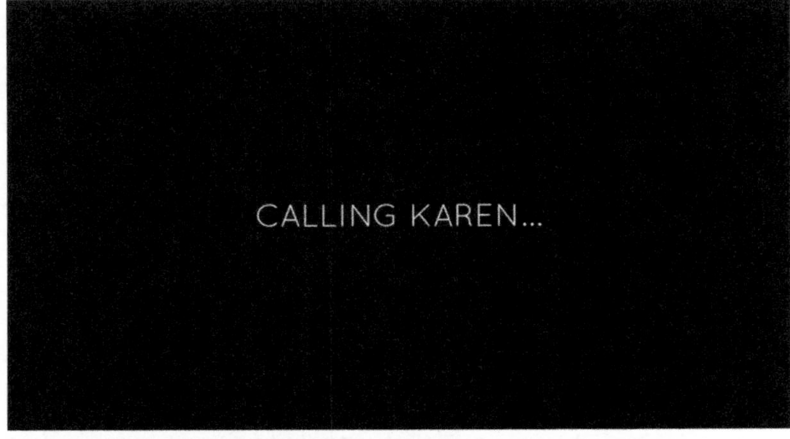

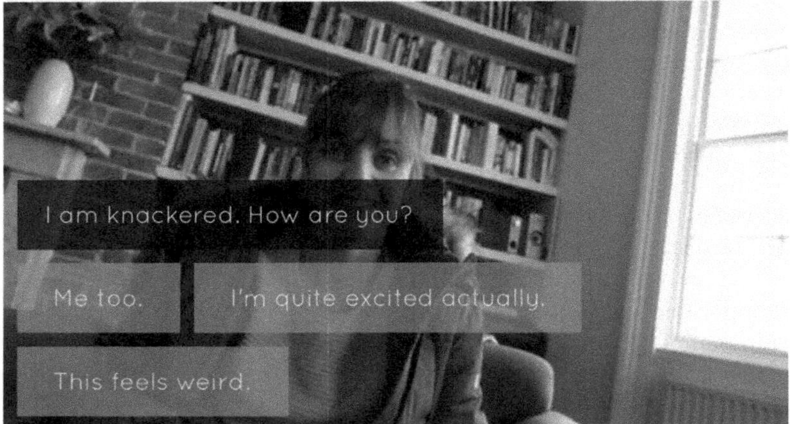

Figure 19.4 Two screenshots from *Karen* (Blast Theory 2015)

returns. Karen asks, 'Give me an hour or two to get my stuff sorted and we'll get started.' She is 'pretty excited about this', she tells users; the proximal deictic reference of 'this' reinforcing the immediacy of the situation. After all, 'How often do you get to open up to a one hundred per cent stranger?' At this point, the video fades, and users see a generic screen with the app's logo along with information about when the next episode is available to them. The episodes are released at intervals so that the *Karen* app lasts one week over which Karen, as your new life coach, asks you a series of questions that develop a collaborative relationship between user and character. She also reveals information about herself which suggests that she is perhaps not as psychologically stable as one might hope a life coach would be. Although *Karen* is an interactive narrative game designed to entertain, the app also collects users' answers and builds psychological profiles that they can access at the end.

In the second episode, Karen sits at a desk. She looks and behaves professionally; as Blast Theory's script states, she is in '[b]usiness-like mode to establish her as competent and professional'. Karen states, 'It's great you've signed up.' The first touch-screen question in this episode asks, 'What would you like me to call you?' Underneath, there is a box for users to write their name. After typing their chosen name, *Karen* returns to the video call and Karen appears to write it down. Although it isn't used in this conversation, the given name will later appear in touch-screen text, thus appearing to personalise the app to each user.

Before the next touch-screen question, Karen says, 'I want to help you with the most important things in your life. That's what I'm here for. Which of the following is most important for you, right now?' The question and following three options appear on the screen:

- I want to take more control of my life
- I want to change my attitude to relationships
- I want to review my life goals

All three statements open with the main clause 'I want', but are differentiated in terms of the subsequent verb phrase. The boulomaic verb 'want' suggests that users should select the statement that best applies to them. Depending on their answer, users then watch a different video segment. Karen thus has three potential responses:

- 'Taking control? God, me too. Well, we can definitely help you to get that sorted. I'm going to pop you a couple of questions and you can tell me about how you see the world'
- 'Relationships is such a great one to choose. Let me pop you a couple of questions and you can tell me about how you see the world'
- 'Gotcha, it's great to bounce life goals off someone and see what it throws up. Let me pop you a couple of questions and you can tell me about how you see the world'

Each of the responses ends in a similar way. This enables the app to continue along the same narrative trajectory, asking all users the same subsequent touch-screen questions. *Karen* as a whole follows this format. It features a more-or-less linear narrative, but users' touch-screen responses affect the exact nature of Karen's response, in terms of her verbal utterances. The personalised nature of the responses maintains the deception of the interaction as real since Karen appears to directly respond to the user.

Before episode 2 ends, Karen gives the user some homework. She says, 'I want you to do something for me.' A touch-screen question then appears: 'Are you at home?' Karen also asks if you're on your own. The tasks, which she hopes you'll do at home and alone, appear on the screen with two response options for the user.

> Take some time to think about something that you're grateful for today. Once you've thought of it, write it down. It can be on a Post-It note, or a message to yourself on your phone. Then I'd like you to read it back to yourself tomorrow morning and call me when you get a chance. OK?
>
> I can't promise Yes, I can do that.

If the user selects, 'I can't promise', another touch-screen quiz replies offering to remind the user ('in ten minutes', 'in an hour', 'in three hours', or 'Don't worry, I'll remember'). If required, the *Karen* app can therefore send the user an alert. In the third episode, Karen then checks your progress, asking you if you completed this task. Users who do complete the task are therefore performing an action in the real world. Doing so once again gives credence to users' interaction with Karen, symbolising their commitment to these fictional life-coaching sessions.

This brief analysis of *Karen*'s opening demonstrates the interactive and in some ways intimate experience that *Karen* offers to users. The fact that *Karen* is a digital app is vital to creating this sense of intimacy. The app messages the user when new episodes become available or if a user ends an episode early. On an iPhone, the messages from *Karen* look and read like text messages, including direct address and colloquial language (see Figure 19.5). These messages further enhance users' impressions of Karen as more than fiction – as a real person (perhaps even a friend) with whom they are interacting. Texts devised specifically for digital platforms are called 'born-digital' texts, and the born-digital nature of *Karen* is vital to the intimate and immersive experience it generates. In the twenty-first century, tablets and mobile phones have become a ubiquitous presence in our day-to-day lives, thus the device is in many ways an extension of the self. Think about the way in which you use your own mobile phone: how often are you without it? Mobiles are, in Farman's words, 'our most intimate technologies' (2014: 5).

Using stylistic analysis, we have shown that interacting with *Karen* feels personal precisely because of its multimodal and multimedial composition. The app's video-call illusion and its evocation of face-to-face conversation between the user and Karen play a big part in this. So, too, does users' interactions with the app and the fact that Karen

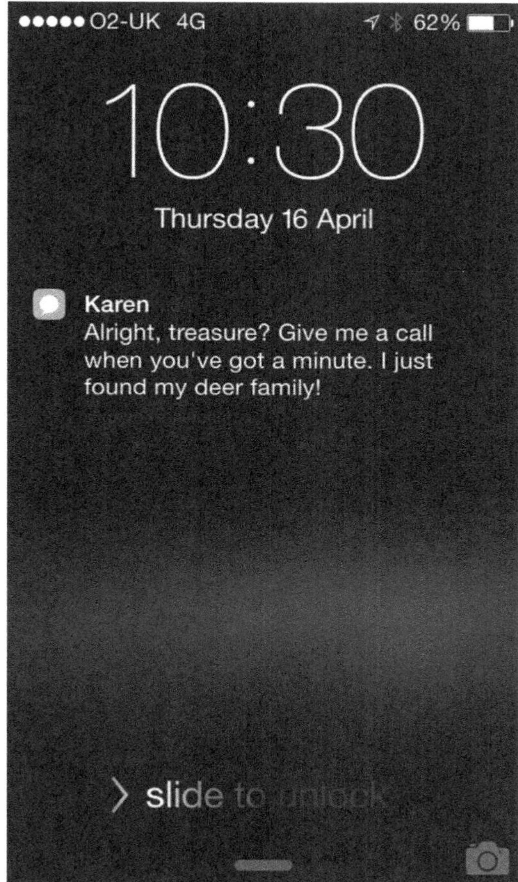

Figure 19.5 Personal iPhone screenshot of a message from *Karen* (Blast Theory 2015)

seems to respond. Discussing the development process of *Karen* in an article for UK newspaper *The Guardian*, Blast Theory artist-creator Matt Adam reveals that the app was improved to boost the interrelationship between the character Karen and users. Interactivity is central to this interrelationship since it makes users feel both included in and as though they contribute to the narrative action. Indeed, when Blast Theory enhanced user involvement by emphasising the personal relationship between users and Karen, real users in test reports used words such as 'intimate' and 'addictive' (Adams 2015) to describe their experience of the app.

Keywords and summary

Area model, intermedial evocation, mode, multimodality.

This chapter started by emphasising that modes should be understood as fluid categories that shift according to usage and reception. Subsequently, the concept of multimodality was introduced and we outlined the conceptual shifts that multimodal texts enact. The composite nature of multimodal literature means that it makes use of various modes – language, image, interaction – to communicate narrative meanings as well as genre. The chapter also explored the types of experiences offered by multimodal, multimedial, and/or digital fictions. The visual dimension of multimodal fictions enables them to show rather than just tell narrative information. In *13, rue Thérèse,* for instance, readers are shown the box and its contents. *13, rue Thérèse* and Blast Theory's app *Karen* also highlight the conceptual shift from reader to a more interactive user of multimodal fictions. Such interaction could be as simple as turning a page in such a way that it has narrative meaning or it could be more dynamic as shown by *Karen* with the text seeming to respond and change as a result of the interaction. Multimodal analysis illuminates the interactions between language and other semiotic modes in readers' narrative experiences.

Activities

1. Find an example of multimodal fiction. You might look, for instance, at the work of Mark Z. Danielewski, Graham Rawle, or Steve Tomasula or the novels *Extremely Loud and Incredibly Close* by Jonathan Safran Foer, *The Raw Shark Texts* by Steven Hall, or *The Selected Works of T. S. Spivet* by Reif Larsen (there are plenty more to choose from). Turn to a page that is multimodal. Make a list of all the different modes being used. How are they interacting with each other? (Do the meanings of different modal elements complement or contradict each other?) How does the multimodality of your chosen text affect your experience as a reader?
2. Figure 19.6 shows page 25 of *Illuminae.* Analyse it using the cognitive poetic model of genre discussed in section 19.3 of this chapter. What genre foundations does it have? How do you read it as a result?
3. Visit the *Electronic Literature Collection* website: http://collection.eliterature.org. Here you will find a vast range of digital texts. Play the texts, and as you do, consider: what kinds of interactions are asked of you by the texts? How do your interactions impact upon the story?

Main Page
Contents
Random
Current
Generation
Contribution
Report
▾ Interface
Sensei
About
Hivemind
Editorial
Review
Make Noise
▸ Tools
▸ Sync
▾ Languages
官话
广州话
Deutsch
Español
Italiano
język polski
русский язык
Edit
Links

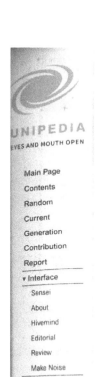

Review Discuss Refute Read Edit Y

BRIEFING NOTE:
Director: Although most of the intel in this dossier was acquired through covert means, we did discover one public channel with surprisingly accurate intel about the Kerenza assault itself—the hacktivist website known as Unipedia. Most readers of Unipedia are probably wearing tinfoil hats in their mothers' basements, but you might want to open a hellgate or two and unleash your lawyers anyway. We've included Unipedia's coverage here for completion's sake.

Kerenza, Battle of

This article is about the Battle of Kerenza IV. Get the gen on the planet and system here.

This historical article is currently unc
because you choobs gobble corp prc
cheap dust at an all-night chuff party
citations for verification purposes. Pl
the Hivemind. Please attribute intelli
mom does not count). And learn to s
[insert appropriate deity name here].

INTRO

The Battle of Kerenza IV was the opening salvo in the ongoing and bafflingly unreported Stellarcorp War. Initiated by BeiTech Industries,[1] the assault targeted illegal hermium mining operations owned by the Wallace Ulyanov Consortium.[2] United Terran Authority vessel *Alexander*[3] answered WUC distress calls, resulting in a three-way throwdown between BeiTech, WUC, and UTA forces.

CONTENTS [HIDE]

BACKGROUND

Kerenza IV is situated in freespace, approximately 34.5 AU from a waypoint leading to static Jump Station *Heimdall*. The planet contains unusually high concentrations of hermium on its polar ice shelf. In violation of the Interstellar Exotic Materials Act of 2514,[4] the Wallace

25 / 599

Figure 19.6 Page image from *Illuminae* (Kaufman and Kristoff 2015: 25)

What effects do the texts have upon you as a user? How do these digital texts compare with printed books?

Further reading and references

The study of multimodality stems from Gunther Kress and Theo van Leeuwen's (2006 [1996]) book *Reading Images: The Grammar of Visual Design* in which they suggest a toolkit for analysing texts with visual elements. Since its inception, the academic study of multimodality has expanded (see Jewitt 2009a), and it is now possible to speak of four distinct approaches. Three of these are identified by Jewitt (2009b: 28): the social semiotic approach (as in Kress and van Leeuwen's work; see also Kress 2009, 2010); a discourse analysis approach (Baldry and Thibault 2006; O'Halloran 2004, 2005; O'Toole 1994); and an interaction analysis approach (Norris 2004; Scollon and Scollon 2003).

The fourth approach is stylistic, and Nørgaard (2014) identifies two strands: the social semiotic (Nørgaard 2010a, 2010b) and the cognitive approach (Borkent 2012; Gibbons 2008, 2010a, 2010b, 2012b, 2014b, 2015, 2016a). Gibbons' (2012a) monograph also features response data, offering empirical insight into how readers interpret multimodality and its impact on imaginative engagements. The edited collection *Multimodal Metaphor* (Forceville and Urios-Aparisi 2009) analyses conceptual metaphors across multimodal text-types whilst conceptual metaphors in multimodal literature are explored by Gibbons (2013) and Hiraga (2005). Hallet's (2009, 2011, 2014) work offers a cognitive narratological angle.

McIntyre (2008) analyses film using multimodal stylistic analysis. For stylistic analyses of digital texts, see: Bell (2010, 2014), Bell and Ensslin (2011, 2012), Ciccoricco (2012), Ensslin (2010, 2012a, 2012b, 2014), Gibbons (2012c), Trimarco (2014), as well as the essays collected in Bell et al. (2014a). The cognitive approach has been shown capable of analysing other multimodal text-types, such as mobile narratives (Gibbons 2014a) and immersive theatre (Gibbons 2016a).

The study of multimodality and genre is introduced by Bateman (2008, 2014), and developed by Francesconi (2014) and Hiippala (2016) as well as Gibbons (2016b) who takes a specifically cognitive poetic approach. Typography has been categorised by: Nørgaard (2009), Stöckl (2005, 2009, 2014), and van Leeuwen (2005, 2006).

20 Understanding emotions

20.1 Emotional involvement in reading

As well as engaging our cognitive capacities of attention, perception, knowledge, and inferencing, literary works involve our feelings and emotions. The early phases of cognitive science, and the early stages of cognitive stylistics, studied cognition as information processing, separate from processes of emotion and motivation. In contemporary cognitive science there is more recognition of the interactions between emotion and cognition in our everyday experience of the world, and similarly, cognitive stylisticians have begun to investigate ways of modelling and accounting for the emotional aspects of literary reading.

There is a long history of debate about *why* readers have emotional reactions to fictional or remote situations that they know are not real. Some philosophers have questioned whether the emotions we experience in response to fictional events can even be thought of as 'real' emotions. As we have seen in Parts IV and V, a central tenet of the cognitive approach to literature is that the embodied, cognitive processes used in our everyday interactions with the world are also used when we read. Even the simulated experiences we generate with our imaginations engage the physical and sensory aspects of our human experience. The emotions we experience in literary reading are thought to arise through the same emotion processes involved in 'real-life' situations.

One of the challenges involved in the investigation of emotion is the lack of scholarly agreement over how emotion is defined. One popular theory regards emotions as physiological responses that occur when we 'appraise' (or evaluate) a particular event or situation as being relevant to our goals, plans, expectations, or desires. This appraisal triggers the bodily changes, sensations, actions, and expressions that typically occur when we experience an emotion. From this perspective, emotions function to activate bodily resources and direct our attention so that we are able to modify or cope with the situation that triggered the appraisal.

Other theories emphasise the role of emotion in our interpersonal relationships, viewing emotions as having a communicative function as part of the roles or identities that we adopt in relation to others. As well as disagreement about what constitutes an emotion and what the functions of emotion are, there is also disagreement over the relationship between 'emotion' and other concepts such as 'feeling' and 'affect' which are sometimes used differently and sometimes interchangeably.

In this chapter, we consider 'emotion' as an umbrella term for a range of experiential phenomena that involve relatively brief but intense felt experiences. Emotions are experiences with different levels of **intensity** (or strength) and **valence**. Emotions with a positive valence (e.g. joy) give rise to more pleasurable experiences than those with a negative valence (e.g. sadness). Emotions also involve different **action tendencies**: some emotions are characterised by attraction or movement towards something (e.g. love), whilst others are characterised by aversion and movement away (e.g. fear). Movement through space is integral to the way we conceptualise emotion. For instance, everyday phrases such as 'we're really close' or 'she's being really distant' are underpinned by the conceptual metaphor EMOTIONAL RELATIONSHIP IS DISTANCE BETWEEN TWO ENTITIES (Kövecses 2000; Stockwell 2005a: 148). Since emotions are often discussed using spatial metaphors, stylistic frameworks that draw on a 'text-as-world' metaphor or have a spatial metaphor as their basis, such as Text World Theory and Deictic Shift Theory, have been particularly useful for the consideration of emotional responses.

20.2 Psychological projection and mind-modelling

Emotional responses to literary texts are underpinned by projection, our ability to shift our viewpoint as we process language. In Chapter 13, this was referred to as deictic projection, as it originates from the linguistic theory of deixis. The broader term **psychological projection** is used to capture the sense that projection is more than just a relocation of deictic coordinates, but also the means by which we imaginatively construct and experience fictional or remote worlds. Stockwell (2009a) characterises psychological projection in terms of another important cognitive ability: conceptual mapping. As discussed in Chapter 16 on metaphor, the human mind is adept at taking a familiar domain and mapping from it in order to understand another less familiar domain. When we project into other viewpoints during literary reading, we do so by mapping (to various degrees) from our own sense of self and mind. This mapping occurs across an ontological boundary: from the real reader in the actual world onto the enactors populating the imagined fictional world. Projection is therefore thought to contribute to readers' feelings of **immersion** and involvement in literature.

Psychological projection also enables us to imaginatively construct the minds of literary characters during reading. In everyday life, we do not have direct access to other people's minds, yet we regularly attribute thoughts, emotions, attitudes, and goals to them based on their behaviour and speech. For example, if you walked into your housemate's room and found them sitting at their book-strewn desk with their head in their hands, you would automatically 'read' their body language and infer that they are upset about something, or extremely tired; because the books are open, you might infer that their studies are the source of their distress. Even though they are not always accurate, these attributions are a fundamental part of social interaction and would determine your next interactional move. As Stockwell (2009a: 132) explains: 'we assume that others are, in basic mechanics, the same as us, and we anticipate their beliefs, motives, speech and actions accordingly by projecting them in their circumstances'. When we read literature, our imaginative construction of the minds of literary characters is thought to occur using the same attribution processes which, in a literary context, is known as **mind-modelling**.

Consider this extract from Sunjeev Sahota's novel *The Year of the Runaways* (2015: 112; sentences numbered for analysis). Passionate teenage lovers Avtar and Lakhpreet have been meeting secretly for the past few months, but Lakhpreet's family is about to move four hours away, making it harder for them to see each other. Here, they bid each other farewell before the move. As you read the passage, consider how the couple feel about the goodbye:

> (1) They walked to Jalianwala Bagh Road and kissed for several minutes behind the gates to the museum, tongues thick, hips fighting. (2) Then Avtar called over an idling auto-rickshaw. (3) 'PCO me when you arrive, acha?'
>
> (4) 'Try and come every month,' she said and climbed into the ripped seats of the auto. (5) She was looking away. (6) He put his hand on her cheek and turned her face towards him. (7) Her white chunni had fallen off her head and her eyes were brimming. (8) He went round and gave the driver her address.

The passage is narrated in the third person with variable focalisation. Much of the scene is externally focalised but there is a sense of focalisation through Avtar's visual perspective in S5 and S7 as our viewpoint is limited to what he can see. Although the feelings of the characters are not explicitly narrated, it is easy to imagine their feelings based on narrative cues that describe the characters' physical behaviour and speech, combined with our schematic knowledge about relationships. This mind-modelling enables readers to flesh out the narrative and imagine the emotional lives of the characters.

Lakhpreet's sadness or distress is indicated through her body language: she looks away from Avtar, her eyes are brimming with tears, and she is absentminded about her dress which suggests she is struggling to keep her emotional composure. Contrastingly, Avtar appears entirely composed, focused on performing practical actions such as calling and directing the rickshaw and planning their communications once she's gone. However, Avtar's focus on perfunctory actions and lack of responsiveness to Lakhpreet are also suggestive of his own sadness and distress. These inferences about the minds of the characters are fuelled by our experience of the prior narrative (in which the two are very much in love) as well as schematic knowledge about romantic relationships (lovers want to be together, being apart causes emotional pain) and perhaps even memories of painful goodbyes or teenage romances from our own lives. Although no emotion is mentioned explicitly in the extract, the scene is emotional (and evoked an emotional response in us) due to these mind-modelling inferences. The way the scene is narrated contributes to readers' involvement in the scene: in order to interpret these purely physical descriptions of the characters' behaviour and actions, we have to model their minds.

Mind-modelling is an integral part of world-building (discussed in Chapter 17), as it is the means by which readers use their own inferences to give psychological substance to characters. It is also considered important in readers' emotional experience of narrative, because it enables them to imagine textual entities as 'real' people (people like us) who have 'real' thoughts, emotions, and reactions. If readers are able to imagine characters as real people, this goes some way to explaining how these characters' vicissitudes can also involve a reader's own emotions.

20.3 Identification and resistance

The particularities of a reader's emotional response to a piece of literature are thought to be linked to the extent of the projection and mind-modelling undertaken during reading: for instance, the extent of their immersion in the fictional world, the kinds of features mapped between the reader and the text, and the richness of the mappings.

The mapping between self and other performed during mind-modelling has the potential to lead to processes of comparison – in which a reader recognises either similarities or marked differences between themselves and a particular character. A reader's recognition of a similarity between themselves and character is called **identification**. Hogan (2003) suggests that the similarities between readers and characters might be of two broad types. **Categorical similarities** relate to a reader's self-concept and identity: for instance, facts about their gender, nationality, sexuality, personal history, abilities, weaknesses, physical characteristics, and so on. **Situational similarities** are based on personal memories of particular experiences, such as 'my tenth birthday', or 'my wedding day', or 'being in high school'. The perception of categorical, situational, or both types of similarities can underpin readers' identification with characters.

The extract below comes from the first chapter of Tom McCarthy's novel *Satin Island* (2015: 6). The narrator, U, a male corporate anthropologist, is waiting in a noisy airport lounge for a delayed flight, and describes a childhood memory. As you read the passage, consider the extent to which you can identify with the narrator. How does this influence your response to the passage?:

> To a soundtrack, incongruous, of looped, recorded messages and chimes, a fruit machine's idle-tune, snatches of other people's conversations and the staggered, intermittent hiss, quieter or louder, of steam-arms at espresso bars dotted about the terminal, a memory came to me: of freewheeling down a hill as a child, riding my second bike. It wasn't a specific memory of riding down the hill on such-and-such a day: more a generic one in which hundreds of hill-descents, accumulated over two or three years, had all merged together. Where my first bike had had a footbrake, activated by the pedal, this one, fitted with a handbrake instead, allowed back-pedalling. This struck me, I remembered, as nothing short of miraculous. That you could move one way while rotating the crank in the opposite direction contravened my fledgling understanding not only of motion but also of time – as though this, too, could be laced with a contraflow lodged right inside its core. Whenever I hurtled, back-pedalling, down the hill, I'd feel exhilaration, but also vertigo – vertigo tinged with a slight nausea. It wasn't an entirely pleasant feeling. Recalling the manoeuvre now reproduced – in the crowded terminal, in my head and stomach – the same awkward sense of things being out of sync, out of whack.

The passage is narrated in the first person and involves two time zones: the speaker-now in which the narrator is sitting in an airport recounting his memory, and the memory itself in which the narrator is a child riding his new bike. As such, there are two minds to model in the extract: that of the adult-narrator and that of the narrator-as-child. The extract is rich with sensory description that facilitates mind-modelling.

The first sentence features several long noun phrases with heavy pre- and post-modification in order to give detailed description of the sounds that the adult-narrator can hear around him. The narration of the memory describes the emotional and sensory experience of the narrator-as-child: their excitement about the 'miraculous' bike and the 'exhilaration' and 'vertigo tinged with a slight nausea' that they felt when back-pedalling it down a hill. Neuroscientific research into embodied cognition has found evidence to suggest that the sensorimotor areas of the brain, which are involved in performing actions, are also active when we perceive and imaginatively simulate actions. In the extract, the narrator's memory reproduces the sensation of vertigo as he sits in the airport lounge, and for one of us (Sara), when reading the passage for the first time, the passage also induced mild vertigo – coupled with a thrill of recognition and affinity towards the narrator-as-child. The narrator's memory of backpedalling a bike chimed with Sara's own childhood memory (which she had forgotten about until she read the passage). Such recognition of similarity between self and narrator is identification, founded on the recognition of situational similarities ('backpedalling a bike as a child'). Interestingly, the narrator describes his memory as 'generic' rather than anchored in one specific autobiographical moment, and here this seems to makes it easier to recognise broad similarities between reader and character.

A glance at online reviews of *Satin Island* suggests that not all readers' experiences of the novel are characterised by identification with the narrator. On the book recommendation website Goodreads, readers offer polarised evaluations of the text. Readers who rate the novel highly (above 3 stars out of 5) often portray some identification with the novel's contents. For instance, 'Maxwell' suggests that the novel gives expression to experiences he recognises, and 'RitaSkeeter' implicitly compares herself to the internet-surfing narrator:

> 'at some points [in the book] there is nothing that exceptional. But at others it delivers these moments of clarity and insight that I have never seen put down in words before.' (Maxwell, Goodreads, Sep 25 2015, 3 stars)

> 'Ever gone to do a quick look-up of something on Wikipedia, and 5 hours later you're still there following links to things you never realised you had an interest in until just then? Yeah, me either *shifty eyes*.' (RitaSkeeter, Goodreads, Dec 19 2015, 4 stars)

Readers who give the novel lower ratings often emphasise their dislike and difference from the narrator. 'Barry Pierce' found the pondering narration boring, rather than involving. 'Vanessa' took 'nothing away' from her reading, unlike the 'moments of clarity' described by 'Maxwell' above. 'Sam Quixote' equates U with a class of people ('anthropologists') whom he regards as pretentious in real life:

> 'What an utterly boring and navel-gazing novel. [. . .] we follow a character named U, no really, he's called fucking *U*, while he wonders and ponders for 200ish pages. I applaud this novel on its brevity, any longer and I would have *literally* died of boredom.' (Barry Pierce, Goodreads, Jul 30 2015, 1 star)

> 'For the most part this was a snore-fest and I took nothing away from it.' (Vanessa, Goodreads, Oct 4 2015, 1 star)

> 'One of the most pretentious people I ever met was an anthropologist (the person would literally sniff and turn their noses up after making a point), so it's no surprise to me that a novel featuring an anthropologist would turn out to be a load of pretentious crap.' (Sam Quixote, Goodreads, Mar 17 2005, 2 stars)

The latter three reviewers express some resistance to the novel. **Resistance** is the flipside of identification, when readers perceive difference between themselves and a literary entity, or are not willing or able to make the self-implicating connections that characterise identification. Just like identification, resistance involves projection and the interaction between textual cues and a reader's sense of self, but whilst identification is characterised by attraction and positive valence, resistance is characterised by aversion and negative valence.

People's emotional responses to texts are likely to differ because *people* differ, yet it is worth remembering that literary texts are written in order to encourage or facilitate particular emotional responses in their audiences. Broadly speaking, readers are likely to be motivated towards identification with literary characters, and literary works which inspire such identification are usually evaluated more positively. However, resistance is also an important component of literary response, and can be equally responsible for the evocation of emotion during reading. Rather than being an all-or-nothing phenomenon, it is likely that identification and resistance are also scalar and can fluctuate during reading experiences in order to contribute to nuanced emotional effects.

The acts of comparison and recognition which underpin identification and resistance are also thought to be the basis for feelings of empathy and sympathy. Broadly speaking, these terms refer to an emotional experience which arises from a particular relationship between the experiencer and another person (or literary character). Sanford and

Emmott (2012: 221) suggest that both empathy and sympathy involve some moral stance or judgement in relation to an 'other'. **Empathy** is often characterised by a sense of emotional similarity and proximity to another person, the sense that the experiencer is 'feeling with' someone else, and therefore it is clear how it might arise through identification. Some researchers (e.g. Keen 2007; Sklar 2013) suggest that empathy is a spontaneous sharing of (what the experiencer believes to be) the emotions of others. In Sara's reading of the passage from *Satin Island*, her spontaneous sharing of the narrator's feeling of being 'out of sync' might be considered an empathic response. **Sympathy** is often characterised as 'feeling for' someone else, and although it involves the experience of emotions in response to another person's plight (sympathy is often discussed as a response to perceived suffering), it involves greater distance, evaluation, or judgement between the sympathiser and the object of their sympathy.

20.4 Narrative perspective and positioning

One might assume that first-person narration is the ultimate emotion-generating style because of the access it grants readers to characters' minds and emotions. However, empirical studies have not supported this. Narrative perspective affects levels of empathy, but not in a straightforward way. Narratives operate on multiple communicative levels. On one level (the discourse-world in Text World Theory terms), a real author addresses a real reader (although they tend to be separated in space and time). On another level, formed by the text, an implied author addresses an implied reader. Implied authors and readers are distinct from real authors and readers because they are generated by the language of the text (and exist in the minds of readers) rather than being flesh-and-blood beings. In other words, this level and all subsequent levels are imagined text-worlds. Next, a narrator addresses a narratee, and at a further level, characters exist and interact with other characters. These levels, and the communicative roles they hold, are summarised in Figure 20.1.

Cognitive stylistic theories of emotional response suggest that it is possible for 'real readers' to engage in different levels of psychological projection, mind-modelling, identification, empathy, sympathy, and resistance in relation to each of the other roles. Continuing the spatial metaphor established at the beginning of this chapter, the emotional texture of reading can be seen to arise from readers' **positioning** in relation to the multiple entities evoked by a text. These positions correlate with the degree of 'support, acquiescence or resistance' in the reading

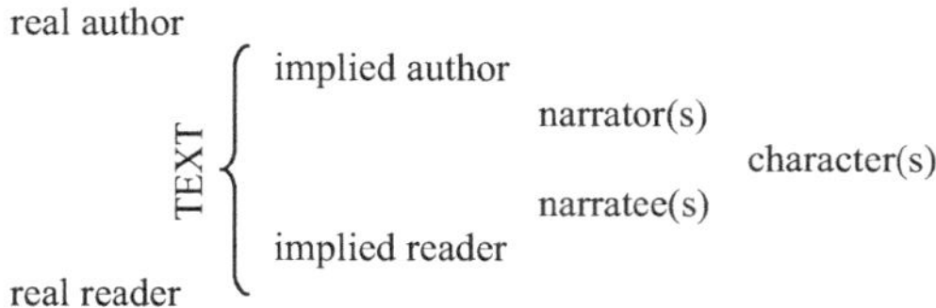

Figure 20.1 Roles involved in literary communication

(Stockwell 2009a: 160). The language of the text contributes to positioning readers in these relationships and therefore influences readers' emotional experiences.

The extract below is the opening of Ethan Hawke's novel *Ash Wednesday* (2002: 3), a romantic drama set in the USA. The extract establishes the first-person narration of one of the novel's main characters, Jimmy Heartsock. We first saw this extract in Chapter 9 where we analysed modal shading in order to account for our impressions of the narrator's conflicted character. There, we argued that the modality in the text contributes to creating the impression of an opinionated, gregarious narrator who is also insecure. Here, our cognitive stylistic analysis attempts to account for a reader's emotional response to that character – providing a framework for discussing the interaction between reader and text in greater detail. How do you feel about Jimmy?:

> I was driving a '69 Chevy Nova four-barrel with mag wheels and a dual exhaust. It's a kick-ass car. I took the muffler out so it sounds like a Harley. People love it. I was staring at myself through the window into the driver's-side mirror; I do that all the time. I'll stare into anything that reflects. That's not a flattering quality, and I wish I didn't do it, but I do. I'm vain as hell. It's revolting. Most of the time when I'm looking in the mirror, I'm checking to see if I'm still here or else I'm wishing I was somebody else, a Mexican bandito or somebody like that. I have a mustache. Most guys with mustaches look like fags, but I don't. I touch mine too much, though. I touch it all the time. I don't even know why I am telling you about it now. I just stare at myself constantly and I wish I didn't. It brings me absolutely no pleasure at all.
>
> My fingers were frozen around the steering wheel. Albany in February is a black sooty slab of ice. The woman on the radio announced the time and temperature: eight forty-two and twenty-three degrees. Christy and I had broken up fifteen hours earlier, and I was in a tailspin. I had my uniform on, the dress one; it's awesome. Military uniforms make you feel like somebody, like you have a purpose, even if you don't. You feel special, connected to the past. You're not just an ordinary person, a *civilian* – you're noble. The downside of this Walk of Pride is, it's a lie.

The use of first-person narration establishes the role of a narrator located in an unspecified time/place, and this automatically implies the corresponding presence of a narratee (someone being addressed by the narrator). This narratee is addressed explicitly by the second-person reference in L8–9: 'I don't even know why I am telling you about it now.' Broadly speaking, the narrator seems to shift rapidly between two main topics: recounting an event from his past, when he was sitting in a cold car after breaking up with his girlfriend (this is indicated by the past progressive and simple tenses in L1 'I was driving', L2–3 'I was staring', L11–14 'My fingers were frozen . . .'), and offering more general summaries or statements about his habitual characteristics (indicated by temporal locatives and the present simple; e.g. 'I do that all the time' L3, 'Most of the time' L5, 'I just stare at myself constantly' L9). The narrative shifts between these topics and time zones, creating multiple text-worlds which represent different locations in time and space (or different story-nows). Jimmy spends much of this opening talking about himself – offering a representation of himself to the unnamed narratee. The text-worlds he creates are populated with different versions (or enactors) of himself, so that he is a character in his own narrative.

When mind-modelling the narrator, Jimmy Heartsock, the rapid topic shifts and preoccupation with self-representation leads to the attribution of personality traits and emotions to Jimmy: he seems rather self-obsessed and also somewhat nervous and jumpy. We experience a lack of identification with this narrator in terms of categorical similarities – neither of us is American or male, and the references to American cars (Chevy Nova) are unfamiliar. Other aspects of Jimmy-the-character's experiences are more relatable, however. Jimmy represents himself as vain and prone to stare at himself in reflective surfaces – and this evokes some situational identification – we know what it is like to do this! This makes Jimmy-the-narrator's harsh self-criticism (he describes himself as 'revolting' and 'vain') less easy to relate to. Other aspects of Jimmy-the-character evoke resistance, particularly his use of homophobic language and cultural stereotypes (L7–8). Thus, we experience fluctuating positioning in relation to Jimmy Heartsock as narrator and character: sometimes experiencing mild identification and other times feeling resistant.

In addition to the narrator and character roles evoked by this extract, the implied author role may also be significant for readers' emotional positioning. The real author of the novel, Ethan Hawke, is a Hollywood actor with a diverse filmography which includes sci-fi and cop movies (e.g. *Gattaca*, *Training Day*), but who is also known for his roles in cult dramas *Dead Poets Society*, *Reality Bites*, *Boyhood* and romances such as *Before Sunset*, *Before Sunrise*, and *Before Midnight*. In the latter movies, Hawke plays articulate male characters struggling with aspects of masculinity and the complexities of human relationships. In the media, Hawke's real-life marriages and divorces are widely reported and he is often represented as holding liberal political values: he is quoted celebrating Democrat wins and recorded a video in support of gay marriage. For readers who possess it, this knowledge of the real-world Ethan Hawke is likely to contribute to the mind-modelling inferences they make about the implied author of the novel. The perception of an authorial presence 'behind' the text also gives rise to the sense of an implied reader, who is being addressed by that author. Figure 20.2 summarises the narrative roles involved in the extract from *Ash Wednesday*.

Our idea of the author Ethan Hawke as a sensitive and politically liberal American is projected onto our sense of the implied author of the novel. Hawkes' associations with American culture and masculinity add a sense of authenticity to his creation of Jimmy's narrative voice, but Jimmy's use of homophobic language signals characterisation and distinguishes Jimmy the narrator from the implied author. There is a sense that the implied author and the implied reader know more than the character and are in a position to judge him together. Taken together, the passage encourages sympathy for the character-narrator but not necessarily empathy: whilst we judge him as a particular type of macho American male, we also perceive some glimmer of common humanity in him (through the representation of his suffering, disillusionment, and minor flaws).

This analysis has shown how textual cues evoke a number of textual entities who are involved in the rhetorical act of the narrative. Cognitive stylistic analysis encourages us to be aware of the narrative levels involved in a text and the way language contributes to the characterisation of different roles at these levels. It also emphasises the role that a reader's knowledge and personality may play in their emotional reactions to texts.

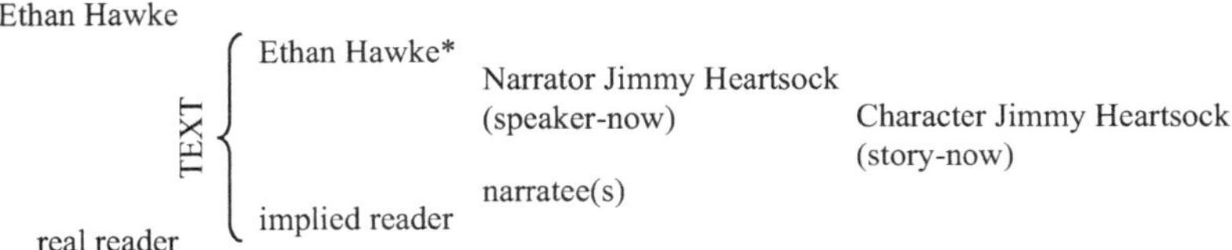

Figure 20.2 Roles involved in the opening passage of *Ash Wednesday*

* distinguishes the reader's mental model of Ethan Hawke from the real Ethan Hawke, who most readers will not know personally or have any real-world access to

Keywords and summary

Categorical similarities, emotion (intensity, valence, action tendencies), empathy, identification, immersion, mind-modelling, positioning, psychological projection, resistance, situational similarities, sympathy.

This chapter has introduced some of the key ideas underpinning cognitive stylistic attempts to understand emotions in literary reading. Analysing emotional involvement in literature is complex because literary works are multi-layered, and readers are all different. There is not a guaranteed one-to-one correspondence between textual feature and emotional effect. However, there are often similarities between readers' emotional responses to texts. Studying emotion involves paying close attention to narrative perspective, to the resources which readers contribute to imaginatively realising the narrative, and the multiple positions they can adopt in relation to the tellers and the story. Whilst offering accounts of your own introspective emotional responses to a text (as we have here) can be interesting, there is an increasing tendency for researchers to examine the responses of readers other than themselves in order to try and understand emotional experience during reading. In Chapter 22, we provide more details about the methods used to gather data from other readers for use in stylistic analysis.

Activities

1. The extract below comes from the end of *The Fault in Our Stars* by Tom Green (2012: 263–6). The main character Hazel has recently learnt that her boyfriend Augustus has died from cancer. What mind-modelling inferences do you make about the character? How do textual cues and your own knowledge contribute to these inferences? Consider the positions you adopt in relation to the enactors in the novel. Do you experience any identification, resistance, empathy, or sympathy and if so, why?:

> I lay still and alone in my bed staring at the ceiling, the waves tossing me against the rocks then pulling me back out to sea so they could launch me again into the jagged face of the cliff, leaving me floating faceup on the water, undrowned.
>
> Finally I did call him. His phone rang five times and then went to voice mail. "You've reached the voice mail of Augustus Waters," he said, the clarion voice I'd fallen for. "Leave a message." It beeped. The dead air on the line was so eerie. I just wanted to go back to that secret post-terrestrial third space with him that we visited when we talked on the phone.

I waited for that feeling, but it never came: The dead air on the line was no comfort, and finally I hung up.

I got my laptop out from under my bed and fired it up and went onto his wall page, where already the condolences were flooding in. The most recent one said:

I love you, bro. See you on the other side.

... Written by someone I'd never heard of. In fact, almost all the wall posts, which arrived nearly as fast as I could read them, were written by people I'd never met and whom he'd never spoken about, people who were extolling his various virtues now that he was dead, even though I knew for a fact they hadn't seen him in months and had made no effort to visit him. [...] I knew these people were genuinely sad, and that I wasn't really mad at them. I was mad at the universe.

2. Read these four Goodreads responses about *The Year of the Runaways*. What types of emotional experiences are exhibited in the reviews? Are they empathetic? Sympathetic? Identificatory? Resistant? Which linguistic features in the reviews support your assessment of the readers' emotional responses?:

   - I found myself doing a lot of yelling – out loud, and in my head – at the characters in this novel about four young Indian immigrants who find their way separately, and together, to Sheffield, England. What's so compelling about this book is the way Sahota brings together four individuals from different backgrounds, castes, and socio-economic levels, and shows how they did, or would have interacted at home in India, and how that differs from their experience together in England. Sadly, both at home and abroad, life is filled with hardship and tragedy for all four of them, despite the differences in their backgrounds, and the varying degrees of privilege they start out with. [...] It's impossible not to feel for them, even as you shake your head at their behavior. I found the ending a bit unsatisfying, if only because I would have liked to follow these characters into old age. (Sue, Goodreads, May 01 2016, 4 stars)
   - Good but utterly grim. I'm a migrant but my life's been a doddle compared to the experiences of these 3 young men. Bit slow in places and suddenly it comes together at the end. Also: they ate a lot of roti in this book. (Kinga, Mar 21 2017, 4 stars)
   - The problem is with the characters – the situations they're in feel realistic, they're certainly grim enough, but the characters themselves feel unreal. Two of them are same-y, two of them are not good people, two are silent and mysterious (and these are the ones who are not the

same), the girl – I can't understand her at all – I mean, I can figure that she's naive enough to think she can make a difference, but I don't understand which god fearing Indian girl would treat marriage so lightly, to be able to divorce one and marry another, no matter what her motivations are. (Chaitra, Goodreads, Sep 29 2016, 2 Stars)

- The plot follows a group of Indian men as they try to find work and livelihood in modern-day Britain. This whole novel is a character study of these men as we follow their lives for one year in 400ish pages. Sadly, this novel is so lacking in engaging prose or fully-rounded characters that one does not read this novel, they stare and wait for it to end. I did not care about any of these characters. There was nothing there to care about. And since I didn't care, I didn't derive any enjoyment from this. I was utterly bored from page 20 onwards. Such a pity. (Barry Pierce, Goodreads, Nov 08 2015, 1 star)

3. Pick a text which evoked a strong emotion in you, and one that didn't. Can you account for your responses using the concepts of identification and resistance described in this chapter? To what extent does the language of the text affect your response? Are there any aspects of your emotional experience that can't be accounted for using the ideas in this chapter?

Further reading and references

Other cognitive stylistic analyses of emotional response can be found in: Burke (2011a), Freeman (2009), Gavins (2007), Jeffries (2001), Lahey (2005), Nuttall (2015, 2017), Semino (1997), Stewart-Shaw (2017), Stockwell (2005a, 2009a), van Peer (1997), and Whiteley (2011a, 2014, 2015). Sanford and Emmott (2012: 191–232) offer a useful review of work on emotion, empathy, and suspense in narrative. Palmer (2004), Stockwell (2009a), and Zunshine (2006) discuss mind modelling. Keen (2007) and Sklar (2013) discuss empathy and sympathy in literature; Browse (2018) and Stockwell (2009a) discuss resistance. Phelan's (1996, 2005, 2007) work in rhetorical narratology discusses literary roles and positioning in relation to narrative ethics. Classic work discussing narrative levels can be found in: Booth (1961, 1988), Genette (1980), Leech and Short (2007 [1981]: 206–30), and Stanzel (1984). Experiments investigating the influence of perspective on reader empathy include: Bray (2007a, 2007b), Sotirova (2006), and van Peer and Pander Maat (1996, 2001).

Eysenk and Keane (1995) and Griffiths (1998) offer useful introductions to emotion in cognitive psychology. Arnold (1960), Frijda (1986), and Moors et al. (2013) are good starting points for psychological work on appraisal theory. Oatley (1994, 1999a, 1999b, 2002, 2009), Oatley and Gholamain (1997), and Robinson (2005) apply appraisal theory in the discussion of literary emotion. Psychological work which views emotion from a social perspective includes: Oatley (2009), Oatley and Johnson-Laird (1987, 1996), Parkinson (1995), and Parkinson et al. (2005). Other influential psychological work on emotion and literature includes: Gerrig (1993, 1996), Kuiken et al. (2004), Miall (2006), and Oatley (2003); see also Albritton and Gerrig (1991), Gerrig and Rapp (2004), Prentice et al. (1997), and Rapp and Gerrig (2002, 2006). For more on the philosophical debate about the status of our emotional responses to fiction, see: Currie (1997), Levinson (1997), Walton (1997), and Yanal (1999).

Part VII

Reading as data

21 Corpus stylistics

21.1 Corpus linguistics, stylistics, and corpora

The chapters in this Part of the book cover two areas of data-driven stylistic analysis: this chapter considers texts as data to be explored using computers, and Chapter 22 discusses the use of reader response data in stylistic analysis. Both approaches use methodological innovations to test and develop stylistic claims and provide new perspectives on texts and reading.

Corpus linguistics is an area of linguistics which capitalises on relatively recent developments in computing, specifically the power of computers to identify patterns in large stretches of language. **Corpus stylistics** applies these computational methods to address stylistic concerns. Fundamental to corpus linguistics and stylistics is a mixed methodology that is both quantitative and qualitative. **Quantitative methods** gather numerical data that can be used for precise, statistical comparisons and are therefore seen as objective measurements. **Qualitative methods** tend to be text- or picture-based and are more subjective because they require additional interpretive work from the researcher. By the end of this chapter, you will have used both methods and thus learnt how they are combined in corpus stylistics. For now, it suffices to say that because the computational dimension of the corpus approach yields quantitative data, it is seen to introduce a greater degree of analytical objectivity into stylistic analysis. This objectivity means it has the potential to reveal patterns in the texts that might otherwise have gone unnoticed.

The term '**corpus**' refers to a collection of data. However, when used to describe approaches in linguistics and stylistics, it usually also implies that this data is stored on a computer. The data is analysed using corpus tools, that is – computational procedures. There are a number of different corpus software programs. Some require a fee for a single-user licence or annual subscription, such as Wordsmith and

WMatrix. In this chapter, we'll be using AntConc, which is free to download and compatible with Windows, Linux, and Mac (links to all three programs are provided in the 'Corpus programs' section of this book's references). You should therefore be able to use AntConc for your own research.

The type of corpus used in a piece of research will depend on the research question. Corpus linguistic studies are often interested in the spread and use of a particular language feature (for instance, sentence initial connectives such as 'And' or 'But'), and as such need to look at a large **general corpus** like the British National Corpus (BNC), which contains 100 million words from spoken and written British English, or the Corpus of Contemporary American English (COCA), which contains 520 million words from spoken and written American English. In comparison, corpus stylistics tends to use smaller, **specialised corpora**, which can be designed specifically for the research project or created by focusing on a particular aspect of a general corpus. For instance, you could restrict your search of COCA by genre to fiction. You could also select a particular time period – fiction from 1990 to 2000. In corpus stylistics, specialised corpora might focus on: a particular author, as in the CLiC Dickens project which uses Charles Dickens' fiction as its corpus (see Mahlberg 2013); or a particular text, such as in Ho's (2011) study of John Fowles' *The Magus* or in Lahey's (2015) exploration of REMEMBER and FORGET in Dan Brown's *Angels and Demons*.

As a guide for how to conduct corpus research, we have adapted a methodological approach suggested by Rayson (2008: 519–21), shown in Table 21.1. The most obvious way to conduct corpus research is to have a research question in mind before you start your project (step 1). However, your analysis might reveal new insights or yield unexpected results, so the model allows you to modify the research aims (step 5). We'll pursue these steps throughout this chapter. If you want to follow along, now would be a good point to download and install AntConc on your computer (http://www.laurenceanthony.net/software/antconc).

21.2 Corpus stylistics and word lists

To demonstrate the methodological steps of corpus research in action, we're going to use a case study and examine the language of a particular short story: 'Blood Story' by Melvin Burgess (n.d.). 'Blood Story' is divided into two parts, both named after their first-person narrators. In the first part, Grace sits on a blanket outdoors, watching her twin brothers playing; in the second part, Captain Tom watches Grace and her brothers. As your reading of 'Blood Story' progresses, it

Table 21.1 Methodological steps in corpus research (adapted from Rayson 2008; see also Mahlberg 2013: 13)

Methodological steps in corpus research		
1.	Devise	What is your research question or hypothesis? What is it that you want to find out about your data?
2.	Build	Design and compile your corpus.
3.	Annotate	Manual or automatic analysis of the corpus.
4.	Retrieve	Quantitative and Qualitative analyses of corpus.
5.	Question	If you did not devise a research question (step 1), do so now with your results in mind. Alternatively, revisit your question.
6.	Interpret	Manual interpretation of your results. How do they answer your research question, or prove/disprove your hypothesis?

becomes increasingly clear that it is set in an alternate reality, in which a new breed of humans has come into being. Grace and her family are members of this new species – half-human, half-dog. Captain Tom, on the other hand, is watching them because he wants to assassinate them. The story represents the same narrative events but from different points of view, to create some interesting effects.

We are interested in how the same narrative events are presented by two different characters, and so our research questions are something like: what are the similarities/differences in the narrators' representations of the scene? What does this suggest about their characterisation? How does this inform the story's effects? To address these questions, we need to build an appropriate corpus. In this case, the corpus is simply the whole short story. The scale of your research question will influence how many examples you need. For instance, it would be possible to broaden the corpus to include all of Burgess' writing, or several examples of short stories with shifting focalisation – but these corpora would in turn address much broader research questions (about Burgess' style in general, or focalisation patterns in short stories).

'Blood Story' is available online through the BookTrust website so we downloaded it from there. It is only five pages long so we recommend that you take this opportunity to read Burgess' story. As you do so, think about your experience of the text and the characterisation of the two narrators. You will then be able to see if our corpus analysis confirms your impressions of 'Blood Story' or reveals anything you hadn't noticed. To undertake corpus analysis, we need our data in electronic format. We already have 'Blood Story' as a Word file (.doc or .docx) but even though Word documents look as though they consist only of words, there is also a lot of 'behind the scenes' data such as formatting (font, paragraphing, bold, italics, etc.). We need to strip this out, so we must convert the story into a plain text file (.txt). Actually, because we want to compare the two parts of the short story, we will separate them into two .txt files, one for each part (Grace.txt and CaptainTom.txt).

It is at this point that you complete the third methodological step in corpus research: annotate. Whether you do this and what you do will again depend on your research question. If you're interested in specific parts of speech (POS) – that is, grammatical categories – you would **annotate** or **tag** each word with its POS label. Some programs have automatic software to do this, such as WMatrix's corpus annotation tool CLAWS (which can also be used free online to tag small amounts of text). Since we're interested in content rather than syntax, we will skip the annotation step and now load our two .txt files into AntConc, using the 'Open file' command. To check these files have loaded properly, go to the 'File View' tab, click on the file, and you should be able to see the text.

An essential tool in, and starting point for, corpus analysis is the **word list**. This generates a list of all the words in your corpus and shows their **frequency** (the number of times each word occurs) and rank order. To generate a word list, click on the 'Word List' tab and then hit 'Start'. Figure 21.1 is a screenshot of AntConc's word list output for 'Blood Story'. In the left pane, you can see that we have opened both files, so this word list is for the whole short story. In the first instance, we can describe our corpus in terms of the number of types and tokens it contains. The number of **tokens** represents the total number of words in the corpus; the number of **types** is the total number of *unique* words. Figure 21.1 shows that 'Blood Story' consists of 2080 tokens, but only 645 types; 'the' is the most frequent word in 'Blood Story' because there are 84 occurrences, but it is only counted as 1 type.

Simply generating a word list isn't very revealing. As you can see, the most frequent types in 'Blood Story' are all grammatical words. Grammatical words are most frequent in almost any corpus because of the central role they play in language. There are two things we can do to fine-tune our word list. Firstly, we can use a **stop list**, a list of words for the program to ignore or remove from its searches. The most common stop list is for grammatical words (the list we used is shown in Table 21.2). Save these words in a text file (.txt) in order to import them into AntConc. Another useful tool is a **lemma list**. A **lemma** is a set of words that share a stem (also referred to as the head word or the canonical form of the word). For instance, the lemma FEEL consists of the stem 'feel' as well as its inflected forms 'feels', 'feeling', 'felt'. The

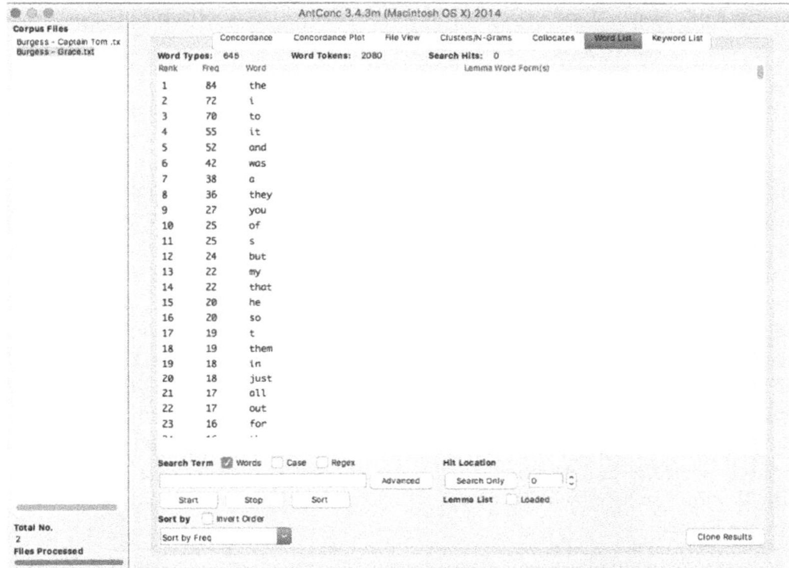

Figure 21.1 Screenshot of AntConc's word list for 'Blood Story'

lemma list tells the corpus software to group all the related lexemes under the lemma. We used Anthony's (n.d.) 'AntBNC Lemma List', available from the AntConc Homepage, but made one modification to it. We removed the lemma string for the verb inflections 'pup -> pups pup pupped' and added the lexemes 'pup' and 'pups' to the lemma string with noun inflections 'puppy -> puppy puppies puppys'. This is because we know from reading 'Blood Story' that it contains the lexemes 'pup' and 'pups' but uses them as nouns in the lemma string PUPPY. This kind of human intuition is sometimes required in corpus research in order to tailor computer tools to fit the particular object of the study.

To apply both your stop list and lemma list to the word list tool in AntConc, you'll need to open 'Tool Preferences' which can be found in the same level as the 'File' menu. If you use Anthony's 'AntBNC Lemma List', you will also need to go into 'Global Settings' (also in the main menu), select 'Token Definition' in the left-hand category pane, and tick 'Use Following Definition' and 'append the following definition': in the latter box, type a hyphen (-) and apostrophe (') (e.g. -').

We can now generate more insightful word lists. Because we're interested in the differences between Grace's and Captain Tom's narration, we're going to do this for each part of the story in turn. First, then, with

Table 21.2 Stop list for grammatical words (from http://99webtools.com/blog/list-of-english-stop-words)

Stop list words
a, able, about, across, after, all, almost, also, am, among, an, and, any, are, as, at, be, because, been, but, by, can, cannot, could, dear, did, do, does, either, else, every, for, from, get, got, had, has, have, he, her, hers, him, his, how, however, i, if, in, into, is, it, its, just, least, let, like, likely, may, me, might, must, my, neither, no, nor, not, of, off, often, on, only, or, other, our, own, rather, said, say, says, she, should, since, so, some, than, that, the, their, them, then, there, these, they, this, tis, to, too, twas, us, wants, was, we, were, what, when, where, which, while, who, whom, why, will, with, would, yet, you, your, ain't, aren't, can't, could've, couldn't, didn't, doesn't, don't, hasn't, he'd, he'll, he's, how'd, how'll, how's, i'd, i'll, i'm, i've, isn't, it's, might've, mightn't, must've, mustn't, shan't, she'd, she'll, she's, should've, shouldn't, that'll, that's, there's, they'd, they'll, they're, they've, wasn't, we'd, we'll, we're, weren't, what'd, what's, when'd, when'll, when's, where'd, where'll, where's, who'd, who'll, who's, why'd, why'll, why's, won't, would've, wouldn't, you'd, you'll, you're, you've

only the 'Grace' file open, navigate to the 'Word List' tab in AntConc and hit 'Start'. Once you have your word list, press the 'Clone Results' button on the bottom right. This will open a new window with your 'Grace' word list results. Navigate back into AntConc, close the 'Grace' file, and 'Clear all Tools'; then open the 'Captain Tom' file and repeat the process. You'll now be able to compare the results. If you've been doing this in AntConc while reading, take a moment to consider your two word lists.

The top ten lemmas for the 'Grace' and 'Captain Tom' narratives are shown in Table 21.3. (Because our corpus – 'Blood Story' – is so small, the difference between frequencies is not significant, and thus our decision of where to draw the line for 'top' lemmas was very arbitrary.) Both lists include verbs of perception and epistemic knowledge, such as SEE, LOOK, KNOW, and THINK. This perhaps makes sense since, as first-person narratives, both parts of 'Blood Story' present characters' consciousness. There are, however, also differences. Most notably, Grace's worldview seems to be quite family-oriented with MUM and DAD, and BOY all appearing as lemmas at the top of the word list; in contrast, while GIRL appears in Captain Tom's list, the highest-ranking lemma is PUPPY and (although not shown in Table 21.3) further down, we also find DOG (three instances). This does make sense if you've read 'Blood Story': the PUPPY and DOG lemmas suggest Captain Tom's interest in the half-dog species that he is watching in order to assassinate.

Table 21.3 Word lists for 'Grace' and 'Captain Tom' parts of Burgess' 'Blood Story'

GRACE				CAPTAIN TOM		
Freq.	Lemma forms	Lemma	Rank	Lemma	Lemma forms	Freq.
12	out(12)	out	1	puppy	pup(1), pups(5)	6
11	know(7), knowing(1), known(1), knows(1), knew(1)	know	2	look	look(2), looked(1), looking(2)	5
11	up(11)	up	3	out	out(5)	5
9	looked(2), looking(2)	look	4	way	way(5)	5
8	dad(8)	dad	5	girl	girl(4)	4
8	mum(8)	mum	6	know	knew(1), know(3)	4
7	see(4), seeing(1), saw(3)	see	7	never	never(4)	4
7	day(3), days(4)	day	8	take	taken(2), took(2)	4
6	think(2), thought(5)	think	9	up	up(4)	4
6	boy(2), boys(6)	boy	10	away	away(3)	3

21.3 Keywords and keyness

The two word lists shown in Table 21.3 begin to offer quantitative insight into 'Blood Story'. On the one hand, we can say that there is a difference between the two narratives in terms of content; on the other, this isn't actually surprising (we would necessarily expect the two parts to differ). Although we could speculate that the different content might be due to the narrator-focalisers, our word list doesn't provide any real evidence. There are limits to the value of word lists: some of the lemmas shown are quite unremarkable and we don't know if readers will notice the differing emphases of the two narratives. What we need is a way to extract the most significant words, rather than simply the most frequent. To do this, we'll use another tool: the keyword list. Generating our word list, though, was not a wasted step because AntConc needs to produce a word list before it can create a keyword list.

To use the keyword tool, you need to provide AntConc with a reference corpus. Strictly speaking, the corpus program views a **reference corpus** as a collection of data to use in making comparisons. We could for instance, compare Grace's narrative with Captain Tom's. However, this would be a somewhat atypical understanding of a reference corpus. A typical reference corpus is a larger, general corpus that is representative of language use. We are going to use the BNC Baby corpus, a 4 million word sample from the 100 million word BNC. We need our reference corpus to be appropriate to our **study corpus** though, so we will only use BNC Baby's fiction subcorpus. If you want to continue following the analysis, you can download the BNC Baby corpus at: http://ota.ox.ac.uk/desc/2553.

We're going to create a keywords list for both parts of the narrative and for 'Blood Story' as a whole. In AntConc, in the 'File' main menu, click 'Clear all Tools and Files'. Before you begin, make sure your stop and lemma lists are still loaded. Then, open one of the files (e.g. Grace.txt). Go into 'Tool Preferences' again and navigate to the 'Keyword List' category. Under 'Reference Corpus', tick the 'Use RAW files' box and then underneath that, click on 'Add files'. Add the files in the fiction folder of BNC Baby and click 'Load'. Once the load bar is full, click 'Apply' and close tool preferences. First, make a word list for Grace.txt, then in the keyword list tab, hit start (AntConc should be set to 'Sort by keyness'). Once you have your keyword list for Grace.txt, clone results, and repeat the process for CaptainTom.txt and then repeat with both files open. You should now have three key word lists, similar to those in Table 21.4. We disregarded some lemmas from the list, namely 'bull' and 'turner', which are the names of a character, as well as 're' and 'didn', which are fragments.

A **keyword list** is a list of words that are unusually frequent in your study corpus in comparison with their frequency in your chosen reference corpus. The **keyness value** is a statistical measurement – using *Chi-square* or *log-likelihood* (LL), which is AntConc's default setting – that represents the unusualness of the word (or lemma) contained in the study corpus. Keyness measurements are related to probability or *p*-values. A ***p*-value** represents how probable it is that your result occurred by accident (e.g. that it is a 'false positive'). Lower *p*-values therefore coincide with higher keyness, and are desirable because they indicate that it is less likely that your result is the product of random error. We can equate LL keyness to *p*-values as shown in Table 21.5 (Rayson n.d.), where '<' means 'less than'. As a stylistician, you must decide what level is significant or, in other words, how much potential error you are comfortable with. Quantitative, experimental research in the humanities generally classes $p < 0.05$ as significant and $p < 0.01$ as very significant (van Peer et al. 2012 [2007]: 207). Corpus linguistics usually accepts a maximum of $p < 0.01$ (LL keyness: 6.63).

Keyness values are important because, in Baker's words, a keyword list therefore 'gives a measure of *saliency*, whereas a simple word list only provides *frequency*' (2006: 125; original emphasis). In 'Blood Story', all of the lemmas shown in Table 21.4 have very high keyness values (with $p < 0.0001$), suggesting high significance. We do, however, have to be

Table 21.4 Keywords lists using BNC Baby fiction reference corpus

	GRACE			CAPTAIN TOM			'BLOOD STORY'		
Rank	Freq.	Keyness	Lemma	Freq.	Keyness	Lemma	Freq.	Keyness	Lemma
1	8	79.569	mum	6	99.006	puppy	8	115.208	puppy
2	8	76.385	dad	3	35.153	clever	17	80.026	out
3	6	59.664	hide	5	31.885	way	14	74.571	look
4	3	57.9	halfman	2	31.568	pant	8	73.497	mum
5	12	56.711	out	4	30.696	girl	8	70.389	dad
6	11	52.484	know	3	30.003	dog	15	70.206	know
7	11	49.845	up	3	29.474	check	15	66.168	up
8	9	46.452	look	5	28.366	look	6	55.209	hide
9	6	45.452	boy	2	27.591	fro	8	53.197	girl
10	4	44.575	twin	2	26.553	spit	11	50.315	see
11	3	44.405	pee	4	25.969	never	7	50.16	boy
12	7	42.115	day	3	23.75	run	3	47.448	halfman
13	3	38.835	wreck	4	23.431	take	10	45.141	think
14	2	38.6	yow	5	23.387	out	8	44.622	day
15	3	37.428	fur	2	22.478	meat	8	43.85	never
11	8	37.185	see	1	21	bloodline	5	42.974	dog
12	6	34.555	old	1	21	halfmen	3	42.271	pant
13	6	32.688	still	1	21	kick	5	42.137	check
14	4	31.835	play	1	21	poof	4	41.733	twin
15	7	31.597	think	1	21	shrapnel	6	41.37	run

Table 21.5 LL keyness and *p*-value equation

LL keyness	p-value
3.84	$p < 0.05$
6.63	$p < 0.01$
10.83	$p < 0.001$
15.13	$p < 0.0001$

somewhat sceptical as our high keyness values are partly an effect of our small study corpus. Nevertheless, we can see that lemmas related to canine animals (PUPPY, DOG, PANT) and to the new species (HALFMAN/ HALFMEN, BLOODLINE, PANT) emerge as significant in both parts of the narrative when compared with fiction generally. Some of the lemmas from our original word lists remain significant: MUM and DAD in Grace's narrative and PUPPY in Captain Tom's. There are also some new, unexpected keywords, such as HIDE in Grace's narrative and CLEVER in Captain Tom's. We will therefore look at these – and some other keywords – in more detail in the next section.

21.4 Concordances and collocations

The word and keyword lists have provided us with quantitative data about the frequency and keyness of particular sets of words within 'Blood Story'. However, we have no sense of *how* those words are used. We therefore also need to undertake some qualitative analysis by looking at the keywords in context (KWIC) using concordance lines. A **concordance** is another form of list, showing all occurrences of a particular keyword. The keyword is displayed centrally with immediate co-text on either side. Let's start by looking at PUPPY since it is the most significant keyword in 'Blood Story'. In the keyword list for the whole story in AntConc, place the cursor over the lemma PUPPY and it will become a pointing finger icon. When you click, AntConc will switch to the concordance tab, which should show two concordance lines with the word 'puppy' in blue. We know from our keyword list that there were eight occurrences of the lemma PUPPY; we're therefore only seeing the two 'puppy' lexemes. To solve this, we can use the * (asterisk) symbol: The corpus software will interpret this as standing in for any character or string of characters (this is called a **wildcard**). In the concordance tab of AntConc, type 'pup*' into the search bar and click 'Start'. AntConc will now show all eight concordance lines, as shown in Figure 21.2. Concordance lines will automatically be listed in the order in which they appear in your corpus. However, using the KWIC sort

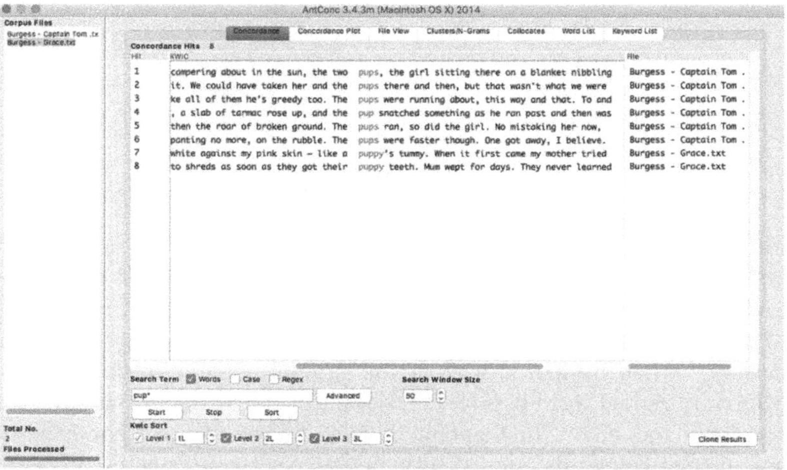

Figure 21.2 Screenshot of AntConc's concordance lines for *pup** in 'Blood Story'

menu underneath, you can adjust the three levels to sort your concordance lines based on their co-text. This will help you to see patterns in your data. The PUPPY lexemes, for instance, are almost always preceded by an article ('the', 'a') or possessive determiner 'their'.

Another thing you can do with KWIC is to look at a **concordance plot** (also called a **dispersion plot**). If you click on the 'Concordance Plot' tab in AntConc, you can see how the lexemes for puppy are distributed throughout Grace's and Captain Tom's narratives. When we read 'Blood Story', we didn't initially realise that Grace was not human (this is the principle of minimal departure, as discussed in Chapter 14); it only became clear gradually. The concordance plot, shown in Figure 21.3, reveals why this was the case, because lexemes related to puppy occur infrequently in Grace's narrative, and become more frequent in Captain Tom's.

The lemma CLEVER was the second most significant keyword in Captain Tom's narrative. Because this lemma was unexpected, let's look at its concordance lines: either click on CLEVER in keywords or type it directly into the search box in the 'Concordance' tab. All three occurrences are in Captain Tom's narrative. If we click on each, we can also see them in their narrative context (in 'File View'). How is Captain Tom using the word 'clever'?

> They might look human, but underneath the <u>clever</u> talk and the pretty face, they are just animals in disguise.
> They were <u>clever</u> – <u>clever</u> in that animal way some halfmen are.

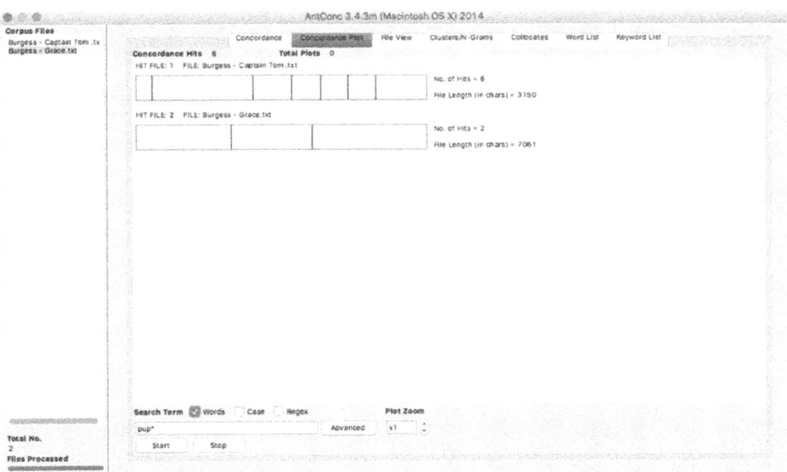

Figure 21.3 Screenshot of AntConc's concordance plot for *pup** in 'Blood Story'

In each case, clever co-occurs near the word 'animal'; it is attributed to the new species. However, although 'clever' is usually understood as a positive personality trait, looking at KWIC reveals that Captain Tom uses it in a more negative manner (more akin to synonyms like 'shrewd' or 'manipulative'). It is therefore indicative of his disdain for the new species.

In the two concordance lines above, we also find the word 'look', which was the second most significant keyword in 'Blood Story' overall. The concordance lines for 'look*' are shown in Figure 21.4. You can also see how we've sorted them, first by the first word to the left, then by the first and second words to the right (1L 1R 2R). When LOOK appeared in our word list, we thought this was probably due to the fact that first-person narratives recount the perceptions of their narrators. The concordance lines reveal that this is only sometimes the case: LOOK does relate to the perceptions and feelings of Grace (hits 5, 7, 8, 13), Captain Tom (1), and the description of other characters' expressions (4, 11, 12) in eight instances. However, on the other six occasions (2, 3, 6, 9, 10, 14), LOOK serves a different function, used to signify the deceptive nature of appearances. The two occurrences of the active verb 'looking' (2, 14) suggest a form of assessment, in this case judging whether someone is human or 'halfman'. This is supported by the recurrence of 'girl' and 'human' in the co-text of hits 2, 3, 6, 9, and 10. The cognitive nature of the assessment is also suggested by the presence of

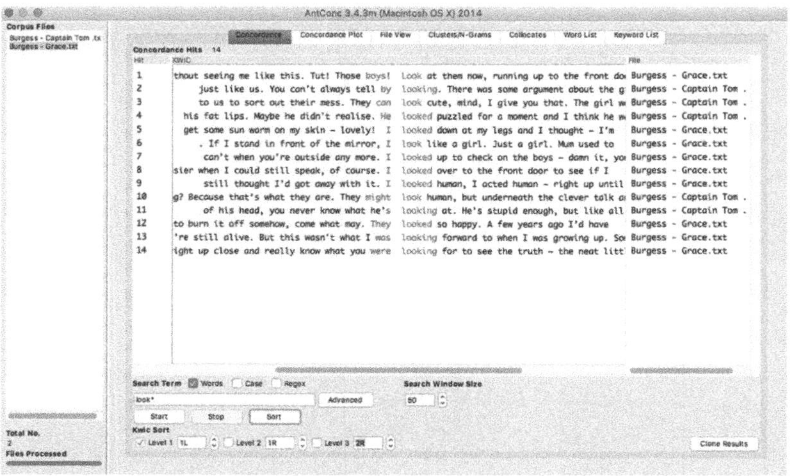

Figure 21.4 Screenshot of AntConc's concordance lines for *look** in 'Blood Story'

modal auxiliaries such as 'can't' (2), 'can' (3), and 'might' (10) as well as epistemic verbs such as 'tell' (2), 'know' (14), and the noun 'argument' (2) which suggests considered debate. As such, qualitative analysis of the word LOOK is beneficial, since it reveals a theme in its usage of which we were previously unaware.

We will look finally at the other keyword that surprised us, the lemma HIDE which was the third most significant keyword in Grace's narrative and seventh in 'Blood Story' overall. After clicking 'hide' in the keyword list tab of AntConc, the concordance view reminds us that to find all the lexemes of HIDE, we need to use the wildcard * to see all six KWICs. Every instance of HIDE is in Grace's narrative, immediately telling us something about her life: as a 'halfman', she must hide to protect herself. This is reinforced by the two-time co-occurrence of HIDE with a preposition in immediate right co-text (1R), as in 'hidden away' and 'hide in'.

Another twice-recurring phrase, however, strikes us as odd, and it is a phrase that we found strange when we first read 'Blood Story'. The short story starts: 'The twins were playing <u>hide and catch</u> around the wrecks' (Burgess n.d.; our emphasis). 'Hide and Seek' is a well-known children's game and as such, it is also a well-known collocation. **Collocations** are words that frequently co-occur together (roughly within five words left and/or right) and thus start to influence meaning and interpretation. This is precisely what happened in our experience of the text: reading 'Hide and . . .', we expected the phrase to be completed as 'Hide and Seek', especially since in the first occurrence, 'hide and catch' is preceded by the verb 'playing'. To make sure that we're not only relying on our intuitions, we can use corpus methods to test the strength of collocations. To do this, we'll consult the full BNC. Open your web browser and navigate to http://corpus.byu.edu/bnc/. After clicking on the 'Collocates' tab, type in 'hide and'. Table 21.6 shows the top ten collocates, occurring within four words either side. 'Seek' is the most frequent, whilst lexis relating to the semantic field of game-playing is also recurrent. If we return to the search page and now search the BNC for 'hide and catch', we are told, 'Sorry, there are no matching records.' This shows the atypical nature of the word string 'hide and catch' and explains why it caught our attention. This deviation of 'Hide and Seek' as 'hide and catch' is slightly disorientating for the reader and creates a defamiliarising difference between a reader's knowledge and experience and that of the character Grace.

This deviation contributes in interesting ways to the ethical situation of the narrative by marking Grace as different in some way from the reader. Our initial reaction to Grace may reflect that perceived

Table 21.6 BNC collocates for 'hide and'

Rank	Collocates
1	seek
2	playing
3	play
4	game
5	behind
6	nothing
7	let
8	crawled
9	games
10	ran

difference, particularly when we learn that she is a half-breed human-dog. When we read Captain Tom's section, however, readers are invited to reassess their positioning in relation to Grace. As such, the story dramatises an important ethical question: how do we respond to others whom we perceive as different to ourselves?

Having used both quantitative (word lists, keyword lists) and qualitative (concordances, collocates) methods in our analysis, we can now return to our research question: what are the similarities/differences in the narrators' representations of the scene? What does this suggest about their characterisation? How does this inform the story's effects? Our analysis speaks most strongly to the issue of characterisation but to refine our question further: what are the differences in the mind styles of the two narrators? Mind style was defined in Chapter 2 as the rendering of a character's mind through distinctive linguistic features.

In 'Blood Story', our corpus analysis shows up the differences in the characterisation and mind styles of Grace and Captain Tom. Word lists demonstrate that Grace's worldview is family-oriented whilst keyword analysis and concordancing suggests that the importance of family to Grace was perhaps not so much a worldview but a necessary restriction: as a member of the new species, Grace and her family are in danger and therefore live in hiding. In contrast, Captain Tom's preoccupation with the new species and his disdain for them is clear from the keyness of PUPPY and our interpretation of its co-occurrence with CLEVER in concordance analysis. Finally, concordance plots for PUPPY showed that Burgess gradually introduces this dystopic aspect into the fiction whilst our collocation analysis of 'hide and' helped to confirm the deviance of the phrase 'hide and catch' and its role in reinforcing the unusualness of the world in which Grace lives compared with readers' reality.

Keywords and summary

Annotate/tag, concordance, concordance plot, corpus/corpora (generalised, specialised, reference, study), corpus linguistics, corpus stylistics, dispersion plot, keyness value, keyword list, lemma list, p*-value, qualitative methods, quantitative methods, stop list, wildcard, word list (frequency, tokens, types).*

Corpus methods can be used to direct and support stylistic analysis, and this chapter has introduced you to some key tools and terms needed to begin exploring this form of analysis. Quantitative methods allow us to extract information from our corpus about frequency and significance whilst qualitative measures such as concordancing and collocations help us to see patterns in our data. Whilst corpus methods may appear to remove our own researcher bias, in reality they only reduce it. This is because the decisions a researcher makes (about significance levels, reference corpus, etc.) still affect the results. As we have demonstrated here, to use corpora in stylistic analysis it is always necessary to move beyond corpus search results to a consideration of the text as a piece of literature (i.e. involving representations of characters, points of view, and readers' influences and emotions), which inevitably involves the subjective insights of the researcher.

One of the big advantages of corpus methods lies in the opportunity it offers for moving beyond the close analysis of small chunks of text. The example we have given here is necessarily short to allow us to talk you through corpus methods. However, when applied to a whole novel, or whole oeuvres, which would take years to analyse by hand, the power of corpus methods is clear. Used sensitively, corpus programs can be valuable tools for stylistic research, supporting intuitions and providing surprising analytical insights.

Activities

1. Design a hypothetical corpus study around one of the following research projects:
    - You have an intuition that a text features lexis from two central semantic fields (for instance, war and nature). How would you examine this?
    - You think a text includes lots of deviant expressions. How could you ascertain how unusual these word or phrase choices are?

- You are analysing a poem that repeats the phrase 'like a peach'. How would you find out what connotations this word tends to evoke?
- What kind of specialised corpus would you need if you wanted to examine the stylistic similarities (and differences) between Ted Hughes' and Sylvia Plath's poetry?

2. Choose another short story from the BookTrust website (http://www.booktrust.org.uk/books/adults/short-stories/stories/). After you've read it, create a .txt version of it and analyse it using AntConc and the corpus methods we've discussed in the chapter. How does your corpus analysis help to evidence your interpretation or experience of the short story? Does corpus analysis reveal anything new?
3. CLiC Dickens is a useful resource for investigating both Dickens' words as well as other nineteenth-century novels. Visit the site (http://clic.bham.ac.uk) and do some concordance searches. For instance, you could see how certain body parts function in Dickens. Start by looking up the word 'brow'.

Further reading and references

You can download most corpus software programs online. Links can be found for AntConc, Wordsmith, and WMatrix in the 'Corpus programs' section of this book's references. Important reading in the fundamentals of corpus linguistics is: Baker (2006), Carter (2004), McEnery and Hardy (2012), Sinclair (2004), and Wynne (2005). Further readings in corpus stylistics include: Adolphs and Carter (2002), Burrows (1987), Culpeper (2002), Ho (2011), Hori (2004), Lahey (2015), Louw (1997, 2008), McIntyre and Archer (2010), Mahlberg (2007, 2010, 2013), Mahlberg and McIntyre (2011), Mahlberg and Smith (2012), Mahlberg et al. (2013), Partington (1995), Semino (2014), Semino and Short (2004), Starcke (2006), Stubbs (2005), van Peer (1989), and Wynne et al. (1998). Mastropierro (2017) develops the corpus stylistic approach in relation to translation studies, whilst Mahlberg et al. (2014) incorporate psycholinguistic insights into corpus study to learn more about how textual structures influence readers' experiences. Van Peer et al. (2012 [2007]) is an useful introduction to empirical research.

22 Investigating readers

22.1 Collecting data about readers and reading in stylistics

Stylistic analysis is dependent upon the notion of a reader: a literate human who engages with a text's language in order to make meaning. Stylisticians regularly make claims about what 'the reader' or 'readers' (or audience/viewers/users) do or think when they engage with a text. Often, this 'reader' is a largely theoretical construct, based partly on the analyst's own interpretations, partly on the linguistic theory being used, and partly on ideas about how the text might be received by others.

In order to investigate the responses of other readers, it is common for stylisticians to engage with published criticism and reviews about a literary work (indeed, this is often a very good starting point for a stylistic analysis), or offer descriptions of reader reactions they have observed first-hand during seminars or conferences. It is also possible to use formal **empirical methods** in order to collect and analyse **extra-textual data** (Swann and Allington 2009) about reader responses. Empirical methods investigate the responses of other readers through direct observation, investigation, or experiment. The data is called 'extra-textual' because it involves going beyond the language of a literary text in order to examine evidence of readers' responses to it. This empirical **reader response research** is used to inform stylistic analysis of a literary text, and to explore whether stylistic assumptions and frameworks are supported by evidence from real (rather than largely theoretical) readers. It can also be used to develop stylistics by generating new insights into the workings of reading and interpretation. One of the interesting things about reading is that people will always interpret texts slightly differently. However, as Short points out, for stylisticians, 'the fascinating thing that needs to be explained is that we often agree on our understanding of poems, plays and novels *in spite* of the fact that we are all different' (1996: xi; original emphasis). Thus, in their analyses of textual style, stylisticians are often particularly interested in accounting for points of interpretative overlap between readers.

There are lots of ways to investigate real readers' responses to texts, and choosing which method to use depends entirely on the aims of a particular study. Most commonly, reading is studied through the collection of **verbal data** in which readers (via various means) provide written or spoken descriptions of their experiences. It is also possible to study reading through the observation of non-verbal features such as reading time and eye movement, although this tends to involve specialist equipment. Our focus here is on methods that gather verbal data as part of **exploratory data collection**. The aim of exploratory data collection is not to prove or disprove a particular hypothesis or theory – as is usually the case in traditional, scientific, and experimental paradigms. Instead, exploratory data is collected in order to offer new perspectives on a topic of interest. You can use exploratory data to inform a stylistic analysis of a text, and to reveal interesting things about the nature of reading.

Reading is a complex activity that takes place through time, and different empirical methods tap into different phases in the act of reading. As Steen (1991) notes, reading can be seen to involve two overlapping phases: the moments when a reader first runs their eyes over a page and generates meanings, impressions, and sensations, known as the **reception phase**; and a subsequent **post-processing phase** when these initial interpretations are refined and readers arrive at 'a sense of the text which is personally acceptable' (Stockwell 2002a: 8). Arguably, this 'post-processing' phase continues indefinitely, as readers might think about or discuss a text days, weeks, or years after putting it down. There is also, perhaps, a 'selection' phase before reception in which the text is selected and various expectations about it are formed. Figure 22.1 offers a schematic model of the act of reading, reflecting the main actions and phases.

This chapter introduces three methods of verbal data collection that tap into various moments in the post-processing phase of reading: thinking aloud, questionnaires, and online book reviews. These methods involve different levels of researcher intervention in the reading process, and different levels of researcher control over the data collected, as will be discussed below. These methods are among the easiest to implement in small-scale studies such as student projects. Our aim is to give you a sense of what each method involves and the type of data it might yield, so that you can consider trying out one of these methods yourself. It is important to note you should never begin collecting data from human participants without first checking your institution's ethics

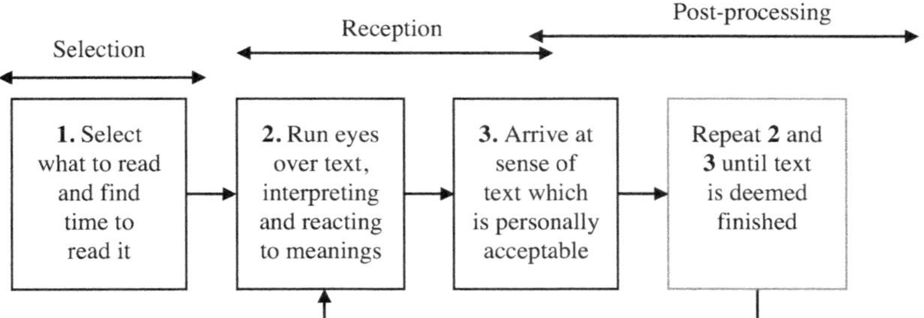

Figure 22.1 Schematic representation of the act of reading

policy: it is likely that you will need to obtain approval before you begin (see Table 22.5).

22.2 Thinking aloud

The model of reading outlined in Figure 22.1 suggests a distinction between the immediate act of making sense of a text, and the subsequent post-processing of these initial interpretations. Often, by the time we reach the end of a text, we have rejected, discarded, or extended many of our initial interpretations, and may well be unable to recall or articulate their original form. Thinking aloud is a method that tries to access and record those initial reception-phase interpretations as a reader moves through a text. Participants are asked to read a text in sections (line by line or paragraph by paragraph) and speak or write about their thought processes at the end of each section. The verbal data created by participants in think-aloud tasks are called **protocols**. Protocols provide insights into the development of meanings during reading, and the kinds of interpretative activities that readers perform at different moments in a text.

Think-aloud tasks work best with short texts such as poems, short stories, or extracts of prose. Think-aloud tasks can be conducted in a low-tech fashion using a few pieces of paper or in a more high-tech fashion by presenting the text and response boxes on a computer. Spoken responses could also be recorded but this would require you to later transcribe them for analysis. In the low-tech version, each participant needs: a copy of the printed textual stimuli, with sections divided by clear line marks; one blank piece of paper to cover the first, which can be moved down to each line in order to reveal the next section of text; and a third piece of paper with section numbers and a space for participants to write their responses. It is good to explain to your participants how long the text they will be reading is, and what you want them to do, for example:

> *You are about to be presented with a poem, line by line. In each section of the task, a new line will be added.*
> *The poem is called 'Inversnaid' by Gerard Manley Hopkins, and consists of four stanzas containing four lines each.*
> *Please write down your thoughts in the text boxes as you read the poem.*
> *Note that there are no 'correct' answers in this task; we are simply interested in capturing your immediate responses.*

The data in Table 22.1 offers an example of what think-aloud protocols might look like. In this study, third-year stylistics students were given the poem 'Inversnaid' by Gerard Manley Hopkins ([1881] 2014) line by line on a computer, and asked to write their initial thoughts in a text box below each new line. Here is the first stanza of the (sixteen-line) poem:

1 This darksome burn, horseback brown,
2 His rollrock highroad roaring down,
3 In coop and in comb the fleece of his foam
4 Flutes and low to the lake falls home.

One interesting feature of this poem is its use of Scots dialect terms, such as 'burn' (L1) meaning a small stream. Very crudely, the first stanza describes the movement of the stream as it flows from the mountains into a lake. Even though the participants in the study had permission to look things up in dictionaries if they wished, most did not identify the Scots meaning of the word 'burn'. This seemed to affect the way they read the poem: rather than demonstrating a clear sense of the poem's narrative from the outset, participants were engaged in inferring a range of possible meanings from the other language and imagery.

The protocols in Table 22.1 were written in relation to the third line of the poem. As you read them, consider the similarities and differences between the responses. These protocols illustrate both the messy and diverse nature of think-aloud data, and the intriguing overlaps between readers' responses to the same line of a poem.

When analysing the content of protocols such as this, it is necessary to find ways to reduce the data and notice patterns within it, for instance by grouping the data together in different ways. This process is part of **qualitative content analysis**. For stylistic purposes, one important way to approach think-aloud protocols is to consider the interpretative content provided by readers and group the interpretative similarities

Table 22.1 Think-aloud protocols for L3 of 'Inversnaid'

Protocols for L3: 'In coop and in comb the fleece of his foam'	
Participant	Protocol
A	Rhythm, line divided in 2, internal rhyme of *comb* and *foam.* Farming situation?
B	Fluffy jacket, sea.
C	Internal rhyme.
D	Nature, reminds me of western, cowboy, etc.
E	Farmyard/countryside. *Coop* = chickens and *fleece* = sheep. Rhyme and alliteration could show the horse riding through the countryside – rhythm of the ride.
F	*Coop* suggests confinement in a small space. *Fleece* suggests a comforting layer, could be referring to the horse.
G	Rhyme. *Coop, fleece* – chickens? animals?
H	*Coop* – chicken? Theme of breaking free? Of escape?
I	The word *foam* maybe suggests water?
J	Chickens, sheep. Horse foaming at the mouth from speed of galloping.

Table 22.2 Similarities and differences in protocols for L3 of 'Inversnaid'

Similarities	Disagreements
• 5 readers associate the line with farmyards, especially farm animals such as sheep and chicken • 4 readers note the internal rhyme	• 1 reader makes a western/cowboy association rather than farming
• 3 readers make a connection to 'the horse' they identified earlier in the poem (L1) • 2 readers associate 'fleece' with a jacket/comforting layer • 2 readers associate the line with water • 2 readers associate the line with confinement/escape	• Connections to 'the horse' differ – one saw the foam as the horse's mouth, one saw the fleece as the horse's fur, one saw the rhyme/rhythm as the motion of the horse

and disagreements across the data. Some of the similarities and differences that can be perceived in the protocols for L3 of 'Inversnaid' are shown in Table 22.2.

Short and van Peer (1989) offer a detailed stylistic analysis of 'Inversnaid', and note the presence of vocabulary with strong ANIMAL connotations throughout the text (1989: 50). They suggest that this vocabulary has the effect of personifying the stream. Our think-aloud data shows that readers recognise these ANIMAL connotations and use them to generate meaning as they move through the poem, even if they do not pick up on the meaning of the term 'burn'. For the readers in our study, the animacy and the natural references still contribute to some sense of the poem's meaning. The data has some intriguing implications for the stylistic analysis of reading, because they show readers making meaning – in some cases, quite coherent meaning (e.g. in protocols E, F, H, and J) – even if particular vocabulary items are 'missed'.

Another way to examine think-aloud protocol data is to consider what kind of strategies of meaning-making readers are employing at different moments in a text. Table 22.3 summarises some of the reading strategies you might find in protocols. If these categories are applied to the data in A–J in Table 22.1 above, it emerges that the majority of readers (nine out of ten) are involved in reconstructing meaning by making inferences, particularly from the semantic meaning of the vocabulary of the poem (all but C offer some reconstructive inferencing). Participants exhibit varying levels of confidence in their inferences – from strongly asserted associations (e.g. 'fluffy jacket, sea' (B)

Table 22.3 Reading strategies you might find in protocols (adapted from Andringa 1990)

Reading act/Strategy	Code	Explanation/Examples
Emotive reaction/attitude	emo	Expressions of negative/positive emotions related to content of text, the behaviour of characters, the basic ideas underlying a text or the style of the text
(Re)construction	rec	Making inferences, drawing conclusions, building representations of a text by selecting/focusing on information, summarising, offering causal explanations, suggesting motives/intentions/qualities of characters or narrator
Bridging	bri	Forming connections between parts of the text, the text and the external world, or the text and other texts
Elaboration	ela	Making associations related to personal experiences, imagining alternative events in the text
Identification	ide	Identifying period/genre/author or linguistic/stylistic/structural aspects of text

or 'chickens, sheep' (J)) to weaker ones (e.g. which are modalised 'could show' (E), 'maybe suggests' (I) or feature question marks (A, G, H, I)). There is also some bridging evident in four responses (D, E, F, J) where readers link L3 to the horse they perceived earlier in the poem. Responses A, C, E, G feature the identification of stylistic features such as rhyme and rhythm.

It is useful to track the strategies which are evident across the protocol data you collect, as shifts in strategies might be linked to textual features. For instance, the data in Table 22.1 demonstrates readers early on in the text primarily trying to make sense of the poem's vocabulary both within and across lines. By the final stanza, these readers demonstrate more certainty in their interpretations and make connections between the poem and the external world – and this coincides with a shift in the text's style in which the poetic voice adopts direct address to proclaim that the wilderness should be preserved.

Thinking aloud can yield particularly interesting data if the texts used involve some stylistic shift or repeated intriguing stylistic feature to which you would expect readers to react. It can be interesting to first perform a stylistic analysis of a text by yourself, and then compare this analysis with some think-aloud data from other readers. Do other readers arrive at similar interpretations to you? When and how are these interpretations formed? Is there anything your stylistic analysis did not account for? It is not necessary to collect a lot of data in order to find interesting points of comparison and things to discuss. You can use think-aloud data to reflect on the meaning of the text, the nature of reading, or the nature of stylistic analysis.

22.3 Questionnaires

Questionnaires are a very flexible way of collecting reader response data. They can be administered at different moments in the post-processing phase (e.g. as part of a think-aloud study, or after an entire text/extract has been read). They are best suited to the examination of relatively short texts or extracts. They also allow researchers to exercise control over the type of data they collect: making it easy to collect comparable data from multiple respondents in the same replicable way. The flipside of this is that they always constrain your data by shaping readers' responses in some way (this can be both a useful or limiting characteristic).

Questionnaires can consist of open or closed questions. **Closed questions** offer participants a fixed set of responses, which are typically easier and quicker for them to answer and for researchers to analyse. Some common closed question types are listed in Table 22.4.

Table 22.4 Closed question types

Question type	Examples
Multiple choice	Would you like to continue reading the novel? (a) Yes (b) No (c) Don't know
Semantic differential scale: provides participants with pairs of adjectives with opposite meanings at either end of a scale	boring – – – – interesting ugly – – – – beautiful
Likert scale/Attitude scale: provides participants with a numerical scale to illustrate their attitudes/opinions	I enjoyed this poem. 1 2 3 4 5 6 7 strongly agree · neither agree nor disagree · strongly disagree
Ranking scale: ask people to rank a list of things according to what is most important/most influences them, etc.	Below are some reasons for selecting a book. Based on your usual experience, please rank them in order of importance with 1 being the most important and 5 being the least important: ☐ cover ☐ blurb ☐ friend's recommendation ☐ prize winner ☐ bookshop/library recommendation
Matched guise/cloze technique: ask participants to complete a sentence	I have known her ______ three years now. (a) whilst (b) for (c) since (d) besides (e) at

Open questions invite a lengthier, unstructured response from participants and therefore can be more time consuming for participants to complete and for researchers to analyse. The researcher has minimal control over those responses, and must interpret them during analysis (the data will need reducing through qualitative content analysis, like the think-aloud protocols in section 22.2). Examples of open questions include:

- Did you get any particular impression about any of the characters, and if so what?
- How would you describe the atmosphere created by the poem?
- List five words that describe the narrator.

Many questionnaires combine open and closed questions to collect both easily analysable data and the freer responses of participants, as both can be useful for exploration of a topic.

Questionnaires should be kept short (we think no more than ten questions – preferably fewer). It is very easy to put participants off by boring them or by asking them ambiguous questions. Questions should be expressed clearly and simply, avoiding jargon (don't use stylistic or literary terms). Always think ahead to consider how you are going to analyse the responses to the questions. Every question must be there for a good reason (ask yourself, 'why am I asking this question?'). *Always* **pilot test** a questionnaire (run a test version with a couple of participants) before you administer it in your main study in order to check that the questionnaire is comprehensible and provides the kind of data you want.

Questionnaires work best when you have identified a text or extract with an interesting effect (created by its stylistic features), and want to explore how readers respond to it. The trick, however, is to avoid revealing your own views about the text's effects in the way you phrase your questions. Take care to *avoid* loaded questions which have an underlying assumption built in. For instance: 'At the end of stanza 1, what kind of emotional response did you experience?' is loaded because it assumes that an emotion *was* experienced then. A less loaded alternative might be to ask participants to indicate whether they experienced emotional responses, and if so at what point in the text. It is also good to *avoid* leading questions where the wording suggests a 'right' answer, such as: 'Did you recognise that the narrator is male?' An alternative might be: 'In your view, what is the gender of the narrator?'

Gibbons (2012a: 183–97) uses a questionnaire to explore readers' responses to a multimodal novel, *Woman's World* by Graham Rawle (2005). The novel is a collage, constructed from words cut out of 1960s women's magazines. Gibbons' multimodal stylistic analysis argues that the visual style of the text influences its meanings and effects (see Chapter 19). To see whether there was any evidence of this in readers' responses, Gibbons presented participants with a page from the novel and a questionnaire. First, the questionnaire asked readers to annotate the text as they read, to see which parts they picked out to comment upon. Then information about participants' age, education, and reading habits was collected using closed questions, before a combination of closed and open questions was posed about participants' views of the text. Questionnaires enable analysts to hone in on particular aspects of reader response which they are interested in. For example:

> Q8. Do you think that the way the novel is presented, in collage form, affected your reading?
>
> Yes [ ] Don't know [ ] No [ ]
>
> If so, how?

> Q11. Did you get any particular impression about any of the characters (the narrator, Mr Hands, the woman, the poodle) and if so, what?

The questionnaire results offered support for Gibbons' argument that the multimodal presentation of the text affected the reading experience, and gave her examples of precisely how it was affected. For example, some of the answers to Q8 were:

> 'The size of the typing made me hear the words like they would be spoken e.g. larger was louder.' (R-11)

> 'The way the whole paragraph has been written feels very disjointed, almost emphasising it not being spoken by the same person, i.e. phrases/words taken from the different articles and put together to form the above paragraph.' (R-13)

This suggests that the typographical design of the novel impacts particularly upon readers' sense of 'voice' in the narrative (Gibbons 2012a: 193). Other responses suggest that the source texts used in the collage also affected readers' interpretations: the annotations revealed readers making links to old-fashioned home decor and advertising texts. Gibbons uses the reader response data to inform and support an analysis of the 'layering of worlds and contexts' (2012a: 187) in this multimodal work.

22.4 Post-processing: 'Naturalistic' data

Both thinking aloud and questionnaires are methods that somehow intervene in the reading process and the articulation of readers' responses. Thinking aloud requires readers to pause continually during reading to articulate their thoughts, and questionnaires ask readers focused questions related to a researcher's interests. This high level of researcher intervention, characteristic of **experimental methods**, is not the only way to access reader responses. Reader responses to literature are also visible in everyday social interactions. As Stockwell (2005a: 144) notes, talk about reading can happen anywhere: 'in bookshops and bus stations, in reading groups and at parties, at the next table in the restaurant and the seat behind you on the train'. **Naturalistic methods** (Swann and Allington 2009: 248) are those which try to tap into this kind of habitual reading behaviour, and study readers interacting with each other about literature in their usual environments.

One convenient source of naturalistic reader response data is the internet. There are several open access platforms dedicated to the discussion of literature (key English-speaking sites include Goodreads and LibraryThing), as well as booksellers who permit reader reviews of their products (e.g. Amazon). These sites sometimes contain hundreds of thousands of words of reader reviews, discussion forums, ratings, and other commentary about particular literary works. Rather than being prompted by researchers in empirical tasks, this online discourse shows readers discussing literature in interaction with friends and fellow book-lovers, or businesses and their customers (there are consequently ethical considerations to bear in mind: see Table 22.5). There could be a number of factors motivating readers to leave online reviews; Milota (2014) argues that a desire for recognition is an important drive behind such posts.

This online data is located firmly in the post-processing phase, at some considerable distance from a text's initial reception. This means that it cannot be seen to provide access to that initial moment of reading. Instead, online posts contain post-hoc representations and more considered reactions to a work, which are tailored to the particular online context. Whilst thinking aloud and questionnaires can provide you with information about how particular textual features influence reader reactions, online review data rarely links reactions to particular sections of a text. It is still possible to use this data in stylistic analysis, but to do so the analyst has to argue for connections between the general trends in online responses and the language of the text – the data itself is unlikely to provide evidence of this.

For stylisticians, these posts offer a way of gaining insights into the interpretations, evaluations, effects, and other issues or reactions associated with particular literary works, which can form a useful starting point for stylistic analysis, and offer an easy way to compare your own interpretations with those of other readers. Because the researcher has no control over online data, it avoids the **observer's paradox** in which a researcher obscures that which they study through the act of studying it. The flipside is that you can only work with what is there. Researchers must 'take the reading process as it comes' and follow the lead of the contributors rather than imposing an agenda on them (Swann and Allington 2009: 249).

In order to begin exploring and collecting online data, simply search for a particular literary work within the search bar of websites mentioned above, or use an internet search engine. Bear in mind that the lack of researcher control means that online data can be wide-ranging and time-consuming to sift through and analyse. For literary texts which have reams of commentary, it will be necessary to decide on a way to limit the amount of data you will focus on by sampling the comments in some way (e.g. looking only at the first ten from each site, or the ten most recent, or only reviews which mention a particular thing). We'd recommend copying and pasting the text into a word-processing document so that you can annotate it and search it during your analysis, taking care to keep a record of the origin of the review.

As a rough guide, in online reviews it is customary to find discussion of things like: plot, setting, characters, moral messages/themes of a work, the author, style (though not in stylistic terms, of course), a reader's emotional responses, and relevant personal anecdotes/memories. You are likely to find a range of responses to any text, but also a relatively finite set of recurring points which suggest broad patterns in reader reactions and which might merit further investigation. After collection it might be necessary to reduce the data using qualitative content analysis. It can be interesting, as in section 22.2, to consider similarities and differences between commentaries. It can also be interesting to examine points of polarity or controversy and consider the extent to which it is possible to account for both responses in a stylistic analysis of the text.

Chapter 14 (section 14.3) discussed the opening of the novel *The Unconsoled* by Kazuo Ishiguro (2005 [1995]) in which the narrator Ryder arrives in a hotel. After he has been checked in, a porter escorts him to his room in an elevator, but time and space begin behaving strangely: the elevator journey lasts an inordinate amount of time, and Ryder fails to notice another character in the enclosed space with them. We argued that the novel was 'unusual' and 'challenging' because of the way it disrupts readers' schemas, and posited that readers are likely to engage in processes of downgrading in order to explain or make sense of the unusual events in the narrative. For instance, readers might attribute Ryder's failure to notice the other occupant of the elevator to his tiredness or jet lag. The kind of schema disruption discussed in Chapter 14, and readers' search for an explanation of the unusual occurrences, continues throughout the novel.

A survey of online discussions provides insights into readers' views about the meanings and effects of *The Unconsoled.* The data below was collected as part of a study of literary discussions (Whiteley 2010) and therefore focused on posts on online discussion threads. Posts about *The Unconsoled* were located within threads about more general issues such as Ishiguro's works as a whole, or lists of favourite and least favourite books. This meant it took some time to sift out relevant data. Brief mentions of the novel were discounted, and only comments that were part of an exchange between several participants and/or which featured lengthy comments about the novel were included in the sample.

Across the sampled posts, the experience of reading the novel was a central topic. Readers associated the novel with emotional effects such as frustration, bewilderment, stress, and also humour:

- 'I had to remind myself to remain calm because it was "just a book". Every page is endlessly frustrating [. . .] a novel about stress turns the reading experience itself into stress'
- '[it] makes your innards squirm with confusion and teeth-gritting frustration'
- '*The Unconsoled* [. . .] [leaves] a person more and more bewildered'
- 'I found this so disturbing [. . .] that I preferred to give up and try something less demanding'
- 'I'm surprised more people don't mention that it's absolutely hilarious in places'
- 'patently unreal and uneasily real, both pathetically sad and absurdly funny'

Emotional reactions associated with confusion and the experience of incongruity might be expected in a schema-disrupting text. Thus, the schema disruption discussed in the stylistic analysis in section 14.3 could go some way to accounting for these emotional responses.

The online data also provides insight into the downgrading strategies readers use to explain the schema-disrupting aspects of the narrative. In our analysis in section 14.3 we explained the unreliability of Ryder's perception by associating it with his tiredness. Online, the majority of readers attribute an altered state of consciousness to Ryder – declaring that he is dreaming or suffering amnesia:

- 'what seemed clear to me as I read the book was that it was a dream story'
- 'it's all a dream (this becomes obvious after the first 10–20 pages)'
- 'The story reads like someone relating a dream, but this dream goes on and on'
- 'This book is halfway between a dream (or nightmare) and reality'
- 'As we read through the novel it becomes increasingly dreamlike [. . .] Perhaps it isn't dreamlike, maybe it's more his insanity'
- 'The effect of a dream was created through confused logic'
- 'At first, you think Ryder is suffering from some sort of amnesia [. . .] [then] a new explanation presents itself. He's dreaming'

This suggests that, when reading the entire novel (rather than just the short extract discussed in section 14.3), different and more extensive explanations for the schema disruption and narratorial unreliability are required.

It would be difficult to organise an experimental task that required readers to engage with the entirety of this strange, 500-page novel. Naturalistic online data, however, provides access to readers who have engaged with the entire text in their normal circumstances. Their comments can be used to support and inform stylistic analysis in dialogue with our own interpretations.

Online responses can also provide information about how readers position themselves in relation to the characters and contents of a literary text, and therefore are often used in work on reader emotions. A final thing to note about online reader response data is that analysts should look not only at *what* readers say, but also at *how* they say it. Consider this example from a review of *I Am Legend* by Richard Matheson on Goodreads (cited in Nuttall 2015: 25):

> 'The novel had me so tense in places that I was almost screaming out at the pages of the book. I felt the main character's pain, solitude and deep sadness at the loss of his love, life and the horrific existence he now endured [. . .] Despite that I found it hard to like him. Maybe I wasn't suppose[d] to like him'

The reader's comments here are clearly relevant to a study of empathy and emotional positioning in the novel, but the reader does not use the word 'empathy'. It is implicit in the statement 'I felt the main character's pain'. Similarly, positioning is also implicit in the comment 'I found it hard to like him' – which suggests some resistance to the character. The reader exhibits conflict in their empathy for and also resistance to the character – and (if shared by several readers) this suggests a closer look at the style of the novel, and the way it encourages or problematises empathy, could be a profitable focus of a stylistic analysis (see Nuttall 2015).

Keywords and summary

Empirical methods (experimental methods, naturalistic methods), exploratory data collection, extra-textual data, pilot test, post-processing phase, qualitative content analysis, questionnaires (closed questions, open questions), reader response research, reception phase, research ethics, thinking aloud (protocols), verbal data.

This chapter has introduced three methods of reader response research: thinking aloud, questionnaires, and online reviews. These methods tap into different moments of reading and are well suited to small-scale exploratory projects. Reader response research can be used to inform stylistic textual analysis and provide you with additional responses (beyond your own).

LIBRARY, UNIVERSITY OF CHESTER

Table 22.5 Ethical considerations for reader response data collection

	Thinking aloud and questionnaires	Online reviews
Ethical concerns	Be sure to obtain informed consent from your participants before they take part in the task. They should understand the basic purpose of your study and how you will use the data. You should ask participants to sign or otherwise indicate that they consent to take part in the study. Consider the texts you use: is there sensitive material which might upset people? If so, you should warn them. Consider whether it is necessary to collect personal data from participants (e.g. names, addresses, birthdates, etc.). How will this information be stored securely? How long will it be kept? Consult your university's ethics policy for further guidance.	Many researchers collect data from publicly available online review sites – i.e. ones you can view without needing a log-in password – without obtaining informed consent from the authors. However, as noted above, it is questionable whether online contributors realise that they could be used in academic research when they post on these sites. As such, always use the data respectfully. You might consider anonymising the data (removing the posters' names) in your write-up, although not all researchers deem this necessary. Do not use data from sites which are not publicly available without obtaining permission from the authors. Consult your university's ethics policy for further guidance, as rules about internet data are continually being updated.

Research into readers must always be carried out according to the principles of **research ethics**. These principles ensure that no one is harmed or damaged by taking part in academic research, and are an integral part of research planning and design. Before you carry out any research using human participants, you must obtain ethics approval from your institution – ask to find out about the procedure that applies to you. Some of the main ethical considerations associated with the methods in this chapter are summarised in Table 22.5.

Here are some final tips if you are considering reader response research:

1. Remember there is no 'right' or perfect method for data collection – each method has advantages and disadvantages; you just need to make the right choices based on what you want to achieve.

2. Do not collect more data than you can handle. Always think about how you will analyse the data *before* you collect it (e.g. what kinds of things do you expect you will look for?), so that you can gauge how much is appropriate for the timeframe of your project.
3. *Always* conduct a pilot study to test out your method before you begin the main phase of data collection. This will help you to spot problems which could render your data unusable if not corrected.
4. For thinking aloud and questionnaires, you will need to recruit some willing participants to take part in the tasks. Think about how you will do this as part of your research design. How many people can you feasibly ask to be involved?
5. Always follow the ethical procedures of your institution.

Activities

1. Conduct a think-aloud study with one or two participants using the poem 'One Perfect Rose' by Dorothy Parker (2011 [1926]). Print the poem with double-spaced lines on a piece of paper, and lay a blank piece of paper on top. Ask participants to write their initial responses to each line on a separate piece of paper, moving the blank masking paper down a line at a time. What kinds of meanings did the participants generate? Simpson (2014 [2004]: 100–2) provides a stylistic analysis of the poem: do the stylistic features Simpson identifies seem to map on to the reader responses you collected? Ask your participants to reflect on the experience of completing the task. To what extent did it capture their normal way of reading?
2. Choose the opening of a novel or a short story in which you get a sense of the main character, such as *The Book Thief* by Marcus Zusak (2008) or one of the extracts we discussed in Chapter 9. Conduct a stylistic analysis of its point of view and consider how your impressions of the character are generated by the text's language. Then, devise a questionnaire to investigate other readers' responses to the character, and test it out on a small group of participants. As part of your questionnaire, ask readers to describe the narrator's attributes or qualities. Did other readers have the same impression of the character as you? Do they describe other reactions, and if so, can you still account for them stylistically? If you re-did your questionnaire, would you change anything about its design?
3. Visit the Goodreads and Amazon websites and search for readers' reviews and ratings about *Satin Island* by Tom McCarthy (2015)

(which we briefly discussed in Chapter 20). Have a look at the first few reviews you find on each site and consider:

- At first glance, what kinds of things do the readers on these websites say about *Satin Island*? Are there recurring themes/ideas in the posts? What are the similarities/differences?
- Although you may be unfamiliar with the novel, what kind of questions about the language of the text might you generate from these reviews (which you could investigate further with stylistic analysis using the frameworks discussed in this book)? For instance, do readers talk about particular responses to the characters, plot, or style? Does a particular scene or aspect of the novel seem significant? Where would you start with a stylistic analysis of the novel?
- Looking at a few reviews, is it possible to gauge anything about the readers' identities? Do they seem to come from a particular country, or be a specific gender? Is it sometimes hard to tell (and is this a problem)?
- Are there differences between the types of posts which appear on the different sites? So, for instance, do the Amazon reviews seem to function differently than the ones on Goodreads, etc.? At first glance, why do you think readers post reviews onto these online sites? Have you ever contributed to one?

Further reading and references

For short overviews of empirical methods in stylistics, see: Peplow and Carter (2014), van Peer and Hakemulder (2015), and Whiteley and Canning (2017). The distinction between reception and post-processing comes from Steen (1991), who also offers a comprehensive survey of reader response methods. Van Peer et al. (2012 [2007]) is a book-length overview of empirical methods in the humanities, offering extensive treatment of quantitative and hypothesis-testing approaches which are not discussed here. Short and van Peer (1989) offer think-aloud data and stylistic analysis of 'Inversnaid', and was the inspiration for the data collected in section 22.2. Other stylistic work that uses thinking aloud includes: Alderson and Short (1989), Jeffries (2002), and Short et al. (2011). Andringa (1990) discusses reading strategies in thinking aloud, and for other empirical work using think-aloud methods, see: Davis and Andringa (1995), Miall (1990), and Miall and Kuiken (2002). For stylistic work that uses questionnaire methods, see: Bray (2007a, 2007b), Burke (2011a), Cui (2017), Gibbons (2012a: 183–97), Macrae (2016b),

Sotirova (2006), van Peer (1986), and van Peer and Pander Maat (1996, 2001). Allington and Swann (2009) and Swann and Allington (2009) discuss the distinction between experimental and naturalistic methods, and see also Hall (2008). For stylistic work that uses online reviews, see: Gavins (2013: 10–57), Nuttall (2015, 2017), Whiteley (2016); and other naturalistic methods (reading groups), see Peplow et al. (2016: 30–60) and Whiteley (2011a, 2014). Milota (2014) offers an interesting overview of online data. Further information on qualitative content analysis can be found in Schrier (2014). For stylistic work that uses experimental methods from psychology, see: Emmott et al. (2006) and Sanford and Emmott (2012); and for wider reading about the experimental study of literature, see Bortolussi and Dixon (2003) and Miall (2006).

Part VIII

Conclusion

23 Future stylistics

23.1 Past resonances

Contemporary stylistics is a composite approach to analysing texts and the experiences that stem from them. It studies the language of literature in context, using knowledge about linguistic structures and the cognitive processes involved in reading and comprehension. Linguistic structures, in turn, influence interpretation, along with the personal knowledge that readers bring to texts. It is only through the integrated analysis of language, interpretation, cognition, and context that we can account for the experience of literary reading.

In this book, we have introduced analytical frameworks in contemporary stylistics. After introducing stylistics as an interdisciplinary method of analysis in Part I, we moved in Part II to an exploration of the ways in which traditional linguistic analysis (considering phonology, morphology, syntax, and textual patterning) can be used to underpin interpretations. Part III repositioned focus to the study of texts as discourse, presenting frameworks that allow us to explore the way texts can be structured to portray different points of view, such as offering an insight into character consciousness or reflecting power relations and ideological stances.

Part IV introduced frameworks that bring a cognitive dimension into stylistic analysis. The concepts introduced in Parts IV and V – such as cognitive deixis, schemas, and conceptual metaphor amongst others – represent ways in which stylistics as a discipline has responded to advances in the cognitive sciences. Such advances allow greater insight into the embodied nature of cognition and the way in which the human mind works. Contemporary stylistics has put these to good use in order to further our understanding of the processes involved in reading literature and the nature of literary experience.

Like us, some stylisticians believe that cognitively informed frameworks have the potential to provide valuable new perspectives on the concerns established in Parts II and III. However, critics of cognitive stylistics argue that in some cases new sets of terms are simply relabelling existing ideas. For instance, the cognitive framework of figure and ground is designed to explore attentional prominence, an idea that is also at the heart of foregrounding. Rather than one framework outdating the other or both acting as competing frameworks, we see foregrounding and figure and ground as complementary. Whilst foregrounding focuses on textual patterns such as parallelism and deviation, figure and ground advances our understanding of the dynamic processes of reading by drawing on human sensory perception. The relationships and resonances between early and more recent frameworks in contemporary stylistics are something you can reflect on. We believe that it is important to refresh the labels we use to describe linguistic phenomena if they better reflect current thinking about language and the mind.

Stylistics is a progressive discipline and wants to make use of linguistic theories which are current in other fields as well as its own, though the frameworks and terms inspired by non-cognitive linguistic theories continue to offer useful insights into textual meaning. Contemporary stylisticians are those who are able to consider all available options and choose the best 'tools' for the analytical 'job' they are undertaking; the ones which facilitate the production of interesting textual analysis and have explanatory power in accounting for textual effects. Regardless of how established frameworks are, the work of testing and refining approaches in stylistics is never complete. Stylisticians must, and do, continue to test frameworks by applying them to different, and increasingly challenging, text types – and now that you have read this book, you are equipped to continue this work yourself. Parts VI and VII again relocated the level of analysis to experience and empiricism. Chapter 19 considered how different semiotic modes (printed type, but also graphology, visual elements, and the materiality of a book) interact to create meaning and impact the reading experience whilst Chapter 20 explored the way in which texts evoke emotional responses, both through stylistic composition and as evidenced in reader responses. Chapters 21 and 22 introduced empirical approaches, employing computational methods to analyse texts and using reader response data to learn more about how real readers experience literature. These chapters cover the most recent frontiers of stylistics, and ensure that this book is up to date.

Contemporary stylistics – as we mentioned in Chapter 1 – prides itself on being a discipline that does not stand still. Its continued evolution means that whilst the fundamental principles of stylistic analysis remain the same, its dominant approaches may change. To see this in practice, we can look back at the first edition of Stockwell's (2002a) *Cognitive Poetics: An Introduction*, the first textbook in the emerging field of cognitive stylistics. Stockwell had the task of charting the parameters of the discipline based on which advances in the cognitive sciences he thought – at that time – were the most valuable for exploring literary reading. In this book, *Contemporary Stylistics*, written over a decade later, we have also made choices about what to include and exclude based on our current impression of the most significant frameworks in the discipline. We have included some of the same cognitive frameworks as Stockwell (2002a), whilst omitting others. Possible Worlds Theory is one such omission. This is not because we think Possible Worlds Theory is unimportant; on the contrary, it continues to be used in inventive ways (for instance, see Bell 2010; Bell and Ryan forthcoming). However, Possible Worlds Theory is predominantly a philosophical model of ontology rather than a *cognitive* model of discourse like Text World Theory, and as such the latter now seems to sit more centrally within the discipline of contemporary stylistics.

With a view to the continued evolution of the discipline, the remainder of this chapter offers some examples of present trends and future directions in contemporary stylistic research.

23.2 Present trends

In Chapter 1, we mentioned that classical rhetoric influenced stylistics, particularly in terms of the study of the way linguistic structures induce social and emotional effects. The social dimension of style has become an increasingly important aspect of contemporary stylistics. Indeed, there are points of mutual overlap between stylistic and sociolinguistic research. Coopland, in fact, calls his (2007) sociolinguistic study of language variation (including accent and dialect, idiolect and social repertoires) *Style*. 'Literary style', Coopland argues, 'relates to the crafting of linguistic text in literary genres and to an aesthetic interpretation of text' (2007: 2) whereas 'social style' – a term he takes from Machin and van Leeuwen (2005) – is concerned with 'style *in speech* and about *ways of speaking*' (2007: 2; original emphasis). Despite the differing foci, Coopland emphasises 'it would be wrong to force these areas of study too far apart' (2007: 2). Indeed, like stylistics, Coopland's work draws on Systemic Functional Linguistics, such as the work of Halliday. Moreover, the influence of sociolinguistics is evident in discourse-focused stylistic frameworks, such as the employment of conversation analysis to analyse speech in fiction (Chapter 7) and the analysis of literary representations of accent and dialect (Chapter 11).

Another reason for the increased emphasis on social meanings and social context in contemporary stylistics is that cognition itself is fundamentally social. As Fiske and Taylor state, social cognition is 'the study of how people make sense of other people and themselves' (2017: 2). When we read fiction, our understanding of characters and how they relate to each other and to the world is not isolated from our own everyday interactions and cognitions. The social nature of cognition in literary reading is evidenced, for instance, in Whiteley's (2011a) study of reader responses to *Remains of the Day* as well as in Chapter 20's account of the ways in which readers emotionally position themselves whilst reading. Moreover, contemporary stylistic frameworks have been used to analyse what might traditionally be seen as sociolinguistic data. Van der Bom (2016), for instance, applies Text World Theory to interview data whilst reader response analysis in contemporary stylistics often explores social interaction in reading groups (Peplow 2016; Peplow et al. 2016).

The current interest in sociolinguistic style is complemented by increased attention to empirical research, particularly in terms of investigation into the responses of real readers (or audiences/viewers/users/participants). Chapter 22 offered you an insight into how to collect data in the post-processing phase of reading. Within naturalistic methods which study online review data and reading groups, for instance, there is a clear move to understanding literary meaning not as an individual solipsistic experience but as a fundamentally social endeavour that takes place beyond the literary page (Peplow 2016; Peplow and Carter 2014; Peplow et al. 2016; Whiteley 2011a, 2011b, 2016). This is also evident in Mason's work (forthcoming) on intertextuality.

Stylistics has traditionally been used to analyse language in literary contexts, yet as the above discussion of socio-stylistic and empirical stylistic research demonstrates, the discipline is moving beyond the literary work. Another current trend in contemporary stylistics is the relationship between stylistic research and education. Cognitive stylistic approaches have been used to analyse classroom discourse as well as to offer cognitive stylistic tools as models of best practice for teachers (Clark 2016; Giovanelli 2016a; Giovanelli and Mason 2015; Macrae 2016a; Mason 2016). The stylistic approach has also been used to analysis the discourse of education more generally (Berry 2016; Solly 2015), paratextual pedagogical material in literary textbooks such as questions for readers placed before each chapter (Mason and Giovanelli 2017), as well as students' and schoolchildren's interpretations of stylistic features (Cushing 2018; Unsworth and Macken-Horarik 2015). Such work is of course preceded by a history of research in pedagogical stylistics (see Brumfit and Carter 1986; Burke et al. 2012; Clark and Zyngier 2003; Short 1989; Widdowson 1975).

Current cognitive frameworks in contemporary stylistics do remain biased towards particular aspects of cognition that are most relevant to written and text-based contexts. However, as well as moving beyond the literary work, stylistics is moving beyond an exclusive focus on language and the printed page. This is most clear in multimodal stylistics, which was the subject of Chapter 19. Increasingly, stylisticians are analysing composite texts with multiple modes (which may or may not include printed language). Stylistics has therefore been applied to printed multimodal fiction (Gibbons 2008, 2010a, 2010b, 2012b, 2015, 2016b; Nørgaard 2010a, 2010b, 2014), visual poetry (Borkent 2012; Hiraga 2005), film (McIntyre 2008), digital fictions and computer games (Bell 2010, 2014; Bell and Ensslin 2011, 2012), theatre and participatory narratives (Gibbons 2014a, 2016a), and songs and song lyrics (Morini 2013).

A final current trend in contemporary stylistics is the project of scaling up cognitive grammar. As discussed in Chapter 14, Cognitive Grammar was originally conceived by Langacker (1987) as a means of analysing clauses. However, stylisticians both have transferred its application to a new, literary context and are adapting the framework for analysis at the discourse level (Giovanelli and Harrison forthcoming; Hamilton 2003; Harrison 2017; Harrison et al. 2014; Nuttall 2015; Stockwell 2009a). It has also been used to analyse political discourse and combined with empirical research to investigate resistant reading (Browse 2018).

Taken together, these present trends question the related ideas of text, author, and readers. Texts, including literature, are no longer confined to the printed page. They can be multimodal and multimedial; more than this, social discourse such as reading group conversations, political speeches, and educational tools can be texts in themselves. Relatedly, authors and readers are no longer seen as individual; rather the production of textual meaning is negotiated and the acts of writing and reading are fundamentally collaborative processes of creativity and interpretation.

23.3 Future directions: Situated contemporary stylistics

Stylistics is a forward-thinking discipline and in this section of the chapter, we consider future directions for cutting-edge stylistic research. In discussing current advancements to cognitive grammar, we briefly mentioned that it was being applied to political discourse. As an applied discipline, linguistics and stylistics have often undertaken critical forms of discourse analysis (for instance, see Jeffries

2010b). Just as an ethical and socio-political turn is being felt within cultural studies and literary criticism more broadly, it is similarly manifesting itself in contemporary stylistics. Recent analyses of conceptual metaphor, for instance, have considered its use in language surrounding the 2008 financial crash (Browse 2016a, 2016b) and other forms of political discourse (Giovanelli 2016b); how it is employed by Facebook or YouTube users in religious speech (Pihlaja 2010, 2011, 2013, 2014, 2017); and how it appears in healthcare contexts such as in the language of healthcare professionals and patients (Demjén et al. 2016; Demmen et al. 2015; Potts and Semino 2017; Semino et al. 2016; Semino et al. 2017), in counselling (Beger 2015), and newspaper reports about cancer (Williams Camus 2015). Another example of socially and ethically conscious research in linguistics and stylistics is the 'Language in Conflict' project based at the University of Huddersfield, which explores how linguistic approaches can contribute to studies of conflict resolution.

We believe that contemporary stylistics has an ethical and social responsibility, and therefore our role as stylisticians carries accountability and influence. Critical linguistic approaches, such as critical discourse analysis and critical stylistics, have always understood the role of linguistic analysis in raising awareness about ideological biases and injustice. Likewise, contemporary stylistics can be employed in analysis – of both literary and non-literary texts – to raise consciousness and conscience about particular socio-cultural and political issues. In her doctoral research, for instance, Hanna has conducted interviews with asylum seekers. Her project analyses both the linguistic make-up of the personal narratives of the asylum seekers interviewed as well as the responses to these narratives from members of the general public within discussion groups held in local libraries (see Hanna 2016). The study therefore not only captures the 'voices' of marginalised members of society but also brings their voices into social dialogue. Similarly, Browse's (2018) work on political discourse considers the production of political speeches and public talk (both in terms of their multiple authors and linguistic and rhetorical structures) as well as the processes of political reception and interpretation by members of the voting public.

Both Hanna and Browse practise what we see – and advocate – as a form of situated stylistics; 'situated' in the sense that it entails stylistics analysis that, on the one hand, is critically contextualised and ideologically attuned and, on the other hand, triangulates data from various related sites and sources. Context has always been important to stylistic analysis. As such, the form of situated stylistics we are promoting builds on 'contextualised stylistics', defined by Bex et al. as involving

> the co-text, which surrounds the part of the text that is being analysed, the social and cultural backgrounds, which bring a text into being, and the social, cultural and cognitive positionings of those readers who interpret the text and give it meaning. (Bex et al. 2000: i)

Contextualised stylistics maintains an emphasis on the literary text as the central focus of analysis, whilst situated stylistics displaces the literary text by using it as one element within a larger network of data (often empirical response data) and intertexts. Doing so balances attitudes from multiple sources (that may exist in tension) and results in a cumulative stylistic analysis that is situated within the wider socio-political context of the data, that is a situated interpretation of larger discursive event. Gibbons (forthcoming), for instance, investigates the court case surrounding the Egyptian novelist Ahmed Naji's multimodal novella *Using Life* (originally published in Arabic as *Istikhdam al-Hayat*). In February 2016, Naji was sentenced to two years in prison for 'violating public modesty' after a reader complained that shocking, taboo content in an extract from the novel compromised his health (Naji was later released). In her analysis, Gibbons analyses Naji's trial in its socio-political context, considering the legal arguments, public discourse surrounding the case, and style of the translated excerpt. In doing so, she explores what a situated, politicised stylistics can contribute to the study of freedom of expression as well as language and discrimination.

The situated form of contemporary stylistics we are advocating here can also be applied to empirical studies of reception. Doing so can produce enriching results for researchers as well as the readers who participate in such studies. Canning (2017), for instance, led a read-aloud literary project ('read.live.learn') with a group of inmates in Northern Ireland's only female prison. During the readings, Canning would pause to allow participants to respond to the text(s) and to generate discussion about their own real-life experiences with which the text may have resonated. Analysing the data she collected through observational notes, interviews, and questionnaire responses, Canning's research develops understanding of the interaction between discourse-world and text-world contexts thus leading to an enhancement of the Text World Theory framework. Furthermore, in the process of conducting her research, Canning's read-aloud sessions had an impact on the participants themselves, showing that – in her words – 'literary fiction can help unlock inaccessible or challenging personal narratives' (2017: 185).

Studies of emotional responses to literature and to the experiential textures of reading already situate interpretation by incorporating the views of multiple readers, either through discussion group data (e.g. Whiteley 2011a; Peplow et al. 2016), or by gathering a sample of representative responses from online sites such as Goodreads (for instance, Gavins 2013; Stewart-Shaw 2017; Stockwell 2005a). By combining textual analysis, our own intuitions as the analyst, and the attitudes of real readers, situated empirical stylistics presents what Stewart-Shaw calls a 'multidimensional approach' that is 'at times objective, subjective, and intersubjective' (2017: 180). As Stockwell observes, initially cognitive poetics followed the norm of cognitive science in focusing on the individual mind and thus 'the solitary reader' (2002a: 169), but this is a tendency which is now being resisted in contemporary stylistic studies of reading in social contexts. The notion of the solitary, isolated reader with a single isolated reading is also being challenged by empirical research into re-reading (Harrison and Nuttall 2016).

Two final, connected tendencies in forward-thinking research in contemporary stylistics are the use of mixed methods of analysis and collaboration. Thus, not only is the reader a more social being, so too is the academic researcher. Through the course of this section, we've already touched upon work that incorporates readers and stakeholders as part of the research process as well as studies that incorporate numerous data sources. Additionally, the use of mixed methods of analysis enhances the rigour and reliability of contemporary stylistics. This is particularly seen in the empirical field in which participant responses might, for example, be analysed using corpus methods as well as forms of thematic analysis (for instance, tagging the data using software such as NVivo). The use of mixed methods is one reason for the rise of collaborative research, allowing researchers to contribute different expertise to a venture.

Collaboration is a process that works in the interest of advancing the discipline. Contemporary stylistics is not the isolated, lonely work of individual scholars, but is fundamentally collaborative. Even research produced by a single author is in dialogue with existing research in the field. The project of contemporary stylistics is by no means finished. Knowing its history and knowing its scope allows you to identify where gaps still remain in existing provision. You now have the contemporary stylistic toolkit with which to build the next future-thinking, cutting-edge study.

References

Literary works

Poetry

Armitage, S. (2001 [1999]) 'Meanwhile, Somewhere in the State of Colorado' [originally printed in *Killing Time* (1999)], in *Selected Poems*, London: Faber & Faber, pp. 153–5.

Burns, R. (1953 [1794]) 'A Red, Red Rose', in Meikle, H. W. and Beattie, W. (eds) *Robert Burns*, Harmondsworth: Penguin, p. 228.

Causley, C. (2000) 'I Am the Song', in *Collected Poems 1951–2000*, Basingstoke: Picador, p. 420.

Cope, W. (1992) 'Valentine', in *Serious Concerns*, London: Faber & Faber, p. 12.

Copus, J. (2003) 'In Defence of Adultery', in *In Defence of Adultery*, Newcastle upon Tyne: Bloodaxe Books, p. 41.

Copus, J. (2012) 'This Is the Poem in which I Have Not Left You', in *The World's Two Smallest Humans*, London: Faber & Faber, p. 3.

cummings, e. e. (1994 [1938]) 'The Mind's(' [originally published in *Collected Poems* (1938)], in Firmage, G. J. (ed.) *e. e. cummings: Complete Poems 1904–1962*, revised, corrected, and expanded edition containing all the published poetry, New York: Liveright, p. 474.

cummings, e. e. (1994 [1958]) 'unlove's the heavenless hell and homeless home' [originally published in *Poems* (1958)], in Firmage, G. J. (ed.) *e. e. cummings: Complete Poems 1904–1962*, revised, corrected, and expanded edition containing all the published poetry, New York: Liveright, p. 765.

Faber, M. (2016) *Undying: A Love Story*, Edinburgh: Canongate.

Gay, R. (2011) 'The Lion and the Gazelle', in *Bringing the Shovel Down*, Pittsburgh: University of Pittsburgh Press, pp. 17–19.

Goldsmith, S. (2012) 'Received Pronunciation', in Lehoczky, A., Piette, A., Sansom, A. and Sansom, P. (eds) *The Sheffield Anthology: Poems from the City Imagined*, Sheffield: Smith/Doorstop, pp. 93–4.

Harvey, M. (2000) 'In Defense of Our Overgrown Garden', in *Pity the Bathtub Its Forced Embrace of the Human Form*, Farmington, ME: Alice James Books, p. 29.

Hopkins, G. M. ([1881] 2014) 'Inversnaid', in *Poems of Gerard Manley Hopkins*, London: Createspace Publishing, p. 24.

Leonard, T. (1995 [1976]) 'The Six O'Clock News', in *Intimate Voices: Selected Works 1965–83*, London: Vintage, p. 88.

MacNeice, L. (1966 [1925–9]) 'River in Spate', in Dodds, E. R. (ed.) *The Collected Poems of Louis MacNeice*, London: Faber & Faber, pp. 5–6.

Marinetti, F. T. (2010 [1914]) 'Zong Toomb Toomb' [originally published as 'Zang Tumb Tumb', 1912–13; 1914)], in *F. T. Marinetti: Selected Poems and Related Prose*, selected by Luce Marinetti, trans. Elizabeth R. Napier and Barbara R. Studholme, New Haven, CT: Yale University Press, pp. 55–82.

McCaffery, S. (2000) 'Sixteen' [originally published in *Intimate Distortions* (1979)], in *Seven Pages Missing: Volume One: Selected Texts 1969–1999*, Toronto: Coach House Books, p. 138.

McDaniel, J. (2008) 'don't touch it!', in *The Endarkenment*, Pittsburgh: University of Pittsburgh Press, p. 34.

Morgan, E. (1990 [1977]) 'Space Sonnet & Polyfilla', in *Edwin Morgan: Collected Poems 1949–1987*, Manchester: Carcanet Press, p. 341.

Nichols, G. (1984) 'Shopping', in *The Fat Black Woman's Poems*, London: Virago Press, p. 31.

Normal, H. (1993) 'The House Is Not the Same since You Left', in *Nude Modelling for the Afterlife*, Newcastle upon Tyne: Bloodaxe Books, p. 21.

Parker, D. (2011 [1926]) 'One Perfect Rose', in *The Collected Dorothy Parker*, London: Penguin Classics, p. 104.

Poe, E. A. (1992 [1831]) 'The City in the Sea', in *The Collected Tales and Poems of Edgar Allan Poe*, New York: Modern Library, pp. 963–5.

Sidney, Sir P. (1994 [1580]) *The Countess of Pembroke's Arcadia (The Old Arcadia)*, Oxford: Oxford University Press, p. 167.

Strand, M. (2014 [1970]) 'Tomorrow' [originally published in *Darker* (1970)], in *Collected Poems*, New York: Alfred A. Knopf, p. 94.

Taylor, M. (2014) 'Hypothetical', in Hannah, S. (ed.) *The Poetry of Sex*, London: Viking, pp. 45–6.

Welton, M. (2003) 'The Book of Matthew', in *The Book of Matthew*, Manchester: Carcanet Press, pp. 40–78.

Young, D. (2005) 'Facet', in *Elegy on Toy Piano*, Pittsburgh: University of Pittsburgh Press, p. 10.

Zephaniah, B. (1995) 'Dis Poetry', in *City Psalms*, Newcastle upon Tyne: Bloodaxe Books, p. 12.

Prose

Adams, S. (2013) *A Modern Family*, New York: Bluemoose Books.

Austen, J. (1992 [1813]) *Pride and Prejudice*, Ware: Wordsworth Editions.

Brontë, E. (1995 [1847]) *Wuthering Heights*, London: Penguin.

Burgess, Melvin (n.d.) 'Blood Story', BookTrust, <http://fileserver.booktrust.org.uk/usr/library/documents/main/blood-story-final-1.docx> (last accessed 17 November 2016).

Castro, B. (2009 [2003]) *Shanghai Dancing*, New York: Kaya Press.

Chbosky, S. (1999) *The Perks of Being a Wallflower*, London: Pocket Books.

Cleave, C. (2016) *Everybody Brave Is Forgiven*, London: Hodder & Stoughton.

Coleman, E. H. (1997 [1930]) *The Shutter of Snow*, Normal, IL: Dalkey Archive Press.

Corman, A. (1977) *Kramer versus Kramer*, Glasgow: Fontana.

Edwards, K. (2005) *The Memory Keeper's Daughter*, London: Penguin Books.

Eggers, D. (2000) *A Heartbreaking Work of Staggering Genius*, London: Picador.

Eggers, D. (2006) *What Is the What: An Autobiography of Valentino Achak Deng, A Novel*, London: Penguin.

Eggers, D. (2007) 'The New Rules' [looseleaf insert], in Eggers, D., Manguso, S. and Unferth, D. O. (authors) *One Hundred and Forty Five Stories in a Small Box: Hard to Admit and Harder to Escape, How the Water Feels to the Fishes, and Minor Robberies*, San Francisco: McSweeneys.

Ellis, B. E. (1991) *American Psycho*, London: Picador.

Ferris, J. (2007) *Then We Came to the End*, London: Viking.

Ferris, J. (2014) *To Rise Again at a Decent Hour*, London: Penguin.

Filer, N. (2013) *The Shock of the Fall*, London: HarperCollins.

Flanagan, R. (2014) *The Narrow Road to the Deep North*, London: Chatto & Windus.

Foer, J. S. (2010) 'Here We Aren't, So Quickly', *The New Yorker*, 14/21 June, pp. 72–3. Reprinted in Treisman, D. (ed.) (2010) *20 under 40: Stories from the New Yorker*, New York: Farrar, Straus and Giroux, pp. 139–44.

Forster, M. (2016) *How to Measure a Cow*, London: Chatto & Windus.

Frey, J. (2003) *A Million Little Pieces*, London: John Murray.

Gay, R. (2014) *An Untamed State*, New York: Black Cat.

Green, T. (2012) *The Fault in Our Stars*, London: Penguin Books.

Hamid, M. (2013) *How to Get Filthy Rich in Rising Asia*, London: Hamish Hamilton.

Handler, D. (2011) *Why We Broke Up*, New York: Little, Brown.

Hawke, E. (2002) *Ash Wednesday*, London: Bloomsbury.

Hawkins, P. (2015) *The Girl on the Train*, London: Black Swan.

Heti, S. (2013) 'The Cherry Tree', *The White Review*, 3 June, <http://www.thewhitereview.org/fiction/the-cherry-tree/> (last accessed 5 February 2014).

Hickey, E. (2005) *The Painted Kiss*, New York: Washington Square Press.

Ishiguro, K. (2005 [1995]) *The Unconsoled*, London: Faber & Faber.

Jacobson, H. (2010) *The Finkler Question*, London: Bloomsbury.

James, E. L. (2012) *Fifty Shades of Grey*, London: Arrow.

Johnson, B. S. (2004 [1964]) *Albert Angelo*, London: Picador.

Kaufman, A. and Kristoff, J. (2015) *Illuminae: The Illuminae Files_01*, London: Rock the Boat.

Kieser, C. (1997) 'Completely Overloaded', in Corrigan, S. (ed.) *Typical Girls*, London: Sceptre, pp. 75–92.

Kunzru, H. (2013) *Memory Palace*, London: V&A.

Kureshi, H. (1998) *Intimacy*, London: Faber & Faber.

Larsen, N. (2004 [1929]) *Passing*, Mineola, NY: Dover Publications.

Lawrence, D. H. (1985) *Mr. Noon*, ed. Vasey, L., Cambridge: Cambridge University Press.

Lawrence, D. H. (1995 [1915]) *The Rainbow*, London: Penguin.

Lockhart, E. (2014) *We Were Liars*, London: Hot Key Books.

Lodge, D. (1993 [1975]) 'Changing Places', in *A David Lodge Trilogy*, London: Penguin, pp. 1–218.

McCarthy, C. (2006) *The Road*, London: Picador.

McCarthy, T. (2015) *Satin Island*, London: Vintage.

Martin, S. (2003) *The Pleasure of My Company*, New York: Hyperion.

Meno, J. (2006) *The Boy Detective Fails*, Chicago: Planet Punk Books.

Mitchell, D. (2004) *Cloud Atlas*, London: Hodder & Stoughton.

Mitchell, D. (2014) *The Bone Clocks*, London: Hodder & Stoughton.

Moody, R. (2003) 'Circulation', in Cassini, M. and Testa, M. (eds) *The Burned Children of America*, London: Hamish Hamilton, pp. 265–79.

Moore, S. (1995) *In the Cut*, New York: Plume.

Mukherjee, N. (2014) *The Lives of Others*, London: Chatto & Windus.

Rawle, G. (2005) *Woman's World*, London: Atlantic Books.

Richardson, S. (2009–13 [1740]) *Pamela, or Virtue Rewarded*, Project Gutenberg e-book, produced by Tapio Riikonen and David Widger, <https://www.gutenberg.org/files/6124/6124-h/6124-h.htm> (last accessed 14 August 2015).

Rifaat, Alifa (1985) 'An Incident in the Ghobashi Household', trans. Denys Johnson-Davies, in Achebe, C. and Innes, C. L. (eds) (1987) *African Short Stories*, Harlow: Heinemann, pp. 86–9.

Rourke, L. (2010) *The Canal*, New York: Melville House Publishing.

Rule, J. (1970) *This Is Not for You*, London: Pandora.

Sahota, S. (2015) *The Year of the Runaways*, London: Picador.

Shapiro, E. M. (2011) *13, rue Thérèse*, New York; Boston; London: Back Bay Books.

Smith, A. (2008) 'Astute Fiery Luxurious', in *The First Person and Other Stories*, London: Penguin Books, pp. 165–87.

Strout, E. (2016) *My Name Is Lucy Barton*, London: Viking.

Thirlwell, A. (2015) *Lurid & Cute*, New York: Farrar, Straus and Giroux.

Thomas, D. (1954) *Under Milk Wood: A Play for Voices*, London: J. M. Dent & Sons.

Tillman, L. (2002) 'Living with Contradictions', in *This Is Not It: Stories*, New York: Distributed Art Publishers, pp. 81–4.

Unferth, D. O. (2007) 'Deb Olin Unferth', in *Minor Robberies*, San Francisco: McSweeney Books, pp. 21–4.

Winterson, J. (1992) *Written on the Body*, London: Jonathan Cape.

Zusak, M. (2008) *The Book Thief*, London: Black Swan.

Other media

Blast Theory (2015) *Karen*. App for iOS and Android [script for *Karen* shared with authors by Blast Theory, though at times the in-app dialogue varies slightly from the script].

Fresh Meat Series 2, Episode 7, Channel 4 television, first broadcast 20 November 2012.

Fresh Meat Series 3, Episode 2, Channel 4 television, first broadcast 13 November 2013.

House of Cards Season 2, Episode 5, Netflix Original (2014). Directed by John Coles. Based on the novels by Michael Dobbs, based on the mini-series by Andrew Davies, created for television by Beau Willimon, written by Kenneth Lin.

'My Blackberry Is Not Working', *The One Ronnie* (2010) BBC, first broadcast 25 December 2010. Directed by Geoff Posner, multiple writers, <https://www.youtube.com/watch?v=6dmhF1rqaZk> (last accessed 22 July 2016).

Critical works

Adams, M. (2015) 'How We Made Experiential Life-Coaching App, Karen', *The Guardian*, 15 August, <https://www.theguardian.com/culture-professionals-network/2015/aug/14/how-we-made-life-coaching-app-karen-blast-theory> (last accessed 14 September 2016).

Adamson, S. (1999) 'Literary Language', in Lass, R. (ed.) *The Cambridge History of the English Language, 1476–1776, Vol. 3*, Cambridge: Cambridge University Press, pp. 539–653.

Adamson, S. (2001) 'The Rise and Fall of Empathetic Narrative: A Historical Perspective on Perspective', in van Peer, W. and Chatman, S. (eds) *New Perspectives on Narrative Perspective*, New York: State University of New York Press, pp. 83–99.

Adolphs, S. and Carter, R. (2002) 'Point of View and Semantic Prosodies in Virginia Woolf's *To the Lighthouse*', *Poetica* 58: 7–20.

Albritton, D. W. and Gerrig, R. J. (1991) 'Participatory Responses in Text Understanding', *Journal of Memory and Language* 30(5): 603–26.

Alderson, J. C. and Short, M. (1989) 'Reading Literature', in Short, M. (ed.) *Reading, Analysing and Teaching Literature*, London: Longman, pp. 72–119.

Allan, K. (1986) *Linguistic Meaning*, 2 vols, London: Routledge & Kegan Paul.

Allington, D. and Swann, J. (2009) 'Researching Literary Reading as Social Practice', *Language and Literature* 18(3): 219–30.

Altendorf, U. and Watt, D. (2008) 'The Dialects in the South of England: Phonology', in Kortmann, B. and Upton, C. (eds) *Varieties of English 1: The British Isles*, Berlin: Mouton de Gruyter, pp. 194–222.

Anderson, E. R. (1998) *A Grammar of Iconism*, Cranbury, NJ; London; Mississauga: Associated University Presses.

Andringa, E. (1990) 'Verbal Data on Literary Understanding: A Proposal for Protocol Analysis on Two Levels', *Poetics* 19: 231–57.

Anthony, L. (n.d.) 'AntConc Homepage', <http://www.laurenceanthony.net/software/antconc> (last accessed 17 November 2016).

Arnold, M. B. (1960) *Emotion and Personality: Vol. 1, Psychological Aspects*, New York: Columbia University Press.

Attridge, D. (1982) *The Rhythms of English Poetry*, Harlow: Longman.

Attridge, D. (1988) *Peculiar Language: Literature as Different from the Renaissance to James Joyce*, London: Methuen.

Auer, A., González-Díaz, V., Hodson, J. and Sotirova, V. (eds) (2016) *Linguistics and Literary History: In Honour of Sylvia Adamson*, Amsterdam: John Benjamins.

Austin, J. L. (1962) *How to Do Things with Words*, Oxford: Clarendon Press.

Baker, P. (2006) *Using Corpora in Discourse Analysis*, London: Continuum.

Bakhtin, M. (1981 [1934–5]) 'Discourse in the Novel', in *The Dialogic Imagination*, trans. Emerson, C. and Holquist, M., ed. Holquist, M., Austin, TX: University of Texas Press, pp. 258–422.

Baldry, A. and Thibault, P. (2006) *Multimodal Transcription and Text Analysis*, London; Oakville: Equinox.

Banfield, A. (1982) *Unspeakable Sentences: Narration and Representation in the Language of Fiction*, Boston: Routledge & Kegan Paul.

Barney, T. (2010) 'Public House Confidence: The Indispensability of Sound Patterns', in McIntyre, D. and Busse, B. (eds) *Language and Style*, Basingstoke: Palgrave Macmillan, pp. 133–42.

Barsalou, L. (1983) 'Ad-hoc Categories', *Memory and Cognition* 11: 211–27.

Barsalou, L. W. (2003) 'Situated Simulation in the Human Conceptual System', *Language and Cognitive Processes* 18(5–6): 513–62.

Bartlett, F. C. (1995 [1932]) *Remembering: A Study in Experimental and Social Psychology*, Cambridge: Cambridge University Press.

Bateman, J. A. (2008) *Multimodality and Genre: A Foundation for the Systematic Analysis of Multimodal Documents*, Basingstoke: Palgrave Macmillan.

Bateman, J. A. (2014) 'Genre in the Age of Multimodality: Some Conceptual Refinements for Practical Analysis', in Allori, P. E., Bateman, J. and Bhatia, V. K. (eds) *Evolution in Genre: Emergence, Variation, Multimodality*, Bern: Peter Lang, pp. 237–69.

Beal, J. C. (2006) 'Dialect Representation in Texts', in Brown, K. (ed.) *Encyclopedia of Language and Linguistics*, 2nd edn, Oxford: Elsevier, pp. 531–7.

Beal, J. (2008) 'English Dialects of the North of England: Phonology', in Kortmann, B. and Upton, C. (eds) *Varieties of English 1: The British Isles*, Berlin: Mouton de Gruyter, pp. 122–44.

Beaugrande, R. de (1980) 'Informativity', in *Text, Discourse and Processes: Toward a Multidisciplinary Science of Texts*, Norwood, NJ: Ablex, pp. 103–31.

Beger, A. (2015) 'Metaphors in Psychology Genres: Counseling vs. Academic Lectures', in Berenike Herrmann, J. and Berber Sardinha, T. (eds) *Metaphor in Specialist Discourse*, Amsterdam: John Benjamins, pp. 53–76.

Bell, A. (2010) *The Possible Worlds of Hypertext Fiction*, Basingstoke: Palgrave Macmillan.

Bell, A. (2014) 'Schema Theory, Hypertext Fiction and Links', *Style* 48(2): 140–61.

Bell, A. and Ensslin, A. (2011) '"I know what it was. You know what it was": Second-Person Narration in Hypertext Fiction', *Narrative* 19(3): 311–29.

Bell, A. and Ensslin, A. (2012) '"Click = Kill": Textual *you* in Ludic Digital Fiction', *Storyworlds: A Journal of Narrative Studies* 4: 49–73.

Bell, A., Ensslin, A. and Rustad, H. (eds) (2014a) *Analyzing Digital Fiction*, London; New York: Routledge.

Bell, A., Ensslin, A. and Rustad, H. (2014b) 'From Theorizing to Analyzing Digital Fiction', in Bell, A., Ensslin, A. and Rustad, H. (eds) *Analyzing Digital Fiction*, London; New York: Routledge, pp. 3–17.

Bell, A. and Ryan, M.-L. (forthcoming) *Possible Worlds Theory and Contemporary Narratology*, Lincoln, NE: University of Nebraska Press.

Bergen, B. K. (2004) 'The Psychological Reality of Phonaesthemes', *Language* 80(2): 290–311.

Berry, M. (2016) 'Systemic Functional Linguistics and Teachers' Knowledge about Students' Writing', in Giovanelli, M. and Clayton, D. (eds) *Knowing about Language: Linguistics and the Secondary English Classroom*, London; New York: Routledge, pp. 173–85.

Bex, T., Burke, M. and Stockwell, P. (2000) 'Foreword', in Bex, T., Burke, M. and Stockwell, P. (eds) *Contextualized Stylistics: In Honour of Peter Verdonk*, Amsterdam: Rodopi, pp. i–v.

Biber, D. and Conrad, S. (2009) *Register, Genre, and Style*, Cambridge: Cambridge University Press.

Birch, D. (1989) *Language, Literature and Critical Practice: Ways of Analysing Text*, London: Routledge.

Black, E. (1993) 'Metaphor, Simile and Cognition in Golding's *The Inheritors*', *Language and Literature* 2(1): 37–48.

Blake, N. E. (1981) *Non-Standard Language in English Literature*, London: Andre Deutsch.

Blake, N. (1990) *An Introduction to the Language of Literature*, London: Longman.

Blast Theory (2015) 'Press Release', <http://www.blasttheory.co.uk/wp-content/uploads/2015/04/press_release_karen.pdf> (last accessed 14 September 2016).

Bloomsfield, L. (1984 [1933]) *Language*, Chicago; London: University of Chicago Press.

Bloor, M. (2007) *The Practice of Critical Discourse Analysis: An Introduction*, London: Hodder Education.

Boase-Beier, J. (2003) 'Mind Style Translated', *Style* 37(3): 253–65.

Bockting, I. (1994) 'Mind Style as an Interdisciplinary Approach to Characterisation in Faulkner', *Language and Literature* 3(3): 157–74.

Booth, W. C. (1961) *The Rhetoric of Fiction*, Chicago: University of Chicago Press.

Booth, W. C. (1988) *The Company We Keep: An Ethics of Fiction*, Berkeley: University of California Press.

Borkent, M. (2012) 'Illusions of Simplicity: A Cognitive Approach to Visual Poetry', in Dancygier, B., Sander, J. and Vandelanotte, L. (eds) *Textual Choices in Discourse: A View from Cognitive Linguistics*, Amsterdam; Philadelphia: John Benjamins, pp. 5–24.

Bortolussi, M. and Dixon, P. (2003) *Psychonarratology: Foundations for the Empirical Study of Literary Response*, Cambridge: Cambridge University Press.

Bousfield, D. (2015) 'Politeness Theory', in Tracy, K., Ilie, C. and Sandel, T. (eds) *The International Encyclopedia of Language and Social Interaction*, Chichester: Wiley Blackwell.

Bradford, R. (1997) *Stylistics*, London: Routledge.

Brandt, P. A. (2004) *Spaces, Domains, and Meaning: Essays in Cognitive Semiotics*, Bern: Peter Lang.

Brandt, L. and Brandt, P. A. (2005) 'Making Sense of a Blend: A Cognitive-Semiotic Approach to Metaphor', *Annual Review of Cognitive Linguistics* 5: 216–49.

Bray, J. (2003) *The Epistolary Novel: Representations of Consciousness*, London; New York: Routledge.

Bray, J. (2007a) 'The Effects of Free Indirect Discourse: Empathy Revisited', in Lambrou, M. and Stockwell, P. (eds) *Contemporary Stylistics*, London; New York: Continuum, pp. 56–67.

Bray, J. (2007b) 'The "Dual Voice" of Free Indirect Discourse: A Reading Experiment', *Language and Literature* 16(1): 37–52.

Bray, J. (2010) 'Writing Presentation, the Epistolary Novel and Free Indirect Thought', in McIntyre, D. and Busse, B. (eds) *Language and Style: In Honour of Mick Short*, Basingstoke: Palgrave Macmillan, pp. 388–401.

Bray, J. (2014a) 'A Portrait of Historical Stylistics', in Stockwell, P. and Whiteley, S. (eds) *The Cambridge Handbook of Stylistics*, Cambridge: Cambridge University Press, pp. 485–99.

Bray, J. (2014b) 'Speech and Thought Presentation in Stylistics', in Burke, M. (ed.) *The Routledge Handbook of Stylistics*, London; New York: Routledge, pp. 222–36.

Brinton, L. (1980) '"Represented Perception": A Study in Narrative Style', *Poetics* 9(4): 363–81.

Brown, P. and Levinson, S. C. (1978) 'Universals in Language Usage: Politeness Phenomena', in Goody, E. N. (ed.) *Questions and Politeness*, Cambridge: Cambridge University Press.

Brown, P. and Levinson, S. C. (1987) *Politeness: Some Universals in Language Use*, Cambridge: Cambridge University Press.

Browse, S. (2014) 'Resonant Metaphor in Kazuo Ishiguro's *Never Let Me Go*', in Harrison, C., Nuttall, L., Stockwell, P. and Yuan, W. (eds) *Cognitive Grammar in Literature*, Amsterdam: John Benjamins, pp. 69–82.

Browse, S. (2016a) 'Revisiting Text World Theory and Extended Metaphor: Embedding and Foregrounding Metaphor in the Text-Worlds of the 2008 Financial Crash', *Language and Literature* 25(1): 8–3.

Browse, S. (2016b) '"This is not the end of the world": Situating Metaphor in the Text-Worlds of the British Financial Crisis', in Gavins, J. and Lahey, E. (eds) *World Building: Discourse in the Mind*, London; New York: Bloomsbury, pp. 183–201.

Browse, S. (2018) *Cognitive Rhetoric: The Cognitive Poetics of Political Discourse*, Amsterdam: John Benjamins.

Brumfit, C. and Carter, R. (eds) (1986) *Literature and Language Teaching*, Oxford: Oxford University Press.

Buck, R. and Austin, T. R. (1995) 'Dialogue and Power in E. M. Forster's *Howard's End*', in Verdonk, P. and Weber, J. J. (eds) *Twentieth-Century Fiction: From Text to Context*, London; New York: Routledge, pp. 63–77.

Bühler, K. (1982 [1932]) 'The Deictic Field of Language and Deictic Worlds', in Jarvella, R. and Klein, W. (eds) *Speech, Place and Action: Studies in Deixis and Related Topics*, Chichester: John Wiley, pp. 9–30.

Burke, M. (2001) 'Iconicity and Literary Emotion', *European Journal of English Studies* 5(1): 31–46.

Burke, M. (2011a) *Literary Reading, Cognition and Emotion: An Exploration of the Oceanic Mind*, London: Routledge.

Burke, M. (2011b) 'A Cognitive Stylistic Analysis of *The Great Gatsby* at Closure', in *Literary Reading, Cognition and Emotion: An Exploration of the Oceanic Mind*, London: Routledge, pp. 202–30.

Burke, M. (ed.) (2014a) *The Routledge Handbook of Stylistics*, London; New York: Routledge.

Burke, M. (2014b) 'Introduction: Stylistics: From Classical Rhetoric to Cognitive Neuroscience', in Burke, M. (ed.) *The Routledge Handbook of Stylistics*, London; New York: Routledge, pp. 1–7.

Burke, M., Csabi, S., Week, L. and Zerkowitz, J. (2012) *Pedagogical Stylistics: Current Trends in Language, Literature and ELT*, London: Continuum.

Burrows, J. F. (1987) *Computation into Criticism: A Study of Jane Austen's Novels and an Experiment in Method*, Oxford: Clarendon Press.

Burton, D. (1982) 'Through the Glass Darkly, through Dark Glasses', in Carter, R. (ed.) *Language and Literature: An Introductory Reader*, London: Allen & Unwin, pp. 195–214.

Busse, B. (2014) '(New) Historical Stylistics', in Burke, M. (ed.) *The Routledge Handbook of Stylistics*, London; New York: Routledge, pp. 101–17.

Busse, B. and McIntyre, D. (2010) 'Language, Literature and Stylistics', in McIntyre, D. and Busse, B. (eds) *Language and Style*, Basingstoke: Palgrave Macmillan, pp. 3–12.

Cameron, D. (2001) *Working with Spoken Discourse*, London: Sage.

Canning, P. (2008) '"The bodie and the letters both": "Blending" the Rules of Early Modern Religion', *Language and Literature* 17(3): 187–203.

Canning, P. (2017) 'Text World Theory and Real World Readers: From Literature to Life in a Belfast Prison', *Language and Literature* 26(2): 172–87.

Canovas, C. P. and Jenson, M. F. (2013) 'Anchoring Time-Space Mappings and Their Emotions: The Timeline Blend in Poetic Metaphors', *Language and Literature* 22(1): 45–59.

Carter, R. (1982) 'Introduction', in Carter, R. (ed.) *Language and Literature: An Introductory Reader in Stylistics*, London: George & Allen, pp. 1–17.

Carter, R. (1993) 'Between Languages: Grammar and Lexis in Thomas Hardy's "The Oxen"', in Verdonk, P. (ed.) *Twentieth-Century Poetry: From Text to Context*, London: Routledge, pp. 57–67.

Carter, R. (2004) *Language and Creativity: The Art of Common Talk*, London: Routledge.

Carter, R. (2010) 'Methodologies for Stylistic Analysis: Practices and Pedagogies', in McIntyre, D. and Busse, B. (eds) *Language and Style*, Basingstoke: Palgrave Macmillan, pp. 55–68.

Carter, R. (2014 [1989]) 'What Is Stylistics and Why Can We Teach It in Different Ways?', in Simpson, P. (2014 [2004]) *Stylistics: A Resource Book for Students*, 2nd edn, Abingdon; New York: Routledge, pp. 176–82.

Carter, R. and Stockwell, P. (2008) 'Stylistics: Retrospect and Prospect', in Carter, R. and Stockwell, P. (eds) *Language and Literature Reader*, Abingdon; New York: Routledge, pp. 291–302.

Chapman, R. (1973) *Linguistics and Literature: An Introduction to Literary Stylistics*, London: Edward Arnold.

Chapman, S. (2002) '"From their point of view": Voice and Speech in George Moore's *Esther Waters*', *Language and Literature* 11(4): 307–23.

Chomsky, N. (2002 [1957]) *Syntactic Structures*, 2nd edn, Berlin; New York: Mouton de Gruyter.

Ciccoricco, D. (2012) 'Focalization and Digital Fiction', *Narrative* 20(3): 255–76.

Clark, B. (2016) 'Pragmatics', in Giovanelli, M. and Clayton, D. (eds) *Knowing about Language: Linguistics and the Secondary English Classroom*, London; New York: Routledge, pp. 64–76.

Clark, H. H. and Clark, E. V. (1977) *Psychology and Language: An Introduction to Psycholinguistics*, New York: Harcourt Brace Jovanovich.

Clark, U. (1996) *An Introduction to Stylistics*, Cheltenham: Stanley Thornes.

Clark, U. and Zyngier, S. (2003) 'Towards a Pedagogical Stylistics', *Language and Literature* 12(4): 339–51.

Coates, J. (1983) *The Semantics of the Modal Auxiliaries*, London: Longman.

Cohn, D. (1966) 'Narrated Monologue: Definition of a Fictional Style', *Comparative Literature* 18(2): 97–112.

Cook, G. (1994) *Discourse and Literature*, Oxford: Oxford University Press.

Coopland, N. (2007) *Style: Language Variation and Identity*, Cambridge: Cambridge University Press.

Cornis-Pope, M. (1994) 'From Cultural Provocation to Narrative Cooperation: Innovative Uses of the Second Person in Raymond Federman's Fiction', *Style* 28(3): 411–31.

Coulson, S. (2001) *Semantic Leaps: Frame-Shifting and Conceptual Blending in Meaning Construction*, Cambridge: Cambridge University Press.

Coulson, S. and Oakley, T. (2000) 'Blending Basics', *Cognitive Linguistics* 11(3/4): 175–96.

Crisp, P. (2003) 'Conceptual Metaphor and Its Expression', in Gavins, J. and Steen, G. (eds) *Cognitive Poetics in Practice*, London: Routledge, pp. 99–113.

Crisp, P. (2008) 'Between Extended Metaphor and Allegory: Is Blending Enough?', *Language and Literature* 17(4): 291–308.

Croft, W. (2001) *Radical Construction Grammar: Syntactic Theory in Typological Perspective*, Oxford: Oxford University Press.

Croft, W. and Cruse, D. A. (2004) *Cognitive Linguistics*, Cambridge: Cambridge University Press.

Crowley, T. (2003) *Standard English and the Politics of Language*, Basingstoke: Palgrave Macmillan.

Cruikshank, T. and Lahey, E. (2010) 'Building the Stages of Drama: Towards a Text-World Theory Account of Dramatic Play-Texts', *Journal of Literary Semantics* 39: 67–91.

Cruse, D. A. (1986) *Lexical Semantics*, Cambridge: Cambridge University Press.

Crystal, D. (1995) *The Cambridge Encyclopedia of the English Language*, Cambridge: Cambridge University Press.

Cui, Y. (2014) 'Parentheticals and the Presentation of Multipersonal Consciousness: A Stylistic Analysis of *Mrs Dalloway*', *Language and Literature* 23(2): 175–87.

Cui, Y. (2017) 'Reader Responses to Shifts in Point of View: An Empirical Study', *Language and Literature* 26(2): 122–36.

Culler, J. (1975) *Structural Poetics*, London: Routledge & Keegan Paul.

Culpeper, J. (2001) *Language and Characterisation: People in Plays and Other Texts*, London: Longman.

Culpeper, J. (2002) 'Computers, Language and Characterisation: An Analysis of Six Characters in Romeo and Juliet', in Melander-Marttala, U., Östman, C. and Kytö, M. (eds) *Conversation in Life and in Literature*, Uppsala: Universitetstryckeriet, pp. 11–30.

Culpeper, J., Short, M. and Verdonk, P. (eds) (1998) *Exploring the Language of Drama: From Text to Context*, London: Routledge.

Cureton, R. (1979) 'e. e. cummings: A Study of the Poetic Use of Deviant Morphology', *Poetics Today* 1(1/2): 213–44.

Cureton, R. (1981) 'e. e. cummings: A Case Study of Iconic Syntax', *Language and Style* 14(3): 183–215.

Cureton, R. (1986) 'Visual Form in e. e. cummings' "No Thanks"', *Word & Image* 2(3): 245–77.

Currie, G. (1997) 'The Paradox of Caring: Fiction and the Philosophy of Mind', in Hjort, M. and Laver, S. (eds) *Emotion and the Arts*, Oxford: Oxford University Press, pp. 63–77.

Cushing, I. (2018) '"Suddenly, I am part of the poem": Texts as Worlds, Reader-Response and Grammar in Teaching Poetry', *English in Education* 52(1): 1–13. https://doi.org/10.1080/04250494.2018.1414398

Cutting, J. (2002) *Pragmatics and Discourse: A Resource Book for Students*, London: Routledge.

Dancygier, B. (2005) 'Blending and Narrative Viewpoint: Johnathan Raban's Travels through Mental Spaces', *Language and Literature* 14(2): 99–127.

Dancygier, B. (2006) 'What Can Blending Do for You?', *Language and Literature* 15(1): 5–15.

Davies, D. (2005) *Varieties of Modern English*, Harlow: Longman.

Davies, M. (2007) 'The Attraction of Opposites: The Ideological Function of Conventional and Created Oppositions in the Construction of In-Groups and Out-Groups in News Texts', in Jeffries, L., McIntyre, D. and Bousfield, D. (eds) *Stylistics and Social Cognition*, Amsterdam: Rodopi, pp. 79–100.

Davies, M. (2013) *Opposition and Ideology in News Discourse*, London: Bloomsbury.

Davis, S. and Andringa, E. (1995) 'Narrative Structure and Emotional Response', in Rusch, G. (ed.) *Empirical Approaches to Literature*, Siegen: Lumis, pp. 50–60.

Demjén, Z., Semino, E. and Koller, V. (2016) 'Metaphors for "Good" and "Bad" Deaths: A Health Professional View', *Metaphor and the Social World* 6(1): 1–19.

Demmen, J. E., Semino, E., Demjén, Z., Koller, V., Hardie, A., Rayson, P. and Payne, S. (2015) 'A Computer-Assisted Study of the Use of Violence Metaphors for Cancer and End of Life by Patients, Family Carers and Health Professions', *International Journal of Corpus Linguistics* 20(2): 205–31.

Douthwaite, J. (2000) *Towards a Linguistic Theory of Foregrounding*, Turin: Edizioni dell'Orso.

Dry, H. A. (1988) 'Timeline, Event Line, and Deixis', *Language and Style* 21(4): 399–410.

Dry, H. A. (1995) 'Free Indirect Discourse in Doris Lessing's "One off the Short List": A Case of Designed Ambiguity', in Verdonk, P. and Weber, J. J. (eds) *Twentieth-Century Fiction: From Text to Context*, London; New York: Routledge, pp. 96–112.

Duchan, J. F., Bruder, G. A. and Hewitt, L. E. (eds) (1995) *Deixis in Narrative: A Cognitive Science Perspective*, Hillsdale, NJ: Lawrence Erlbaum.

Dummett, M. (1993) *Grammar and Style*, London: Duckworth.

Emmott, C. (1999) 'Responding to Style: Cohesion, Foregrounding and Thematic Interpretation', in Louwerse, M. and van Peer, W. (eds) *Thematics: Interdisciplinary Perspectives*, Amsterdam: John Benjamins, pp. 91–118.

Emmott, C. and Alexander, M. (2010) 'Detective Fiction, Plot Construction, and Reader Manipulation: Rhetorical Control and Cognitive Misdirection in Agatha Christie's *Sparkling Cyanide*', in McIntyre, D. and Busse, B. (eds) *Language and Style: In Honour of Mick Short*, Basingstoke: Palgrave Macmillan, pp. 328–346.

Emmott. C., Alexander, M. and Marszalek, A. (2015) 'Schema Theory in Stylistics', in Burke, M. (ed.) *Routledge Handbook of Stylistics*, London; New York: Routledge, pp. 268–83.

Emmott, C., Sanford, A. J. and Alexander, M. (2010) 'Scenarios, Role Assumptions, and Character Status: Readers' Expectations and the Manipulation of Attention in Narrative Texts', in Eder, J., Jannedis, F. and Schneider, R. (eds) *Characters in Fictional Worlds: Understanding Imaginary Beings in Literature, Film and Other Media*, Berlin: de Gruyter, pp. 377–99.

Emmott, C., Sanford, A. J. and Alexander, M. (2013) 'Rhetorical Control of Readers' Attention: Psychological and Stylistic Perspectives on Foreground and Background in Narrative', in Bernaerts, L., de Geest, D., Herman, L. and Vervaeck, B. (eds) *Stories and Minds: Cognitive Approaches to Literary Narrative*, Lincoln, NE: University of Nebraska Press, pp. 39–57.

Emmott, C., Sanford, A. J. and Dawydiak, E. J. (2007) 'Stylistics Meets Cognitive Science: Studying Style in Fiction and Readers' Attention from an Inter-disciplinary Perspective', *Style* 41: 204–26.

Emmott C., Sanford, A. J. and Morrow, L. I. (2006) 'Capturing the Attention of Readers? Stylistic and Psychological Perspectives on the Use and Effect of Text Fragmentation in Narratives', *Journal of Literary Semantics* 35: 1–30.

Ensslin, A. (2010) 'Respiratory Narrative; Multimodality and Cybernetic Corporeality in "Physio Cybertext"', in Page, R. (ed.) *New Perspectives on Narrative and Multimodality*, New York; London: Routledge, pp. 155–65.

Ensslin, A. (2012a) *The Language of Gaming*, Basingstoke: Palgrave Macmillan.

Ensslin, A. (2012b) '"I want to say I may have seen my son die this morning": Unintentional Unreliable Narration in Digital Fiction', *Language and Literature* 21(2): 136–49.

Ensslin, A. (2014) *Literary Gaming*, Cambridge, MA: MIT Press.

Eppler, E. D. and Ozón, G. (2013) *English Words and Sentences: An Introduction*, Cambridge: Cambridge University Press.

Erlich, S. (1990) *Point of View: A Linguistic Analysis of Literary Style*, London: Routledge.

Erlich, V. (1965) *Russian Formalism: History, Doctrine*, Berlin: Mouton.

Evans, V. and Green, M. (2006) *Cognitive Linguistics: An Introduction*, Edinburgh: Edinburgh University Press.

Eysenk, M. W. and Keane, M. T. (1995) *Cognitive Psychology*, 3rd edn, Hove: Psychology Press.

Fabb, N. (1997) *Linguistics and Literature*, Oxford: Blackwell.

Fabb, N. (2002) *Language and Literary Structure: The Linguistic Analysis of Form in Verse and Narrative*, Cambridge: Cambridge University Press.

Fairclough, N. (2010) *Critical Discourse Analysis: The Critical Study of Language*, 2nd edn, Harlow: Longman.

Fairley, I. (1981) 'Stylistic Deviation and Cohesion', in *Essays in Modern Stylistics*, London; New York: Methuen, pp. 123–37.

Farman, J. (2014) 'Site-Specificity, Pervasive Computing, and the Reading Interface', in Farman, J. (ed.) *The Mobile Story: Narrative Practices with Locative Media*, New York: Routledge, pp. 3–16.

Fauconnier, G. (1994 [1985]) *Mental Spaces: Aspects of Meaning Construction in Natural Language*, Cambridge: Cambridge University Press.

Fauconnier, G. and Turner, M. (2002) *The Way We Think: Conceptual Blending and the Mind's Hidden Complexities*, New York: Basic Books.

Fetterley, J. (1977) *The Resisting Reader: A Feminist Approach to American Literature*, Bloomington: Indiana University Press.

Firth J. R. (1930) *Speech*, London: Ernest Benn.

Firth, J. R. (1957) *Papers in Linguistics (1934–1951)*, Oxford: Oxford University Press.

Fischer, O. and Nänny, M. (eds) (1999a) *Form Miming Meaning: Iconicity in Language and Literature*, Amsterdam; Philadelphia: John Benjamins.

Fischer, O. and Nänny, M. (1999b) 'Iconicity as a Creative Force in Language', in Fischer, O. and Nänny, M. (eds) *Form Miming Meaning: Iconicity in Language and Literature*, Amsterdam; Philadelphia: John Benjamins, pp. xv–xxxvi.

Fish, S. (1980 [1973]) 'What Is Stylistics and Why Are They Saying Such Terrible Things About It?', in *Is There a Text in This Class?*, Cambridge, MA: Harvard University Press, pp. 68–96.

Fiske, S. T. and Taylor, S. E. (2017) *Social Cognition: From Brains to Culture*, 3rd edn, London: Sage.

Flowerdew, J. and Mahlberg, M. (eds) (2009) *Lexical Cohesion and Corpus Linguistics*, Amsterdam; Philadelphia: John Benjamins.

Fludernik, M. (1993) *The Fictions of Language and the Languages of Fiction*, New York; London: Routledge.

Fludernik, M. (1994a) 'Second-Person Narrative and Related Issues', *Style* 28(3): 281–311.

Fludernik, M. (1994b) 'Second-Person Narrative as a Test Case for Narratology: The Limits of Realism', *Style* 28(3): 445–79.

Fludernik, M. (1996) 'Linguistic Signals and Interpretive Strategies: Linguistic Models in Performance, with Special Reference to Free Indirect Discourse', *Language and Literature* 5(2): 93–113.

Forceville, C. and Urios-Aparisi, E. (eds) (2009) *Multimodal Metaphor*, Berlin; New York: Mouton de Gruyter.

Fowler, R. (1971) *The Languages of Literature: Some Linguistics Contributions to Criticism*, New York: Barnes & Noble.

Fowler, R. (1977) *Linguistics and the Novel*, London: Methuen.

Fowler, R. (1981) *Literature as Social Discourse*, London: Batsford.

Fowler, R. (1986) *Linguistic Criticism*, Oxford: Oxford University Press.

Fowler, R. (1991) *Language in the News: Discourse and Ideology in the Press*, London: Routledge.

Fowler, R. (1996) *Linguistic Criticism*, 2nd edn, Oxford: Oxford University Press.

Francesconi, S. (2014) *Reading Tourism Texts: A Multimodal Analysis*, Bristol; Buffalo; Toronto: Channel View Publications.

Freeman, D. (1995) *A Course Book in English Grammar: Standard English and the Dialects*, 2nd edn, Basingstoke: Palgrave.

Freeman, M. H. (2005) 'The Poem as Complex Blend: Conceptual Mappings of Metaphor in Sylvia Plath's "The Applicant"', *Language and Literature* 14(1): 25–44.

Freeman, M. H. (2006) 'Blending: A Response', *Language and Literature* 15(1): 107–17.

Freeman, M. (2009) 'Minding: Feeling, Form, and Meaning in the Creation of Poetic Iconicity', in Brône, G. and Vandaele, J. (eds) *Cognitive Poetics: Goals, Gains and Gaps*, Berlin: Mouton de Gruyter, pp. 169–96.

Freund, E. (1987) *The Return of the Reader: Reader Response Criticism*, London: Methuen.

Frijda, N. (1986) *The Emotions*, Cambridge: Cambridge University Press.

Fromkin, V., Rodman, R. and Hyams, N. (2014) *An Introduction to Language*, International Edition, Wadsworth: Cengage Learning.

Furniss, T. and Bath, M. (2007 [1996]) *Reading Poetry: An Introduction*, 2nd edn, Harlow: Pearson Longman.

Galbraith, M. (1995) 'Deictic Shift Theory and the Poetics of Involvement in Narrative', in Duchan, J. F., Bruder, G. A. and Hewitt, L. E. (eds) *Deixis in Narrative: A Cognitive Science Perspective*, Hillsdale, NJ: Lawrence Erlbaum, pp. 19–59.

Gardelle, L. and Sorlin, S. (eds) (2015) *The Pragmatics of Personal Pronouns*, Amsterdam: John Benjamins.

Garvin, P. L. (ed.) (1964) *A Prague School Reader on Aesthetics, Literary Structure and Style*, Washington DC: Georgetown University Press.

Gavins, J. (2000) 'Absurd Tricks with Bicycle Frames in the Text World of *The Third Policeman*', *Nottingham Linguistic Circular* 15: 17–33.

Gavins, J. (2003) 'Too Much Blague? An Exploration of the Text Worlds of Donald Barthelme's *Snow White*', in Gavins, J. and Steen, G. (eds) *Cognitive Poetics in Practice*, London: Routledge, pp. 129–44.

Gavins, J. (2005) '(Re)thinking Modality: A Text-World Perspective', *Journal of Literary Semantics* 34(2): 79–93.

Gavins, J. (2006) 'Text World Theory', in Brown, K. (ed.) *Encyclopedia of Language and Linguistics*, 2nd edn, Oxford: Elsevier, pp. 628–30.

Gavins, J. (2007) *Text World Theory: An Introduction*, Edinburgh: Edinburgh University Press.

Gavins, J. (2010) '"Appeased by the certitude": The Quiet Disintegration of the Paranoid Mind in *The Mustache*', in McIntyre, D. and Busse, B. (eds) *Language and Style*, Basingstoke: Palgrave Macmillan, pp. 402–18.

Gavins, J. (2013) *Reading the Absurd*, Edinburgh: Edinburgh University Press.

Gavins, J. and Lahey, E. (eds) (2016) *World Building: Discourse in the Mind*, London; New York: Bloomsbury.

Gavins, J. and Steen, G. (2003) 'Contextualising Cognitive Poetics', in Gavins, J. and Steen, G. (eds) *Cognitive Poetics in Practice*, London: Routledge, pp. 1–12.

Genette, G. (1980) *Narrative Discourse: An Essay in Method*, trans. Jane E. Lewin, Ithaca, NY: Cornell University Press.

Genette, G. (1988) *Narrative Discourse Revisited*, trans. Jane E. Lewin, Ithaca, NY: Cornell University Press.

Gerrig, R. J. (1993) *Experiencing Narrative Worlds: On the Psychological Activities of Reading*, New Haven, CT: Yale University Press.

Gerrig, R. J. (1996) 'Participatory Aspects of Narrative Understanding', in Kreuz, R. J. and MacNealy, M. S. (eds) *Empirical Approaches to Literature and Aesthetics*, Norwood, NJ: Ablex, pp. 127–42.

Gerrig, R. J. and Rapp, D. N. (2004) 'Psychological Processes Underlying Literary Impact', *Poetics Today* 25(2): 265–81.

Gibbons, A. (2008) 'Multimodal Literature "Moves" Us: Dynamic Movement and Embodiment in *VAS: An Opera in Flatland*', *HERMES: Journal of Language and Communication Studies* 41: 107–24.

Gibbons, A. (2010a) '"I contain multitudes": Narrative Multimodality and the Book that Bleeds', in Page, R. (ed.) *New Perspectives on Narrative and Multimodality*, New York; London: Routledge, pp. 99–114.

Gibbons, A. (2010b) 'Narrative Worlds and Multimodal Figures in *House of Leaves*: "-find your own words; I have no more"', in Grishakova, M. and Ryan, M.-L. (eds) *Intermediality and Storytelling*, Berlin: Walter de Gruyter, pp. 285–311.

Gibbons, A. (2011) 'This Is Not for You', in Bray, J. and Gibbons, A. (eds) *Mark Z. Danielewski*, Manchester: Manchester University Press, pp. 17–32.

Gibbons, A. (2012a) *Multimodality, Cognition, and Experimental Literature*, London; New York: Routledge.

Gibbons, A. (2012b) 'Multimodal Literature and Experimentation', in Bray, J., Gibbons, A. and McHale, B. (eds) *Routledge Companion to Experimental Literature*, London; New York: Routledge, pp. 420–34.

Gibbons, A. (2012c) '"You've never experienced a novel like this": Time and Interaction when Reading *TOC*', *Electronic Book Review*, special festschrift edition on Steve Tomasula, <http://www.electronicbookreview.com/thread/fictionspresent/linear> (last accessed 22 August 2017).

Gibbons, A. (2013) 'Multimodal Metaphors in Contemporary Experimental Literature', *Metaphor in the Social World* 3(2): 180–98.

Gibbons, A. (2014a) 'Fictionality and Ontology', in Stockwell, P. and Whiteley, S. (eds) *The Cambridge Handbook of Stylistics*, Cambridge: Cambridge University Press, pp. 410–25.

Gibbons, A. (2014b) 'Multimodality in Literature: An Analysis of Jonathan Safran Foer's "A Primer for the Punctuation of Heart Disease"', in Norris, S. and Maier, C. D. (eds) *Interactions, Images and Texts: A Reader in Multimodality*, Berlin; New York: Mouton de Gruyter, pp. 369–75.

Gibbons, A. (2015) 'Creativity and Multimodal Literature', in Jones, R. H. (ed.) *Routledge Handbook of Language and Creativity*, London; New York: Routledge, pp. 293–306.

Gibbons, A. (2016a) 'Building Hollywood in Paddington: Text World Theory, Immersive Theatre, and Punchdrunk's *The Drowned Man*', in Gavins, J. and Lahey, E. (eds) *World Building: Discourse in the Mind*, London; New York: Bloomsbury, pp. 71–89.

Gibbons, A. (2016b) 'Multimodality, Cognitive Poetics, and Genre: Reading Grady Hendrix's novel *Horrorstör*', *Multimodal Communication* 5(1): 15–29.

Gibbons, A. (forthcoming) 'Uses and Abuses of Reading Life: Situated Stylistics, Freedom of Expression, and the Case of Ahmed Naji' [working title], *Journal of Language and Discrimination* 2.

Gibbons, A. and Macrae, A. (eds) (2018) *Pronouns in Literature: Positions and Perspectives in Language*, Basingstoke: Palgrave Macmillan.

Gibbs, R. W. (ed.) (2008) *The Cambridge Handbook of Metaphor and Thought*, Cambridge: Cambridge University Press.

Gibbs, R. W. and Steen, G. J. (eds) (1999) *Metaphor in Cognitive Linguistics*, Amsterdam; Philadelphia: John Benjamins.

Giovanelli, M. (2016a) 'Text World Theory as *Cognitive Grammatics*: A Pedagogical Application in the Secondary Classroom', in Gavins, J. and Lahey, E. (eds) *World Building: Discourse in the Mind*, London; New York: Bloomsbury, pp. 109–26.

Giovanelli, M. (2016b) 'Activating Metaphors: Exploring the Embodied Nature of Metaphorical Mapping in Political Discourse', *Communication Teacher* 30(1): 39–44.

Giovanelli, M. and Harrison, C. (forthcoming) *Cognitive Grammar in Stylistics: A Practical Guide*, London: Bloomsbury.

Giovanelli, M. and Mason, J. L. (2015) '"Well I don't feel that": Schemas, Worlds and Authentic Reading in the Classroom', *English in Education* 49(1): 41–55.

Givón, T. (1979) *On Understanding Grammar*, New York: Academic Press.

Givón, T. (1993) *English Grammar: A Function-Based Introduction*, Amsterdam: John Benjamins.

Goatly, A. (1997) *The Language of Metaphors*, London: Routledge.

Goldberg, A. (1995) *Constructions: A Construction Grammar Approach to Argument Structure*, Chicago: University of Chicago Press.

Grady, J. E., Oakley, T. and Coulson, S. (1999) 'Blending and Metaphor', in Gibbs, R. W. and Steen, G. J. (eds) *Metaphor in Cognitive Linguistics*, Amsterdam; Philadelphia: John Benjamins, pp. 101–24.

Green, K. (ed.) (1995) *New Essays in Deixis: Discourse, Narrative, Literature*, Amsterdam: Rodopi.

Gregoriou, C. (2003) 'Criminally Minded: The Stylistics of Justification in Contemporary American Crime Fiction', *Style* 37(2): 144–59.

Gregoriou, C. (2007) *Deviance in Contemporary Crime Fiction*, Basingstoke: Palgrave.

Gregoriou, C. (2009) *English Literary Stylistics*, Basingstoke: Palgrave Macmillan.

Gregoriou, C. (2011) 'The Poetics of Deviance in *The Curious Incident of the Dog in the Night-Time*', in Effron, M. (ed.) *The Millennial Detective: Essays on Trends in Crime Fiction, Film and Television, 1990–2010*, Jefferson, NC: McFarland, pp. 97–111.

Gregoriou, C. (2014) 'Voice', in Stockwell, P. and Whiteley, S. (eds) *The Cambridge Handbook of Stylistics*, Cambridge: Cambridge University Press, pp. 165–78.

Griffiths, P. E. (1998) 'Emotions', in Bechtel, W. and Graham, G. (eds) *A Companion to Cognitive Science*, Oxford: Blackwell, pp. 197–243.

Grundy, P. (2000) *Doing Pragmatics*, 2nd edn, London: Arnold.

Gutwinski, W. (1976) *Cohesion in Literary Texts: A Study of Some Grammatical and Lexical Features of English Discourse*, Paris: Mouton.

Haber, R. and Hershenson, M. (1980) *The Psychology of Visual Perception*, 2nd edn, New York: Holt, Rinehart & Winston.

Hall, G. (2008) 'Empirical Research into the Processing of Free Indirect Discourse and the Imperative of Ecological Validity', in Zyngier, S., Bortolussi, M., Chesnokova, A. and Auracher, J. (eds) *Directions in Empirical Literary Studies: In Honor of Willie van Peer*, Amsterdam: John Benjamins, pp. 21–33.

Hallen, C. (ed.) (2007) *Emily Dickinson Lexicon*, Brigham Young University, <http://edl.byu.edu/index.php> (last accessed 22 August 2017).

Hallet, W. (2009) 'The Multimodal Novel: The Integration of Modes and Media in Novelistic Narration', in Heinenand, S. and Somner, R. (eds) *Narratology in the Age of Cross-Disciplinary Narrative Research*, Berlin: Walter de Gruyter, pp. 129–53.

Hallet, W. (2011) 'Visual Images of Space, Movement and Mobility in the Multimodal Novel', in Brosch, R. (ed.) *Moving Images – Mobile Viewers: 20th Century Visuality*, Berlin: LIT Verlag, pp. 227–48.

Hallet, W. (2014) 'The Rise of the Multimodal Novel: Generic Change and Its Narratological Implications', in Ryan, M.-L. and Thon, J.-N. (eds) *Storyworlds across Media: Towards a Media-Conscious Narratology*, Lincoln, NE: University of Nebraska Press, pp. 151–72.

Halliday, M. A. K. (1973) 'Linguistic Function and Literary Style: An Enquiry into the Language of William Golding's "The Inheritors"', in *Explorations in the Functions of Language*, London: Edward Arnold, pp. 103–43.

Halliday, M. A. K. (1978) *Language as Social Semiotic: The Social Interpretation of Language and Meaning*, London: Edward Arnold.

Halliday, M. A. K. and Hasan, R. (1976) *Cohesion in English*, London: Longman.

Halliday, M. A. K. and Hasan, R. (1989 [1985]) *Language, Context, and Text: Aspects of Language in a Semiotic Perspective*, Oxford: Oxford University Press.

Halliday, M. A. K., McIntosh, A. and Strevens, P. (1964) *The Linguistic Sciences and Language Teaching*, London: Longman.

Halliday, M. A. K. and Matthiessen, C. M. I. M. (2014) *An Introduction to Functional Grammar*, 4th edn, London: Routledge.

Halter, P. (1999) 'Iconic Rendering of Motion and Process in the Poetry of William Carlos Williams', in Fischer, O. and Nänny, M. (eds) *Form Miming Meaning: Iconicity in Language and Literature*, Amsterdam; Philadelphia: John Benjamins, pp. 235–49.

Hamilton, C. (2002) 'Conceptual Integration in Christine de Pizan's *City of Ladies*', in Semino, E. and Culpeper, J. (eds) *Cognitive Stylistics: Language and Cognition in Text Analysis*, Philadelphia: John Benjamins, pp. 1–22.

Hamilton, C. (2003) 'A Cognitive Grammar of "Hospital Barge" by Wilfred Owen', in Gavins, J. and Steen, G. (eds) *Cognitive Poetics in Practice*, London: Routledge, pp. 55–66.

Hanna, R. (2016) 'The Role of Evaluation in Telling and Reading the "Real-Life Stories" of Asylum Seekers', conference paper presented at Poetics And Linguistics Association (PALA) 2016 Conference, 28 July 2016, University of Cagliari.

Harrison, C. (2017) *Cognitive Grammar in Contemporary Fiction*, Amsterdam: John Benjamins.

Harrison, C. and Nuttall, L. (2016) 'The Cognitive Grammar of Re-reading', paper presented at *Style & Response: Minds, Media, Methods*, Sheffield Hallam University, 12 November.

Harrison, C., Nuttall, L., Stockwell, P. and Yuan, W. (eds) (2014) *Cognitive Grammar in Literature*, Amsterdam: John Benjamins.

Hávranek, B. (1964 [1932]) 'The Functional Differentiation of the Standard Language', in Garvin, P. L. (trans. and ed.) *A Prague School Reader on Aesthetics, Literary Structure and Style*, Washington DC: Georgetown University Press, pp. 3–16.

Heoy, M. (1991) *Patterns of Lexis in Texts*, Oxford: Oxford University Press.

Heoy, M. (2005) *Lexical Priming: A New Theory of Words and Language*, Abingdon; New York: Routledge.

Herman, D. (1994) 'Textual *you* and Double Deixis in Edna O'Brien's *A Pagan Place*', *Style* 23(3): 378–410.

Herman, D. (2002) *Story Logic: Problems and Possibilities of Narrative*, Lincoln, NE; London: University of Nebraska Press.

Hidalgo Downing, L. (2000a) *Negation, Text Worlds and Discourse: The Pragmatics of Fiction*, Stamford, CT: Ablex.

Hidalgo Downing, L. (2000b) 'Negation in Discourse: A Text-World Approach to Joseph Heller's *Catch-22*', *Language and Literature* 9(4): 215–40.

Hidalgo Downing, L. (2002) 'Creating Things that Are Not: The Role of Negation in the Poetry of Wislawa Szymborska', *Journal of Literary Semantics* 30(2): 113–32.

Hidalgo Downing, L. (2003) 'Negation as a Stylistic Feature in Joseph Heller's *Catch-22*: A Corpus Study', *Style* 37(3): 318–41.

Hiippala, T. (2016) *The Structure of Multimodal Documents: An Empirical Approach*, London; New York: Routledge.

Hiraga, M. K. (2005) *Metaphor and Iconicity: A Cognitive Approach to Analysing Texts*, Basingstoke; New York: Palgrave Macmillan.

Ho, Y. (2011) *Corpus Stylistics in Principles and Practice: A Stylistic Exploration of John Fowles'* The Magus, London; New York: Continuum.

Hodson, J. (2014) *Dialect in Film and Literature*, Basingstoke: Palgrave Macmillan.

Hodson, J. (2016) 'Talking Like a Servant: What Nineteenth Century Novels Can Tell Us about the Social History of the Language', *Journal of Historical Sociolinguistics* 2(1): 27–46.

Hodson, J. and Broadhead, A. (2013) 'Developments in Literary Dialect Representation in British Fiction 1800–1836', *Language and Literature* 22(4): 315–32.

Hogan, P. C. (2003) *The Mind and Its Stories: Narrative Universals and Human Emotion*, Cambridge: Cambridge University Press.

Holland, N. (1975) *Five Readers Reading*, New Haven, CT: Yale University Press.

Holub, R. C. (1984) *Reception Theory: A Critical Introduction*, London: Methuen.

Hoover, D. L. (1999) *Language and Style in* The Inheritors, Lanham, MD: University Press of America.

Hoover, D. L. (2004) 'Altered Texts, Altered Worlds, Altered Styles', *Language and Literature* 13(2): 99–118.

Hori, M. (2004) *Investigating Dickens' Style: A Collocational Analysis*, Basingstoke: Palgrave Macmillan.

Horn, L. (1989) *A Natural History of Negation*, Chicago: University of Chicago Press.

Hucklesby, D. (2016) 'Reading Technologies, Literary Innovation, and a New Fiction', unpublished doctoral thesis, De Montfort University, Leicester, <https://www.dora.dmu.ac.uk/xmlui/bitstream/handle/2086/14168/David%20Hucklesby%20E-Thesis%20Submission.pdf?sequence=1> (last accessed 22 August 2017).

Hughes, A., Trudgill, P. and Watt, D. (2012) *English Accents and Dialects: An Introduction to Social and Regional Varieties of British English*, London: Hodder Arnold.

Hurst, M. J. (1987) 'Speech Acts in Ivy Compton-Burnett's *A Family and a Fortune*', *Language & Style* 20(4): 342–58.

Ikeo, R. (2007) 'Unambiguous Free Indirect Discourse? A Comparison between "Straightforward" Free Indirect Speech and Thought Presentation and Cases Ambiguous with Narration', *Language and Literature* 16(4): 367–87.

Ikeo, R. (2014) 'Connectives "but" and "for" in Viewpoint Shifting in Woolf's *To the Lighthouse*', *Language and Literature* 23(4): 331–46.

Iser, W. (1974) *The Implied Reader: Patterns of Communication in Prose Fiction from Bunyan to Beckett*, Baltimore: Johns Hopkins University Press.

Iser, W. (1978) *The Act of Reading: A Theory of Aesthetic Response*, Baltimore: Johns Hopkins University Press.

Jakobson, R. (1987) *Language in Literature*, ed. Pomorska, K. and Rudy, S., Cambridge, MA; London: Belknap Press of Harvard University Press.

Jakobson, R. and Waugh, L. R. (1979) *The Sound Shape of Language*, Brighton: Harvester Press.

Jauss, H. R. (1982) *Toward an Aesthetics of Reception*, trans. Timothy Bahti, Minneapolis: University of Minnesota Press.

Jeffries, L. (2001) 'Schema Affirmation and White Asparagus: Cultural Multilingualism among Readers of Texts', *Language and Literature* 10(4): 325–43.

Jeffries, L. (2002) 'Meaning Negotiated: An Investigation into Reader and Author Meaning', in Csabi, S. and Zerkowitz, J. (eds) *Textual Secrets: The Message of the Medium*, Budapest: Eotvos-Lorand University, pp. 241–61.

Jeffries, L. (2008) 'The Role of Style in Reader Involvement: Deictic Shifting in Contemporary Poems', *Journal of Literary Semantics* 37: 69–85.

Jeffries, L. (2010a) *Opposition in Discourse: The Construction of Oppositional Meaning*, London: Continuum.

Jeffries, L. (2010b) *Critical Stylistics: The Power of English*, Basingstoke: Palgrave Macmillan.

Jeffries, L. and McIntyre, D. (2010) *Stylistics*, Cambridge: Cambridge University Press.

Jewitt, C. (2009a) 'An Introduction to Multimodality', in Jewitt, C. (ed.) *The Routledge Handbook of Multimodal Analysis*, London; New York: Routledge, pp. 14–27.

Jewitt, C. (2009b) 'Different Approaches to Multimodality', in Jewitt, C. (ed.) *The Routledge Handbook of Multimodal Analysis*, London; New York: Routledge, pp. 28–39.

Johnson, M. (1987) *The Body in the Mind: The Bodily Basis of Meaning, Imagination, and Reason*, Chicago: University of Chicago Press.

Jones, L. and Mills, S. (2014) 'Analysing Agency: Reader Responses to *Fifty Shades of Grey*', *Gender and Language* 8(2): 225–44.

Kacandes, I. (1994) 'Narrative Apostrophe: Reading, Rhetoric, Resistance in Michel Butor's *La Modification* and Julio Cortazar's "Graffiti"', *Style* 28(3): 329–49.

Kacandes, I. (2001) *Talk Fiction: Literature and the Talk Explosion*, Lincoln, NE; London: University of Nebraska Press.

Keen, S. (2007) *Empathy and the Novel*, Oxford: Oxford University Press.

Kennedy, C. (1982) 'Systemic Grammar and Its Use in Literary Analysis', in Carter, R. (ed.) *Language and Literature: An Introductory Reader in Stylistics*, London: George Allen & Unwin, pp. 83–99.

Kennedy, D. (2010) '"Now", "now", "even now": Temporal Deixis and the Crisis of the Present in Some Northern Irish Poems of the Troubles', *Irish Studies Review* 18(1): 1–16.

Kennedy, D. (2012) 'Here Is/Where There/Is: Some Observations of Spatial Deixis in Robert Creeley's Poetry', *Journal of American Studies* 46(1): 73–87.

Kortmann, B. and Upton, C. (eds) (2008) *Varieties of English 1: The British Isles*, Berlin: Mouton de Gruyter.

Kövecses, Z. (1988) *The Language of Love*, Lewisburg, PA: Associated University Press.

Kövecses, Z. (1990) *Emotion Concepts*, New York: Springer.

Kövecses, Z. (2000) *Metaphor and Emotion: Language, Culture, and Body in Human Feeling*, Cambridge: Cambridge University Press.

Kövecses, Z. (2002) *Metaphor: A Practical Introduction*, Oxford: Oxford University Press.

Kress, G. (2009) 'What Is Mode?', in Jewitt, C. (ed.) *The Routledge Handbook of Multimodal Analysis*, London; New York: Routledge, pp. 54–67.

Kress, G. (2010) *Multimodality: Exploring Contemporary Methods of Communication*, London; New York: Routledge.

Kress, G. and van Leeuwen, T. (2006 [1996]) *Reading Images: The Grammar of Visual Design*, 2nd edn, London: Routledge.

Kuiken, D., Miall, D. S. and Sikora, S. (2004) 'Forms of Self-Implication in Literary Reading', *Poetics Today* 25(2): 171–203.

Labov, W. (1969) 'The Logic of Non-Standard English', in *Language in the Inner City: Studies in the Black English Vernacular*, Oxford: Blackwell, pp. 201–22.

Lahey, E. (2003) 'Seeing the Forest for the Trees in Al Purdy's "Trees at the Arctic Circle"', *BELL: Belgian Journal of Language and Literatures* 1: 73–83.

Lahey, E. (2004) 'All the World's a Sub-world: Direct Speech and Sub-world Creation in "After" by Norman MacCraig', *Nottingham Linguistic Circular* 18: 21–8.

Lahey, E. (2005) 'Text-World Landscapes and English Canadian National Identity in the Poetry of Al Purdy, Milton Acorn and Alden Nowlan', unpublished PhD thesis, University of Nottingham.

Lahey, E. (2006) '(Re)thinking World-Building: Locating the Text-Worlds of Canadian Lyric Poetry', *Journal of Literary Semantics* 35: 145–64.

Lahey, E. (2014) 'Stylistics and Text World Theory', in Burke, M. (ed.) *The Routledge Handbook of Stylistics*, London: Routledge, pp. 284–96.

Lahey, E. (2015) 'remember and forget in Dan Brown's *Angels and Demons*: A Corpus-Informed Account', *Language and Literature* 24(4): 292–306.

Lakoff, G. (1987) *Women, Fire, and Dangerous Things: What Categories Reveal about the Mind*, Chicago: University of Chicago Press.

Lakoff, G. (2004) *Don't Think of an Elephant*, White River Junction, VT: Chelsea Green Publishing.

Lakoff, G. and Johnson, M. (1980) *Metaphors We Live By*, Chicago: University of Chicago Press.

Lakoff, G. and Turner, M. (1989) *More than Cool Reason: A Field Guide to Poetic Metaphor*, Chicago: University of Chicago Press.

Langacker, R. W. (1987) *Foundations of Cognitive Grammar Vol. 1: Theoretical Prerequisites*, Stanford: Stanford University Press.

Langacker, R. W. (1991a) *Concept, Image, Symbol: The Cognitive Basis of Grammar*, New York: Mouton de Gruyter.

Langacker, R. W. (1991b) *Foundations of Cognitive Grammar Vol. 2: Descriptive Application*, Stanford: Stanford University Press.

Langacker, R. W. (2002) *Concept, Image, Symbol: The Cognitive Basis of Grammar*, 2nd edn, Berlin: Mouton de Gruyter.

Langacker, R. W. (2007) 'Cognitive Grammar', in Geeraerts, D. and Cuyckens, H. (eds) *The Oxford Handbook of Cognitive Linguistics*, Oxford: Oxford University Press, pp. 421–62.

Langacker, R. (2008) *Cognitive Grammar: A Basic Introduction*, Oxford: Oxford University Press.

Langacker, R. W. (2009) *Investigations in Cognitive Grammar*, Berlin: Mouton de Gruyter.

Lecercle, J.-J. (1993) 'Briefings, 3: The Current State of Stylistics', *The European English Messenger* 2(1): 14–18.

Leech, G. (1969) *A Linguistic Guide to English Poetry*, London: Longman.

Leech, G. (2007) 'Style in Fiction Revisited: The Beginning of *Great Expectations*', *Style* 41(2): 117–32.

Leech, G. (2008) *Language in Literature: Style and Foregrounding*, Harlow: Longman.

Leech, G. and Short, M. (2007 [1981]) *Style in Fiction: A Linguistic Introduction to English Fictional Prose*, 2nd edn, Harlow: Longman.

Lemon, L. and Reis, M. J. (eds) (1965) *Russian Formalist Criticism: Four Essays*, Lincoln, NE: University of Nebraska Press.

Levin, S. R. (1962) *Linguistic Structures in Poetry*, The Hague: Mouton.

Levinson, J. (1997) 'Emotion in Response to Art: A Survey of the Terrain', in Hjort, M. and Laver, S. (eds) *Emotion and the Arts*, Oxford: Oxford University Press, pp. 20–36.

Levinson, S. C. (1983) *Pragmatics*, Cambridge: Cambridge University Press.

Lippi-Green, R. (1997) *English with an Accent: Language, Ideology, and Discrimination in the United States*, London; New York: Routledge.

Ljungberg, C. (2001) 'Iconic Dimensions in Margaret Atwood's Poetry and Prose', in Nänny, M. and Fischer, O. (eds) *The Motivated Sign: Iconicity in Language and Literature 2*, Amsterdam; Philadelphia: John Benjamins, pp. 351–66.

Louw, B. (1997) 'The Role of Corpora in Critical Literary Appreciation', in Wichman, A., Fligelstone, S., McEnery, T. and Knowles, G. (eds) *Teaching and Language Corpora*, Harlow: Addison Wesley Longman, pp. 240–51.

Louw, B. (2008) 'Consolidating Empirical Method in Data-Assisted Stylistics: Towards a Corpus-Attested Glossary of Literary Terms', in Zyngier, S., Bortlussi, M., Chesnokova, A. and Auracher, J. (eds) *Directions in Empirical Literary Studies*, Amsterdam: John Benjamins, pp. 243–64.

Lugea, J. (2013) 'Embedded Dialogue and Dreams: The Worlds and Accessibility Relations of *Inception*', *Language and Literature* 22: 133–53.

Lyons, J. (1982) 'Deixis and Subjectivity: *Loquor ergo sum*', in Jarvella, R. and Klein, W. (eds) *Speech, Place and Action: Studies in Deixis and Related Topics*, Chichester: Wiley, pp. 101–24.

McAlister, S. (2006) '"The explosive devices of memory": Trauma and the Construction of Identity in Narrative', *Language and Literature* 15(1): 91–106.

McEnery, T. and Hardy, A. (2012) *Corpus Linguistics: Method, Theory and Practice*, Cambridge: Cambridge University Press.

McHale, B. (1978) 'Free Indirect Discourse: A Survey of Recent Accounts', *Poetics and Theory of Literature* 3: 249–87.

Machin, D. and van Leeuwen, T. (2005) 'Language Style and Lifestyle: The Case of a Global Magazine', *Media, Culture and Society* 27(4): 577–600.

McIntyre, D. (2004) 'Point of View in Drama: A Socio-pragmatic Approach', *Language and Literature* 13(2): 139–60.

McIntyre, D. (2005) 'Logic, Reality and Mind Style in Alan Bennett's *The Lady in the Van*', *Journal of Literary Semantics* 34(1): 21–40.

McIntyre, D. (2006) *Point of View in Plays: A Cognitive Stylistic Approach to Viewpoint in Drama and Other Text-Types*, Amsterdam; Philadelphia: John Benjamins.

McIntyre, D. (2007) 'Deixis, Cognition and the Construction of Point of View', in Lambrou, M. and Stockwell, P. (eds) *Contemporary Stylistics*, London; New York: Continuum, pp. 118–30.

McIntyre, D. (2008) 'Integrating Multimodal Analysis and the Stylistics of Drama: A Multimodal Perspective on Ian McKellan's *Richard III*', *Language and Literature* 17(4): 309–34.

McIntyre, D. and Archer, D. (2010) 'A Corpus-Based Approach to Mind Style', *Journal of Literary Semantics* 39(2): 167–82.

Mackay, R. (1996) 'Mything the Point: A Critique of Objective Stylistics', *Language and Communication* 16(1): 81–93.

McLoughlin, N. (2013) 'Negative Polarity in Eaven Boland's "The Famine Road"', *New Writing* 10(2): 219–27.

MacMahon, B. (2007) 'The Effects of Sound Patterning in Poetry: A Cognitive Pragmatic Approach', *Journal of Literary Semantics* 36: 103–20.

Macrae, A. (2010) 'Enhancing the Critical Apparatus for Understanding Metanarration: Discourse Deixis Refined', *Journal of Literary Semantics* 39: 119–42.

Macrae, A. (2012) 'Readerly Deictic Shifting to and through *I* and *you*: An Updated Hypothesis', in Kwaitkowska, A. (ed.) *Texts and Minds: Papers in Cognitive Poetics and Rhetoric*, Frankfurt am Main: Peter Lang, pp. 41–56.

Macrae, A. (2016a) 'Stylistics', in Giovanelli, M. and Clayton, D. (eds) *Knowing about Language: Linguistics and the Secondary English Classroom*, London; New York: Routledge, pp. 51–63.

Macrae A. (2016b) 'You and I, Past and Present: Cognitive Processing of Perspective', *Diegesis* 5(1): 64–80.

Maeder, C., Fischer, O. and Herlofsky, W. J. (eds) (2005) *Outside-In – Inside-Out: Iconicity in Language and Literature 4*, Amsterdam; Philadelphia: John Benjamins.

Mahlberg, M. (2007) 'Corpus Stylistics: Bridging the Gap between Linguistic and Literary Studies', in Hoey, M., Mahlberg, M., Stubbs, M. and Teubert, W. (eds) *Text, Discourse and Corpora*, London: Continuum, pp. 219–46.

Mahlberg, M. (2010) 'Corpus Linguistics and the Study of Nineteenth-Century Fiction', *Journal of Victorian Literature* 15(2): 292–8.

Mahlberg, M. (2013) *Corpus Stylistics and Dickens's Fiction*, London: Routledge.

Mahlberg, M., Conklin, K. and Bisson, M.-J. (2014) 'Reading Dickens's Characters: Textual Patterns and Their Cognitive Reality', *Language and Literature* 23(4): 369–88.

Mahlberg, M. and McIntyre, D. (2011) 'A Case for Corpus Stylistics: Analysing Ian Fleming's *Casino Royale*', *English Text Construction* 4(2): 204–27.

Mahlberg, M. and Smith, C. (2012) 'Dickens, the Suspended Quotation and the Corpus', *Language and Literature* 21(1): 51–65.

Mahlberg, M., Smith, C. and Preston, S. (2013) 'Phrases in Literary Contexts: Patterns and Distribution of Suspensions in Dickens's Novels', *International Journal of Corpus Linguistics* 18(1): 35–56.

Margolin, U. (2001) 'Collective Perspective, Individual Perspective, and the Speaker in between: On "We" Literary Narratives', in van Peer, W. and Chatman, S. (eds) *New Perspectives on Narrative Perspective*, Albany, NY: State University of New York Press, pp. 241–53.

Mason, J. (2016) 'Narrative Interrelation, Intertextuality and Teachers' Knowledge about Students' Reading', in Giovanelli, M. and Clayton, D. (eds) *Knowing about Language: Linguistics and the Secondary English Classroom*, London; New York: Routledge, pp. 162–72.

Mason, J. (forthcoming) *Intertextuality in Practice*, Amsterdam: John Benjamins.

Mason, J. and Giovanelli, M. (2017) '"What do you think?" Let Me Tell You: Discourse about Texts and the Literature Classroom', *Changing English* 24(1): 318–29.

Mastropierro, L. (2017) *Corpus Stylistics in* Heart of Darkness *and Its Italian Translations*, London: Bloomsbury.

Matejka, L. and Pomorska, K. (eds) (1971) *Readings in Russian Poetics: Formalist and Structuralist Views*, Cambridge, MA; London: MIT Press.

Mey, J. (1998) *When Voices Clash: A Study in Literary Pragmatics*, Berlin: Mouton de Gruyter.

Miall, D. S. (1990) 'Readers' Responses to Narrative: Evaluating, Relating, Anticipating', *Poetics* 19: 323–39.

Miall, D. S. (2006) *Literary Reading: Empirical and Theoretical Studies*, New York: Peter Lang.

Miall, D. S. and Kuiken, D. (1994) 'Foregrounding, Defamiliarisation, and Affect: Response to Literary Stories', *Poetics* 22: 389–407.

Miall, D. S. and Kuiken, D. (2002) 'A Feeling for Fiction: Becoming What We Behold', *Poetics* 30: 221–41.

Mills, S. (1995a) *Feminist Stylistics*, London: Routledge.

Mills, S. (1995b) 'Working with Sexism: What Can Feminist Text Analysis Do?', in Verdonk, P. and Weber, J. J. (eds) *Twentieth-Century Fiction: From Text to Context*, London; New York: Routledge, pp. 206–19.

Milota, M. (2014) 'From "compelling and mystical" to "makes you want to commit suicide": Quantifying the Spectrum of Online Reader Responses', *Scientific Study of Literature* 4(2): 178–95.

Minsky, M. (1975) 'A Framework for Representing Knowledge', in Winston, P. (ed.) *The Psychology of Computer Vision*, New York: McGraw-Hill, pp. 211–77.

Montoro, R. (2010a) 'A Multimodal Approach to Mind Style: Semiotic Metaphor vs. Multimodal Conceptual Metaphor', in Page, R. (ed.) *New Perspectives on Narrative and Multimodality*, New York; London: Routledge, pp. 31–49.

Montoro, R. (2010b) 'Multimodal Realisations of Mind Style in *Enduring Love*', in Piazza, R., Fossi, F. and Bednarek, M. (eds) *Telecinematic Discourse: An Introduction to the Fictional Language of Cinema and Television*, Amsterdam; Philadelphia: John Benjamins, pp. 69–83.

Moors, A., Ellsworth, P. C., Scherer, K. R. and Frijda, N. (2013) 'Appraisal Theories of Emotion: State of the Art and Future Development', *Emotion Review* 5(3): 119–24.

Morini, M. (2013) 'Towards a Musical Stylistics: Movement in Kate Bush's "Running Up That Hill"', *Language and Literature* 22(4): 283–97.

Mukařovsky, J. (1964 [1932]) 'Standard Language and Poetic Language', in Garvin, P. L. (trans. and ed.) *A Prague School Reader on Aesthetics, Literary Structure and Style*, Washington DC: Georgetown University Press, pp. 17–30.

Müller, W. G. and Fischer, O. (eds) (2003) *From Sign to Signing: Iconicity in Language and Literature 3*, Amsterdam; Philadelphia: John Benjamins.

Myers-Schulz, B., Pujara, M., Wolf, R. C. and Koenigs, M. (2013) 'Inherent Emotional Quality of Human Speech Sounds', *Cognition and Emotion* 27(6): 1105–13.

Naciscione, A. (2010) *Stylistic Use of Phraseological Units in Discourse*, Amsterdam; Philadelphia: John Benjamins.

Nahajec, L. (2009) 'Negation and the Creation of Implicit Meaning in Poetry', *Language and Literature* 18(2): 109–27.

Nahajec, L. (2012) *Evoking the Possibility of Presence: Textual and Ideological Effects of Linguistic Negation in Written Discourse*, PhD thesis, University of Huddersfield, <http://eprints.hud.ac.uk/17537/1/lnahajecfinalthesis.pdf> (last accessed 22 August 2017).

Nahajec, L. (2014) 'Negation, Expectation and Characterisation: Analysing the Role of Negation in Character Construction in *To Kill a Mockingbird* (Lee 1960) and *Stark* (Elton 1989)', in Chapman, S. and Clark, B. (eds) *Pragmatic Literary Stylistics*, Basingstoke: Palgrave Macmillan, pp. 111–31.

Nänny, M. and Fischer, O. (eds) (2001) *The Motivated Sign: Iconicity in Language and Literature* 2, Amsterdam; Philadelphia: John Benjamins.

Nash, W. (1989) 'Changing the Guard at Elsinore', in Carter, R. and Simpson, P. (eds) *Language, Discourse and Literature*, London: Unwin Hyman, pp. 23–41.

Nash, W. (1990) *Language in Popular Fiction*, London: Routledge.

Neary, C. (2014) 'Stylistics, Point of View and Modality', in Burke, M. (ed.) *The Routledge Handbook of Stylistics*, London; New York: Routledge, pp. 175–90.

Nørgaard, N. (2007) 'Disordered Collarettes and Uncovered Tables: Negative Polarity as a Stylistic Device in Joyce's "Two Gallants"', *Journal of Literary Semantics* 36: 35–52.

Nørgaard, N. (2009) 'The Semiotics of Typography in Literary Texts: A Multimodal Approach', *Orbis Litterarum* 64(2): 141–60.

Nørgaard, N. (2010a) 'Multimodality: Extending the Stylistic Tool-Kit', in McIntyre, D. and Busse, B. (eds) *Language and Style*, Basingstoke: Palgrave Macmillan, pp. 433–48.

Nørgaard, N. (2010b) 'Multimodality and the Literary Text: Making Sense of Safran Foer's *Extremely Loud and Incredible Close*', in Page, R. (ed.) *New Perspectives on Narrative and Multimodality*, New York; London: Routledge, pp. 115–26.

Nørgaard, N. (2014) 'Multimodality and Stylistics', in Burke, M. (ed.) *The Routledge Companion to Stylistics*, London; New York: Routledge, pp. 471–84.

Nørgaard, N., Busse, B. and Montoro, R. (2010) *Key Terms in Stylistics*, London; New York: Continuum.

Norris, S. (2004) *Analysing Multimodal Interaction*, New York; London: Routledge.

Nuttall, L. (2014) 'Constructing a Text World for *The Handmaid's Tale*', in Harrison, C., Nuttall, L., Stockwell, P. and Yuan, W. (eds) *Cognitive Grammar in Literature*, Amsterdam: John Benjamins, pp. 83–100.

Nuttall L. (2015) 'Attributing Minds to Vampires in Richard Matheson's *I Am Legend*', *Language and Literature* 24(1): 23–39.

Nuttall, L. (2017) 'Online Readers between the Camps: A Text World Theory Analysis of Ethical Positioning in *We Need to Talk about Kevin*', *Language and Literature* 26(2): 153–71.

Oatley, K. (1994) 'A Taxonomy of the Emotions of Literary Response and a Theory of Identification in Fictional Narrative', *Poetics* 23: 53–74.

Oatley, K. (1999a) 'Meetings of Minds: Dialogue, Sympathy and Identification in Reading Fiction', *Poetics* 26: 439–54.

Oatley, K. (1999b) 'Why Fiction May Be Twice as True as Fact: Fiction as Cognitive and Emotional Simulation', *Review of General Psychology* 3(2): 101–17.

Oatley, K. (2002) 'Emotions and the Story Worlds of Fiction', in Green, M. C., Strange, J. J. and Brock, T. C. (eds) *Narrative Impact*, London: Lawrence Erlbaum, pp. 36–69.

Oatley, K. (2003) 'Writingandreading: The Future of Cognitive Poetics', in Gavins, J. and Steen, G. (eds) *Cognitive Poetics in Practice*, London: Routledge, pp. 161–73.

Oatley, K. (2009) 'Communications to Self and Others: Emotional Experience and Its Skills', *Emotion Review* 1(3): 206–13.

Oatley, K. and Gholamain, M. (1997) 'Emotions and Identification, Connections between Readers and Fiction', in Hjort, M. and Laver, S. (eds) *Emotion and the Arts*, Oxford: Oxford University Press, pp. 263–79.

Oatley, K. and Johnson-Laird, P. N. (1987) 'Towards a Cognitive Theory of Emotions', *Cognition and Emotion* 1: 29–50.

Oatley, K. and Johnson-Laird, P. N. (1996) 'The Communicative Theory of Emotions: Empirical Tests, Mental Models, and Implications for Social Interaction', in Martin, L. L. and Tesser, A. (eds) *Striving and Feeling: Interactions among Goals, Affects and Self-Regulation*, Mahwah, NJ: Lawrence Erlbaum, pp. 363–93.

O'Halloran, K. L. (ed.) (2004) *Multimodal Discourse Analysis: Systemic Functional Perspectives*, London; New York: Continuum.

O'Halloran, K. L. (2005) *Mathematical Discourse: Language, Symbolism, and Visual Images*, London: Continuum.

Ortony, A. (ed.) (1993) *Metaphor and Thought*, 2nd edn, Cambridge: Cambridge University Press.

O'Toole, M. (1994) *The Language of Displayed Art*, Leicester: Leicester University Press.

Page, N. (1987) *Speech in the English Novel*, London: Longman.

Page, R. (2010) 'Introduction', in Page, R. (ed.) *New Perspectives on Narrative and Multimodality*, New York; London: Routledge, pp. 1–13.

Päivärinta, A. (2014) 'Foregrounding the Foregrounded: The Literariness of Dylan Thomas's "After the Funeral"', in Harrison, C., Nuttall, L., Stockwell, P. and Yuan, W. (eds) *Cognitive Grammar in Literature*, Amsterdam: John Benjamins, pp. 133–44.

Palmer, A. (2004) *Fictional Minds*, Lincoln, NE: University of Nebraska Press.

Palmer, F. R. (1986) *Mood and Modality*, Cambridge: Cambridge University Press.

Parkinson, B. (1995) *Ideas and Realities of Emotion*, London: Routledge.

Parkinson, B., Fischer, A. H. and Manstead, A. S. R. (2005) *Emotion in Social Relations: Cultural, Group and Interpersonal Processes*, New York: Psychology Press.

Partington, A. (1995) 'Kicking the Habit: The Exploitation of Collocation in Literature and Humour', in Payne, J. (ed.) *Linguistic Approaches to Literature*, English Language Research Journal 17, Birmingham: University of Birmingham, pp. 35–44.

Pascal, R. (1977) *The Dual Voice: Free Indirect Speech and Its Functioning in Nineteenth Century European Novels*, Manchester: Manchester University Press.

Peplow, D. (2016) *Talk About Books: A Study of Reading Groups*, London: Bloomsbury.

Peplow, D. and Carter, R. (2014) 'Stylistics and Real Readers', in Burke, M. (ed.) *The Routledge Handbook of Stylistics*, Abingdon: Routledge, pp. 440–54.

Peplow, D., Swann, J., Trimarco, P. and Whiteley, S. (2016) *The Discourse of Reading Groups: Integrating Cognitive and Sociocultural Perspectives*, London: Routledge.

Perkins, M. R. (1983) *Modal Expressions in English*, London: Pinter.

Phelan, J. (1996) *Narrative as Rhetoric: Technique, Audience, Ethics, and Ideology*, Columbus: Ohio State University Press.

Phelan, J. (2005) *Living to Tell about It: A Rhetoric and Ethics of Character Narration*, Ithaca, NY: Cornell University Press.

Phelan, J. (2007) 'Rhetoric/Ethics', in Herman, D. (ed.) *The Cambridge Companion to Narrative*, Cambridge: Cambridge University Press, pp. 203–16.

Pihlaja, S. (2010) 'The Pope of YouTube: Metaphor and Misunderstanding in Atheist–Christian YouTube Dialogue', *The Journal of Inter-Religious Dialogue* 3: 25–35, <http://irdialogue.org/journal/issue03/the-pope-of-youtube-metaphor-and-misunderstanding-in-atheist-christian-youtube-dialogue-by-stephen-pihlaja/> (last accessed 13 May 2017).

Pihlaja, S. (2011) 'Cops, Popes, and Garbage Collectors: Metaphor and Antagonism in an Atheist/Christian YouTube Video Thread', *Language@Internet* 8: article 1, <http://www.languageatinternet.org/articles/2011/Pihlaja/> (last accessed 13 May 2017).

Pihlaja, S. (2013) '"It's all red ink": The Interpretation of Biblical Metaphor among Evangelical Christian YouTube Users', *Language and Literature* 22(2): 103–17.

Pihlaja, S. (2014) *Antagonism on YouTube: Metaphor in Online Discourse*, London: Bloomsbury.

Pihlaja, S. (2017) '"When Noah built the ark . . .": Metaphor and Biblical Stories in Facebook Preaching', *Metaphor and the Social World* 7(1): 88–105.

Plett, H. R. (2010) *Literary Rhetoric: Concepts – Structures – Analyses*, Leiden; Boston: Brill.

Potts, A. and Semino, E. (2017) 'Health Professionals' Online Use of Violence Metaphors for Care at End of Life in the US: A Corpus-Based Comparison with the UK', *Corpora* 12(1): 55–84.

Prentice, D. A., Gerrig, R. J. and Bailis, D. S. (1997) 'What Readers Bring to the Processing of Fictional Texts', *Psychonomic Bulletin and Review* 4(3): 416–20.

Preston, D. R. (1985) 'The Li'l Abner Syndrome: Written Representations of Speech', *American Speech* 60(4): 328–36.

Preston, D. R. (2000) 'Mowr and mowr bayud spellin': Confessions of a Sociolinguist', *Journal of Sociolinguistics* 4(4): 614–21.

Punter, D. (2007) *Metaphor*, London: Routledge.

Rapp, D. N. and Gerrig, R. J. (2002) 'Readers' Reality-Driven and Plot-Driven Analyses in Narrative Comprehension', *Memory and Cognition* 30(5): 779–88.

Rapp, D. N. and Gerrig, R. J. (2006) 'Predilections for Narrative Outcomes: The Impact of Story Contexts and Reader Preferences', *Journal of Memory and Language* 54: 54–67.

Raskin, V. (1985) *Semantic Mechanisms of Humour*, Dordrecht: Reidel.

Rauh, G. (1983) 'Aspects of Deixis', in Rauh, G. (ed.) *Essays on Deixis*, Tübingen: Gunter Narr Verlag, pp. 9–60.

Rayson, P. (2008) 'From Key Words to Key Semantic Domains', *International Journal of Corpus Linguistics* 13(4): 519–49.

Rayson, P. (n.d.) 'How to Calculate Log Likelihood', *UCREL* [Web pages for Lancaster University's Centre for Computer Corpus Research on Language], <http://ucrel.lancs.ac.uk/llwizard.html> (last accessed 19 November 2016).

Richardson, B. (1991) 'The Poetics and Politics of Second-Person Narrative', *Genre* 24: 309–30.

Richardson, B. (1994) 'I etcetera: On the Poetics and Ideology of Multipersoned Narratives', *Style* 28(3): 312–28.

Richardson, B. (2006) *Unnatural Voices: Extreme Narration in Modern and Contemporary Fiction*, Columbus: Ohio State University Press.

Richter, D. (1985) 'Two Studies in Iconic Syntax: Tennyson's "Tears, Idle Tears", and Williams's "The Dance"', *Language and Style* 18(2): 136–51.

Ricks, C. (1963) *Milton's Grand Style*, Oxford: Oxford University Press.

Robinson, J. (2005) *Deeper than Reason: Emotion and Its Role in Literature, Music, and Art*, Oxford: Clarendon Press.

Rosch, E. (1975) 'Cognitive Representations of Semantic Categories', *Journal of Experimental Psychology: General* 104: 193–233.

Rosch, E. (1977) 'Human Categorisation', in Warren, N. (ed.) *Studies in Cross-Cultural Psychology Vol. 1*, London: Academic Press, pp. 1–49.

Rosch, E. (1978) 'Principles of Categorisation', in Rosch, E. and Lloyd, B. (eds) *Cognition and Categorisation*, Hillsdale, NJ: Lawrence Erlbaum, pp. 27–48.

Rubin, E. (1958 [1915]) 'Figure and Ground', in Beardslee, D. C. and Wertheimer, M. (eds) *Readings in Perception*, Princeton, NJ: D. Van Nostrand, pp. 194–203.

Rundquist, E. (2014) 'How Is Mrs Ramsay Thinking? The Semantic Effects of Consciousness Presentation Categories within Free Indirect Style', *Language and Literature* 23(2): 159–74.

Ryan, M.-L. (1991) *Possible Worlds, Artificial Intelligence and Narrative Theory*, Bloomington: Indiana University Press.

Sacks, H., Schegloff, E. A. and Jefferson, G. (1974) 'A Simplest Systematics for the Organization of Turn Taking in Conversation', *Language* 50(4): 696–735.

Sanford, A. J. and Emmott, C. (2012) *Mind, Brain, and Narrative*, Cambridge: Cambridge University Press.

Schank, R. and Abelson, R. (1977) *Scripts, Plans, Goals, and Understanding: An Inquiry into Human Knowledge Structures*, Hillsdale, NJ: Lawrence Erlbaum.

Schiffrin, D. (1994) *Approaches to Discourse*, Oxford: Blackwell.

Schrier, M. (2014) 'Qualitative Content Analysis', in Flick, U. (ed.) *The SAGE Handbook of Qualitative Data Analysis*, London: Sage, pp. 170–81.

Scollon, R. and Scollon, S. W. (2003) *Discourses in Place: Language in the Material World*, London; New York: Routledge.

Scott, J. (2009) *The Demotic Voice in Contemporary British Fiction*, Basingstoke: Palgrave Macmillan.

Searle, J. R. (1969) *Speech Acts*, Cambridge: Cambridge University Press.

Searle, J. R. (1991 [1965]) 'What Is a Speech Act?', in Davis, S. (ed.) *Pragmatics*, Oxford: Oxford University Press, pp. 254–64.

Semino, E. (1997) *Language and World Creation in Poems and Other Texts*, London: Longman.

Semino, E. (2002a) 'A Cognitive Stylistics Approach to Mind Style in Narrative Fiction', in Semino, E. and Culpeper, J. (eds) *Cognitive Stylistics: Language and Cognition in Text Analysis*, Amsterdam; Philadelphia: John Benjamins, pp. 95–122.

Semino, E. (2002b) 'Stylistics and Linguistic Variation in Poetry', *Journal of English Linguistics* 30(1): 28–50.

Semino, E. (2006) 'Blending and Characters' Mental Functioning in Virginia Woolf's "Lappin and Lapinova"', *Language and Literature* 15(1): 55–72.

Semino, E. (2007) 'Mind Style 25 Years On', *Style* 41(2): 153–73.

Semino, E. (2014) 'Language, Mind and Autism in Mark Haddon's *The Curious Incident of the Dog in the Night-Time*', in Fludernik, M. and Jacob, D. (eds) *Linguistics and Literary Studies*, Berlin: de Gruyter, pp. 279–303.

Semino, E. and Culpeper, J. (eds) (2002) *Cognitive Stylistics: Language and Cognition in Text Analysis*, Philadelphia: John Benjamins.

Semino, E., Demjén, Z. and Demmen, J. E. (2016) 'An Integrated Approach to Metaphor and Framing in Cognition, Discourse and Practice, with an Application to Metaphors of Cancer', *Applied Linguistics*: 1–16.

Semino, E., Demjén, Z., Demmen, J., Koller, V., Payne, S., Hardie, A. and Rayson, P. (2017) 'The Online Use of Violence and Journey Metaphors by Patients with Cancer, as Compared with Health Professionals: A Mixed Methods Study', *BMJ Supportive and Palliative Care* 7(1): 60–6.

Semino, E. and Short, M. (2004) *Corpus Stylistics: Speech, Writing, and Thought Presentation in a Corpus of English Writing*, London; New York: Routledge.

Semino, E. and Swindlehurst, K. (1996) 'Metaphor and Mind Style in Ken Kesey's *One Flew Over the Cuckoo's Nest*', *Style* 30(1): 143–66.

Šhklovsky, V. (1965 [1917]) 'Art as Technique', in Lemon, L. and Reis, M. J. (trans. and eds) *Russian Formalist Criticism: Four Essays*, Lincoln, NE: University of Nebraska Press, pp. 3–24.

Short, M. (ed.) (1989) *Reading, Analysing and Teaching Literature*, London: Longman.

Short, M. (1996) *Exploring the Language of Poems, Plays and Prose*, Harlow: Longman.

Short, M. (2000) 'Graphological Deviation, Style Variation and Point of View in *Marabou Stork Nightmares* by Irvine Welsh', *Journal of Literary Studies/Tydskrif vir Literatuur Wetenskap* 15(3/4): 305–23.

Short, M. (2003) 'A Corpus-Based Approach to Speech, Thought, and Writing Presentation', in Wilson, A., Rayson, P. and McEnery, T. (eds) *Corpus Linguistics by the Lune: A Festschrift for Geoffrey Leech*, Frankfurt am Main: Peter Lang, pp. 242–71.

Short, M. (2012) 'Discourse Presentation and Speech (and Writing, but Not Thought) Summary', *Language and Literature* 21(1): 18–32.

Short, M. (2014) 'Analysing Dialogue', in Stockwell, P. and Whiteley, S. (eds) *The Cambridge Handbook of Stylistics*, Cambridge: Cambridge University Press, pp. 344–59.

Short, M., Freeman, D. C., van Peer, W. and Simpson, P. (1998) 'Stylistics, Criticism, Mythrepresentation Again: Squaring the Circle with Ray Mackay's Subjective Solution for All Problems', *Language and Literature* 7(1): 39–50.

Short, M., McIntyre, D., Jeffries, L. and Bousfield, D. (2011) 'Processes of Interpretation: Using Meta-analysis to Inform Pedagogic Practice', in Jeffries, L. and McIntyre, D. (eds) *Teaching Stylistics*, Basingstoke: Palgrave Macmillan, pp. 69–94.

Short, M., Semino, E. and Culpeper, J. (1996) 'Using a Corpus for Stylistics Research: Speech and Thought Presentation', in Thomas, J. A. and Short, M. (eds) *Using Corpora for Language Research*, London; New York: Longman, pp. 110–31.

Short, M. and van Peer, W. (1989) 'Accident! Stylisticians Evaluate: Aims and Methods in Stylistic Analysis', in Short, M. (ed.) *Reading, Analysing and Teaching Literature*, London: Longman, pp. 22–71.

Simpson, P. (1992) 'Teaching Stylistics: Analysing Cohesion and Narrative Structure in a Short Story by Ernest Hemingway', *Language and Literature* 1(1): 47–67.

Simpson, P. (1993) *Language, Ideology, and Point of View*, London: Routledge.

Simpson, P. (1997) *Language through Literature: An Introduction*, London; New York: Routledge.

Simpson, P. (1998) 'Odd Talk, Studying Discourses of Incongruity', in Culpepper, J., Short, M. and Verdonk, P. (eds) *Exploring the Language of Drama: From Text to Context*, London: Routledge, pp. 34–53.

Simpson, P. (2000) 'Satirical Humour and Cultural Context: With a Note on the Curious Case of Father Todd Unctuous', in Bex, T., Burke, M. and Stockwell, P. (eds) *Contextualized Stylistics: In Honour of Peter Verdonk*, Amsterdam: Rodopi, pp. 243–66.

Simpson, P. (2003) *On the Discourse of Satire: Towards a Stylistic Model of Satirical Humour*, Amsterdam: John Benjamins.

Simpson, P. (2014 [2004]) *Stylistics: A Resource Book for Students*, 2nd edn, Abingdon; New York: Routledge.

Simpson, P. and Canning, P. (2014) 'Action and Event', in Stockwell, P. and Whiteley, S. (eds) *The Cambridge Handbook of Stylistics*, Cambridge: Cambridge University Press, pp. 281–99.

Sinclair, J. (2004) *Trust the Text: Language, Corpus and Discourse*, London: Routledge.

Sklar, H. (2013) *The Art of Sympathy in Fiction: Forms of Ethical and Emotional Persuasion*, Amsterdam: John Benjamins.

Solly, M. (2015) *The Stylistics of Professional Discourse*, Edinburgh: Edinburgh University Press.

Sotirova, V. (2004) 'Connectives in Free Indirect Style: Continuity or Shift?', *Language and Literature* 13(3): 216–34.

Sotirova, V. (2005) 'Repetition in Free Indirect Style: A Dialogue of Minds?', *Style* 39(2): 123–36.

Sotirova, V. (2006) 'Reader Responses to Narrative Point of View', *Poetics* 34(2): 108–33.

Sotirova, V. (2010) 'The Roots of a Literary Style: Joyce's Presentation of Consciousness in Ulysses', *Language and Literature* 19(2): 131–49.

Sotirova, V. (2011) *D. H. Lawrence and Narrative Viewpoint*, London: Continuum.

Sotirova, V. (2013) *Consciousness in Modernist Fiction: A Stylistic Study*, Basingstoke: Palgrave Macmillan.

Stanzel, F. K. (1984) *A Theory of Narrative*, trans. C. Goedsche, Cambridge: Cambridge University Press.

Starcke, B. (2006) 'The Phraseology of Jane Austen's *Persuasion*: Phraseological Units as Carriers of Meaning', *ICAME Journal* 30: 87–104.

Steen, G. (1991) 'The Empirical Study of Literary Reading', *Poetics* 20: 559–75.

Steen, G. (1994) *Understanding Metaphor in Literature*, London: Routledge.

Steen, G. (2003) '"Love Stories": Cognitive Scenarios in Love Poetry', in Gavins, J. and Steen, G. (eds) *Cognitive Poetics in Practice*, London: Routledge, pp. 67–82.

Steen, G. (2011) 'Genre between the Humanities and the Sciences', in Callies, M., Keller, W. R. and Lohöfer, A. (eds) *Bi-directionality in the Cognitive Sciences: Avenues, Challenges, Limitations*, Amsterdam; Philadelphia: John Benjamins, pp. 21–41.

Stewart-Shaw, L. (2017) 'The Cognitive Poetics of Horror Fiction', unpublished PhD thesis, University of Nottingham.

Stöckl, H. (2005) 'Typography: Body and Dress of a Text – A Signing Mode between Language and Image', *Visual Communication* 4(2): 204–14.

Stöckl, H. (2009) 'The Language-Image-Text – Theoretical and Analytical Inroads into Semiotic Complexity', *AAA – Arbeitan aus Anglistik und Amerikanistik* 34(2): 203–26.

Stöckl, H. (2014) 'Typography', in Norris, S. and Maier, C. D. (eds) *Interactions, Images and Texts: A Reader in Multimodality*, Berlin; New York: Mouton de Gruyter, pp. 281–95.

Stockwell, P. (1999) 'The Inflexibility of Invariance', *Language and Literature* 8(2): 125–42.

Stockwell, P. (2000a) *The Poetics of Science Fiction*, Harlow: Longman.
Stockwell, P. (2000b) '(Sur)real Stylistics: From Text to Contextualizing', in Bex, T., Burke, M. and Stockwell, P. (eds) *Contextualized Stylistics: In Honour of Peter Verdonk*, Amsterdam: Rodopi, pp. 15–38.
Stockwell, P. (2002a) *Cognitive Poetics: An Introduction*, London: Routledge.
Stockwell, P. (2002b) 'Miltonic Texture and the Feeling of Reading', in Culpeper, J. and Semino, E. (eds) *Cognitive Stylistics: Language and Cognition in Text Analysis*, Amsterdam; Philadelphia: John Benjamins, pp. 73–94.
Stockwell, P. (2003) 'Surreal Figures', in Gavins, J. and Steen, G. (eds) *Cognitive Poetics in Practice*, London: Routledge, pp. 13–26.
Stockwell, P. (2004) 'Cognitive Stylistics and the Theory of Metaphor', in Simpson, P. *Stylistics: A Resource Book for Students*, Abingdon; New York: Routledge, pp. 211–17.
Stockwell, P. (2005a) 'Texture and Identification', *European Journal of English Studies* 9(2): 143–54.
Stockwell, P. (2005b) 'On Cognitive Poetics and Stylistics', in Veivo, H., Pettersson, B. and Polvinen, M. (eds) *Cognition and Literary Interpretation in Practice*, Helsinki: Helsinki University Press, pp. 267–82.
Stockwell, P. (2006) 'Invented Language in Literature', in Brown, K. (ed.) *Encyclopedia of Language and Linguistics*, 2nd edn, vol. 6, Oxford: Elsevier, pp. 3–10.
Stockwell, P. (2009a) *Texture: A Cognitive Aesthetics of Reading*, Edinburgh: Edinburgh University Press.
Stockwell, P. (2009b) 'The Cognitive Poetics of Literary Resonance', *Language and Cognition* 1(1): 25–44.
Stockwell, P. (2014a) 'Atmosphere and Tone', in Stockwell, P. and Whiteley, S. (eds) *The Cambridge Handbook of Stylistics*, Cambridge: Cambridge University Press, pp. 360–74.
Stockwell, P. (2014b) 'War, Worlds and Cognitive Grammar', in Harrison, C., Nuttall, L., Stockwell, P. and Yuan, W. (eds) *Cognitive Grammar in Literature*, Amsterdam: John Benjamins, pp. 19–34.
Stockwell, P. (2016) *The Language of Surrealism*, London; New York: Palgrave.
Stockwell, P. and Whiteley, S. (eds) (2014) *The Cambridge Handbook of Stylistics*, Cambridge: Cambridge University Press.
Stoddard, S. (1991) *Text and Texture: Patterns of Cohesion*, Norwood, NJ: Ablex.
Stoddart, J., Upton, C. and Widdowson, J. A. (1999) 'Sheffield Dialect in the 1990s: Revisiting the Concept of NORMS', in Foulkes, P. and Docherty, G. (eds) *Urban Voices: Accent Studies in the British Isles*, London: Arnold, pp. 72–89.
Stubbs, M. (2005) 'Conrad in the Computer: Examples of Quantitative Stylistics Methods', *Language and Literature* 14(1): 5–24.
Swann, J. and Allington, D. (2009) 'Reading Groups and the Language of Literary Texts: A Case Study in Social Reading', *Language and Literature* 18(3): 247–64.
Sweetser, E. E. (2006a) 'Negative Spaces: Levels of Negation and Kinds of Spaces', in Bonnefille, S. and Salbayre, S. (eds) *Proceedings of the Conference*

'Negation: Form, Figure of Speech, Conceptualization', Publication du groupe de recherches anglo-américaines de l'Université de Tours, Tours: Publications universitaires François Rabelais, pp. 313–32.

Sweetser, E. (2006b) 'Whose Rhyme Is Whose Reason? Sound and Sense in *Cyrano de Bergerac*', *Language and Literature* 15(1): 29–54.

Talmy, L. (2000) *Towards a Cognitive Semantics, Volume 1: Conceptual Structuring Systems*, Cambridge, MA: MIT Press.

Terblanche, E. (2010) 'Iconicity and Naming in e. e. cummings's Poetry', in Conradie, C. J., Johl, R., Beukes, M., Fischer, O. and Ljungberg, C. (eds) *Signergy*, Iconicity in Language and Literature 9, Amsterdam; Philadelphia: John Benjamins, pp. 179–91.

Thompson, G. (2004) *Introducing Functional Grammar*, 2nd edn, London: Arnold.

Thompson, S. A. (1994) 'Aspects of Cohesion in Monologue', *Applied Linguistics* 15: 58–75.

Thornborrow, J. and Wareing, S. (1998) *Patterns in Language: An Introduction to Language and Literary Style*, London: Routledge.

Tobin, V. (2006) 'Ways of Reading *Sherlock Holmes*: The Entrenchment of Discourse Blends', *Language and Literature* 15(1): 73–90.

Tompkins, J. P. (ed.) (1980) *Reader-Response Criticism: From Formalism to Post-Structuralism*, Baltimore; London: Johns Hopkins University Press.

Toolan, M. (1985) 'Analysing Fictional Dialogue', *Language and Communication* 5(3): 193–206.

Toolan, M. (1990) *The Stylistics of Fiction*, London: Routledge.

Toolan, M. (ed.) (1992a) *Language, Text and Context: Essays in Stylistics*, London: Routledge.

Toolan, M. (1992b) 'The Significations of Representing Dialect in Writing', *Language and Literature* 1(1): 29–46.

Toolan, M. (1996 [1990]) 'Stylistics and Its Discontents; or, Getting off the Fish "Hook"', in J. J. Weber (ed.) *The Stylistics Reader: From Roman Jakobson to the Present*, London: Edward Arnold, pp. 117–35.

Toolan, M. (1998) *Language in Literature: An Introduction to Stylistics*, London: Arnold.

Toolan, M. (2014) 'The Theory and Philosophy of Stylistics', in Stockwell, P. and Whiteley, S. (eds) *The Cambridge Handbook of Stylistics*, Cambridge: Cambridge University Press, pp. 13–31.

Trask, R. L. (1997) *A Student's Dictionary of Language and Linguistics*, London: Arnold.

Traugott, E. and Pratt, M. L. (1980) *Linguistics for Students of Literature*, New York: Harcourt Brace Jovanovich.

Trimarco, P. (2014) 'Stylistics and Hypertext Fiction', in Burke, M. (ed.) *The Routledge Handbook of Stylistics*, London; New York: Routledge, pp. 500–15.

Turner, M. (1991) *Reading Minds: The Study of English in the Age of Cognitive Science*, Princeton, NJ: Princeton University Press.

Turner, M. (2006) 'Compression and Representation', *Language and Literature* 15(1): 17–27.

Ungerer, F. and Schmidt, H.-J. (1996) *An Introduction to Cognitive Linguistics*, London: Longman.

Ungerer, F. and Schmidt, H.-J. (2006) *An Introduction to Cognitive Linguistics*, 2nd edn, Harlow: Pearson.

Unsworth, L. and Macken-Horarik, M. (2015) 'Interpretive Responses to Images in Picture Books by Primary and Secondary School Students: Exploring Curriculum Expectations of a "Visual Grammatics"', *English in Education* 49(1): 56–79.

Uspensky, B. (1973) *A Poetics of Composition*, trans. V. Zavarin and S. Wittig, Berkeley: University of California Press.

van der Bom, I. (2016) 'Speaker Enactors in Oral Narrative', in Gavins, J. and Lahey, E. (eds) *World Building: Discourse in the Mind*, London; New York: Bloomsbury, pp. 91–108.

van Leeuwen, T. (2005) 'Typographic Meaning', *Visual Communication* 4(2): 137–43.

van Leeuwen, T. (2006) 'Towards a Semiotics of Typography', *Information Design Journal & Document Design* 14(2): 139–55.

van Peer, W. (1986) *Stylistics and Psychology: Investigations of Foregrounding*, New York: Croom Helm.

van Peer, W. (1987) 'Top-Down and Bottom-Up: Interpretative Strategies in Reading e. e. cummings', *NLH* 18(3): 597–609.

van Peer, W. (1989) 'Quantitative Studies of Style: A Critique and an Outlook', *Computers and the Humanities* 23: 301–7.

van Peer, W. (1996) 'Typographical Foregrounding', *Language and Literature* 2(1): 49–61.

van Peer, W. (1997) 'Towards a Poetics of Emotion', in Hjort, M. and Laver, S. (eds) *Emotion and the Arts*, Oxford: Oxford University Press, pp. 215–24.

van Peer, W. (2007) 'Introduction to Foregrounding: A State of the Art', *Language and Literature* 16(2): 99–104.

van Peer, W. and Hakemulder, F. (2015) 'Empirical Stylistics', in Sotirova, V. (ed.) *The Bloomsbury Companion to Stylistics*, London: Bloomsbury, pp. 189–207.

van Peer, W., Hakemulder, F. and Zyngier, S. (2012 [2007]) *Scientific Methods for the Humanities*, Amsterdam; Philadelphia: John Benjamins [originally published as *Muses and Measures: Empirical Research Methods for the Humanities*, Cambridge: Cambridge Scholars Publishing].

van Peer, W. and Pander Maat, H. (1996) 'Perspectivation and Sympathy: Effects of Narrative Point of View', in Kreuz, R. J. and MacNealy, M. S. (eds) *Empirical Approaches to Literature and Aesthetics*, Norwood, NJ: Ablex, pp. 143–54.

van Peer, W. and Pander Maat, H. (2001) 'Narrative Perspective and the Interpretation of Characters' Motives', *Language and Literature* 10(3): 229–41.

Verdonk, P. (ed.) (1993) *Twentieth-Century Poetry: From Text to Context*, London: Routledge.

Verdonk, P. (2002) *Stylistics*, Oxford: Oxford University Press.

Verdonk, P. (2006) 'Style', in Brown, K. (ed.) *Encyclopedia of Language and Linguistics*, 2nd edn, vol. 12, Oxford: Elsevier, pp. 196–210.

Verdonk, P. and Weber, J. J. (eds) (1995) *Twentieth-Century Fiction: From Text to Context*, London; New York: Routledge.

Wales, K. (1993) 'On the Stylistics of Jean-Jacques Lecercle', *The European English Messenger* 2(2): 30–31.

Wales, K. (1996) *Personal Pronouns in Present-Day English*, Cambridge: Cambridge University Press.

Wales, K. (1998) 'Cohesion and Coherence in Literature', in Mey, J. L. (ed.) *Concise Encyclopedia of Pragmatics*, Amsterdam: Elsevier, pp. 134–6.

Wales, K. (2006) 'Stylistics', in Brown, K. (ed.) *Encyclopedia of Language and Linguistics*, 2nd edn, vol. 12, Oxford: Elsevier, pp. 213–17.

Wales, K. (2011 [1990]) *A Dictionary of Stylistics*, 3rd edn, Harlow: Pearson.

Wales, K. (2014) 'The Stylistic Tool-Kit: Methods and Sub-disciplines', in Stockwell, P. and Whiteley, S. (eds) *The Cambridge Handbook of Stylistics*, Cambridge: Cambridge University Press, pp. 32–45.

Walsh, C. (2007) 'Schema Poetics and Crossover Fiction', in Lambrou, M. and Stockwell, P. (eds) *Contemporary Stylistics*, London; New York: Continuum, pp. 106–17.

Walton, K. L. (1997) 'Spelunking, Simulation, and Slime: On Being Moved by Fiction', in Hjort, M. and Laver, S. (eds) *Emotion and the Arts*, Oxford: Oxford University Press, pp. 37–49.

Wareing, S. (1994) 'And then He Kissed Her: The Reclamation of Female Characters into Submissive Roles in Contemporary Fiction', in Wales, K. (ed.) *Feminist Linguistics in Literary Criticism*, Woodbridge: Boydell & Brewer, pp. 117–36.

Warner, C. (2009) 'Speaking from Experience: Narrative Schemas, Deixis, and Authenticity Effects in Verena Stefan's Feminist Confessions *Shedding*', *Language and Literature* 18(1): 7–23.

Wason, P. C. (1961) 'Response to Affirmative and Negative Binary Statements', *British Journal of Psychology* 52: 133–42.

Watson, G. (1999) 'Something Will Come of Nothing: An Empirical Model of Negation for Prose Literature', *Journal of Literary Semantics* 15(3/4): 377–406.

Webster (1999) '"singing is silence": Being and Nothing in the Visual Poetry of e. e. cummings', in Fischer, O. and Nänny, M. (eds) *Form Miming Meaning: Iconicity in Language and Literature*, Amsterdam; Philadelphia: John Benjamins, pp. 199–214.

Wells, J. C. (1982) *Accents of English 1: Introduction*, Cambridge: Cambridge University Press.

Werth, P. (1984) *Focus, Coherence and Emphasis*, London: Croom Helm.

Werth, P. (1995a) 'How to Build a World (in a Lot Less than Six Days and Using only What's in Your Head)', in Green, K. (ed.) *New Essays on Deixis: Discourse, Narrative, Literature*, Amsterdam: Rodopi, pp. 48–80.

Werth, P. (1995b) '"World enough and time": Deictic Space and the Interpretation of Prose', in Verdonk, P. and Weber, J. J. (eds) *Twentieth-Century Fiction: From Text to Context*, London; New York: Routledge, pp. 181–205.

Werth, P. (1997a) 'Conditionality as Cognitive Distance', in Athanasiadou, A. and Dirven, R. (eds) *On Conditionals Again*, Amsterdam: John Benjamins, pp. 243–71.

Werth, P. (1997b) 'Remote Worlds: The Conceptual Representation of Linguistic Would', in Nuyts, J. and Pederson, E. (eds) *Language and Conceptualization*, Cambridge: Cambridge University Press, pp. 84–115.

Werth, P. (1999) *Text Worlds: Representing Conceptual Space in Discourse*, Harlow: Longman.

Whiteley, S. (2010) 'Text World Theory and the Emotional Experience of Literary Discourse', unpublished PhD thesis, University of Sheffield.

Whiteley, S. (2011a) 'Text World Theory, Real Readers and Emotional Responses to *The Remains of the Day*', *Language and Literature* 20(1): 23–42.

Whiteley, S. (2011b) 'Talking about "An Accommodation": The Implications of Discussion Group Data for Community Engagement and Pedagogy', *Language and Literature* 20: 236–55.

Whiteley, S. (2014) 'Ethics', in Stockwell, P. and Whiteley, S. (eds) *The Cambridge Handbook of Stylistics*, Cambridge: Cambridge University Press, pp. 393–407.

Whiteley, S. (2015) 'Emotion', in Sotirova, V. (ed.) *The Bloomsbury Companion to Stylistics*, London: Bloomsbury, pp. 507–22.

Whiteley, S. (2016) 'Building Resonant Worlds: Experiencing the Text-Worlds of *The Unconsoled*', in Gavins, J. and Lahey, E. (eds) *World Building: Discourse in the Mind*, London; New York: Bloomsbury, pp. 165–81.

Whiteley, S. and Canning, P. (2017) 'Reader Response Research in Stylistics', *Language and Literature* 26(2): 71–87.

Widdowson, H. G. (1975) *Stylistics and the Teaching of Literature*, London: Longman.

Williams Camus, J. T. (2015) 'Metaphor, News Discourse, and Knowledge', in Berenike Herrmann, J. and Berber Sardinha, T. (eds) *Metaphor in Specialist Discourse*, Amsterdam: John Benjamins, pp. 245–69.

Wolf, W. (2005) 'Intermediality', in Herman, D., Jahn, M. and Ryan, M.-L. (eds) *Routledge Encyclopedia of Narrative Theory*, London; New York: Routledge, pp. 252–6.

Wright, L. and Hope, J. (1996) *Stylistics: A Practical Coursebook*, London: Routledge.

Wynne, M. (ed.) (2005) *Developing Linguistic Corpora: A Guide to Good Practice*, Oxford: Oxbow Books [full text available free online at <http://www.ahds.ac.uk/linguistic-corpora/>].

Wynne, M., Short, M. and Semino, E. (1998) 'A Corpus-Based Investigation of Speech, Thought and Writing Presentation in English Narrative Texts', in Renouf, A. (ed.) *Explorations in Corpus Linguistics*, Amsterdam: Rodopi, pp. 233–47.

Yanal, R. J. (1999) *Paradoxes of Emotion and Fiction*, Pennsylvania: Pennsylvania State University Press.

Zunshine, L. (2006) *Why We Read Fiction: Theory of Mind and the Novel*, Columbus: Ohio State University Press.

Corpus programs

AntConc [created by Laurence Anthony], 'AntConc Homepage', <http://www.laurenceanthony.net/software/antconc> (last accessed 17 November 2016).

CLAWS 'Free CLAWS WWW Tagger', <http://ucrel.lancs.ac.uk/claws/trial.html> (last accessed 17 November 2016).

WMatrix [initially developed by Laurence Anthony], <http://ucrel.lancs.ac.uk/wmatrix> (last accessed 17 November 2016).

WordSmith [created by Mike Scott and published by Lexical Analysis Software and Oxford University Press since 1996], <http://www.lexically.net/wordsmith> (last accessed 17 November 2016).

Index